NEEDLESS DEATHS IN THE GULF WAR

Civilian Casualties During the Air Campaign and Violations of the Laws of War

A Middle East Watch Report

Human Rights Watch

New York • Washington • Los Angeles • London

Cover design by Patti Lacobee

Needless deaths in the Gulf War: civilian casualties during the air
    campaign and violations of the laws of war.
            p. cm -- (A Middle East Watch report)
            Includes bibliographical references.
            ISBN 1-56432-029-4
            1. Persian Gulf War, 1991--United States. 2. Persian Gulf War,
1991--Atrocities. 3. War victims--Iraq. 4. War--Protection of civilians.
I. Human Rights Watch (Organization) II. Series.
DS79.72.N44 1991
956.704'3--dc20   91-37902
                                                                CIP

CONTENTS

Acknowledgments ix
Preface xi
Introduction and Summary of Conclusions 1

PART I: THE LEGAL STANDARDS

CHAPTER ONE
The Legal Regime Governing the Conduct of Air Warfare 25
    A. International Humanitarian Law 28
    B. Military Necessity and the Principle of Humanity 29
    C. U.N. General Assembly Resolution 2444 30
    D. Customary Law and Protocol I: Civilian Immunity and the
    Principle of Distinction 31
    E. General Restrictions on Air Warfare 31
    F. Restraints on Attacks: Prohibition of Disproportionate and
    other Indiscriminate Attacks 41
    G. Precautionary Measures 49
    H. Verification of Military Objectives 53
    I. Collateral Casualties and Damage 54
    J. The Rule of Proportionality 55
    K. Cancellation or Suspension of Attacks 55
    L. Warning Requirement 56
    M. Special Legal Protection 57
    N. Prohibition Against Starvation of the Civilian Population 57
    O. Special Protection for Civilian Defense Shelters 62

PART II: THE AIR WAR AGAINST IRAQ

Background: Operation Desert Storm 69

CHAPTER TWO
U.S. Public Statements 75

CHAPTER THREE
The Means and Methods of Attack 89
    A. U.S. Public Statements 90

B. Daytime Bomb and Missile Attacks on Targets in Populated
Areas 95
    1. One Hundred Killed in Daytime Attack on Bridge in
    Southern City 96
    2. Scores of Civilians Killed in Flawed Attack on Bridge
    in Western Iraq 97
    3. Denials and then Admissions by the Allies about the
    Attack 100
    4. Scores of Civilians Killed in Daytime Attack on Bridge
    near Market in Southern City 102
    5. Scores of Workers Killed in Market Area of
    Southeastern City 104
    6. Morning Bombing Near Crowded Market Area in
    Basra 105
    7. Daytime Bombing of Bridges in Basra 107
    8. Scores of Civilians, Waiting for Cooking Gas, Killed
    and Injured During Daytime Attack 108
    9. Civilian Factory in Southern City Bombed in
    Afternoon; Seven Killed 109
    10. Legal Standards, Conclusions and Unanswered
    Questions 110
C. "Smart" Bombs, "Dumb" Bombs, and Inaccurate Attacks on
Targets in Civilian Population Centers 113
D. The Lack of Warning Prior to Attack: The Ameriyya Air Raid
Shelter 128

CHAPTER FOUR
Objects Attacked: The Need for Full Disclosure and Accountability 149
    A. Target Selection: The Need for Public Disclosure 154
    B. Reports of Attacks on Food, Agricultural and Water-Treatment
    Facilities 160
    C. The Crippling of the Electrical System 171
    D. Civilian Vehicles on Highways 193
        1. U.S. Public Statements 195
        2. An Inquiry by Middle East Watch 199
        3. Eyewitness Accounts: Attacks on Civilian Vehicles
        Carrying Evacuees to Jordan 201
            a. Two cars directly hit by diving aircraft in
            daytime attack, killing two families 202
            b. 30 killed in attack on bus 204
            c. Cluster bomb falls meters from two cars in
            dawn attack 205

        d. Strafing of Buses on Highways During
        Daytime 206
        e. Southern Iraq: 31 Dead in Daytime Attack on
        Civilian Vehicles 208
   4. Legal Standards and Conclusions 210
   5. Attacks on Jordanian Civilian Oil Tankers 213
   6. Jordan's Dilemma: Dependence on Imported Oil214
   7. Civilian Trucker Casualties: Eyewitness
   Testimony 219
        a. Convoy of Four Tankers Attacked 219
        b. 28-truck convoy hit in nighttime attack . 220
        c. One Driver Killed, Others Injured, when
        Aircraft Machine-gunned Five-truck
        Convoy 220
        d. Cluster Bomb Dropped at Truck Stop in
        Afternoon Attack 221
        e. Two Tankers Destroyed at Intersection . 221
        f. Cluster Bomb Dropped in Daytime Attack,
        Two Injured 222
        g. Refrigerator Truck Attacked Near
        Border 223
        h. Other Accounts of Strafing of Trucks by Allied
        Aircraft 224
   8. Legal Standards and Conclusions 224
 E. Attacks on Bedouin Tents 227

CHAPTER FIVE
The View from the Ground: Eyewitness Accounts of Civilian Casualties
and Damage 231
 A. Summary of Findings 232
 B. Baghdad 245
   1. Bombing in the Bataween Quarter: What Were the
   Targets? 257
   2. Cruise Missiles in the Karada and Masbah Quarters:
   What were the Targets? 259
   3. Destruction of the Central Bank 262
   4. Civilians Killed in Attack on Major Bus Station . 262
   5. Five to Six Houses Totally Destroyed in the Working-
   class Quarter 263
   6. Six Houses in Residential Neighborhood Sustain Direct
   Hit 264

7. Commercial Area in Residential Neighborhood bombed; Four Homes Damaged 265

8. Five Homes Collapse, Killing Family of Six . . . 266

9. Five Residential Buildings in Vicinity of Doura Oil Refinery completely destroyed 266

10. Reports of Damage Near Bridges 268

    a. Restaurant Destroyed, Civilians Killed, Near Sarafiya Bridge 268

    b. Five Houses Damaged, Civilians Injured and Killed, Near Sarafiya Bridge 269

    c. Shops and Two Cinemas Damaged near Jumhouriyya Bridge 271

    d. Restaurant Destroyed near Jumhouriyya Bridge 272

C. Basra 273

1. Two Missiles Crash into Crowded Market in Daytime Attack 276

2. Ashshar Market Area in Downtown Basra Sustains Damage from Two Missiles 276

3. 25 Houses Destroyed in Middle-class Neighborhood During Nighttime Attack; at Least 11 Killed 278

4. About 60 Homes Damaged in Several Attacks in al-Ma'qil Neighborhood 279

5. Eight Adobe Houses Destroyed in al-Zubayr . . . 280

6. Only Hospital in al-Zubayr Destroyed 281

7. Mosque Damaged 282

8. Bombs Miss Small Bridge, Hit Hospital 282

9. Small Bridge Missed Again 285

10. 50 Homes Damaged, Ten Killed, as Bombs Miss Telecommunications Tower in Daytime Attack . . . 285

11. Nighttime Bombing of Railroad Station 286

12. Soda-bottling Plant Destroyed 287

13. Reports of Attacks on Oil-industry Administrative Buildings 288

D. Other Cities and Towns in Southern Iraq 291

1. 20 Houses Destroyed in an Agricultural Village 291

2. 36 Houses Destroyed or Damaged in Nighttime Attack 293

3. Three Houses Destroyed in an Agricultural Village 294

4. Two-story Medical Clinic Destroyed 294

5. Three Residential Buildings Destroyed 296

6. Two-story House Destroyed as Bomb Misses Bridge by 500 Meters 296
7. Bomb Misses Bridge by 500 Meters, Falls in Residential Quarter, Six Killed 297
8. Bridge Missed Again, One Killed 298
9. Health Clinic and Several Houses Destroyed in Bombing of Bridges 299
10. Bomb Misses Telecommunications Tower; at least 20 Killed in Two-story House 299
11. Telecommunications Tower Missed; 11 Killed When Hotel is Destroyed 301
12. Civilian Casualties in Bombing of Bus Station in Hilla 301
13. Civilian Casualties and Damage in Samawa from Cluster Bombs 302
E. Cities and Towns in Western and Northern Iraq 304
1. Bomb Hits House in Early Evening, Killing Five 305
2. Airplane Opens Fire, Killing Members of Wedding Party 305
3. Bomb Hits House in Midnight Attack, Injured Family of 14 Survives 306
4. School Completely Destroyed, Hotel Damaged, at least Three Civilians Killed 307
5. 23 Houses in Agricultural Area Hit with Bombs in Two Separate Attacks, No Survivors 308
6. Reports from Northern Iraq 309

PART III: IRAQ'S MISSILE ATTACKS AGAINST ISRAEL AND THE GULF STATES

Overview 317

CHAPTER SIX
Targets in Israel and the Gulf States: Iraq's Public Statements . . . 327

CHAPTER SEVEN
Means and Methods of Attack and Defense 335

CHAPTER EIGHT
Civilian Casualties and Damage: Israel 347
A. The First Attack: Early Morning Hours of January 18 . 352
B. The Second Attack: January 19 355

C. The Third and Most Damaging Attack: January 22 ... 358
D. No Casualties in the Fourth Attack: January 23 361
E. Wide Collateral Damage in the Fifth Attack: January 25 362
F. The Sixth Attack on January 26: Varying Figures, Unknown Targets 366
G. Two Missiles Land in Occupied West Bank: January 28 and January 31 368
H. No Casualties or Damage Reported: Attacks on Night of February 2-3 370
I. Iraq Claims Another Attack: February 6 371
J. Civilian Damage in the Eleventh Attack: February 9 ... 372
K. Two Attacks in Rapid Succession: February 11 and February 12 373
L. An Apparently Harmless Attack: February 16 376
M. The Fifteenth Attack: February 19 378
N. Sixteenth Attack: February 23 378
O. The Last Missiles: Early Morning Hours of February 25 379

CHAPTER NINE

Civilian Casualties and Damage: Saudi Arabia 385
A. The First Attacks: Dhahran Air Base 387
B. First Missiles Fired at Riyadh on January 21, 12 Injured 389
C. Conflicting Information About the Cause of Damage on the Ground 389
D. The Second Attack on Riyadh, No Civilian Casualties .. 392
E. Five Missiles Fired on January 23, No Civilian Casualties Reported 393
F. First Civilian Killed as Missile Levels Wing of Interior Ministry Building in Riyadh on January 25, 30 Injured 394
G. The Next Two Attacks: No Reported Casualties or Damage 396
H. 29 Injured in Riyadh: February 3 397
I. No Casualties in February 8 Attack 397
J. Two Foreign Workers Injured in Riyadh: February 11 . 398
K. Four Slightly Injured in Daytime Attack on Hafr al-Batin: February 14 399

MAPS

Western and Northern Iraq 67
Southern Iraq 68
Disposition of Military Forces at the Commencement of the Ground War 316

ACKNOWLEDGMENTS

Virginia N. Sherry, associate director of Middle East Watch, had overall responsibility for this report. She also wrote Chapters Two to Five, on the air war against Iraq, and Chapters Six, Seven and Nine, on Iraq's missile attacks against Israel and the Gulf states.

Jemera Rone, counsel to Human Rights Watch, conducted the wartime field research, and subsequently provided additional legal analysis and factual research.

Robert Kogod Goldman, professor of law at the Washington College of Law of the American University in Washington, D.C., and a member of the Middle East Watch Committee, wrote Chapter One on the legal standards, and provided guidance on international humanitarian law for the report as a whole. Andrew Whitley, executive director of Middle East Watch, conducted field research and wrote Chapter Eight on the Iraqi missile attacks against Israel. Jacqueline Williams and Yuval Ginbar conducted the interviews in London in May 1991 that are cited in the report.

Kenneth Roth, deputy director of Human Rights Watch, contributed to the legal analysis and edited the report.

Middle East Watch extends special thanks to Lauren Fishman, who carried out research for Chapters Eight and Nine. Thanks are also due to Christina Derry and Paige Wilhite, who provided invaluable production assistance on this report. Finally, Middle East Watch acknowledges with deep appreciation the contributions of those expert readers who commented on the draft manuscript while it was in preparation.

PREFACE

This report applies the rules of war governing international armed conflicts to examine civilian casualties and damage to civilian objects from bomb and missile attacks carried out by the allied forces against Iraq during Operation Desert Storm, and from missile attacks by Iraq against Israel, Saudi Arabia, Bahrain and Qatar. The report does not address civilian deaths and injuries, or damage to civilian objects, during the Iraqi occupation of Kuwait, the subject of previous and upcoming Middle East Watch (MEW) reports. Nor does it address possible violations of humanitarian law, or the laws of war, against combatants on either side in the conflict. Also beyond the scope of this report are the environmental damage and regional health hazards caused by the fires set in Kuwait's oil wells and the massive release of oil into the Persian Gulf.

The purpose of this report is to contribute to the public debate about the conduct of the Persian Gulf War and to draw attention to violations and possible violations of humanitarian law. In some cases it draws conclusions, and in others it requests from the U.S. Department of Defense and other allied military commands, additional information that is important in assessing the allies' compliance with the laws of war governing aerial bombardment. Further, the report raises questions that Middle East Watch believes should be addressed to the Pentagon and publicly discussed.

Middle East Watch hopes that this report will be useful to members of the U.S. Congress in evaluating the two Department of Defense reports on the conduct of the Persian Gulf conflict. These documents -- the first preliminary report was released on July 16, 1991,[*] and the second and final report is due no later than January 15, 1992 -- are to be submitted by the U.S. Secretary of Defense, in consultation with the Chairman of the Joint Chiefs of Staff and the Commander-in-Chief of the United States Central Command, to the congressional defense

---

[*] U.S. Department of Defense, *Conduct of the Persian Gulf Conflict/An Interim Report to Congress*, July 1991 [hereinafter Pentagon Interim Report].

committees, pursuant to legislation enacted in March 1991.[*] These reports -- which will include classified and unclassified versions -- are required to address a range of issues. The issues related to subjects in this report are:

- the use and performance of United States military equipment, weapon systems, and munitions;

- the role of the law of armed conflict in the planning and execution of military operations by U.S. and coalition forces, including collateral damage and civilian casualties;

- the rules of engagement for the coalition forces; and

- estimates of military and civilian casualties sustained by Iraq and by nations not directly participating in the hostilities in the conflict.

Middle East Watch has included material from the Pentagon's July 1991 preliminary report in this report. While we acknowledge the Pentagon's prominent caveat that the interim report contains preliminary information subject to change as additional information is received by the Defense Department, nevertheless we find -- regrettably -- that numerous questions related to the issues noted above remain unanswered.

CIVILIAN CASUALTIES AND DAMAGE IN IRAQ: METHODOLOGY

This report uses the same methodological framework as other Human Rights Watch investigative reports on violations of the rules of war in Afghanistan, Angola, Burma, Cambodia, El Salvador, Ethiopia, India, Mozambique, Nicaragua, Peru, the Philippines, Somalia, Sri Lanka and Sudan. As has been the case with many of these reports, Middle East

---

[*] Title Five (Report on the Conduct of the Persian Gulf Conflict) of the Persian Gulf Conflict Supplemental Authorization and Personnel Benefits Act of 1991, March 21, 1991.

Watch was obliged to rely on testimony from those who had fled the country where the violations of the rules of war were committed. Despite repeated requests beginning February 7, 1991, MEW did not receive permission from the Iraqi government to visit the country and conduct on-site investigations of the sites of allied bomb and missile attacks. However, as this report was going to press in October, the Iraqi Red Crescent Society extended an invitation for a delegation to visit Iraq, a mission we hope to undertake in the near future.

The interviews with former residents of Iraq and other eyewitnesses to allied bomb damage cited in this report were conducted by Middle East Watch representatives during the war in Jordan, and after the war in Kuwait, Saudi Arabia, the United Kingdom and the United States. Most of the interviews cited in this report were conducted in Jordan during the war by Jemera Rone, counsel to Human Rights Watch. Ms. Rone has undertaken similar field work in Africa, Asia, Europe and Latin America over a six-year period.

Ms. Rone visited Jordan from February 11 to March 2, and conducted interviews with randomly selected persons who had arrived in Jordan from Iraq during the air war. Most of those interviewed were "evacuees" -- foreign workers, typically males from Africa and South Asia, who had fled Iraq after living there for at least one year and in some cases over 10 years. Pakistanis and Indians typically were employed by large construction or other companies and lived in compounds provided by their employers; others had lived among Iraqis, often in poor neighborhoods.

The Jordanian government and international humanitarian organizations were well prepared for an exodus of refugees and evacuees far greater than what actually materialized during the war. By the time the air war started, they had readied tents, supplies and transport systems that were more than adequate for the needs of the 22,000-plus evacuees who crossed into Jordan from Iraq between January 17 and February 27.[*] The system of repatriation of the evacuees had become so efficient

---

[*] In the early weeks of the air war, some 5,000 to 10,000 evacuees and Jordanians were blocked by the Iraqi authorities from crossing into Jordan on the grounds that they did not have exit permits. For the most part, the evacuees

that evacuees, after spending the night at the Ruwayshid facility near the Jordan-Iraq border, typically stayed only a few days in Azraq before being repatriated or only overnight in Aqaba before being taken by ferry to Egypt. The evacuees in many cases left Jordan within a few days and the incoming evacuees thus had no opportunity to talk to them about the contents of the interviews -- conditions which are superior for fact-finding purposes, compared to situations that usually exist in camps where refugees spend months together.

Ms. Rone interviewed the evacuees in private, without the presence of government officials. The Jordanian authorities granted permission for Ms. Rone to travel to four sites where the evacuees were housed while awaiting transport to their countries of origin: the Ruwayshid evacuee facility, the sole Jordanian crossing point on the Iraqi border; the Azraq evacuee facility near Azraq, Jordan, 60 km east of Amman; the Andalus transit facility outside of Amman; and the Rabia evacuee facility in Aqaba. The evacuees usually remained only overnight at Ruwayshid and then moved to Azraq or, in the case of Egyptians, to Aqaba, to await transport to their countries of origin. The evening before they departed by plane, they were moved to the Andalus facility.

Ms. Rone also interviewed Jordanians and Palestinians who had returned from Iraq. A few had been in Kuwait before or during the war: some had lived in Kuwait; some went to help other Jordanians in Kuwait and Iraq pack up and move to Jordan; and others went to Iraq to provide medical assistance during the war. As it did during the 1980-88 Gulf War, Iraq barred its citizens from leaving during this conflict. With the exception of one Bedouin -- whose tent in western Iraq was bombed -- interviewed by Ms. Rone at a hospital in Jordan, she met no Iraqis who

---

could not return to Baghdad to secure the permits because they lacked gasoline and money. Moreover, the highway was very dangerous because of frequent allied air attacks. As a result of international pressure, the Iraqis relented and those stranded at the frontier without proper food or shelter and in sub-zero nighttime temperatures finally were permitted to cross into Jordan. (*See* David Hirst and Wafa Amr, "Refugees cross into Jordan as Baghdad reopens border," *The Guardian*, January 29, 1991.) The only exceptions to this apparently were Egyptians, who massed on the border until mid-February when their crossing was allowed, also without exit permits.

had entered Jordan since the bombing began. Ms. Rone also did not encounter in her random selection any evacuees who had come from Kuwait after the air war started.

Ms. Rone questioned all interviewees about the day, time and place of bombing incidents that caused civilian casualties or damage; the physical details of the damage inflicted, including bomb craters; the wounded or dead persons actually seen; and the distance of the site of the damage from military or possible military targets. Distances, where they are noted in this report, were roughly calculated by the interviewees. Judging by the way the interviewees answered, they considered the questioning process to be serious and made efforts to recall the precise information that was sought. They did not have prepared stories -- much of the information had to be elicited by questioning; they also were patient with repeated requests for details, such as their meaning if they described a house as "completely destroyed." Ms. Rone asked some but not all the interviewees to provide their names, with the understanding that the names would not be published, and some volunteered their names.

CIVILIAN CASUALTIES AND DAMAGE
IN ISRAEL AND THE GULF STATES:
METHODOLOGY

The information gathered by Middle East Watch on civilian casualties and damage in Israel from Iraq's missile attacks came from a variety of private and public sources. Andrew Whitley, the executive director of Middle East Watch and a former Israel bureau chief for the London *Financial Times*, conducted a fact-finding mission to Israel from June 2 to 4, 1991. He spoke with dozens of Israeli citizens who lived in the affected areas and others, such as journalists, who gathered information about Iraq's missile attacks as they occurred but have been prevented by Israeli censorship from speaking publicly.

Mr. Whitley concentrated his field research on the greater Tel Aviv metropolitan area, where the majority of missiles landed and where most civilian casualties and damage occurred. Mr. Whitley visited sites where damage had taken place, and interviewed bystanders, local residents and, where appropriate, shopkeepers and other workers. It was explained to them why Middle East Watch was conducting this research. Most interviewees were cooperative, volunteering information about such matters as the extent of warning they had received from air raid sirens, how much damage had been caused and whether there had been any casualties. However, it should be emphasized that the sampling was not scientific and the picture obtained from these eyewitnesses was not necessarily complete. Some respondents were suspicious about the inquiries, preferring not to talk to a foreign human rights worker without official permission.

Official sources of information were releases from the Government of Israel Press Office, *Ricochet*, a published compilation of statements issued during the war by the Israel Defense Forces Spokesman, data from the Press Communications Center set up temporarily during the war, and news broadcasts on the government-controlled Israel Radio and Television networks. *Maariv*, a mass circulation daily newspaper, also published a useful, detailed chart of those missile attacks about which official information was disclosed.

Middle East Watch did not undertake fact-finding in Saudi Arabia to document civilian casualties and damage there from Iraq's missile attacks during the war. The information presented on this subject has been drawn from official Saudi Press Agency reports, independent press accounts and other sources indicated in Chapter Nine.

MEDIA ACCOUNTS

This report also draws in part on reports filed by journalists who were based in Iraq, Saudi Arabia and Israel during the war. Despite the control of movement by the authorities on both sides, and the clearance of dispatches by Iraqi government or U.S. military censors, Middle East Watch found the reporting of journalists in the region to be valuable to our ongoing work. We salute their efforts and persistence under extremely difficult conditions.

INTRODUCTION AND SUMMARY OF CONCLUSIONS

According to U.S. Secretary of Defense Richard Cheney, the 43-day U.S.-led international military campaign to oust Iraq from Kuwait, Operation Desert Storm, was spearheaded by "the most successful air-campaign in the history of the world." In some respects, this claim seems justified. The allies assembled a gigantic airborne armada that quickly and easily established air superiority over Iraqi military forces. Allied aircraft bombed wherever and whenever they wanted. Their arsenals were equipped with technologically sophisticated weapons that proved capable of astonishing precision. By means of the bombing campaign, the allies overwhelmed the foe to the point where -- once the long-dreaded ground war got underway -- it quickly became a rout and coalition forces suffered mercifully few casualties.

Yet Secretary Cheney's assertion of unequalled success went even further. Implicitly it included the contention -- made explicit by President Bush and other Pentagon officials -- that never before had such care been taken to avoid harm to the opposing side's civilian population. Further, U.S. and other allied spokespersons claimed at every turn that the effort to minimize damage to civilians had succeeded. Though occasionally acknowledging that some civilian casualties were inevitable, the impression was created by statement after statement and television image after image that, so far as the allied performance was concerned, it was a near-perfect war, with as little harm to civilian life and property as humanly possible.

This impression was reinforced by a deliberate policy on the part of the United States and its allies to manage the news of the war in a manner designed to suggest that all feasible precautions in fact had been taken to avoid harm to civilians. Restrictions placed on journalists attempting to cover the war and the selective presentation of information about the conduct of the war, in part through elaborately rehearsed military briefings, left the press unable to probe the extent of the precautions actually adopted. Parallel curbs on the foreign press imposed by Iraq exacerbated the difficulty of penetrating the veils that blocked the view of the actual conduct of the war.

It is Middle East Watch's purpose in this report to break through this carefully constructed image of perfection to examine how closely U.S. and allied claims conform to the reality on the ground, as measured by the standards established by the laws of war. Primarily through interviews conducted during the war with scores of Iraqi residents of various nationalities who had fled the aerial bombardment for the safety of Jordan, we have assembled a detailed picture of the allied campaign as it affected civilians. Although this image is still incomplete -- both because of information held exclusively by the Pentagon and other allied commands which they have not released, and because Iraq refused during the period when this report was being prepared to permit Middle East Watch investigators to enter the country -- we believe that the accounts we have been able to collect are sufficiently comprehensive to draw certain conclusions regarding the allied conduct of the air war and to direct other questions to allied commanders which we believe should be answered to allow independent assessment of allied conduct.

We have evaluated the allied bombing campaign under the laws of war, primarily the standards set forth in the First Additional Protocol of 1977 to the 1949 Geneva Conventions. Although the United States has not ratified Protocol I, it has recognized most of the pertinent provisions as declarative of customary international law and thus as legally binding. As is our practice, we have also examined the performance of the other side -- the Iraqi missile attacks, primarily against Israel and Saudi Arabia. We hold all sides in military conflicts to the same standards, because the laws of war impose an independent duty of compliance regardless of deviations by the other side.

This study is part of a series of reports relating to the Persian Gulf conflict which have been issued by Middle East Watch and the other divisions of Human Rights Watch. In February 1990 -- six months before the Iraqi invasion of Kuwait -- Middle East Watch issued *Human Rights in Iraq*, which detailed systematic abuses committed by Saddam Hussein's forces against Kurds and perceived and actual dissidents in Iraq. Once the invasion took place, Middle East Watch issued several reports documenting Iraqi abuses in occupied Kuwait and toward foreigners under Iraqi control. Middle East Watch also issued reports addressing the humanitarian-law limits to the U.N.-mandated sanctions against Iraq, and describing war-related restrictions on human rights in Egypt, the United Kingdom and the Israeli occupied territories. Once hostilities between

Iraq and the allied coalition began, the Fund for Free Expression, another division of Human Rights Watch, issued a report on restraints placed by the allies on press coverage of the war. Following the end of the war, Middle East Watch issued an appeal to allied and Iraqi forces regarding the release of prisoners of war and other detainees and the duty to provide proper documentation and burial of the dead. In September 1991, Middle East Watch published *A Victory Turned Sour: Human Rights in Kuwait Since Liberation.* Middle East Watch is also completing research into abuses committed by Iraqi and resistance forces during the uprising in March 1991.

THE ALLIED AIR WAR

In assessing allied conduct of the air war as it affected civilians, Middle East Watch starts from the following premises:

- The standard to which the United States and its allies publicly aspired, and which they claim to have met, was the appropriate one: to take every feasible measure to avoid harm to civilians.

- The overwhelming air superiority quickly established by the United States and its allies heightened their ability to take all feasible steps to avoid harm to civilians. That is, from early in the war the allies were never driven by urgent military imperatives to take steps that might have imposed greater risk of harm on civilians. They had the opportunity and resources to plan and carry out their attacks with scrupulous care to avoid civilian casualties.

- The precision weapons and surveillance technology available to the United States and its allies increased their capacity still further to avoid harm to civilians.

Despite this exceptional opportunity to conduct the allied bombing campaign in strict compliance with the legal duty to take all feasible precautions to avoid civilian harm, we find that the actual conduct of the war fell short of this obligation in several significant respects. This divergence between legal duty and actual practice emerged both in the choice of the means and methods to prosecute the air war and in the selection of targets for attack. All of these shortcomings appear to have involved deliberate decisions by allied commanders to take less than the maximum feasible precautions necessary to avoid harm to civilians.

In noting these discrepancies between duty and conduct, we do not suggest that the allies in general violated the requirements of the laws of war. To the contrary, in many if not most respects the allies' conduct was consistent with their stated intent to take all feasible precautions to avoid civilian casualties. At the same time, the existence of these shortcomings in allied conduct reveals that the effort of U.S. and allied commanders to portray the bombing campaign as a near-perfect attempt to avoid civilian harm was not entirely accurate, and that in some instances coalition forces appear to have violated the laws of war. We believe these findings are important both for understanding the extent to which the suffering of Iraqi civilians might have been lessened and for avoiding similar deficiencies in any future air war.

MEANS AND METHODS OF ATTACK

The following summarizes our findings of deficiencies in the allies' choice of the means and methods of attack:

Daytime v. Nighttime Bombing

One shortcoming arose in the allies' choice of the time of day to execute certain attacks in urban areas. The customary-law principle reaffirmed in Article 57 of Protocol I requires parties to "take all feasible precautions in the choice of means and methods of attack with a view to avoiding, or in any event to minimizing, incidental" civilian casualties. One obvious precaution in attacking targets in urban areas near markets or busy thoroughfares where many civilians can be expected to be found during daytime hours is to bomb these areas at night. Certainly the allies had the technological capacity to conduct aerial attacks at night. There were also more than enough targets away from populated areas to keep allied bombers in the 24-hour-per-day campaign busy during daytime hours. Nevertheless, in several attacks in urban areas, allied planes dropped their bombs during the day, needlessly killing hundreds. For example:

- A mid-afternoon attack on a bridge in Nasiriyya in southern Iraq killed scores of people -- 100, according to a local doctor, with 80 others injured -- who were crossing the bridge at the time.

- A daytime British attack on a bridge in Falluja, a town west of Baghdad on the Euphrates River, killed 130 civilians, according to Iraqi authorities.

- During a daytime attack on one of the bridges in Samawa, a city on the Euphrates River in southern Iraq, bombs fell near a crowded market, in an open area at the edge of the river, killing over 100 civilians and injuring others.

- An attack on an underwear-manufacturing plant in Hilla at 2:00 in the afternoon killed seven administrative workers. The casualty toll would have been considerably higher had the normal shift of 200 workers not been dismissed by management at noon that day and told to report back to work five or six days later.

- At 3:30 in the afternoon an oil-storage tank was attacked near a gas-distribution point where civilians were lined up to purchase fuel for cooking and heating. Some 200 people at the site were killed or injured.

The failure in all of these cases to launch the attack at night when fewer civilians were likely to have been in the vicinity -- or, at the very least, to have issued a warning that a target in the area was to be attacked -- suggests a failure by the allies to live up to the duty to take all feasible precautions to avoid civilian casualties, and thus a violation of the laws of war.

"Dumb" v. "Smart" Bombs

Another shortcoming is the allies' apparent use of unguided bombs when attacking urban areas. Repeatedly during the bombing campaign allied commanders suggested that in urban areas where civilian populations were likely to be found, allied air forces were using the most sophisticated munitions at their disposal to minimize the risk of collateral civilian harm. The U.S. Air Force chief of staff, Gen. Merrill A. McPeak, estimated that some 90 percent of these so-called "smart" weapons hit their targets.

Yet according to Gen. McPeak, precision-guided bombs accounted for only 7,400 of the 84,200 tons of munitions dropped by the allies during Operation Desert Storm, or a mere 8.8 percent, some of which was used to attack hardened targets in the Kuwaiti military theater. The remaining 91.2 percent consisted of unguided weaponry -- so-called "dumb" bombs -- with a reported estimated accuracy rate of only 25 percent.

While downtown Baghdad was said to have been attacked with only precision weapons, the Pentagon and its allies have remained silent about the type of munitions used in other urban areas. It appears likely that at least some of the munitions used in urban areas outside of downtown Baghdad were unguided -- "the same dumb iron bombs that fell on Berlin, Pyongyang and Hanoi," in the words of one former U.S. army officer. For example, Basra, which was largely off-limits to foreign reporters during the air war, appears to have suffered considerably more damage to civilian structures than Baghdad, where a small international press force was present.

Middle East Watch calls on the Pentagon and other allied commands, first, to reveal the extent to which dumb bombs were dropped in populated urban areas and, second, to explain how such use accords with the customary-law duty to "take all feasible precautions" to avoid civilian harm. While we recognize that cost and availability are factors in the preference for dumb bombs -- unguided munitions are available in vast quantities and, in the words of one Pentagon official, are "cheaper than hamburger" -- we have asked allied commanders to explain how cost and availability were balanced against the duty to take all feasible precautions to avoid civilian harm. In our view, decisions of this sort, with their potentially deadly consequences for the civilian population, should be subject to independent review now that hostilities have ended.

The Attack on the Ameriyya Air Raid Shelter

The largest loss of civilian life in a single incident occurred in the attack on the Ameriyya civil-defense shelter at approximately 4:30 a.m. on February 13, which killed between 200 and 300 civilians, according to various Iraqi reports. The United States, which was responsible for the attack, claimed it had intercepted signals and made various observations suggesting that the facility was being used as a military command-and-control center. Among the visual observations announced were the building's hardened exterior, the presence of military personnel at the site, the location of camouflage paint on the structure's roof and a barbed-wire fence around the perimeter. U.S. commanders claimed not to have noticed that civilians were using the shelter.

The attack raises several questions about the precautions taken by the United States to verify that the shelter was an appropriate military target. For example, the Pentagon concedes that it knew the Ameriyya facility had been used as a civil-defense shelter during the Iran-Iraq war, but U.S. officials gave no warning that they considered its protected status as a civilian shelter to have ended. Article 65 of Protocol I provides that the special protection afforded civil-defense structures ceases in the event that a shelter is used for military purposes "only after a warning has been given setting, whenever appropriate, a reasonable time-limit, and after such warning has remained unheeded."

Although the United States has not commented one way or the other on whether it views the warning requirement of Article 65 to be a matter of customary international law, a fair interpretation of the recognized customary-law requirement that all feasible precautions be taken to avoid civilian casualties, including by giving "effective advance warning" of attacks which may affect the civilian population unless circumstances do not permit (Article 57 of Protocol I; U.S. Air Force Manual, pp. 5-11), would suggest that such a warning should have been given. The United States' failure to give such a warning before proceeding with the disastrous attack on the Ameriyya shelter was a serious violation of the laws of war.

The United States also has been disturbingly silent about the steps taken to determine that the Ameriyya shelter was an appropriate target for attack. The silence has precluded independent assessment of whether these steps complied with U.S. obligations. It is now well established, through interviews with neighborhood residents, that the Ameriyya structure was plainly marked as a public shelter and was used throughout the air war by large numbers of civilians. That military personnel were observed at the facility is not conclusive in labeling it a military target because Article 65 makes clear that civil-defense functions can be carried out under the control of or in cooperation with military personnel without the facilities used losing their protective status. Although the United States has charged that the civilians were difficult to observe because they must have entered the shelter after dark, U.S. officials have not explained why large numbers of civilians were not observed in the daylight of the morning when they exited the shelter.

TARGETS OF ATTACK

In addition to these deviations from the laws of war in the means and methods of attack, Middle East Watch has documented a series of apparent shortcomings in the allied selection of targets for attack. The following summarizes our findings:

Food, Agricultural and Water-Treatment Facilities

The shortage of food in Iraq resulting from the mandatory sanctions imposed by U.N. Security Council Resolution 661 and subsequent resolutions was exacerbated by allied bombardment of certain Iraqi food and agricultural facilities. For example:

- Four government food warehouses in Diwaniyya, a city south of Baghdad, were bombed.

- A new dairy factory about 30 km north of Basra was attacked.

- Flour-milling facilities and grain-storage warehouses were destroyed.

- Several water-treatment facilities in Basra were damaged, including the destruction beyond repair of the facility serving the densely populated Bratha'iyya quarter of the city.

In none of these cases does the facility appear to have been a legitimate military target, in that it was not making an effective contribution to the enemy's military action and its destruction did not offer a definite military advantage in the circumstances ruling at the time, as required by the customary-law principle reaffirmed in Article 52 of Protocol I. Attacking such targets in itself is a violation of the laws of war.

Moreover, Article 54 of Protocol I, which the United States has accepted as customary international law, states that attacks on foodstuffs and other facilities necessary for the survival of the civilian population (including, according to the International Committee of the Red Cross, drinking-water installations) are prohibited if the purpose of the attack is to deny the "sustenance value" of these objects "to the civilian population...whether in order to starve out civilians, to cause them to move away, or for any other motive." The only exception to this rule is for objects used "as sustenance solely for the members of [an adverse party's] armed forces" or "in direct support of military action," and even then, attacks are prohibited if they "may be expected to leave the civilian population with such inadequate food or water as to cause its starvation or force its movement." In light of the lack of any evidence that these facilities were being used solely by or in direct support of Iraqi troops, these attacks appear to violate the principle set forth in Article 54, particularly in the context of the serious deprivations of food caused by the U.N. embargo.

The Crippling of the Electrical System

It is now well known that the allies virtually destroyed Iraq's electrical system, including four of the country's five hydroelectric facilities. Certainly the crippling of Iraq's electrical production impeded the Iraqi military's ability to communicate, and it undoubtedly also had an effect on war-related production. Moreover, because Iraq's electrical system is an integrated grid, the rerouting of electricity was possible to some extent to compensate for destroyed facilities.

However, the cost to the civilian population of these attacks on the electrical system was severe. Iraq was quickly transformed from a modern, energy-dependent society into, in the now-famous words of the Ahtissari report, a "pre-industrial age." Shortages of food due to the U.N. embargo were exacerbated by the lack of refrigeration and the impairment of Iraq's highly mechanized, irrigation-based agriculture. The nation's electricity-dependent water-purification and sewage-treatment facilities were crippled, creating a serious health hazard. Hospitals and clinics were forced to meet this growing health emergency, and to treat the war wounded, with, at most, erratic electricity supplied by back-up generators. Vaccines and medicines requiring refrigeration deteriorated and were difficult to replace. A UNICEF representative in Iraq noted in late May the "vicious circle" of "poor hygiene, contaminated water and poor diet," which he said left about 100,000 Iraqi children under one year of age vulnerable to diarrhea and dehydration.

Given these serious costs to the entire civilian population, it is appropriate to ask whether allied commanders engaged in the proportionality analysis required by the customary principle codified in Articles 51 and 57 of Protocol I. Did they assure themselves that the civilian costs were not "excessive in relation to the concrete and direct military advantage anticipated"?

At a briefing on January 30, Gen. Norman Schwarzkopf, the U.S. commander in the Gulf region, seemed to recognize that at some point during the destruction of the electrical system the civilian cost indeed did become excessive in relation to the concrete and direct military advantage. He reported that in less than two weeks of bombardment the allies had rendered 25 percent of Iraq's electrical-generating facilities "completely inoperative" and an additional 50 percent "degraded." He went on to say:

> I think I should point out right here that we never had any intention of destroying all of Iraqi electrical power. Because of our interest in making sure that civilians did not suffer unduly, we felt we had to leave some of the electrical power in effect, and we've done that.

But the allied attacks continued -- including the destruction, following Gen. Schwarzkopf's statement, of two of the four hydroelectric facilities hit by allied bombers -- and Iraqi civilians did suffer unduly.

Comments by Pentagon officials since the war give rise to questions about whether inappropriate goals in attacking the electrical system may have yielded an improper balance in applying the rule of proportionality. U.S. Air Force officials involved in planning the air war have indicated that one purpose of destroying the electrical system was to harm civilians and thus encourage them to overthrow Saddam Hussein. For example, one Air Force planner stated in an interview with *The*

Washington Post that the attacks on the country's electrical system were intended to send a message to the Iraqi people: "We're not going to tolerate Saddam Hussein or his regime. Fix that, and we'll fix your electricity."

Whether or not one shares the goal of overthrowing Saddam's regime, it is clearly inappropriate to target the civilian population as a means for achieving that goal, since such attacks conflict with the customary-law duty to distinguish between military targets and the civilian population. As Article 51 of Protocol I provides: "The civilian population as such, as well as individual civilians, shall not be the object of attack." Direct attacks of this sort on civilian morale and well-being are clearly impermissible under the rules of law.

Insofar as the allies wrongly deemed the causing of suffering among Iraq's civilian population to be a legitimate military goal of the attacks on the electrical system, it may have caused allied commanders to misapply the rule of proportionality by giving undue weight to the perceived military advantages of the attacks while according insufficient weight to their civilian cost. To allay suspicions that the civilian cost of the destruction of the electrical system was not properly taken into account, the allies should fully disclose the proportionality calculation undertaken in choosing to continue the attacks on the electrical system.

Civilian Vehicles on Highways

Middle East Watch took testimony of repeated incidents in which civilian vehicles were attacked on Iraqi highways, primarily in Western Iraq in the course of the allied effort to locate and destroy Iraqi mobile missile launchers. These included a series of civilian buses that were hit, with considerable loss of life.

- Some 30-35 Sudanese fleeing Iraq to neighboring Jordan were killed when their bus was bombed 18 miles east of Rutba, in western Iraq.

- At 2:00 p.m. on February 9, a Jordanian bus carrying fleeing Kuwaiti civilians was attacked with rockets by allied planes near the Kuwaiti border, killing 27 in the bus and another four in two cars traveling with the bus. The bus had luggage on the roof.

- At about 4:10 in the afternoon on February 15, a bus carrying 36 Pakistani workers was strafed six miles west of Rutba. The bus, which had luggage piled on top, was attacked four times, at two- to three-minute intervals. Bullets were fired near the bus but it was not hit.

Even if it is assumed that these civilian vehicles were not deliberately targeted, these allied attacks appear to have been indiscriminate, in that they failed to distinguish between military and civilian objects on the highway, as required by the customary-law principle set forth in Article 48 of Protocol I.

The drivers of Jordanian civilian oil tankers were a frequent target of these attacks. Prior to the war, Jordan had imported half of its oil from Saudi Arabia and the remainder from Iraq. When Saudi Arabia cut off oil to Jordan on September 20, citing a financial dispute over payments for previously imported oil, Jordan became dependent on Iraqi oil. On October 15, as its oil reserves were running low, Jordan informed the U.N. Sanctions Committee that it would be importing oil from Iraq, noting that Iraq would generate no income from the sales because the oil would be sold in satisfaction of an Iraqi debt to Jordan.

On February 4, five days after a formal protest from Jordan over attacks on its civilian tankers, U.S. State Department spokeswoman Margaret Tutwiler said that although Iraq's oil exports to Jordan "do violate the sanctions, it is not coalition policy to attack civilian trucks exporting petroleum to Jordan." At the same time, she charged: "[W]e have credible information that war material, including some related to Scud missiles, has been transported in convoy with civilian oil trucks. Such material contributes to Iraq's occupation of Kuwait and is a legitimate military target."

On February 5, Lt. Gen. Thomas Kelly, director of operations for the U.S. Joint Chiefs of Staff, stated that "If a truck chooses to operate in that environment, there is some risk. We're not purposely going after civilian vehicles. [I]f one got hit, it was certainly by mistake." Similarly, Maj. Gen. Robert Johnston, chief of staff at U.S. headquarters in Riyadh, said at a briefing the same day that "we are not specifically targeting Jordanian civilian tankers."

These statements implicitly assert that the allies were capable of distinguishing civilian oil tankers from tankers used to supply Iraqi missiles, particularly after they received formal notice from Jordan that such civilian vehicles were being hit. In light of that assertion, the repeated attacks on Jordanian civilian oil tankers -- in some instances by low-flying aircraft -- evidence a failure to live up to the duty to discriminate between civilian and military objects.

It may be that part of the problem was that some allied bombers -- those firing precision weapons from high altitudes -- may not have been capable of distinguishing civilian tankers from those used for military purposes. If that proves to be the case, the Pentagon must explain why it issued public statements suggesting that discrimination among civilian and military targets was possible and thus lending encouragement to the drivers of civilian tankers who sought to travel on the highways in western Iraq. A general warning that any tanker on the highway was subject to attack would have been more appropriate. While elements of U.S. statements suggest such a warning, their overall thrust was quite the opposite -- to imply that discrimination was possible. Tanker drivers who entered Iraq on the basis of such assurances were thus needlessly and unjustifiably killed.

Bedouin Tents

A similar lack of discrimination characterized several attacks on Bedouin tents in western Iraq. Bedouin in the area traditionally live in long, black, goat-hair tents which are familiar to travelers in the region. Middle East Watch collected information about several Bedouin tents that were attacked in western Iraq, leaving at least 46 dead civilians, including infants and children. In one daytime attack on January 22, the lone survivor told of 12 family members and two others killed; four planes circled over his compound of three 30-meter-long tents, dove down and attacked, firing 12 rockets. The compound was 100 km from the nearest highway, and was surrounded by sheep and goats.

Bedouin tents, as objects which are "normally dedicated to civilian purposes," should fall within the category of objects to which a presumption of civilian use attaches under the customary principle codified in Article 52 of Protocol I. The presumption requires that in case of doubt, pilots should refrain from attacking these objects. It may be that the pilots fired at the long, black tents thinking that they were concealing Iraqi missiles or other war-related materiel. However, given the distance of the tents from a highway (mobile missile launchers are large and presumably would have had considerable difficulty traversing 100 km of undeveloped desert) and the signs of civilian life surrounding the tent compound, there is reason to question whether the pilots, as they dove toward the ground, did "everything feasible to verify that the objectives to be attacked [were] neither civilians nor civilian objects," as required by the customary-law principle reaffirmed in Article 57 of Protocol I.

ALLIED SILENCE ABOUT CIVILIAN CASUALTIES IN IRAQ

During the war, military briefers emphasized the allies' observance of the rules of war and persistently projected the image of a squeaky-clean bombing campaign. U.S. military spokesmen refused to concede that *any* of the allies' combat sorties were flawed. Maj. Gen. Robert B. Johnston, Gen. Schwarzkopf's chief of staff, said on February 4: "I quite truthfully cannot tell you of any reports that I know of that would show inaccurate bombing, particularly north of the Saudi-Kuwaiti border....I cannot tell you of any that I know of that have grossly missed the target."

But the view from the ground in Iraq clearly differed from the images of a near-perfect war promoted by the Pentagon on television screens in the United States and around the world. The reassuring words of allied military briefers and Bush Administration spokesmen about successful pinpoint strikes did not match the often-bloody results of allied bombing in populated areas. In the course of Middle East Watch's fact-finding alone, we found the following civilian objects were damaged or destroyed during the air war: some 400 one- and two-story homes, often in poor neighborhoods;[1] 19 apartment buildings and several hotels; two hospitals and two medical clinics; two schools and one mosque; restaurants and other commercial buildings; and market areas in four cities -- Basra, Falluja, Samawa and al-Kut. By far, the greatest number

---

[1]This is a conservative total in calculating damage to residential buildings, in that it is based on the lowest figure given whenever witnesses reported a range of numbers.

of civilian objects damaged in Iraq during the war were residential buildings.

In many of these cases, witnesses said that they were unaware of any conceivable military target in the vicinity that might have justified the attacks, suggesting that the attacks may have been indiscriminate. In other instances, the presence of a nearby military target suggests that allied bombers and missiles simply missed. Some damage cannot be definitively linked to the allied air campaign, and may have resulted from Iraqi defensive weapons falling back to earth.

Despite persuasive evidence of the messy human dimensions of the bombing campaign, specific damage and casualties sustained by Iraqi civilians from allied bomb and missile attacks have barely been noted by the Pentagon. This silence appears to reflect a deliberate policy not to disclose information in the Pentagon's possession about the extent of harm to civilians and damage to civilian property. Evidence supporting this conclusion includes the following:

- The allies clearly were equipped with the technological capacity to monitor and evaluate the destruction caused by bomb and missile attacks. Bomb-damage information, necessary for continuing military operations, was obtained from a variety of sources: pilots' reports, video and still photographs taken by gun cameras on bombers, and photographs and computer data from satellites and reconnaissance aircraft. Indeed, according to *The Washington Post*, "senior [Pentagon] officers viewed extensive footage of bombs that missed targets -- or hit targets selected in error, such as the civilian building across the street from the Iraqi Interior Ministry -- but the Pentagon has released none of the footage." U.S. Defense Secretary Cheney dismissed the need to release video footage of bombs that missed their targets on the basis that such film would have been "pretty dull, boring stuff."

- To date, the Pentagon has released virtually no information about the war's impact on Iraqi civilians. This silence has extended even to the public version of the interim report, released in July, in which Congress had required the Pentagon to estimate the civilian casualties suffered by Iraq. The two exceptions to this policy of silence were the U.S. justifications for the bombing of the Ameriyya air raid shelter in Baghdad and the British admissions of error in the bombing of a bridge in Fallujah west of Baghdad.

- By contrast, the Pentagon has released highly detailed information about successful "kills" of Iraqi military targets such as individual military trucks and tanks, even though Pentagon spokesman Pete Williams acknowledged that bomb damage to structures was easier to evaluate than damage to dug-in troops and equipment. On January 30, for example, Gen. Schwarzkopf said that among the military targets destroyed or damaged from 12:00 noon on January 29 until 3:00 a.m. on January 30, were 178 trucks, 55 artillery pieces and 52 tanks.

- Similarly, after the war Pentagon officials were not at all reluctant to leak highly detailed bomb-damage-assessment data about damage to civilian objects caused by the Iraqi military in its suppression in March of anti-government insurgents in southern Iraq. On March 19, *The New York Times*, citing one official who said that U.S. air reconnaissance had revealed damage to mosques in the southern city of Karbala caused between March 11 and March 17, reported: "At the al-Hussein mosque, there is a hole in the dome of the mosque and at least two craters from artillery or mortar fire in the courtyard."

Given the numerous U.S. statements about the allied forces' intent to comply fully with the rules of war requiring steps to minimize Iraqi civilian casualties, Middle East Watch believes that the extent of bombing in populated areas inside Iraq in which civilian casualties occurred and civilian property was damaged should be acknowledged, investigated and publicly explained by U.S. and other allied air forces. As part of this process, Middle East Watch calls on the Pentagon to disclose the evidence from U.S. bomb-damage assessments.

THE EXTENT OF CIVILIAN CASUALTIES IN IRAQ

Like the issue of damage to civilian property, the issue of the number of Iraqi civilians killed by allied bombardment was carefully -- and deliberately -- side-stepped by U.S. military officials during the war. To date, neither the U.S. nor other allied forces have offered public estimates of the number of Iraqi civilian casualties during Operation Desert Storm.

Compounding the problem of gaining an accurate assessment of Iraqi civilian casualties from allied bombing and missile attacks was the Iraqi authorities' failure to provide consistent or detailed information during the war. Part of this failure was due to the country's crippled communications system, destroyed by aerial bombardment of telephone and telegraph exchanges. But even during the first days of the air war, the Iraqi government did not issue reports of civilian casualties or damage.

This approach soon changed. Beginning on January 23, the Iraqi government announced civilian-casualty figures, and Baghdad's three dailies featured photographs of damage to civilian areas. Among the information released by the Iraqi government was the following:

- In a January 24 letter to the United Nations Secretary General from then Foreign Minister Tareq Aziz, Iraq provided an accounting of civilian damage and casualties from January 17 to January 21, citing examples from Baghdad and other parts of the country. The details in the letter varied from incident to incident; the total civilian casualties during the five-day period were 324 dead and 416 injured. The letter noted that many of the casualties occurred on January 21, during the bombing of two cities south of Baghdad.

- On February 5, Iraqi newspapers published a letter to the UN Secretary General from Tareq Aziz, in which he stated that 108 civilians had been killed and 250 injured in the bombing that took place between January 21 and January 30. By February 3, Iraq's count of civilian casualties numbered 428 dead and 650 wounded.

- On February 6, Iraq announced additional civilian casualty figures, stating that about 150 people, including 35 children, were killed in a bombing raid on Nasiriyya, a city south of Baghdad on the Euphrates River. U.S. Gen. Richard Neal and British Group Capt. Niall Irving denied that any bombing had taken place in the vicinity of Nasiriyya, which they said included a petroleum refinery and storage facilities. The same day, the Iraqi daily newspaper *al-Thawra* reported that 349 people had been killed in Basra since the war began.

- After the bombing of the Ameriyya civilian shelter in Baghdad on February 13, Iraq began to release figures indicating that civilian casualties had, inexplicably, jumped into the thousands. Substantiation for the dramatic increase in the reported civilian toll was not provided. For example, Iraq's ambassador in Tokyo said on February 14 that an estimated 7,000 civilians had been killed in the allies' bombing raids to date, which had totaled 70,000 sorties.

- Iraq's first deputy minister of health told *The Washington Post* in June that there were "thousands and thousands" of civilian casualties, but refused to provide more specific numbers; he said that the government would announce a figure and that it would be "based on correct data."

In contrast to the statistics issued during the war by government officials, Iraqi doctors provided more modest figures in post-war interviews with visitors and journalists about the number of civilian casualties treated during the war, shedding some light on the extent of injuries from the bombing in Baghdad, though not in other parts of the country. Doctors at Yarmuk Hospital, Baghdad's second largest hospital and a major surgical facility, reported that approximately 600 "war victims" were treated at the hospital. The director of Yarmuk Hospital told members of a visiting U.S. group that, in addition to those injured in the bombing of the Ameriyya air raid shelter in Baghdad, about 1,000 civilians were treated during the war and that between 150 and 200 of them died. According to one member of the U.S. group, the doctor later revised his estimate downward to between 100 and 150 dead. In a subsequent interview with *The Washington Post* in June, he said that he was not allowed to release statistics about the number of people who had died at the hospital during the air war.

The director of the 400-bed al-Kindi Hospital in the Nahda quarter of Baghdad told a representative of the U.S.-based Physicians for Human Rights in March that about 500 civilians were brought to the hospital during the war; about 25 percent were dead on arrival and another 50 percent died of their injuries or septicemia. At Saddam General Hospital, located in the Saddam City suburb of Baghdad, another 400 people were said to have been treated. Statistics were not provided about the number of these patients who died, nor about the total number of civilians treated in the hospitals.

Middle East Watch believes that the truth about civilian casualties may lie somewhere between the high-end statistics provided by Iraqi government officials in February and the modest figures noted by Baghdad doctors after the war ended. Clearly, Baghdad's civilian population was not as hard-hit during the air war as the residents of cities and towns in other parts of the country, especially Basra and other areas of southern Iraq, so the dead and injured in Iraq's largest city are not necessarily indicative of the civilian toll nationwide. Testimony collected at random by Middle East Watch from former residents of Iraq reveals numerous allied attacks in which scores of civilians were killed. In each of six incidents described in this report, the civilian death toll was put at 100 or more.

As noted, these accounts provide only a partial view, not a comprehensive survey, of the civilian casualties during the air war. Middle East Watch concludes that the number of Iraqi civilians killed as a direct result of injury from allied bombs and missiles will ultimately be calculated in the thousands, not the hundreds. At the same time, we are reasonably confident that the total number of civilians killed directly by allied attacks did not exceed several thousand, with an upper limit of perhaps between 2,500 and 3,000 Iraqi dead. These numbers, we note, do not include the substantially larger number of deaths that can be attributed to malnutrition, disease and lack of medical care caused by a combination of the U.N.-mandated embargo and the allies' destruction of Iraq's electrical system, with its severe secondary effects (see Chapter Four).

IRAQ'S MISSILE ATTACKS

Unlike the allied bombing campaign, it is not possible to say that most Iraqi missile attacks against Israel and Saudi Arabia complied with the requirements of the laws of war. It is worth noting, however, that this conclusion in no way depends on the nature of the conflict between Iraq and the countries targeted. While the missile attacks on Saudi Arabia were part of a classic armed conflict between two nations, the strikes against Israel have been subject to various characterizations. Some view the assaults as part of the continuing state of war between Iraq and Israel dating back to the termination of the British Mandate in Palestine and the declaration of the State of Israel in 1948. Quite apart from any formal state of war, others note the long-term military competition between the two nations, usually conducted clandestinely but occasionally, as in Israel's attack on an Iraqi nuclear reactor in 1981, breaking into the open. Still others view Iraq's missile strikes as an act of aggression designed to draw Israel into the Gulf war and split the allied coalition against Iraq.

Middle East Watch takes no position on this issue, both because it is beyond the organization's mandate and because the principles discussed below do not depend on its resolution. We ask not whether the attacks should be condemned as acts of aggression, but rather, whether they complied with the requirements of humanitarian law. The answer to that question is unaffected by how one characterizes the nature of the conflict between Iraq and Israel.

Applying the principles of humanitarian law, we find that, although a substantial number of attacks on Saudi Arabia and even some on Israel appear to have been aimed at or near military targets, Iraq's missile campaign as a whole was characterized by serious violations of humanitarian law. The following summarizes our findings in this regard:

Attacks on Civilian Targets

Many of the Iraqi missiles appear to have been directed at civilian targets. While the use of Patriot missiles to intercept the Iraqi-modified Scud missiles often made it impossible to determine exactly where the Iraqi missiles had been aimed, the repeated launching of relatively inaccurate missiles at targets in Israel's and Saudi Arabia's population centers of Tel Aviv and Riyadh, when a wealth of military targets were available outside heavily populated areas, suggests a deliberate decision to harm civilians. This conclusion is only reinforced by the rhetoric accompanying the missile attacks, described below, which suggests that the Iraqi military was at best indifferent to the plight of the civilian populations of Israel and Saudi Arabia, if not intent on causing as much damage and suffering as possible among those populations. Firing missiles with the purpose of harming civilians flatly violates the customary-law rule that the civilian population shall not be the object of attack, as reaffirmed in Article 51 of Protocol I.

The Use of Indiscriminate Missiles

Even many of the missiles that appear to have been directed toward military targets violated the laws of armed conflict. The customary-law principle codified in Article 51 prohibits attacks as "indiscriminate" which use "method[s] or means of combat which cannot be directed at a specific military objective" and thus "are of a nature to strike military objectives and civilians or civilian objects without distinction." Among the weapons that the provision was designed to forbid are long-range missiles with rudimentary guidance systems that cannot with any reasonable assurance be directed against a military objective, such as the V2 rockets used at the end of the Second World War.

Whether the use of a particular missile is indiscriminate, assuming the object selected for attack is a military target, depends in part on the accuracy of the weapon, the size and location of the military objectives and the target's proximity to civilians and civilian objects. As one respected commentator said, "Those methods and means of combat which would be indiscriminate in a densely populated city, might be lawful in an unpopulated area such as a forest or a desert."

The Iraqi-modified Scud missiles used against Israel and Saudi Arabia had a circular error probable (CEP) of 1000 meters, meaning that 50 percent of the missiles launched could be expected to fall within a 1000-meter radius of the point targeted. While a CEP of this magnitude may be adequate if the military object targeted is either very large or is located in a desolate area without a surrounding civilian population, it is wholly inadequate if used against a relatively small target in a populated urban area, since 50 percent of the missiles would not come within even one kilometer of the target, and additional missiles would miss their targets by lesser amounts. Accordingly, while Iraqi missile attacks on the huge Dhahran air base in Saudi Arabia or the Dimona nuclear facility in the northern Negev Desert in Israel could have been expected to be adequately discriminate, the missile attacks on small military targets in Riyadh and Tel Aviv should have been expected to be indiscriminate given the inaccuracy of Iraq's missiles.

It is worth noting that this conclusion in no way depends on an assessment of Iraq's goals in attacking Israel or Saudi Arabia. Although Iraq might claim in the case of Israel that it sought a military advantage from its missile attacks -- to split the military coalition against it by prompting Israel to attack Iraq -- those objectives do not justify indiscriminate attacks on civilians. Just as it would be illegal for allied forces to harm Iraqi civilians with the aim of encouraging them to overthrow Saddam Hussein, as explained above, so it is improper for Iraq to target or launch indiscriminate attacks against civilians in Israel or Saudi Arabia with the aim of furthering Iraq's military or political objectives.

Terrorizing the Civilian Population

The Iraqi missile attacks against both Israel and Saudi Arabia came amid an outpouring of rhetoric apparently designed to terrorize the civilian population of those countries. For example, an official Iraqi military communique of January 19 described the previous night's attack on Tel Aviv as "missiles pour[ing] out of the sky, making Tel Aviv and other targets a crematorium." A similar image was conjured up by Saddam Hussein in his April 1, 1990 speech, when he threatened to "make fire eat up half of Israel" if it attacked Iraq. An Iraqi military communique issued on January 23 stated that a purpose of an attack the previous night was "to disturb the sleep of the Zionists and blacken their night." Following a missile launching on February 11, Radio Baghdad said that the strike was intended "to sow death and alarm in the hearts of those who have isolated our women and children in the occupied land." The Iraqi Armed Forces General Command stated that the missiles launched against Israel on February 12 were intended "to spread death and terror among those who terrorized our nation."

The language accompanying the attacks on Saudi Arabia, though perhaps somewhat less vivid, was comparable. For example, the Iraqi Armed Forces General Command stated that the missiles launched at

Riyadh on February 8 were intended "to punish the traitor al-Sa'ud family" and "to disturb the sleep of the tyrants."

These comments, when coupled with ongoing missile attacks against Israel and Saudi Arabia and the ever-present possibility that these missiles might be armed with chemical weapons, appear to have been made deliberately to spread terror among the civilian populations, in violation of the customary-law principle codified in Article 51. Such spreading of terror is a violation regardless of whether any particular attack was aimed at a military or civilian target.

Illegal Reprisals

Iraq suggested in several public statements during the war that its missile attacks on Israel and Saudi Arabia were justified as reprisals. For example, missiles were said to have been launched on January 22 "in revenge for the crimes of Zionism." In describing two missile attacks against Tel Aviv on January 25, the Iraqi Armed Forces General Command said that the intent was to "pour fire on the heads of the arrogant Zionists to avenge what their hands have committed." The attacks on Riyadh were frequently accompanied by similar language: the aim of a February 11 attack was "to punish the agent traitors, infidel apostates, the rulers of Saudi Arabia...and to harass the traitors"; the February 8 attack was "[s]o that the rulers of the Sa'ud family may know that their masters' attacks on our civilian targets will not pass unpunished."

Although Article 51 prohibits "[a]ttacks against the civilian population or civilians by way of reprisals," this is new law to which many countries, including the United States, have objected on the grounds that it may encourage violations of humanitarian law by leaving the victim nation without any strong deterrent. In outlining when reprisals might be appropriate by nations who do not subscribe to Article 51, a leading commentary would require, among other things, that the reprisals be in response to specified "grave and manifest violations of the law of armed conflict committed by the other Party," the reprisals be taken for the sole purpose of enforcing future compliance with the laws of war, and the reprisals be preceded by reasonable warning that retaliation will follow if illegal acts do not cease (see Chapter Six).

It is utterly implausible, when judged against these criteria, that Iraq's attacks on civilians could qualify as lawful reprisals. Israel did not even participate in the hostilities during the Gulf conflict, let alone commit the "grave and manifest" violations of the laws of war against Iraq that might have justified reprisals. In the case of Saudi Arabia, even if Iraq believed that the coalition of which Saudi Arabia was a part was committing illegal acts against the Iraqi population, Iraq had a duty both to detail those alleged violations and to issue a warning to the coalition that reprisals might follow unless the alleged illegal acts ended. No such itemization or warning was ever given.

PART I

THE LEGAL STANDARDS

1
THE LEGAL REGIME
GOVERNING THE CONDUCT OF AIR WARFARE

The recently concluded hostilities between the allied coalition and Iraq were a classic example of an international -- that is, interstate -- armed conflict as defined in Article 2 common to the four 1949 Geneva Conventions. As such, the conduct of military operations by all the warring parties in the Gulf was governed by the Geneva Conventions, as well as by the customary laws of war. Since Iraq, as well as many of the key members of the allied coalition, were not Parties to the First Additional Protocol[1] to the Geneva Conventions, that instrument was not applicable to the Gulf conflict as a matter of conventional law. This does not mean, however, that the Protocol was irrelevant, since many of the Protocol's provisions reaffirm, clarify or otherwise codify pre-existing customary-law restraints on methods and means of combat and, thus, are binding on all nations regardless of ratification.

Despite its refusal to ratify Protocol I, the United States has expressed its support for many rules in the Protocol and has declared others to be customary law.[2] Moreover, the U.S. Army, Navy and Air

---

[1] Protocol Additional to the Geneva Conventions of 12 August 1949, and Relating to the Protections of Victims of International Armed Conflicts (Protocol I) of June 8, 1977, *opened for signature* December 12, 1977, U.N. Doc. A/32/144, Annex I, II (1977), *reprinted in* 16 I.L.M. 1391 (1977) [hereinafter Protocol I]. This instrument, which supplements the four 1949 Geneva Conventions for the Protection of War Victims, codifies and updates legal restraints on means and methods of warfare to provide more effective protection to the civilian population against the effects of hostilities in international armed conflicts.

[2] *See* Michael J. Matheson, Deputy Legal Advisor at the U.S. Department of State, "The United States Position on the Relation of Customary International Law to the 1977 Protocols Additional to the 1949 Geneva Conventions," Speech on January 22, 1987 at the 6th Annual American Red Cross - Washington College of Law Conference on International Humanitarian Law: A Workshop on Customary International Law and the 1977 Protocols Additional to the 1949

Force manuals on international law applicable during armed conflict include prescriptions which often track the terminology of Protocol I. This chapter sets forth, albeit not exhaustively,[3] the legal rules and principles governing aerial bombardment[4] during the Gulf war. It focuses, in particular, on customary restraints on methods and means of warfare, and the relation of customary law to codifications of the laws of war in Protocol I.

INTERNATIONAL HUMANITARIAN LAW

The law of war, or international humanitarian law, has developed over centuries. It was largely shaped before the emergence of air power. The 1907 Hague Regulations on land warfare, for example, were designed to apply to a combat zone where hostile land forces confronted each other in close proximity. Air bombardment, while dimly recognized, was thought to be feasible only as close support for ground forces -- a kind of supplement to artillery. The hinterlands of the belligerents were believed to be secure from the effects of hostilities. Rapid technological advances in military air power and its devastating effects during World War II shattered any illusion about the security of areas far from land combat. Although there is no comprehensive treaty on the conduct of air warfare comparable to the 1907 Hague Regulations, aerial bombardment is, like all other forms of combat, governed by certain legal rules which "must be derived from general principles, extrapolated from the law

---

Geneva Conventions, 2 *The American University Journal of International Law and Policy*, Fall 1987, at 419 [hereinafter Matheson].

[3] It does not discuss, for example, prohibitions on the use of chemical, biological and other poisonous weapons; prohibitions against seizure or destruction of enemy property; or the special protections afforded prisoner-of-war camps, medical units and transport, and various other protected objects.

[4] The term aerial bombardment includes, among other things "dropping munitions from manned or unmanned aircraft, strafing, and using missiles or rockets against enemy targets on land." U.S. Dept of the Air Force, Air Force Pamphlet No. 110-31, *International Law -- The Conduct of Armed Conflict and Air Operations*, November 19, 1976, para. 5-1 at 5-1 [hereinafter Air Force Pamphlet].

affecting land or sea warfare, or derived from other sources including the practice of states reflected in a wide variety of sources."[5]

MILITARY NECESSITY AND THE PRINCIPLE OF HUMANITY

Customary legal restraints on warfare are premised on the notion that violence and destruction that are superfluous to actual military necessity are wasteful, politically counterproductive, and immoral. The Air Force Pamphlet defines military necessity as "the principle which justifies measures of regulated force not forbidden by international law which are indispensable for securing the prompt submission of the enemy, with the least possible expenditures of economic and human resources."[6] It notes that this concept embraces the following four basic elements:

> (i) that the force used is capable of being and is in fact regulated by the user; (ii) that the use of force is necessary to achieve as quickly as possible the partial or complete submission of the adversary; (iii) that the force used is no greater in effect on the enemy's personnel and property than needed to achieve his prompt submission (economy of force), and (iv) that the force used is not otherwise prohibited.[7]

---

[5] Air Force Pamphlet, para. 1-3(c) at 1-7. The 1907 Hague Regulations are annexed to Hague Convention (IV) of October 18, 1907, *Respecting the Laws and Customs of War on Land*, 36 Stat. 2227, T.S. 539, *reprinted in* D. Schindler & J. Toman, *The Law of Armed Conflict* 63-68 (1981). The United States is a Party to this Convention which, together with its annexed Regulations, remains the most authoritative source of law for the United States in the conduct of actual military operations.

[6] Air Force Pamphlet, para. 1-3(a)(1) at 1-5-1-6.

[7] *Id.* at 1-6.

Accordingly, the conduct of hostilities "must be carried on within the limits of the prohibitions of international law, including the restraints inherent in the principle of 'necessity'."[8]

The principle of humanity both complements and inherently limits the doctrine of military necessity. The U.S. Air Force Pamphlet states that the principle of humanity "forbids the infliction of suffering, injury or destruction not actually necessary for the accomplishment of legitimate military purposes."[9] More concretely, the principle yields "a specific prohibition against unnecessary suffering, a requirement of proportionality, and . . . [an affirmation of] the basic immunity of civilian populations and civilians from being objects of attack during armed conflict."[10]

U.N. GENERAL ASSEMBLY RESOLUTION 2444

The duty to distinguish and refrain from targeting the civilian population was reiterated in U.N. General Assembly Resolution 2444, *Respect for Human Rights in Armed Conflict*,[11] adopted by unanimous vote on December 18, 1969. The Resolution states in pertinent part:

> a) that the right of Parties to a conflict to adopt means of injuring the enemy is not unlimited;
> b) that it is prohibited to launch attacks against the civilian population as such;
> c) that a distinction must be made at all times between persons taking part in the hostilities and members of the civilian population to the effect that the later be spared as much as possible....

---

[8] *Id.*, para. 1-3 (a) (1) at 1-6.

[9] *Id.*, para. 1-3(a)(2) at 1-6.

[10] *Id.*

[11] G.A.Res. 2444, 23 U.N. GAOR Supp. (No. 18) at 164, U.N. Doc. A/7433 (1968).

The U.S. government has expressly recognized this Resolution as declaratory of existing customary international law.[12] That is, these principles legally govern the conduct of hostilities, including aerial bombardment, by all nations, including the U.S. military.

CUSTOMARY LAW AND PROTOCOL I
CIVILIAN IMMUNITY AND THE PRINCIPLE OF DISTINCTION

Protocol I contains detailed rules, mostly reaffirmations or clarifications of existing customary law, which implement the customary principles that a distinction should be made between combatants and civilians and that civilians and civilian objects may not be the object of attacks. Four different sections of the Protocol are devoted to this task. First are provisions designed to revitalize and strengthen the legal requirement to distinguish military objectives from civilians and civilian objects and to limit attacks to military objectives. Second are provisions clarifying practical steps to be taken in the selection of targets to prevent attacks on civilians and civilian objects, including the rule of proportionality and a prohibition of indiscriminate attacks. Third are provisions regulating the means and methods of *both* attack and defense to avoid or minimize civilian casualties and damage to civilian objects. Fourth are specific provisions limiting or prohibiting attacks on particular objects and specified areas.

GENERAL RESTRICTIONS ON AIR WARFARE

The Basic Rule: The Immunity of Civilians and Civilian Objects

Article 48 of Protocol I is a paraphrase of the basic rules stated in paragraphs 2 and 3 of UNGA Resolution 2444. It states: "In order to ensure respect for and protection of the civilian population and civilian objects, the Parties to the conflict shall at all times distinguish between the civilian population and combatants and between civilian objects and

---

[12] *See* letter from the General Counsel, United States Department of Defense, to Senator Edward M. Kennedy (September 22, 1968), *reprinted in* Rovine, Contemporary Practice of United States Relating to International Law, 67 *American Journal of International Law* at 122-26 (1973).

military objectives and accordingly shall direct their operations only against military objectives." The Air Force Pamphlet's formulation of this basic principle is substantially similar. It states: "The requirement to distinguish between combatants and civilians, and between military objectives and civilian objects, imposes obligations on all the parties to the conflict to establish and maintain the distinctions."[13]

Article 51(2) reaffirms this mandatory distinction by providing: "The civilian population as such, as well as individual civilians, shall not be the object of attack. Acts or threats of violence the primary purpose of which is to spread terror among the civilian population are prohibited." This general immunity does *not* prohibit attacks which may cause civilian casualties. For example, civilians who are located within or near legitimate military targets, while still immune from individualized attack, may be at risk of death or injury as a result of lawful attacks against such targets, although, as noted later, such civilians would retain the benefits of the rule of proportionality as it applies to collateral civilian casualties.

Terror and Morale Attacks
Article 51(2) also prohibits attacks, and threats of such acts, which are launched or threatened with intent to terrorize the civilian population. Specifically, the second sentence of that section provides: "Acts or threats of violence the primary purpose of which is to spread terror among the civilian population are prohibited." This provision is intended to make clear that terror bombing violates the laws of war. However, the fact that attacks upon legitimate military objectives may cause terror among the civilian population does not make such attacks unlawful.

This article also prohibits bombing to attack civilian morale. Although technically there may be a distinction between morale and terror bombing, they are, in practice, treated the same. It has often been observed that what is morale bombing to the attacking force is terror bombing to the civilians who are targeted. In the past, these attacks were carried out by strategic aerial bombardment of the enemy's economic infrastructure. This infrastructure may include a mix of military and civilian targets. To the extent that these attacks are launched or

---

[13] Air Force Pamphlet, para. 5-3 (a)(2)(b) at 5-8.

threatened solely or primarily for political ends, they violate the principles of civilian immunity, proportionality, and humanity. Attacks intended primarily to induce the civilian population to rebellion or to overthrow its leadership would be examples of unlawful attacks.[14]

Prohibited Uses of Civilians

The effort to protect the civilian population would be frustrated if the party in control of the population used civilians to render certain areas immune from military attack. Accordingly, Article 51[15] prohibits the use of civilians to shield a defensive position, to hide military objectives or to screen an attack. Nor may civilians be induced or compelled to leave their homes or shelters to interfere with the movement of the enemy. The Air Force Pamphlet notes that a "party to a conflict which chooses to use its civilian population for military purposes violates its obligations to protect its own civilian population. It cannot complain

---

[14] *See generally* Remarks of Hamilton DeSaussure delivered at the American Red Cross - Washington College of Law Conference on International Humanitarian Law in 31 *The American University Law Review*, Summer 1982 at 883-889; J. Spaight, *Air Power and War Rights* (3d ed. 1947) at 275; J. Spaight, *Air Power in the Cities* (1930) at 110.

[15] Art. 51(7) provides: "The presence or movements of the civilian population or individual civilians shall not be used to render certain points or areas immune from military operations, in particular in attempts to shield military objectives from attacks or to shield, favour or impede military operations. The Parties to the conflict shall not direct the movement of the civilian population or individual civilians in order to attempt to shield military objectives from attacks or to shield military operations."

The *New Rules* states: "The paragraph reaffirms Art. 28 of the Fourth Convention which provides that '[T]he presence of protected persons may not be used to render certain points or areas immune from military operations,' and it extends this provision by enlarging the protected class to all civilians. It also incorporates the concept of movement to the prohibition in order to cover cases in which civilian refugees are herded down a road either as a shield for a moving column of combatants, or to impede the movement of the adversary's columns." (footnote omitted) Bothe, Michael, Karl Josef Partsch, and Waldemar A. Solf, *New Rules for Victims of Armed Conflicts* (Boston: Martinus Nijhoff Publishers, 1982) at 316. [hereinafter *New Rules*].

when inevitable, although regrettable, civilian casualties result."[16] However, as discussed later, such deliberate misuse of civilians to gain a military advantage does not permit the attacking party to disregard customary precautions designed to avoid or minimize incidental civilian casualties.

The U.S. government has expressly recognized Article 51 as customary international law,[17] and the Air Force Pamphlet enjoins attacks against civilians in terms virtually identical to Article 51.[18] The U.S. government also regards as declaratory of customary law other articles in Protocol I which are designed to clarify further the requirement to distinguish between civilians and military objectives. These articles, among others, provide relatively explicit definitions of civilians, the civilian population, military objectives and civilian objects.

Civilians and Civilian Population
Article 50 of Protocol I defines the term "civilian population" as comprising "all persons who are civilians" and defines a civilian as anyone who is not a member of the armed forces or of an organized armed group of a party to the conflict.[19] Thus, civilians and the civilian

---

[16] Air Force Pamphlet, para. 5-3 (a)(2)(b) at 5-8.

[17] Matheson at 426.

[18] Air Force Pamphlet, para. 5-3(a)(1) at 5-7.

[19] Protocol I, Art. 50(l) defines a civilian as "any person who does not belong to one of the categories referred to in article 4 A (l),(2),(3), and (6) of the Third Convention and in article 43 of this Protocol." In pertinent part the persons listed in Article 4(A) of the Third Geneva Convention are: members of the armed forces of a Party to the conflict as well as members of militias or volunteer corps forming part of such armed forces; members of other militias and volunteer corps, provided that they fulfill certain conditions; and members of regular armed forces who profess allegiance to a government or an authority not recognized by the detaining power.
Article 43(1) of Protocol I defines the armed forces of a party as consisting of "all organized armed forces, groups and units which are under a command responsible to that Party for the conduct of its subordinates, even if that Party is represented by a government or an authority not recognized by an

population comprise all persons who are not entitled to, or do not directly, participate in hostilities. This article also stipulates that the "presence within the civilian population of individuals who do not come within the definition of civilians does not deprive the population of its civilian character."[20] The point of this provision, according to the *New Rules*, is that "[t]he presence of a small number of off-duty combatants, or even of some engaged in the transaction of business for the armed forces within a community of civilians would not subject that community to attack."[21]

Military Objectives

Both Article 52(2) of Protocol I and the Air Force Pamphlet[22] employ the same two-pronged test to define military objectives. This test limits military objectives to those objects or targets which by their nature, location, purpose or use contribute effectively to the enemy's military action *and* whose total or partial destruction, neutralization or capture offers a definite military advantage in the circumstances ruling at the time.

The requirement that military objectives effectively contribute to military action does not necessarily require a direct connection with combat operations. As the Air Force Pamphlet states, the "inherent nature of the object is not controlling since even a traditionally civilian object, such as a civilian house, can be a military objective when it is occupied and used by military forces during an armed engagement."[23] The military objective not only must effectively contribute to the enemy's military action, but its destruction, neutralization or capture *must also*

---

adverse Party. Such armed forces shall be subject to an internal disciplinary system . . . . "

[20] Protocol I, Art. 50(3).

[21] *New Rules* at 296.

[22] Air Force Pamphlet, para. 5-3(b)(1) at 5-8-5-9.

[23] Air Force Pamphlet, para. 5-3(b)(2) at 5-9.

offer a "definite military advantage" to the attacking party in the "circumstances ruling at the time."

The official ICRC *Commentary* on Article 52, Protocol I,[24] notes that the concept "definite military advantage in circumstances ruling at the time" means that "it is not legitimate to launch an attack which only offers *potential or indeterminate advantages.* Those ordering or executing the attack must have sufficient information available to take this requirement into account; in case of doubt, the safety of the civilian population, which is the aim of the Protocol, must be taken into consideration."[25] The other authoritative commentary, the *New Rules,* similarly indicates that the adjective "definite" which modifies "military advantage" "is a word of limitation denoting in this context a concrete and perceptible military advantage rather than a hypothetical and speculative one."[26] The requirement that the definite military advantage must be present "in circumstances ruling at time" imposes an additional significant limitation on the attacker's target selection. The *New Rules* states in this regard: "This element emphasizes that in the dynamic circumstances of armed conflict, objects which may have been military objectives yesterday, may no longer be such today and vice versa. Thus, timely and reliable information of the military situation is an important element in the selection of targets for attack."[27]

A leading authority on the laws of war, who was present at the drafting of Protocol I, endorses these interpretations, stating:

> [T]he "definite military advantage" required under the definition must be present "in the circumstances ruling at the time". This element in the definition effectively

---

[24] International Committee of the Red Cross, *Commentary on the Additional Protocols of 8 June 1977 to the Geneva Conventions of 12 August 1949* (Geneva: Martinus Nijhoff Publishers, 1987) at 636 [hereinafter ICRC *Commentary*].

[25] *Id.* (Emphasis added)

[26] *New Rules* at 326.

[27] *Id.*

precludes military commanders from relying exclusively on abstract categorizations in the determination of whether specific objects constitute military objectives ("a bridge is a military objective"; "an object located in the zone of combat is a military objective", etc.). Instead, they will have to determine whether, say, the destruction of a particular bridge, which would have been militarily important yesterday, does, in the circumstances ruling today, still offer a "definite military advantage": if not, the bridge no longer constitutes a military objective and, thus, may not be destroyed.[28]

Whether the required definite military advantage under prevailing circumstances would accrue from a particular attack "must be judged in the context of the military advantage anticipated from the specific military operation of which the attack is a part considered as a whole, and not only from isolated or particular parts of that operation."[29]

Types of Military Objectives

Except for certain objects given special protection, Protocol I does not delineate specific categories of persons or property as military objectives. It is clear, however, that enemy combatants and civilians who assume a combatant's role are legitimate targets. The Air Force Pamphlet identifies as undisputed military objectives the enemy's encampments and his armament, such as military aircraft, tanks, antiaircraft emplacements and troops in the field.[30] The U.S.

---

[28] Frits Kalshoven, "Reaffirmation and Development of International Humanitarian Law Applicable in Armed Conflicts: The Diplomatic Conference, Geneva, 1974-1977," 9 *Netherlands Yearbook of International Law* 107, 111 (1978).

[29] *New Rules* at 324-25.

[30] Air Force Pamphlet, para. 5-3(b)(2) at 5-9.

Army[31] and Navy's[32] lists of military targets are similar, although the Navy's is more expansive.

The ICRC *Commentary* contains the following proposed list of military objectives:

(1) Armed forces . . . and persons who . . . take part in the fighting.

(2) Positions, installations or constructions occupied by the forces . . . as well as combat objectives (that is to say, those objectives which are directly contested in battle between land or sea forces including airborne forces).

(3) Installations, constructions and other works of a military nature, such as barracks, fortifications, War Ministries (e.g. Ministries of Army, Navy, Air Force, National Defence, Supply)

---

[31] "Military objectives include, for example, factories producing munitions and military supplies, military camps, warehouses storing munitions and military supplies, ports and railroads being used for the transportation of military supplies, and other places that are for the accommodation of troops or the support of military operations." Department of the Army, Field Manual 27-10, *The Law of Land Warfare* (July 1956), change no. 1 (15 July 1976), para. 40 (c) [hereinafter Army FM 27-10].

[32] Targets listed as proper for naval attack include such military objectives as "enemy warships and military aircraft, naval and military auxiliaries, naval and military bases ashore, warship construction and repair facilities, military depots and warehouses, POL [petroleum, oil and lubricants] storage areas, docks, port facilities, harbors, bridges, airfields, military vehicles, armor, artillery, ammunition stores, troop concentrations and embarkation points, lines of communication and other objects used to conduct or support military operations. Proper naval targets also include geographic targets, such as a mountain pass, and buildings and facilities that provide administrative and personnel support for military and naval operations such as barracks, communications and command and control facilities, headquarters buildings, mess halls, and training areas." (footnote omitted) Department of the Navy, *Annotated Supplement to The Commander's Handbook on the Law of Naval Operations* (NWP 9 (Rev. A)/ FMFM 1-10) (October 5, 1989), para, 8.1.1 at 8-2 [hereinafter Naval Manual].

and other organs for the direction and administration of military operations.

(4) Stores of arms or military supplies, such as munitions dumps, stores of equipment or fuel, vehicles parks.

(5) Airfields, rocket launching ramps and naval base installations.

(6) Those of the lines and means of communication (railway lines, roads, bridges, tunnels and canals) which are of fundamental military importance;

(7) The installations of broadcasting and television stations; telephone and telegraph exchanges of fundamental military importance;

(8) Industries of fundamental importance for the conduct of the war:

> (a) industries for the manufacture of armaments . . . ;
>
> (b) industries for the manufacture of supplies and material of a military character, such as transport and communications material, equipment for the armed forces;
>
> (c) factories or plant constituting other production and manufacturing centres of fundamental importance for the conduct of war, such as the metallurgical, engineering and chemical industries, whose nature or purpose is essentially military;
>
> (d) storage and transport installations whose basic function it is to serve the industries referred to in (a)-(c);
>
> (e) installations providing energy mainly for national defence, e.g. coal, other fuels, or atomic energy, and plants producing gas or electricity mainly for military consumption.

(9) Installations constituting experimental, research centres for experiments on and the development of weapons and war material.[33]

Civilian and "Dual-Use" Objects

The ICRC's model compilation includes objects that have "dual-uses or functions" in that while they serve the needs of the civilian population, they also are used by the enemy. These objects typically include bridges, power plants, chemical and other factories, fuel-storage depots, railroad and other transportation facilities and systems, vehicles and communications facilities. The Air Force Pamphlet openly concedes that "[c]ontroversy exists over whether, and the circumstances under which, . . . objects, such as civilian transportation and communications systems, dams and dykes can be classified properly as military objectives."[34]

It is important to understand that under customary law civilian objects enjoy general protection against direct attack. Article 52(l) defines civilian objects negatively as all objects that are not military objectives as defined in paragraph 2 of that same article which sets forth the two-fold test for military objectives. Therefore, Article 52 implicitly characterizes all objects as civilian, unless they make an effective contribution to the enemy's military action and unless destroying, capturing, or neutralizing them offers a definite military advantage in the prevailing circumstances.

In doubtful situations, Article 52 creates a presumption that objects normally dedicated to civilian use, such as churches, houses or schools, are not employed to contribute effectively to military action. This presumption attaches only to objects that ordinarily have no significant military use or purpose, not to dual-use objects.[35]

---

[33] ICRC *Commentary*, at 632-33.

[34] Air Force Pamphlet, para. 5-3 (b)(2) at 5-9 (footnote omitted).

[35] *New Rules* at 326.

RESTRAINTS ON ATTACKS:
PROHIBITION OF DISPROPORTIONATE
AND OTHER INDISCRIMINATE ATTACKS

The Rule of Proportionality

The legitimacy of a military target under Article 52 does not provide unlimited license to attack it. The customary principles of military necessity and humanity require that the attacking party always seek to avoid or minimize civilian casualties and, thus, prohibit disproportionate and other kinds of indiscriminate attacks.

Articles 51(5)(b) and 57(2)(a)(iii) and (b) contain the first codification of the customary rule of proportionality as it relates to collateral civilian casualties and damage to civilian objects. Article 51(5)(b) formulates this rule as follows: "an attack which may be expected to cause incidental loss of civilian life, injury to civilians, damage to civilian objects, or a combination thereof, which would be excessive in relation to the concrete and direct military advantage anticipated."

This rule, according to the *New Rules*,

> clearly requires that those who plan or decide upon an attack must take into account the effects of the attack on the civilian population in their pre-attack estimate. They must determine whether those effects are excessive in relation to the concrete and direct military advantage anticipated. Obviously this decision will have to be based on a balancing of:
> (1) the foreseeable extent of incidental or collateral civilian casualties or damage, and
> (2) the relative importance of the military objective as a target.[36]

The U.S. government expressly recognizes the rule of proportionality as a general restraint on the conduct of hostilities.[37]

---

[36] *New Rules* at 310.

[37] Matheson at 426.

Acceptance of this customary law rule is also evidenced by its inclusion in the military manuals of the three U.S. armed services.[38]

Concrete and Direct Military Advantage

The *New Rules* notes that the rule of proportionality imposes "an additional limitation on the discretion of combatants in deciding whether an object is a military objective under para. 2 of Art. 52."[39] If an attack is expected to cause incidental casualties or damage, the requirement of an anticipated "definite" military advantage under Article 52 (one of the minimum requirements for an object to be a proper military target) is heightened to the more restrictive standard of a "concrete and direct" military advantage set forth in Article 51(5)(b). According to the *New Rules*:

> "Concrete" means specific, not general; perceptible to the senses. Its meaning is therefore roughly equivalent to the adjective "definite" used in the two pronged test prescribed by Art. 52(2). "Direct," on the other hand, means "without intervening condition of agency." Taken together the two words of limitation raise the standard set by Art. 52 in those situations where civilians may be affected by the attack. A remote advantage to be gained at some unknown time in the future would not be a proper consideration to weigh against civilian losses.[40]

The ICRC *Commentary* provides a similar interpretation, stating:

> The expression "concrete and direct" was intended to show that the advantage concerned should be substantial and relatively close, and that advantages which are hardly

---

[38] *See* Air Force Pamphlet, para. 5-3 (c)(1)(b)(i)(c) at 5-9 and para. 5-3 (c)(2)(b) at 5-10; Army FM 27-10, at para. 41; Naval Manual, para. 8.1.2.1 at 8-5.

[39] *New Rules* at 360.

[40] *Id.* at 365.

perceptible and those which would only appear in the long term should be disregarded.[41]

While allowing a fairly broad margin of judgment, the *Commentary* notes,

> even in a general attack the advantage anticipated must be a military advantage and it must be concrete and direct; there can be no question of creating conditions conducive to surrender by means of attacks which incidentally harm the civilian population. A military advantage can only consist in ground gained and in annihilating or weakening the enemy armed forces. In addition, it should be noted that the words "concrete and direct" impose stricter conditions on the attacker than those implied by the criteria defining military objectives in Article 52 . . . . [42] (Emphasis added).

The term "concrete and direct military advantage" refers to the advantage expected "from the specific military operation of which the attack is a part taken as a whole and not from isolated or particular parts of that operation."[43]

The military manuals of all three U.S. armed services reflect the "concrete and direct military advantage" language of customary international law. The Air Force Pamphlet, for example, formulates the rule of proportionality as follows:

> Attacks are not prohibited against military objectives even though incidental injury or damage to civilians will occur, but such incidental injury to civilians or damage to civilian objects must not be excessive when compared to *the concrete and direct military advantage* anticipated.

---

[41] ICRC *Commentary* at 684.

[42] ICRC *Commentary* at 685.

[43] *New Rules* at 311 (footnote omitted).

Careful balancing of interests is required between the potential military advantage and the degree of incidental injury or damage in order to preclude situations raising issues of indiscriminate attacks violating general civilian protections. (Emphasis added) [44]

However, in its July 1991 report to Congress on the conduct of the Gulf War, the Defense Department describes the rule of proportionality in somewhat different -- and less restrictive -- terms: "It prohibits military actions in which the negative effects (such as collateral civilian casualties) clearly outweigh the military gain."[45]

This particular statement of the rule of proportionality appears to modify the customary-law formulation of that rule found in the U.S.

---

[44] Air Force Pamphlet at para. 5-3(c)(2)(b) at 5-10. The Naval Manual, para. 8.1.2.1 at 8-5, states:

> It is not unlawful to cause incidental injury or death to civilians, or collateral damage to civilian objects, during an attack upon a legitimate military objective. Incidental injury or collateral damage should not, however, be excessive in light of the military advantage anticipated by the attack. Naval commanders must take all practicable precautions, taking into account military and humanitarian considerations, to keep civilian casualties and damage to the absolute minimum consistent with mission accomplishment and the security of the force. In each instance, the commander must determine whether incidental injuries and collateral damage would be excessive, on the basis of an honest and reasonable estimate of the facts available to him. (footnotes omitted).

The U.S. Army Field Manual 27-10 echoes this:

> loss of life and damage to property incidental to attacks must not be excessive in relation to the concrete and direct military advantage expected to be gained. Those who plan or decide upon an attack, therefore, must take all reasonable steps to insure . . . that those objectives may be attacked without probable losses in lives and damage to property disproportionate to the military advantage anticipated." at para. 41.

[45] Pentagon Interim Report at 12-2.

military manuals and codified in Protocol I. Under the Pentagon's new version of the rule, collateral damage is not evaluated in relation to the "concrete and direct military advantage anticipated" but in terms of the "military gain." This considerably relaxed standard would unduly ease the burden of commanders in their choice of targets.

Because this new formulation, if accepted as Pentagon policy, would amount to a unilateral revision of a fundamental rule of the customary law of armed conflict, long accepted by and *binding* on the United States, it would be in conflict with governing laws. The Pentagon should clarify publicly its position in this regard.

Excessive Collateral Damage

The other side of the proportionality equation is the requirement that the foreseeable injury to civilians and damage to civilian objects not be disproportionate, i.e., "excessive" to the expected "concrete and definite military advantage."

Excessive damage is a relational concept, not quantifiable in terms of a fixed number of civilians dead or injured, or houses destroyed. Such damage need not be so great that it "shock the conscience" of the world. Rather, its avoidance requires a good-faith balancing of disparate probabilities--the foreseeability of collateral damage and the relative importance of a particular military target.

The ICRC *Commentary* provides examples of "excessive" damage: (a) the presence of a soldier on leave cannot serve as a justification to destroy the entire village, and (b) "if the destruction of a bridge is of paramount importance for the occupation or non-occupation of a strategic zone, it is understood that some houses may be hit, but not that a whole urban area be levelled."[46] Of course, the disproportion between losses and damages caused and the military advantages anticipated "raises a delicate problem; in some situations there will be no room for doubt, while in other situations there may be reason for hesitation. In such situations the interests of the civilian population should

---

[46] ICRC *Commentary* at 684.

prevail...."[47] However, the ICRC *Commentary* makes it clear that there is never a justification for excessive civilian casualties:

> The idea has also been put forward that even if they are very high, civilian losses and damages may be justified if the military advantage at stake is of great importance. This idea is contrary to the fundamental rules of the Protocol; in particular it conflicts with Article 48 (*Basic rule*) and with paragraphs 1 and 2 of the present Article 51. The Protocol does not provide any justification for attacks which cause extensive civilian losses and damages. Incidental losses and damages should never be extensive.[48]

Ultimately, compliance with the rule of proportionality depends on the subjective judgment of military commanders in specific situations. Recognizing that decisions are taken in battle "under circumstances when clinical certainty is impossible and when the adversary is striving to conceal the true facts, to deceive and to confuse,"[49] the *New Rules* states:

> The standard for judging the actions of commanders and others responsible for planning, deciding upon or executing attacks, must be based on a reasonable and honest reaction to the facts and circumstances known to them from information reasonably available to them at the time they take their actions and not on the basis of hindsight.[50]

In view of the subjective nature of such decisions, the *New Rules* suggests that parties to the conflict "should curtail the limits within which

---

[47] ICRC *Commentary* at 626.

[48] *Id.* at 626.

[49] *New Rules* at 279.

[50] *Id.* at 279-80.

commanders of operating units exercise their discretion by issuing rules of engagement tailored to the situation prevailing in the area of conflict involved."[51] In this regard, the Defense Department's July 1991 report to Congress contains a section on the rules of engagement for coalition forces, but is utterly silent as to the content of those rules. Since these rules of engagement must be consistent with the law of armed conflict, an important unanswered question pertains to what the rules for Operation Desert Storm provided. Assuming that they are classified, is this still necessary given the successful conclusion of hostilities? Accordingly, Middle East Watch calls on the Pentagon to release these rules of engagement publicly. It is also not clear whether, in discussing the nature of the balance required under the rule of proportionality, the July 1991 Pentagon report's use of the phrase "clearly outweigh" in place of "excessive" -- the term used in Protocol I and the three U.S. military manuals in the passages quoted above -- was meant to signal a substantive change. The Pentagon should clarify the meaning of its new terminology.

Other Kinds of Indiscriminate Attacks
    In addition to disproportionate attacks, Article 5l(5)(a) and (b)[52]

---

[51] *Id.* at 310.

[52] Article 5l states:

> 4. Indiscriminate attacks are prohibited. Indiscriminate attacks are:
>
>> a) those which are not directed at a specific military objective;
>> b) those which employ a method or means of combat which cannot be directed at a specific military objective; or
>> c) those which employ a method or means of combat the effects of which cannot be limited as required by this Protocol; and consequently, in each such case, are of a nature to strike military objectives and civilians or civilian objects without distinction.
>
> 5. Among others, the following types of attacks are to be considered as indiscriminate:

defines and prohibits other kinds of "indiscriminate" attacks. Examples of such attacks are those that are not directed at specific military objectives or that employ a method or means of combat that a party cannot direct at a specific military objective. Thus, the article prohibits parties from attacking military objectives and civilians or civilian objects without distinction.

Article 51(5)(a) characterizes an attack as indiscriminate when it treats a number of clearly separate and distinct military objectives located in a city, town, village, or other area containing a concentration of civilians or civilian objects as a single military objective. A ground assault on a single military objective within that locale, on the other hand, would not constitute an unlawful indiscriminate attack. An attack on an entire populated area to destroy several military objectives that a party could have attacked separately, however, would be indiscriminate under this test. This provision, therefore, would prohibit the target-area aerial bombardment of densely populated civilian centers that occurred during World War II.[53]

Whether the prohibition in Article 51(5)(a) is new law or merely a reaffirmation of existing customary law depends on how the term "clearly separated" is construed. The U.S. and other delegations at the diplomatic conference that elaborated the Protocol "expressed the

---

a. an attack by bombardment by any methods or means which treats as a single military objective a number of clearly separated and distinct military objectives located in a city, town, village or other area containing a similar concentration of civilians or civilian objects; and

b. an attack which may be expected to cause incidental loss of civilian life, injury to civilians, damage to civilian objects, or a combination thereof, which would be excessive in relation to the concrete and direct military advantage anticipated.

[53] The *New Rules* indicates that for this rule to apply the "concentration" of civilians must actually be endangered by the attack. "[T]he rule would not be violated if the civilian population has evacuated the town or city before the attack or if the entire locality is used for military purposes." *Id.* at 309. However, civilians remaining in the town or city would retain the benefits of the rule of proportionality.

understanding that the words "clearly separated" refer not only to a separation of two or more military objectives which can be observed or which are visually separated, but also includes the element of a significant distance. Further, that distance must be at least of such a distance that will permit the individual military objectives to be attacked separately."[54] If construed in accordance with this understanding, the prohibition probably reaffirms customary law.

PRECAUTIONARY MEASURES

Article 57 of Protocol I codifies pre-existing customary law regarding precautions that an attacking party must observe to avoid and minimize collateral civilian casualties and damage to civilian objects.[55]

---

[54] *Id.* (footnote omitted).

[55] Article 57 states:

1. In the conduct of military operations, constant care shall be taken to spare the civilian population, civilians and civilian objects.

2. With respect to attacks, the following precautions shall be taken:
    a) those who plan or decide upon an attack shall:
        i) do everything feasible to verify that the objectives to be attacked are neither civilians nor civilian objects and are not subject to special protection but are military objectives within the meaning of paragraph 2 of Article 52 and that it is not prohibited by the provisions of this Protocol to attack them;
        ii) take all feasible precautions in the choice of means and methods of attack with a view to avoiding, and in any event to minimizing, incidental loss of civilian life, injury to civilians and damage to civilian objects;
        iii) refrain from deciding to launch any attack which may be expected to cause incidental loss of civilian life, injury to civilians, damage

The U.S. Government regards this article as declaratory of existing law:

> We support the principle that all practicable precautions, taking into account military and humanitarian considerations, be taken in the conduct of military operations to minimize incidental death, injury, and damage to civilians and civilian objects, and that effective advance warning be given of attacks which may affect the

---

          to civilian objects, or a combination thereof, which would be excessive in relation to the concrete and direct military advantage anticipated;

b)   an attack shall be canceled or suspended if it becomes apparent that the objective is not a military one or is subject to special protection or that the attack may be expected to cause incidental loss of civilian life, injury to civilians, damage to civilian objects, or a combination thereof, which would be excessive in relation to the concrete and direct military advantage anticipated;

c)   effective advance warning shall be given of attacks which may affect the civilian population, unless circumstances do not permit.

3.   When a choice is possible between several military objectives for obtaining a similar military advantage, the objective to be selected shall be that the attack on which may be expected to cause the least danger to civilian lives and to civilian objects.

4.   In the conduct of military operations at sea or in the air, each Party to the conflict shall, in conformity with its rights and duties under the rules of international law applicable in armed conflict, take all reasonable precautions to avoid losses of civilian lives and damage to civilian objects.

5.   No provision of this article may be construed as authorizing any attacks against the civilian population, civilians or civilian objects.

civilian population, unless circumstances do not permit.[56]

In addition, the Air Force Pamphlet's list of required precautions is also virtually a verbatim transcription of Article 57. The Pamphlet recites these precautions as follows:

(a)   In conducting military operations, constant care must be taken to spare the civilian population, civilians, and civilian objects.

(b)   With respect to attacks, the following precautions must be taken:

   i)   Those who plan or decide upon an attack must:

        (a)   Do everything feasible to verify that the objectives to be attacked are neither civilians nor civilian objects and are not subject to special protection but are military objectives and that it is permissible to attack them;

        (b)   Take all feasible precautions in the choice of means and methods of attack with a view to avoiding, and in any event to minimizing, incidental loss of civilian life, injury to civilians, and damage to civilian objects; and

        (c)   Refrain from deciding to launch any attack which may be expected to cause incidental loss of civilian life, injury to civilians, damage to civilian objects, or a combination thereof, which would be excessive in relation to the concrete and direct military advantage anticipated.

---

[56] Matheson at 426-27.

ii)   An attack must be canceled or suspended if it becomes apparent that the objective is not a military one, or that it is subject to special protection or that the attack may be expected to cause incidental loss of civilian life, injury to civilians, damage to civilian objects, or a combination thereof which would be excessive in relation to the concrete and direct military advantage anticipated;

iii)   Effective advance warning shall be given of attacks which may affect the civilian population unless circumstances do not permit.

c)   When a choice is possible between several military objectives for obtaining a similar military advantage, the objective to be selected shall be that which may be expected to cause the least danger to civilian lives and to civilian objects.[57]

The Pamphlet observes that "[p]recautionary measures are not a substitute for the general immunity of the civilian population, but an attempt to give effect to the immunity of civilians and the requirements of military necessity."[58] These measures in effect impose additional

---

[57] Air Force Pamphlet, para. 5-3(c)(1) at 5-9-5-10.

[58] Air Force Pamphlet para. 5-3(c)(2) at 5-10. The Pamphlet also notes:
Since states have not always separated military activities from civilian activities, a geographical and functional mixture of combatants and civilians and military objectives and civilian objects often results.... Dangers to civilian populations in a given situation vary according to the military objective attacked, configuration of terrain, type of weapons used, meteorological conditions, the presence of civilians at the scene or in the immediate vicinity and a particular combatant's ability and mastery of bombardment techniques as well as the level of the conflict and the type of resistance to be encountered during the attack. Permissible bombardment techniques vary according to such factors. *Id.*

restraints on attacks against legitimate military targets. Thus, the planners of a particular attack must (1) initially verify that the object selected is a lawful military objective; (2) avoid, or at least, minimize incidental civilian casualties and damage; (3) ensure that such casualties and damages are not disproportionate to the "direct and concrete" military advantage anticipated; and (4) do everything feasible to verify that military objectives are in fact being attacked and not civilians or civilian objects.

VERIFICATION OF MILITARY OBJECTIVES

Both Article 57 and the Air Force Pamphlet adopt a "feasible" precautions standard in connection with target verification and the rule of proportionality. The *New Rules* explains that the word "feasible" was understood to mean "that which is practicable or practically possible."[59] The U.S. and its NATO allies at the Diplomatic Conference expressed the understanding that this term means "that which is practicable or practically possible taking into account all the circumstances at the time, including those relevant to the success of military operations."[60]

The *New Rules* indicates that the requirement that the planner do "everything feasible" to verify that the target selected is a military objective involves "a continuing obligation to assign a high priority to the collection, collation, evaluation and dissemination of timely target intelligence. It must be observed, however, that the adverse Party will do its utmost to frustrate target intelligence activity and may be expected to employ ruses to conceal, deceive and confuse reconnaissance means."[61] The Air Force Pamphlet states in this regard: "Sound target intelligence also enhances military effectiveness by insuring that the risks undertaken are militarily worthwhile. It is also a matter of conservation of vital

---

[59] *New Rules* at 362.

[60] *Id.* (footnote omitted). *See also* W. Hays Parks, "Air War and the Law of War," 32 *Air Force Law Review* at 156.

[61] *New Rules* at 363.

resources. Economy of force, concentration of effort and maximization of military advantage support such efforts."[62]

COLLATERAL CASUALTIES AND DAMAGE

The duty under Article 57(2)(a)(ii) and the Air Force Pamphlet to "take all feasible precautions in the choice of means and methods of attack" to avoid or minimize incidental civilian casualties and damage to civilian objects is "an injunction to promote the maximum feasible accuracy in the conduct of bombardments of military objectives situated in populated places."[63]

The Air Force Pamphlet, while indicating that civilian casualties "are to be avoided to the greatest extent possible," states that "international law has long recognized that civilian casualties and damage to civilian objects, although regrettable, do occur in armed conflict."[64]

The *New Rules* suggests that although "it is not possible to regulate all of the infinite variables which may affect military operations," the attacking party has, nonetheless, "an affirmative duty to do what is feasible to promote accuracy and to avoid, or minimize civilian losses."[65] It admonishes that "[t]hese matters should be regulated in detail by the rules of engagement and technical instructions issued by the Parties."[66]

---

[62] Air Force Pamphlet, para. 5-3 (c)(2)(a) at 5-10.

[63] *New Rules* at 364. The term "means" of attack, combat or warfare generally refers to the weapon deployed while the term "methods" of attack generally refers to the way in which such weapons are used. ICRC *Commentary* at 621.

[64] Air Force Pamphlet, para. 5-3 (c)(2)(b) at 5-10.

[65] *New Rules* at 364.

[66] *Id.*

THE RULE OF PROPORTIONALITY

The Air Force Pamphlet and Article 57(2)(a)(ii) both restate and codify the rule of proportionality as a required precautionary measure. As previously explained, this rule prohibits an attack if the foreseeable injury or damage would be excessive or disproportionate compared with the "concrete and direct" military advantage anticipated.

CANCELLATION OR SUSPENSION OF ATTACKS

Customary law and traditional military doctrines, codified in Article 57(2)(b) of Protocol I and the Air Force Pamphlet, require the cancellation or suspension of an attack if it becomes apparent that a given target is not a military objective or that the attack will cause excessive collateral casualties and damage in relation to the concrete and direct military advantage anticipated. The *New Rules* indicates that this obligation is so phrased as to "apply to all commanders who have the authority to cancel or suspend attacks, including those at higher echelons who frequently have better intelligence sources than those actually engaged. But it also applies to the commander of military organizations actually engaged in combat."[67]

The authors of the *New Rules* make the following important point concerning application of the rule of proportionality:

---

[67] *New Rules* at 366 (footnote omitted). The term "attacks" refers to acts of violence, whether offensive or defensive. "The thrust of the term 'attacks' as used in Art. 57 deals with the fire aspect of the operation, not necessarily the movement part." *Id.* (footnote omitted). While offensive operations may be difficult to halt,

> any commander even at the lowest echelon can and must halt fire on a target that he has mistaken as a military objective when he realizes that his target consists of civilians or specially protected objects. Halting fire at a target which does not pose a threat against the attacking element in no way delays the movement of a unit of the armed forces engaged in an offensive military operation. Thus the first clause of subpara. 2(b) causes no problem to combatants who respect the rules applicable in armed conflict. *Id.*

In a co-ordinated military operation, the relative importance of the military objective under attack in relation to the concrete and direct military advantage anticipated is not a matter which can be determined by individual tank leaders, the commanders of lower echelon combat units or individual attacking bomber aircraft. If assigned a fire or bombing mission they must assume that an appropriate assessment has been made by those who assigned the mission. Thus, in this situation, the decision to cancel will have to be made at the level where the decision to initiate the attack was made. Article 85(3) evidences recognition that responsibility for causing excessive loss of civilian lives or injury or excessive damage to civilian objects rests on those who know such consequences to be excessive.[68]

WARNING REQUIREMENT

Both Article 57(2)(c) and the Air Force Pamphlet require the giving of "effective advance warning" of attacks which may affect the civilian population, unless circumstances do not permit. This requirement is based on and reaffirms Article 6 of the Hague Convention No. IX of 1907 relating to Bombardment of Naval Forces.[69]

The *New Rules* notes that since the element of surprise is frequently critical to air operations, "and as a warning serves to alert air defence forces as well as to provide civilians an opportunity to take

---

[68] *Id.* at 366-67 (footnote omitted).

[69] Art. 6 provides "If the military situation permits, the commander of the attacking naval force, before commencing the bombardment, must do his utmost to warn the authorities." (Hague Conventions (IX) of October 18, 1907, *Respecting Bombardment by Naval Forces in Time of War*). The *New Rules* indicates that subparagraph 2(c) of Article 57 "relaxes the warning requirement of Art. 26 of the Hague Regulations of 1907, which permits derogations only in case of assault." *New Rules* at 367. *See also* warning requirement in Air Force Pamphlet, para. 5-3 (c)(2)(d) at 5-11.

shelter, the practice of states during and after World War II has been either to omit warnings or to make them so general and unspecific as not to serve the intended purpose."[70] While the Air Force Pamphlet makes a similar assertion,[71] it does observe, however, that "[m]ore recently, increased emphasis has been placed on the desirability and necessity of prior warnings."[72]

SPECIAL LEGAL PROTECTION

Although Protocol I's provisions on the regulation of attacks are more detailed than those of prior law, they remain to a large extent general principles which require subjective judgment in specific situations. To reduce this subjective realm, the Diplomatic Conference developed a series of specific provisions regulating attacks on particular objects and specific areas.

PROHIBITION AGAINST STARVATION OF THE CIVILIAN POPULATION

By prohibiting starvation of the civilian population as a method of warfare, Article 54 establishes a substantially new rule which has been

---

[70] *New Rules* at 367. "This practice is supported by the negotiating record of the Hague Regulations which suggests that the 'assault' exception includes all cases where surprise is required." (footnote omitted).

[71] The Pamphlet states: "During World War II, practice was lax on warnings because of the heavily defended nature of the targets attacked as well as because of attempts to conceal targets.... Nevertheless, the practice of states recognizes that warnings need not always be given. General warnings are more frequently given than specific warnings, lest the attacking force or the success of its mission be jeopardized." Air Force Pamphlet, para. 5-3 (c)(2)(d) at 5-11.

[72] *Id.*

accepted by the U.S. Government as customary law.[73] This article provides:

1. Starvation of civilians as a method of warfare is prohibited.

2. It is prohibited to attack, destroy, remove or render useless objects indispensable to the survival of the civilian population, such as foodstuffs, agricultural areas for the production of foodstuffs, crops, livestock, drinking water installations and supplies and irrigation works, for the specific purpose of denying them for their sustenance value to the civilian population or to the adverse Party, whatever the motive, whether in order to starve out civilians, to cause them to move away, or for any other motive.

3. The prohibitions in paragraph 2 shall not apply to such of the objects covered by it as are used by an adverse Party:

    a) as sustenance solely for the members of its armed forces; or

    b) if not as sustenance, then in direct support of military action, provided, however, that in no event shall actions against these objects be taken which may be expected to leave the civilian population with such inadequate food or water as to cause its starvation or force its movement.

4. These objects shall not be made the object of reprisals.

5. In recognition of the vital requirements of any party to the conflict in the defence of its national territory against invasion, derogation from the prohibitions contained in paragraph 2 may be made by a Party to the conflict

---

[73] Matheson at 426.

within such territory under its own control where required by imperative military necessity.

Paragraph 1 of Article 54 prohibits starvation as a method of warfare, "i.e., a weapon to annihilate or weaken the population."[74] The ICRC *Commentary* states:

> To use it as a method of warfare would be to provoke it deliberately, causing the population to suffer hunger, particularly by depriving it of its sources of food or of supplies. It is clear that activities conducted for this purpose would be incompatible with the general principle of protecting the population, which the Diplomatic Conference was concerned to confirm and reinforce.[75]

It should be noted that the rule in paragraph 2, which prohibits attacks, destruction, removal or rendering useless covered objects, applies only when such action is taken for the specific purpose of denying these items for their sustenance value to the civilian population of either party, or to a combination of the enemy's forces and the civilian population, but not when damage is the collateral effect of an attack on a military target. The *New Rules* states in this regard:

> This paragraph does not prohibit the incidental distress of civilians resulting from otherwise lawful military operations. It would not, for example, be unlawful to attack or destroy a railroad line simply because the railroad was used to transport food needed to supply the population of a city, if the railroad was otherwise a military objective under Art. 52. Such incidental effects are regulated to some degree by Art. 57 and Arts. 68-71 dealing with relief actions.[76]

---

[74] ICRC *Commentary* at 653.

[75] *Id.*

[76] *New Rules* at 339.

Paragraph 3 specifies the two situations in which the objects covered lose their special protection from direct attack, destruction or removal. Subparagraph 3(a) permits supplies of foodstuffs intended for the sole use of the enemy's armed forces to be attacked or destroyed. The *New Rules* indicates that this exception generally applies "to supplies already in the hands of the adverse party's armed forces because it is only at that point that one could know that they are intended for use only for the members of the enemy's armed forces."[77] However, it would not be permissible to destroy objects "in the military supply system intended for the sustenance of prisoners of war, the civilian population of occupied territory or persons classified as civilians serving with, or accompanying the armed forces."[78]

The ICRC *Commentary* indicates that this permission to target enemy armed forces' foodstuffs "is undoubtedly concerned with foodstuffs and the agricultural areas producing them, crops, livestock, and supplies of drinking water, but not with installations for drinking water or irrigation works."[79] The *Commentary* notes, however, that while "some supplies of foodstuffs or drinking water can serve to sustain the armed forces, this possibility does not seem sufficient reason for depriving such objects of the protection it was agreed to afford them."[80]

The second situation resulting in loss of protection for foodstuffs is set forth in subparagraph (b). This exception permits attacks against objects when used for a purpose other than the subsistence of the enemy's forces and such use is "in direct support of military action." The *New Rules* states that the phrase "direct support of military action" is narrower than the phrase "effective contribution to military action" in Article 52, which could include indirect support.[81]

---

[77] *Id.* at 340.

[78] *Id.* at 340-41.

[79] ICRC *Commentary* at 656.

[80] *Id.* at 657.

[81] *New Rules* at 341.

The ICRC *Commentary* provides examples of military objects used in "direct support of military action": "bombarding a food-producing area to prevent the army from advancing through it, or attacking a food-storage barn which is being used by the enemy for cover or as an arms depot etc."[82] The *New Rules* suggests that this exception "is an extremely narrow one" not likely to be invoked frequently.[83]

Even if action is taken against covered objects under this exception, other provisions of paragraph 3(b) limit such action by prohibiting those "which may be expected to leave the civilian population with such inadequate food or water as to cause its starvation or force its movement."[84] The *New Rules* indicates, however, that "Art. 57 provides the limitations on the effects of the attack, if the purpose of the attack is to deny the adverse Party the direct support to military action afforded by the object (other than its sustenance value) and if the two pronged test of Art. 52 [military objectives] is met."[85]

Both the ICRC *Commentary* and the *New Rules* agree that the term civilian population referred to in paragraph 2(b) does not refer to the civilian population of the country as a whole, but rather to the population of "an immediate area," although the size of the area was not defined by the Diplomatic Conference.[86]

---

[82] ICRC *Commentary* at 657. The *New Rules* gives the following examples of direct support: "an irrigation canal used as part of a defensive position, a water tower used as an observation post, or a cornfield used as cover for the infiltration of an attacking force." (at 341.)

[83] *New Rules* at 341.

[84] *Id.*

[85] *Id.*

[86] *See New Rules* at 341; ICRC *Commentary* at 656.

SPECIAL PROTECTION FOR CIVILIAN DEFENSE SHELTERS

Articles 62-65 of Protocol I create new rules applicable to *civilian* civil defense personnel, activities and objects. Article 62(1)[87] accords general protection from direct attacks against civilian civil defense organizations and personnel. Paragraph 3 provides, among other things, that "[b]uildings and *materiel* used for civil defence purposes and shelters provided for the civilian population are covered by Art. 52 [Protocol I]." While indicating that these facilities are protected to the same extent as civilian objects, the *New Rules* notes:

> A very difficult question in this connection is whether this reference to the protection of civilian objects in general also includes a reference to the definition in Art. 52, para. 2, which could mean that civil defence material making an effective contribution to military action would not be considered as a civilian object and thus not be considered as protected under Art. 52. This is of particular importance for those civil defence functions which are close to military efforts, such as warning and decontamination. The difficulty is, however, perhaps more apparent than real. The question is whether equipment used "to protect the civilian population" within the meaning of the introductory phrase of Art. 61 could

---

[87] Article 62 states:

1. Civilian civil defence organizations and their personnel shall be respected and protected, subject to the provisions of this Protocol, particularly the provisions of this Section. They shall be entitled to perform their civil defence tasks except in case of imperative military necessity.
2. The provisions of paragraph 1 shall also apply to civilians who, although not members of civilian civil defence organizations, respond to an appeal from the competent authorities and perform civil defence tasks under their control.
3. Buildings and *matériel* used for civil defence purposes and shelters provided for the civilian population are covered by Article 52. Objects used for civil defence purposes may not be destroyed or diverted from their proper use except by the Party to which they belong.

ever be considered as "making an effective contribution to military action". The two purposes would be considered as being mutually exclusive. Thus the situation would be similar to that of medical units where their obvious utility for the military effort does not result in a loss of protection. It is only when they are used "outside their humanitarian function" to commit acts harmful to the enemy that they lose their protection. The same holds true for civil defence personnel, organizations and equipment used outside their "proper" task. Thus, civil defence equipment used exclusively for the purposes mentioned in Art. 61 may never be considered as a military objective under Art. 52.[88]

The general protection from attacks enjoyed by civilian civil defense personnel and objects ceases only if "they commit or are used to commit, outside their proper tasks, acts harmful to the enemy."[89] Paragraph 2 of Article 65 lists the following as *not* constituting acts "harmful to the enemy."

(a)   that civil defence tasks are carried out under the direction or control of military authorities;

(b)   that civilian civil defence personnel co-operate with military personnel in the performance of civil defence tasks, or that some military personnel are attached to civilian civil defence organizations;

(c)   that the performance of civil defence tasks may incidentally benefit military victims, particularly those who are *hors de combat*.

However, even in the event that these objects or personnel are used for hostile purposes, Article 65(1) specifies that their protection

---

[88] *New Rules* at 402 (footnote omitted).

[89] Protocol I, Art. 65(1).

against attack ceases "*only* after a warning has been given setting, whenever appropriate, a reasonable time limit, *and* after such warning has remained unheeded." (Emphasis added). The U.S. Government has declared its support for the principle that civilian civil defense organizations and their personnel should be respected and protected as part of the civilian population, but to date has expressed no view on the grounds for cessation of such protection set forth in Article 65.[90]

---

[90] *See* Matheson at 427.

PART II

THE AIR WAR AGAINST IRAQ

Western and Northern Iraq

Elevation in Meters
0
200
500
1000
2000
4000

Airport, Airbase
Major Road

0   100
kilometers

© 1991 Michael S. Miller

Geography based on:
"Operation Desert Storm Planning Graphic",
Defense Mapping Agency

De facto Jordan-Iraq boundary as of 1984 treaty (alignment approximate)

TURKEY

SYRIA

IRAQ

IRAN

JORDAN

Zakhu
Amadiyya
Zummar
Dahuk
Mosul
Mosul
Qayyarah West
al-Qayyara
Arbil
Kirkuk
Suleimaniyya
Tuz
Tikrit
Ba'iji
Samarra West
Tikrit East
Dour
Samarra
Salum
Balal
Kharaqin
BAGHDAD
Salman Pak East
Iskanderiyya
Musayyeb
Karbala
Hilla
Ubaydah
Bin Al Jarrah
al-Kufa
Najaf
Najaf
Diwaniyya
al-Kut
Amara
Amara
Amara

Tigris
Tigris
Tigris
Euphrates

Falluja
Ramadi
Taqaddum
Muhammadi
Hadithah
Asad
Radif Al Khafi
Nukhayb
Mudaysis
al-Qa'im
H2
Rutba
H3
Trebil
Ruwayshid
Ruwayshid

Southern Iraq

Geography based on:
"Operation Desert Storm Planning Graphic",
Defense Mapping Agency

ⓒ 1991 Michael S. Miller

BACKGROUND:
OPERATION DESERT STORM

When the air war began, some 425,000 U.S. military personnel in the Gulf were joined by 265,000 troops from 27 other countries to enforce Iraq's compliance with United Nations Security Council resolutions.[1] Following Iraq's invasion of Kuwait on August 2, 1990, the Security Council adopted eleven resolutions to force Iraqi compliance with Security Council Resolution 660, which condemned the invasion and demanded that Iraq immediately and unconditionally withdraw all its military forces from Kuwait to the positions these forces occupied on August 1, 1990.[2] Resolution 678, adopted by the Security Council on November 29, 1990, sanctioned the use of force against Iraq. It authorized member states cooperating with the Government of Kuwait "to use all necessary means to uphold and implement the Security Council Resolution 660 and all subsequent relevant Resolutions and to restore international peace and security in the area" unless Iraqi withdrew from Kuwait and fully implemented all relevant Security Council resolutions on or before January 15, 1991.[3]

The Department of Defense reported that ultimately the forces participating in Operation Desert Storm totalled over 800,000 military personnel from 36 countries.[4] The following ten countries participated in the air campaign: U.S., Britain, France, Italy, Canada, Kuwait, Saudi Arabia, Bahrain, United Arab Emirates, and Qatar.

---

[1] Andrew Rosenthal, "No Ground Fighting Yet; Call to Arms by Hussein," The New York Times, January 17, 1991.

[2] Resolution 660 was adopted on August 2, 1990 by a Security Council vote of 14 in favor and one opposed.

[3] Resolution 678 was passed by a vote of 12 Security Council members in favor, two opposed (Yemen and Cuba), and one abstention (China).

[4] Pentagon Interim Report, at 15-1.

The U.S. Central Command (Centcom) had overall responsibility for coordination of the non-Arab countries in the military coalition.[5] Immediately after Iraq's invasion of Kuwait in August 1990, Centcom established Central Command Forward headquarters in Riyadh, Saudi Arabia; on the weekend of August 25, Gen. H. Norman Schwarzkopf -- the commander-in-chief of Centcom and commander of the American forces in the Persian Gulf -- and his top aides flew to Riyadh and remained there throughout Operations Desert Shield and Desert Storm. Because Centcom is a unified command, the U.S. military chain-of-command went directly from Gen. Schwarzkopf to Secretary of Defense Cheney to President Bush; Gen. Colin Powell, chairman of the Joint Chiefs of Staff, played an advisory role.[6]

The New York Times said that the air war against Iraq "came after America's allies one by one handed the decision to make war and the ultimate powers of command to Mr. Bush."[7] U.S. officials reportedly spent the day of January 16 "formalizing a command system under which international forces are expected to fight under United Nations auspices but under the actual leadership of the United States."[8] But the U.S.

---

[5] Pentagon Interim Report, at 15-1.

[6] MEW interview with Department of Defense Press Office, September 17, 1991.

The Goldwater-Nichols Department of Defense Reorganization Act of 1986 gave greater responsibility to the commanders-in-chief of regional commands such as CENTCOM, in relationship to the different branches of the U.S. military. According to the Pentagon, "for Desert Shield and Desert Storm, [Gen. Schwarzkopf] was designated the supported [Commander-in-Chief], to be provided with needed assistance and forces from the other [Commanders-in-Chief] and the Services, who assumed supporting roles. These supported and supporting relationships were clarified in [the Goldwater-Nichols Act]." (See Pentagon Interim Report, at 26-1.)

[7] Andrew Rosenthal, "No Ground Fighting Yet; Call to Arms by Hussein," *The New York Times*, January 17, 1991.

[8] *Id.*

Department of Defense public position is that there was no sole overall commander:

> Due to myriad political, military and cultural considerations among countries participating in the Coalition, separate parallel lines of command/authority were established. In general, the Islamic forces were organized into a Joint Forces/Theater of Operations command structure under Saudi Lieutenant General Khalid bin Sultan bin Abdul-Aziz. The Command-in-Chief, Central Command (CINCENT) commanded US and non-Islamic members of the Coalition. However, no single overall commander was designated.[9]

According to the Pentagon, the plan for Operation Desert Storm "envisioned opening the war with a focused, intense air campaign" involving "attacks into Iraq's heartland and against Iraqi forces in the field."[10] The air campaign's goals were as follows:

> The air campaign was developed to attack critical Iraqi centers of gravity -- the heart of what allowed Iraq to maintain its occupation of Kuwait. The strategy was designed to paralyze the Iraqi leadership's ability to command and control the operations of its forces both offensively and defensively, to destroy Iraqi capability to threaten the security and stability of the region, to render Iraqi forces in the [Kuwait theater of operations] ineffective, and to minimize the loss of life.[11]

The air war was planned as a three-phase operation: a strategic bombing campaign, followed by the establishment of air superiority in the Kuwait military theater, followed by attacks on Iraqi troops in the Kuwaiti military theater, termed "battlefield preparation." But rather

---

[9] Pentagon Interim Report at 15-1.

[10] Pentagon Interim Report at 2-6.

[11] Pentagon Interim Report at 2-6.

than implementing these phases sequentially, a decision was made to execute the three phases of the air campaign almost simultaneously, "because of the large number of available aircraft and early attainment of air supremacy."[12] The Pentagon notes that this merging of the phases applied "the greatest amount of pressure from the opening minutes of the war."[13] The Pentagon states that it sought to "weaken signficantly the Saddam Hussein regime by bombing carefully selected targets whose destruciton would collapse vital military capabilities and military-related industrial systems, but leave most of the basic economic infrastructure of the country intact."[14]

About 120,000 sorties were flown by coalition air forces during the 43-day war, of which 60 percent were combat, or attack, missions, according to the Pentagon; the balance were support missions.[15] Over 35,000 combat sorties were flown against targets in the Kuwait-Iraq military theater, leaving approximately 32,200 attack missions presumably executed against targets in "Iraq's heartland."[16] Nearly 60 percent of the sorties were carried out by the U.S. Air Force.[17] Of the total number of U.S. air strikes, 23 percent were conducted by aircraft from the U.S. Navy and the U.S. Marines, according to Adm. Frank B. Kelso, the chief of naval operations.[18]

---

[12] Pentagon Interim Report at 25-1.

[13] Pentagon Interim Report at 2-6.

[14] Pentagon Interim Report at 2-6.

[15] Pentagon Interim Report at 4-5.

[16] Pentagon Interim Report at 4-5.

[17] Gen. Merrill A. Mc Peak, Chief of Staff of USAF, Briefing, March 15, 1991, Transcript at 6 [hereinafter McPeak Briefing].

[18] Molly Moore, "War Exposed Rivalries, Weaknesses in Military," *The Washington Post*, June 10, 1991.

Military briefers in Saudi Arabia reported on February 4 that the allies had been flying one bombing mission per minute against Iraq, on average, since the war began, a tempo that continued until the ceasefire.[19] Some 84,200 tons of ordnance were dropped -- but only 7,400 tons of it precision or "smart" bombs, 90 percent of which was dropped by U.S. aircraft.[20] In addition, 288 sea-launched Tomahawk cruise missiles were fired from surface ships and submarines in the Persian Gulf and the Red Sea.[21]

According to the Pentagon, the rules of engagement that applied for U.S. forces were shared by all members of the military coalition:

> As military command relationships developed among the Coalition, US [Rules of Engagement] became effective for, or were consistent with, all Coalition combatant forces. This compatability was ensured by coordination meetings between US and allied commanders.[22]

---

[19] Philip Shenon, "U.S. Battleship Shells Iraqis in Bunkers on Kuwait Coast," *The New York Times*, February 5, 1991.

[20] McPeak Briefing, Transcript at 6.

[21] Pentagon Interim Report at 6-8.

[22] Pentagon Interim Report at 16-1.

2
U.S. PUBLIC STATEMENTS

THE PUBLIC COMMITMENT
TO MINIMIZE CIVILIAN CASUALTIES AND DAMAGE

The Pentagon described the war against Iraq as "the most important test of American arms in 25 years."[1] It was also a war in which one side explicitly and repeatedly declared its intention to abide by the rules of war with respect to minimizing harm to civilians. This commitment was emphasized throughout the war by the Bush Administration and by U.S. military spokespersons. In its July 1991 preliminary report about the conduct of the conflict, the Defense Department stated:

> The Coalition military campaign will be remembered for its effort, within the bounds of war, to be humane. Coalition airstrikes were designed to be as precise as possible. Coalition pilots took additional risks and planners spared legitimate military targets to minimize civilian casualties.[2]

As was stressed repeatedly during the war, the Pentagon noted in its report that the use of high-technology precision weapons helped minimize Iraqi civilian casualties:

> Careful targeting and expert use of technological superiority -- including precision guided munitions -- throughout the strategic air campaign minimized collateral damage and casualties to the

---

[1] Pentagon Interim Report at 1-1.

[2] Pentagon Interim Report at 1-2.

civilian population, reflecting US policy that Saddam Hussein and his military machine, not the Iraqi people, were the enemy.[3]

While acknowledging that "some" Iraqi civilian casualties and damage occurred, the Pentagon speaks only in terms of Iraq's responsibility for these losses:

> Despite conducting the most discriminate military campaign in history, to include extraordinary measures by US and Coalition aircrews to minimize collateral civilian casualties, some collateral damage and injury did occur. The Government of Iraq located military assets (personnel, weapons, and equipment) in populated areas and adjacent to protected objects (mosques, medical facilities, historical/cultural sites) in an effort to obtain protection for its military forces. Military supplies were stored in mosques, schools, and hospitals in Iraq and Kuwait; a cache of Silkworm surface-to-surface missiles was found inside a school in Kuwait City, for example.[4]

Iraq, the Pentagon argues, used civilian casualties and damage to manipulate public opinion. At the same time, the Pentagon clears coalition forces of any responsibility for unlawful activity:

> Iraq utilized any collateral damage that occurred -- including damage or injury resulting from its own air defenses -- in its disinformation campaign, conveying the impression that the Coalition was targeting populated areas and protected sites. The Coalition's bombing of legitimate Iraqi military targets, notwithstanding that it resulted in collateral injury and damage to civilians and private property, was lawful.[5]

---

[3] Pentagon Interim Report at 4-4.

[4] Pentagon Interim Report at 12-3.

[5] Pentagon Interim Report at 12-3.

As this report shows, the facts do not warrant this facile dismissal of any possiblity that allied forces violated the rules of war.

"THIS IS NOT A WAR AGAINST THE IRAQI PEOPLE"

The policy of the U.S. military during Operation Desert Storm toward civilian objects and the civilian population was clearly articulated by Gen. Schwarzkopf. Echoing earlier statements by President Bush and Defense Secretary Cheney, he said at a briefing on January 18:

> [W]e are doing absolutely everything we possibly can in this campaign to avoid injuring or hurting or destroying innocent people. We have said all along that this is not a war against the Iraqi people.

President George Bush reinforced these comments in a speech on January 28 and went on to spell out the limits imposed on the aerial attacks: "We do not seek the destruction of Iraq," he said. "We have respect for the people of Iraq, for the importance of Iraq in the region. We do not want a country so destabilized that Iraq itself could be a target for aggression." Gen. Schwarzkopf, while noting the inevitability of civilian casualties, stated categorically on January 30 that civilians were not being targeted for attack:

> We never said there won't be any civilian casualties. What we have said is, the difference between us and the Iraqis is we are not deliberately targeting civilians, and that's the difference. There are going to be casualties. Unfortunately, that's what happens when you have a war.[6]

Maj. Gen. Robert Johnston, Gen. Schwarzkopf's deputy, stated at a briefing on February 4 that Iraq was "trying to move their aircraft into residential areas, recognizing that we have avoided civilian targets."[7] He

---

[6] *The Washington Post*, January 31, 1991.

[7] *The New York Times*, February 5, 1991.

cited one case of an airplane hidden in a school, but pledged: "We will not target civilian areas."

THE TARGETS IN IRAQ

Throughout the war, U.S. military and civilian spokespersons repeatedly stressed that indisputable military targets were being attacked, and generally avoided mention of attacks on "dual-use" objects that served military *and* civilian purposes. In a speech from the Oval Office two hours after coalition forces commenced operations against Iraq, President Bush stated that "military targets in Iraq" were under attack. He promised that Iraq's "nuclear bomb potential" and "chemical weapons facilities" would be destroyed. To protect the lives of all the coalition forces, "Saddam's vast military arsenal" would be targeted, the President pledged. In a statement at the Pentagon the same evening, Secretary of Defense Richard Cheney said: "Our focus is on the destruction of Saddam Hussein's offensive military capabilities". He added that the air assaults by U.S., British, Kuwaiti and Saudi forces were undertaken "after months of careful planning." He emphasized that, at the direction of President Bush, "great care has been taken to focus on military targets, to minimize U.S. casualties, and to do everything possible to avoid injury to civilians in Iraq and Kuwait."

Gen. Colin Powell said at a press conference on January 17 that Saddam Hussein himself was not a target, and that the bombing in Baghdad was mainly against military objectives:

> The purpose of our bombing facilities in the vicinity of Baghdad is essentially to go after the command and control system of the Iraqi armed forces. We're looking at principally military targets, command and control installations, air-defense sites that could put our planes at risk, but they are militarily oriented targets.[8]

---

[8] Richard Pyle, *Schwarzkopf/The Man, The Mission, The Triumph* (Signet Books: 1991) at 129 [hereinafter Pyle].

It is worth noting that Gen. Powell chose his words carefully, stating that "principally military targets" in Baghdad were being attacked. He did not mention at this time, for example, that the supply of electricity to civilians in Baghdad -- and elsewhere throughout Iraq -- was being systematically destroyed in allied attacks. A Harvard University on-site investigation established that in the first days of the air war 13 of Iraq's 20 electricity-generating facilities were destroyed or incapacitated.[9]

Allied spokespersons continued to reinforce the public's perception that the bomb and missile attacks were executed against indisputable military targets. At a news briefing on January 23, Defense Secretary Cheney said that in the seven days since the air war began, allied aircraft had flown over 10,000 combat and support sorties. There was no mention of Iraq's electrical system, for example, in Secretary Cheney's description of the targets:

> [W]e began by concentrating on a carefully planned set of military targets that we will continue to hit over the course of the next several days and weeks. We've started with command and control, his communications facilities, his air defense units and radars, his airfields, his Scud missile launchers.
>
> We've gone after the factories where Iraq has produced chemical and biological weapons, and until recently, continued working on nuclear weapons. We've also gone after the mainstay of Saddam's land forces, the Republican Guard units located near the Iraqi-Kuwait border.
>
> All of these targets we chose in advance. The pilots of the allied air forces have operated in accordance with clear instructions to launch weapons only when they are

---

[9] Harvard Study Team, "Public Health in Iraq After the Gulf War," May 1991.

certain they've selected the right targets under correct conditions.[10]

At the end of the second week of Operation Desert Storm, Gen. Schwarzkopf continued the pattern, by selectively noting the targets in Iraq that were under attack:

> In our first phase, what we wanted to do was disrupt the leadership command and control; destroy centralized air-defense command and control; attack combat aircraft in the air and on the ground to achieve air superiority; damage nuclear, biological, and chemical storage and production capability; and commence attack on the Republican Guards. Once we had that done, we planned to go into a second phase, which was to destroy the air-defense radars and missiles in the Kuwaiti theater of operation to achieve undisputed control of the air; and finally, to sever supply lines in the Kuwaiti theater of operation. Once that phase was completed, we planned then to isolate the Kuwaiti theater of operation, continue our attacks on the Republican Guards, and we had other objectives which I will not discuss further.[11]

Gen. Schwarzkopf also announced that 44 airfields had been targeted for attack[12] and that efforts were underway "to isolate the Kuwaiti theater of operations by taking out all the bridges and supply lines that ran between the north and the southern part of Iraq. That was to prevent reinforcements and supplies reaching the southern part of Iraq and Kuwait."[13]

---

[10] *The New York Times*, January 24, 1991.

[11] Pyle at 207-208.

[12] Pyle at 209.

[13] Pyle at 241.

As with the earlier public statements, neither Gen. Schwarzkopf or other U.S. military or civilian officials publicly stated that dual-use installations providing electricity, television and telephone service to Iraqi civilians were being systematically destroyed by allied bombs and missiles. For example, on February 11, White House spokesperson Marlin Fitzwater, chose to emphasize that "military facilities and installations" were the targets of allied attacks:

> We are going to such great lengths to target military facilities and military installations and to not try to do any damage to civilian targets. And it does strike me that Saddam Hussein must be having some impact in trying to convince the world otherwise. And that is disturbing to us, because clearly one of his major objectives is to show that the United States is attacking civilians and not the military, and that is not the case.[14]

The Pentagon reported that allied forces flew a total of 18,000 attack sorties during the war against strategic targets.[15] Yet to date, specific individual targets of coalition forces' bomb and missile attacks in Iraq have not been publicly itemized. The July report only speaks in generic terms:

> The key theater military objectives as stated in Operations Order (OPORD) 91-001, dated 19 January 1991 were: attack Iraqi political-military leadership and command and control; gain and maintain air superiority; sever Iraqi supply lines; destroy known chemical, biological and nuclear production, storage, and delivery capabilities; destroy Republic Guard forces in the [Kuwait theater of operations]; and liberate Kuwait City.[16]

---

[14] Andrew Rosenthal, "President Asserts He Is Putting Off Land War Decision," *The New York Times*, February 12, 1991.

[15] Pentagon Interim Report at 4-2.

[16] Pentagon Interim Report at 2-3.

To carry out these objectives, 12 "target sets" were identified for attack: "leadership command facilities; electrical production facilities powering military systems; command, control and communication nodes; strategic and tactical integrated air defense systems; air forces and airfields; known nuclear, chemical, and biological weapons research and production facilities; Scud production and storage facilities; naval forces and port facilities; oil refining and distribution facilities, as opposed to long-term oil production capability; railroads and bridges connecting Iraqi military forces with logistical support centers; Iraqi military units to include Republican Guard Forces in the [Kuwait theater of operations]; and military storage sites."[17]

OTHER POSSIBLE GOALS OF THE BOMBING CAMPAIGN

There were indications during the war that the bombing of Baghdad and other Iraqi cities was also intended to serve purposes other than those publicly articulated by Pentagon and White House spokesmen. A journalist who was in Baghdad during the early days of the air war wrote that the city after the first night of bombing "did not show much destruction," but added that Iraq's infrastructure appeared to be under systematic attack:

> [I]t was clear that a major objective of the allied raids -- in addition to undermining the Iraqi military capability -- was to shatter normal life. In the first two days, the allied forces destroyed, or at least hit, all the power stations and the telecommunications centres. Telephone lines went dead, there was no electricity and many districts in Baghdad ran short of tap water. Even the central post office was considered "a strategic target." The systematic bombardment of public facilities confirmed that the objective was to destroy the country's infrastructure.[18]

---

[17] Pentagon Interim Report at 4-2.

[18] Lamis Andoni, "Fearful yet defiant," *Middle East International*, February 8, 1991 at 6.

This early analysis was supported by a *Washington Post* correspondent who was in Baghdad toward the war's end:

> In crippling Iraq's infrastructure, the allies paved the way for an overwhelming military victory. But the strategy, familiar to guerrilla armies the world over, also has had the effect of demoralizing Iraq's civilian population.[19]

An experienced war correspondent who was based in Baghdad prior to and during part of the air war told Middle East Watch: "Early on I had the impression that the aim was to destroy the infrastructure, to destroy the country economically."[20]

Statements by Pentagon officials give weight to these journalists' views. One official told *The Washington Post* that the bombing of Baghdad and other Iraqi cities was "a way of letting the [Iraqi] leadership know that we care about them and want to bring the war home to them."[21] He also said that military planners hoped that the unrelenting aerial bombardment would provoke a coup against Saddam Hussein.[22] Gen. Schwarzkopf alluded to the same goal when he said in a television interview with CBS that "the entourage around" Saddam may "crack when they see the devastation that's being wrought on the country and on the armed forces."[23] Information obtained by Middle East Watch suggests that at least two Baghdad neighborhoods may have been attacked by allied bombers in part because top Baath party officials and Saddam Hussein's two sons had homes there (see Chapter Five). In addition, U.S. military briefers refused to provide details, during and after the war,

---

[19] Lee Hockstadter, "Death, Defeat Come Home to Baghdad," *The Washington Post*, March 7, 1991.

[20] MEW telephone interview, July 19, 1991.

[21] Rick Atkinson, "Allies to Intensify Bombing To Prepare for Ground War," *The Washington Post*, February 8, 1991.

[22] *Id.*

[23] *Id.*

about the targets in Baghdad that were the objects of continued bombing raids in the city (see Chapter Five).

One experienced British journalist noted: "The bombing of ministries in Baghdad quite unrelated to the war effort seemed to many to ram home that message, which is in essence that there will be no Iraq left to govern and no means by which to govern it unless Saddam is removed soon."[24]

These views were reinforced by President Bush's remarks on February 15, in reply to the Iraqi Revolution Command Council (RCC) statement about the readiness of Iraq to deal with U.N. Security Council Resolution 660, which demanded that Iraqi military forces withdraw from Kuwait. In rejecting the RCC proposal, the President said: "[T]here's another way for the bloodshed to stop, and that is for the Iraqi military and the Iraqi people to take matters into their own hands and force Saddam Hussein, the dictator, to step aside...."[25] After the war, U.S. Secretary of State James Baker said [on March 17]: "We would like to see a change in that Government. We've made no bones about it."[26]

The goal of encouraging the overthrow of Saddam Hussein's regime apparently was adopted in August 1990, when President Bush signed a secret authorization that permitted the Central Intelligence Agency and other U.S. civilian agencies to engage in covert intelligence operations to "destabilize" the Iraqi government.[27] President Bush at a National Security Council meeting on August 3 reportedly instructed the CIA to begin work on a plan:

---

[24] Martin Woollacott, "Iraq's lost generation," *The Guardian* (London), February 15, 1991.

[25] *The New York Times*, February 16, 1991.

[26] *The New York Times*, March 18, 1991.

[27] Michael Wines, "CIA Joins Military Move to Sap Iraqi Confidence," *The New York Times*, January 19, 1991. Also *see* Bob Woodward, *The Commanders* (Simon & Schuster, New York: 1991) at 282 [hereinafter Woodward].

Bush ordered the CIA to begin planning for a covert operation that would destabilize the regime and, he hoped, remove Saddam from power. He wanted an all-fronts effort to strangle the Iraqi economy, support anti-Saddam resistance groups inside or outside Iraq, and look for alternative leaders in the military or anywhere in Iraqi society.[28]

Less than two weeks later, the President signed the top-secret authorization for the CIA to begin covert operations to overthrow Saddam.[29] According to *The New York Times*, a few senior members of Congress were briefed about the authorization in December 1990. Clearly, the wide-scale disruption of civilian life in Iraq caused by the allied bombing of the country's infrastructure would not be incompatible with the goal of destabilizing Saddam Hussein's regime.

In its July 1991 preliminary report on the conduct of the war, the Department of Defense noted that one of the "five overarching goals" of the air war campaign was to "isolate and incapacitate the Iraqi regime."[30] The report states, for example, that if Saddam and other members of the Iraqi leadership were rendered unable "to maintain a firm grip on their internal population control mechanisms, they might be compelled to comply with Coalition demands."[31] In this respect, it is noteworthy that in the opening hour of the air war, U.S. Stealth bombers struck the headquarters of the internal security and intelligence organizations in Baghdad.[32] The report also notes that the early targeting of Iraq's telecommunications system disrupted the leadership's ability to communicate with the civilian population:

---

[28] Woodward at 237.

[29] Woodward at 282.

[30] Pentagon Interim Report at 2-6.

[31] Pentagon Interim Report at 2-5.

[32] Pentagon Interim Report at 4-3.

Saddam Hussein's internal telecommunications capability was badly damaged so that, while he could broadcast televised propaganda to the world via satellite, he was limited in the use of telecommunications to influence the Iraqi populace.[33]

Did the allies pursue their aim of overthrowing Saddam Hussein's regime by bombing Iraq's infrastructure?

The widespread disruption of civilian life clearly had the effect of destabilizing the Iraqi government. *The Washington Post* reached a similar conclusion, based on interviews after the war with U.S. military officers involved in planning the air war, when it concluded that many of the targets in Iraq "were chosen only secondarily to contribute to the military defeat of Baghdad's occupation army in Kuwait."[34]   One Air Force planner interviewed by the *Post* bluntly stated that the attacks on the country's electrical system were intended to send a message to the Iraqi people: "We're not going to tolerate Saddam Hussein or his regime. Fix that, and we'll fix your electricity."[35]   (See Chapter Four for additional information.)

Although Middle East Watch's mandate allows it to take no position on the propriety of the U.S. effort to destabilize Saddam Hussein's regime, the laws of war outlined in Chapter One, which MEW does seek to uphold, require a critical examination of the means used to pursue this goal. Those laws require as their "basic rule" that all parties to a conflict distinguish the civilian population from combatants, and civilian objects from military objectives, and direct their operations only against military objectives. Deliberately creating hardships for civilians so that they might rise up against their dictatorial leader would violate that essential distinction. This customary-law principle is set forth in Article 51(2) of Protocol I, which states: "The civilian population as such,

---

[33] Pentagon Interim Report at 4-3.

[34] Barton Gellman, "Allied Air War Struck Broadly in Iraq," *The Washington Post*, June 23, 1991.

[35]Id.

as well as individual civilians, shall not be the object of attack. Acts or threats of violence the primary purpose of which is to spread terror among the civilian population are prohibited."

"Bringing the war home to the enemy," to demoralize civilians and lead them to pressure their leaders to surrender, is a tactic that has marked military history. But civilian morale is not a permissible military objective under the laws of war, as discussed in Chapter One. The balance of this report operates from the premise that attacks intended to weaken the morale of the civilian population in order to force capitulation, surrender, or a change of government, are prohibited under the rules set forth in Chapter One of this report. This issue is discussed at greater length in Chapter Four of this report.

3
THE MEANS AND METHODS OF ATTACK

Customary international law, and the U.S. Air Force's own rules, specify that all feasible precautions must be taken in the choice of means and methods of attack to protect civilian life (see Chapter One). The precautions must encompass both the selection of weapons and the way in which the weapons are used.[1] The need for precautions in the choice of means and methods of attack is particularly relevant when targets are located in urban areas; one respected commentary notes that it "is an injunction to promote the maximum feasible accuracy in the conduct of bombardment of military objectives situated in populated places."[2]

Middle East Watch found that in some cases during the war, allied forces fell short of their duty to utilize means and methods of attack to minimize the likelihood of civilian casualties. This failure was particularly evident in decisions to execute daytime attacks on bridges in cities used by civilian pedestrians and motorists and on targets located near crowded urban markets. In such cases, it was inevitable that the civilian casualty toll would be higher than if the same targets were bombed at night when Iraqis typically were at home or in shelters.

In addition, it is still not clear why the nighttime bombing by the U.S. Air Force of the Ameriyya air raid shelter -- an attack which claimed some 200 to 300 civilian lives -- was not preceded by a warning to civilians that the allied forces considered this ordinarily protected facility to have become a legitimate military target subject to attack. Nor has the Pentagon revealed the steps that it took to verify that civilians were not taking shelter in this building during the nightly bombing raids of Baghdad -- an eventuality that should have been anticipated given the Pentagon's admitted knowledge of the facility's original use as a civilian shelter.

---

[1] ICRC *Commentary* at 621.

[2] *New Rules* at 364.

More generally, Middle East Watch believes that numerous unanswered questions remain regarding the type of munitions used by the allied forces to attack targets in close proximity to Iraqi civilians and civilian objects. During the war, allied spokespersons fostered the public impression that in populated areas the war was being fought with high technology and precision-guided "smart" bombs. However, as we note in this chapter, over 90 percent of the total tonnage of munitions used by the allies was unguided "dumb" bombs, with a substantially greater likelihood known to fall wide of their targets, especially when delivered from medium or high altitudes, as was the case during Operation Desert Storm.

A key question therefore is: of the total number of attacks on targets located in proximity to civilian areas, what percent were executed with dumb bombs? The answer to this question may help explain the incidents of reportedly inaccurate bombing that caused Iraqi civilian casualties. Further, if munitions clearly known to be inaccurate were deliberately used in these cases, then the resulting deaths, injuries and damage were potentially avoidable -- given the possibility of selecting alternative and more accurate means and methods of attack. In the absence of additional information from the Pentagon on this subject, it is impossible to assess the allies' compliance with the laws of war in this respect.

U.S. PUBLIC STATEMENTS

Throughout the war, Bush Administration and Pentagon spokesmen repeatedly acknowledged the duty to protect civilian life, emphasizing that the means and methods of attack in Operation Desert Storm were carefully chosen to minimize civilian casualties and damage. U.S. Defense Secretary Cheney stated at a news briefing on January 23 that, in contrast to Iraq's use of "highly inaccurate" Scud missiles, "we've carefully chosen our targets and we've bombed them with precision."

Before Operation Desert Storm began, it was reported that the allies' air-war planning process included efforts to minimize damage to civilian objects:

U.S. experts have spent months planning ways to minimize "collateral damage." For example, military officials have plotted bomb runs so that munitions that fall short or long will miss hospitals, schools and the like. Senior defense officials have stressed recently that only military and military-industrial targets are at risk.[3]

Lt. Gen. Chuck Horner, commander of the U.S. Central Command Air Forces, was described by Gen. Schwarzkopf as "the architect of the entire air campaign."[4] Gen. Horner said in a briefing on January 18 that the weapons chosen to attack every target in Iraq were examined with a view toward avoiding civilian damage:

> Certainly one of the strongest guidance we had from the very start was to avoid any damage to civilian targets and to the holy shrines that happen to be located in Iraq. We've looked at every target from the outset for avenues of approach, the exact type of weapon to cause damage to the target but preclude damage to the surrounding area, and precision delivery.[5]

During the bombing campaign, Gen. Schwarzkopf and other military spokesmen continued to emphasize that the allied forces were taking great care to avoid damage to civilian objects. At a briefing on January 27, Gen. Schwarzkopf said:

> I think we've stated all along that we're being absolutely as careful as we can not only in the way we are going about executing our air campaign, but in the type of armament we're using. We're using the appropriate weapon against the appropriate targets. We're being

---

[3] Rick Atkinson, "War's Course Depends on Air Power," *The Washington Post*, January 17, 1991.

[4] Pyle at 171-2

[5] Pyle at 173.

very, very careful in our direction of attacks to avoid damage of any kind to civilian installations.[6]

In response to Iraqi charges early in the war that civilian objects were being bombed, Gen. Schwarzkopf noted the means he said were being used by the allies to minimize civilian casualties:

> [W]e are absolutely doing more than we ever have, and I think any nation has in the history of warfare, to use our technology...And everybody should clearly understand this, we are probably endangering our pilots more than they would otherwise be by following this course of action. This is something that hasn't been stated. But by requiring that the pilots fly in a certain direction of flight or use a certain type of munitions that requires them to go to altitudes that they normally wouldn't be required to go to, those pilots are at much more risk than they would be otherwise. But we have deliberately decided to do this in order to avoid unnecessary civilian casualties, in order to avoid destroying these religious shrines and that sort of thing....[7]

After this reply, a reporter asked why such care was being taken in the air war and why pilots were being put at risk to avoid civilian casualties. Gen. Schwarzkopf replied that the allied forces had the technological capability to minimize civilian damage:

> The overwhelming part of it is the fact that we have the capability to do that today. Therefore, since we have the capability, the nations that make up this coalition, have deliberately determined to use that capability to limit the

---

[6] *The New York Times,* January 28, 1991.

[7] Pyle at 202-203.

damage against innocent people because we've felt all
along our war is not against the people of Iraq.[8]

The same themes were repeated in the following weeks. At a
briefing in Riyadh on February 2, Maj. Gen. Robert Johnston of the U.S.
Central Command emphasized that the allies' aircraft were "scrupulously
avoiding civilian targets," adding that weapons were being used to
minimize the damage to civilians. On February 4, in an interview with
U.S. correspondents, Gen. Schwarzkopf again said that precautionary
measures were being taken -- such as choice of aircraft, ordnance and
flight paths toward targets -- to minimize civilian damage.[9]

President Bush: Allied Bombing "Fantastically Accurate"

On February 6, Radio Baghdad accused coalition forces of
attempting "to expel Iraq from the 20th century," claiming the bombing
of scientific, economic, cultural and medical installations as well as places
of worship, sacred sites and residential areas.[10] The same day, President
Bush said that the bombing campaign "has been fantastically accurate"
and that he was disturbed by such "statements coming out of
Baghdad."[11] At a news conference at the White House on February 5,
the President said: "We are not trying to systematically destroy...Iraq."[12]
He repeated the allies' policy of minimizing damage to civilians, claiming
great success in the implementation of the policy:

I'd like to emphasize that we are going to extraordinary,
and I would venture to say unprecedented, length to

---

[8] Pyle at 205.

[9] *The New York Times*, February 5, 1991.

[10] Foreign Broadcast Information Service, *Near East and South Asia Daily
Report*, February 6, 1991 at 24 [hereinafter FBIS].

[11] Rick Atkinson, "Gulf Ground War Not Felt Imminent," *The Washington
Post*, February 7, 1991.

[12] Rick Atkinson and Ann Devroy, "Bush 'Skeptical' Air Power Can Prevail
Alone in Gulf," *The Washington Post*, February 6, 1991.

avoid damage to civilians and holy places. We do not seek Iraq's destruction, nor do we seek to punish the Iraqi people for the decisions and policies of their leaders. In addition, we are doing everything possible and with great success to minimize collateral damage, despite the fact that Saddam has now relocated some military functions, such as command and control headquarters, in civilian areas such as schools.[13]

On February 12, President Bush, at the White House with British Defense Minister Tom King, dismissed Iraqi reports of large-scale civilian damage as a "one-sided propaganda machine cranking out a lot of myths and falsehoods."[14] He quickly turned the subject to Iraqi treatment of prisoners-of-war, Scud attacks and environmental terrorism. Defense Minister King added that "tens of thousands of civilians" must have died during the Iraqi occupation of Kuwait.[15]

Radio Baghdad's early claim that the allies' bombing was expelling Iraq from the 20th century was echoed in the report following the war prepared by United Nations Under Secretary General Martti Ahtisaari, who conducted field investigations in Iraq from March 11 to March 16 with representatives from various U.N. agencies to assess urgent humanitarian needs. The report of the mission stated that the war "has wrought near-apocalyptic results upon the economic infrastructure" of Iraq and that the country was "relegated to a pre-industrial age."[16] In response, White House spokesperson Marlin

---

[13] Reuters, February 5, 1991.

[14] *The Washington Post*, February 13, 1991.

[15] Although a substantial number of Kuwaitis missing since the occupation have not been accounted for, Middle East Watch believes that the final tally of Kuwaitis killed by Iraqi forces is unlikely to be significantly greater than 1,000.

[16] "Report to the Secretary-General on humanitarian needs in Kuwait and Iraq in the immediate post-crisis environment by a mission to the area led by Mr. Martti Ahtisaari, Under Secretary-General for Administration and Management, dated 20 March 1991," Annex to Letter Dated 20 March 1991

Fitzwater stated on March 22 that there was "no way of knowing" if the damage in Iraq was as extensive as described in the Ahtisaari report, and added "that certainly was not our intent."[17] He also said: "We fought the war decisively, we fought it well, and we fought it as discriminatingly as we could. You will not find America feeling guilty for Saddam Hussein's invasion and destruction of his own people."

The Pentagon's Preliminary Self-Assessment

The Pentagon's July 1991 report states that the allies "sought to minimize civilian losses through use of precision munitions and various restrictions on the employment of weapons during Desert Storm."[18] The report offers several examples of restrictions that were imposed, with the aim of minimizing civilian losses:

> [T]he Coalition restricted the use of weapons employed near civilian areas, permitting some attacks only during the night when most civilians would be home and not near the target area. Other restrictions included not allowing attacks if targets could not be positively identified and avoiding valid military targets in close proximity to civilian areas, including combat aircraft parked in civilian housing areas or near historic sites.[19]

DAYTIME BOMB AND MISSILE ATTACKS ON TARGETS IN POPULATED AREAS

As indicated in the previous section of this chapter, U.S. military spokesmen repeatedly emphasized during the war that precautions were

---

General Addressed to the President of the Security Council, S/22366, 20 March 1991 at 5 [hereinafter Ahtisaari Report].

[17] Paul Lewis, "United Nations Eases Rules On Food and Fuel for Iraqis," *The New York Times*, March 23, 1991.

[18] Pentagon Interim Report at 27-1.

[19] Pentagon Interim Report at 27-1.

being taken to avoid unnecessary Iraqi civilian casualties. However, bombing by coalition forces during daytime hours of bridges and other targets in populated areas of Iraq suggests a failure to use all possible means to spare the civilian population, particularly because allied aircraft had the capacity to, and did, fly sorties at night. As indicated by the testimony below, a greater number of civilians reasonably could have been expected to be using bridges and shopping in market areas during the day. The lack of electricity in most of Iraq during the war, coupled with the difficulty of securing gasoline for private automobiles, meant that by the time darkness fell most civilians were at home or in air-raid shelters.

The Pentagon's first public report on Operation Desert Storm recognized the importance of nighttime bombing in populated areas as a means of saving civilian lives when it stated that "some attacks" were permitted only "during the night when most civilians would be home and not near the target area." In the incidents described below, however, such restrictions obviously were not applied, resulting in hundreds of needless civilian deaths and injuries. Middle East Watch calls on allied forces to explain this deviation from stated allied policy.

One Hundred Killed in Daytime Attack on Bridge in Southern City
A daytime attack on a bridge in Nasiriyya in southern Iraq in mid-afternoon killed scores of civilians who were crossing the bridge at the time. Dr. Rajha Thamer, who worked in Nasiriyya during the war, told *The New York Times* that his hospital treated 180 casualties from the bombing, 100 of whom died.[20] He noted that many civilians were crossing the bridge when the bomb fell:

> "I was in my office" at 3 pm, he said, just as thousands of civilians were walking home, many of them trekking across the bomb-cratered Euphrates River bridge because it would no longer support vehicles, when the bomb struck. "By the time I got there, there were hundreds of people in the river," Dr. Thamer said.

---

[20] Patrick E. Tyler, "Iraqi Hospitals Struggle With Wounds of War," *The New York Times*, July 5, 1991.

Describing the same incident, one journalist wrote during the war:

> At 3 pm, when traffic was heavy, several fighter bombers
> appeared from nowhere and began to nosedive. By the
> time the sirens let out their warning wail, it was too late.
> The arch of the bridge, torn from the support of its
> metal pillars, fell into the muddy waters of the
> Euphrates, taking with it lorries, cars and people.
> Witnesses said 47 bodies have been found.[21]

British Royal Air Force Tornado fighters were among the allied
aircraft used to bomb bridges. One Tornado squadron leader who
bombed a suspension bridge on February 5 admitted that the bridge was
in the center of a populated area and that his aircraft dropped its laser
bombs in the morning.[22] "Yes, there will be civilian traffic," the pilot
said, purporting to justify the daytime attack by speculating, "but they
could well be civilian contractors working on an airfield."

Scores of Civilians Killed in Flawed Attack on Bridge in Western Iraq
Middle East Watch interviewed three eyewitnesses to the bombing
of a bridge in Falluja, a city on the Euphrates River west of Baghdad, that
left scores of civilians dead. According to a Sudanese worker, 26, who had
lived in Falluja for 14 months and worked at a poultry company, there
are no air raid shelters in the city. He told MEW that in Falluja a new
concrete bridge for vehicles was attacked a week or more before the
February 14 bombing raid in which local residents said some 200 civilians
were killed.[23] The concrete bridge was about one km from the market.

---

[21] Alfonso Rojo, "A bridge too near for civilians as bombers strike," *The
Guardian*, Feb. 8, 1991.

[22] David Sharrock, "Tornado crews defend inflicting injury on civilians," *The
Guardian*, February 6, 1991.

[23] Middle East Watch notes that accounts vary about the number of civilians
killed in this attack. One journalist reported after the war: "Official estimates
have put the death toll at between 40 and 73, the bush telephone in Falluja
counts 200." (*See* Ed Vulliamy, "Limbs and lives blasted away by allied bombs," *The
Guardian*, May 3, 1991.) Vulliamy interviewed members of the Mehsan family in

This bridge was bombed at night and there were no civilian casualties, he said.[24]

The Sudanese saw the aftermath of the inaccurate bombing of a second bridge in Falluja on February 14, in which bombs landed in the main market in the center of Falluja. He said the incident was still vivid to him. During the day, he was outside his house, about two to three km from the market, when he saw three planes at high altitude, too high to see the color. He watched the planes dive down and then rise twice, bombing each time. He said it looked like two of the aircraft dove and bombed, and the third was there to protect the other two. He heard three explosions. He ducked for cover and did not go to the market until about two hours later, because he was afraid.

A steel bridge for vehicles and pedestrians spanned the Euphrates not far from the market; a post office tower was nearby. (The post office was bombed three days later, he said.) The market had hundreds of vendors, mostly women, selling a variety of products: vegetables, food, clothes, shoes, and spare parts. Two bombs fell in the center of the market, according to the Sudanese.

When he went to the site, he saw collapsed stores, some concrete, some cinderblock, and others constructed of flimsy material. By the time he arrived, the authorities were not allowing anyone inside the market because they feared there was an unexploded bomb. He saw many of the injured and dead when the army removed them; Red Crescent ambulances were still carrying away the wounded.

He said it was "a terrible sight" -- people had lost hands, legs, or eyes; others "had their internal organs outside their bodies."[25] There were hundreds of dead and injured, "too much people," he said. The

---

Falluja; in addition to 12-year-old Abdullah Mehsan, whose legs were crushed and amputated from injuries during the attack, three family members were killed in the attack, including Abdullah's father and his 24-year-old brother.

[24] MEW interview, Azraq Evacuee Center, Azraq, Jordan, February 26, 1991.

[25] MEW interview, Azraq Evacuee Center, Azraq, Jordan, February 26, 1991.

market building's zinc roof had collapsed; some walls were completely destroyed and others were still standing. About 200 to 300 meters from the market were homes with damaged doors and windows; civilians had been injured from shrapnel and flying glass.

In a separate interview a week earlier, Middle East Watch talked with two Palestinian truck drivers who had arrived in Falluja from Baghdad shortly after the market was bombed. They had come to the city to deliver medical supplies to Falluja hospital. They arrived at the hospital, located about one km from the market, shortly after the market was bombed. They found the hospital filled with injured and dead civilians, the floors covered with blood. Among the injured were people who had lost arms or legs; others had head injuries. The doctors told them that there were 450 injured and there was no space for all of them. The hospital only had about 50 beds, and lacked electricity and water, the doctors said.

The truckers saw the market, which they described as "rubble." Its zinc roof had covered an area about a half-kilometer square; the one-story market buildings were mostly of cinderblock construction. Bodies were still being removed when they arrived. They walked around to the houses at the rear of the market and saw a two-story home, used as a hotel by Egyptians, which was flattened. They were not sure exactly where the bombs fell because everything was a shambles.

A journalist who visited the site on February 16, two days after this bombing, told Middle East Watch he learned that the first bridge in Falluja, a modern concrete bridge, was hit earlier, on February 10 or 11. The bombers returned to attack that bridge and also targeted the old bridge about 500 to 600 meters from the market, which they missed. The resulting damage was "quite spectacular," he said. A row of modern concrete five- and six-story apartment houses near the market was destroyed, as well as older clay houses with stores on the first floor on that side of the street and across the street. All buildings for 400 meters on both sides of the street, houses and market, were flattened.[26]

---

[26] MEW interview, New York, March 25, 1991.

Denials and then Admissions by the Allies about the Attack

On February 16, reporters were taken by the Iraqi authorities to Falluja to view the damage. The same day, U.S. and British military spokesmen had denied that any bombing had occurred near Falluja on February 14.[27] It was only later in the day on February 16 that a senior allied commander confirmed that a precision bomb dropped from a British bomber had missed its target, a bridge in Falluja, and hit a marketplace instead.[28] Confusingly, at a briefing in Saudi Arabia on February 17, the British military spokesman said that the date of the incident was February 13, not February 14.[29]

RAF Group Capt. Niall Irving said that several of the laser-guided bombs dropped had been "direct hits" on the bridge, but that three "didn't guide for one reason or another," and two fell short into the river and a third veered "off towards the town."[30] Capt. Irving also described the precautions taken by the pilots to minimize civilian damage or casualties:

> Irving said that because the target was in a populated area, pilots had taken extra care to aim their bombs at the center of the bridge, rather than the ends as is normally the case. In addition, he said, the pilots flew straight down the river, "so that if the bombs [didn't] glide in their normal trajectory they [would] either fall short or long, and, one would hope, safely.[31]

---

[27] Eric Schmitt, "2 U.S. Jets Are Shot Down Over Kuwait," *The New York Times*, February 17, 1991.

[28] *The New York Times*, February 17, 1991.

[29] *The New York Times*, February 18, 1991.

[30] John Lancaster, "Tape of Errant Bomb Highlights the PR War Over Civilian Casualties," *The Washington Post*, February 18, 1991.

[31] *Id.*

Capt. Irving also said that there was no evidence to support the Iraqi claim of civilian casualties from the errant bomb, but that if this was verified, Britain "very much regretted" the losses.[32]

Hamid Mehsan, a Falluja merchant who was an eyewitness to the attack and lost his son, brother and nephew, described what he saw:

> It was the first attack here. A bomb hit just over there and as soon as it exploded, the old buildings fell down. The people were buried, and I saw the men digging with their shovels to bring out the dead. I saw people without their throats. Some they did not find: my son Omar was never found, we found only his head.[33]

Mr. Mehsan, who sells kettles, glasses and other household goods at the market, disputed that the bombs from the British aircraft missed:

> This pilot said he had come to hit the bridge, on the television, and it was a mistake. But we're a distance of 1½ kilometers from the bridge. In our minds, we are convinced that the attack was to the market, to kill our people. But anyway, we consider this to be God's will for us.[34]

The London *Financial Times* reported that other laser-guided bombs dropped by Tornado aircraft "fell wide" of their targets; British defense officials provided a broad accuracy range of 75 percent to 90 percent.[35]

---

[32] David White, "Britain admits bomb missed target and hit town," *Financial Times* (London), February 18, 1991.

[33] Ed Vulliamy, "Limbs and lives blasted away by allied bombs," *The Guardian*, May 3, 1991.

[34] *Id.*

[35] David White, "Britain admits bombs missed target and hit town," *Financial Times*, February 18, 1991.

Scores of Civilians Killed in Daytime Attack on Bridge near Market in Southern City

During a daytime attack on one of the bridges in Samawa, a city on the Euphrates River in southern Iraq, bombs fell near a crowded market, in an open area at the edge of the river, killing over 100 civilians and injuring others.

According to former residents interviewed by Middle East Watch, there are three bridges in Samawa, a city on the Euphrates River. During a daytime attack on one of the bridges in February, two eyewitnesses, interviewed separately, described the civilian casualties when bombs fell in an open area at the edge of the river, near a crowded market.

A Sudanese driver who had lived in Samawa for 18 months told MEW that he was in the main market in the city center about 20 to 22 days after the war began when there was an airstrike on the bridge over the Euphrates River that links the market with the residential al-Baath neighborhood, where he lived. (According to testimony taken by MEW, the largest bridge in Samawa, a steel bridge for cars and trucks, was bombed four times. The bridge could no longer be used by vehicles because one attack left a large hole in the middle of the span. The steel bridge is 500 meters from a floating wooden bridge for pedestrians. The steel bridge was bombed before the pedestrian floating bridge was attacked.[36])

The Sudanese told MEW that the floating bridge had a railing on the side; it was not large enough for trucks. The Sudanese saw two aircraft that did what they usually do: first they passed over to be sure there were no antiaircraft guns and then they dived and bombed. One dived at a right angle and the other appeared to be protecting the bomber from antiaircraft fire. He watched the plane dive twice and bomb. The Sudanese was one km inside the market and could not see the bridge at the time it was bombed. After the bombing stopped, he went immediately to see what happened.

He said that the bridge had collapsed in the water and disappeared. He saw "too many" dead floating in the water and on both

---

[36] MEW interview, Azraq Evacuee Center, Azraq, Jordan, February 25, 1991.

sides of the bridge. He saw many ambulances and civilian cars helping the wounded to the hospital. He was told that over 200 people had been killed.

Residents of Samawa make their purchases in the market during the day and the area was crowded. The Sudanese saw bodies on the side of the bridge near the market. There is an open area from the bridge to the market of about 10-15 meters before the covered portion of the market begins. Most of the fatalities he saw were in this open space on the street, near the bridge. He estimated that he saw about 80 people -- children, men and women; some had lost hands or legs and some were severed in two parts. The injured were nearer to the market. All over there were women and children crying. The Sudanese said that this was the first time this area was bombed; there was a siren 15 minutes before the attack.[37]

Another Sudanese, who lived and worked for two years as a truck driver for a construction company hauling cement, gave Middle East Watch a similar account in a separate interview. He was about a half kilometer away from the site where the bombs fell. First there was an air raid siren, followed by two explosions. He looked up and saw two small white planes flying up, together. It was a clear day, he said.

He ran to the site of the bombing to try to help; there was "general chaos." At least two bombs had fallen in an open area at the edge of the river, between the river and the market. He saw two craters -- each about seven meters wide and four meters deep. The area extended about 75 meters from the river to the place where the market's shops began. People usually did their washing at the edge of the river, he said. There were many women there, washing clothes, and children fetching water and playing.

He saw many injured and many dead, "human pieces," as he put it. This spot was about 1.5 km from another bridge which had been totally destroyed before the bombing. There were no military installations

---

[37] MEW interview, Azraq Evacuee Center, Azraq, Jordan, February 25, 1991.

near the area between the market and the riverside where the women and children were killed, he told MEW.[38]

A group of journalists visited Samawa on February 17. One of the group interviewed by MEW said that when they had passed through Samawa on February 10 from Basra to Baghdad, the bridges -- or at least the one they crossed -- were intact. They reported that by February 17 the three bridges had been completely destroyed and people were crossing the river in small boats. They were told that over 100 people were killed when the footbridge was bombed during the day.[39]

Another bridge, in the Shuhada quarter of Samawa, was also bombed during the day, for the first time at 3:00 in the afternoon, according to testimony taken by Middle East Watch from two Sudanese truck drivers who had lived in Samawa for 18 months.[40] The bridge did not collapse, but two nearby houses were damaged. Two days later, the bridge was bombed again at the same time of day. Once again, it did not collapse, but one house and a restaurant were completely destroyed. During a third attack, at 2:00 in the morning, a bomb hit the middle of the bridge and it collapsed into the water. MEW does not have information about the number of casualties, if any, from these subsequent attacks.

Scores of Workers Killed in Market Area of Southeastern City

A Sudanese mechanic interviewed by MEW described a daytime attack on February 5 which killed many civilians in a market area in al-Kut, a city 200 km southeast of Baghdad in Wasit province. The city is six km off the main highway from Baghdad to Basra, and about 3 km from the Tigris River. The mechanic worked at the al-Kut weaving factory, which produced cotton cloth.

He was in Baghdad on the day of the attack, but learned about it from fellow workers when he returned the next day and visited the site

---

[38] MEW interview, Azraq Evacuee Center, Azraq, Jordan, February 15, 1991.

[39] MEW interview, New York, March 25, 1991.

[40] MEW interview, Azraq Evacuee Center, Azraq, Jordan, February 25, 1991.

himself. At about 8:30 am, two planes dropped ordnance on an open yard adjacent to the market area in al-Kut where workers from the factory stop for coffee before reporting to work. He was told that one bomb or missile landed in the open area where the workers were sitting and killed about 150 people, many of them Egyptians and Sudanese.

The mechanic saw a crater in the middle of the area about five meters wide and two meters deep. He also observed that some of the buildings in the market, cinderblock with concrete roofs, had been damaged. He talked to people who had helped evacuate the injured the day before; they told him that 150 people had been killed and over 70 injured, all of whom were taken to the local hospital.

The yard had stands for coffee and tea in one corner. Workers also bought food at the stalls in the market; the workers were accustomed to sitting in the open area and eating between shifts. There were no tall buildings anywhere near the area; all the buildings were one or two stories. The post office was "far away. There were no government or military buildings or emplacements...there was nothing but a market there," the Sudanese said. He said that the weaving factory -- the only factory in al-Kut -- employed 3,000 workers in three shifts. The factory itself, a one-story building, is located about six km from the site of the bombing. The tallest building in al-Kut is three stories.

The Sudanese told MEW that the market area was the only site that was bombed that day, but added that al-Kut had been bombed several times before, sometimes with raids almost on the hour: "We hear the sirens. We do not know if the bombs are targeting this town or another. In the bombings, houses have been hit. The road has not been hit."[41]

Morning Bombing Near Crowded Market Area in Basra

Chapter Five contains testimony about two missiles that landed in the Ashshar market near downtown Basra in January: the first at night and the second just before noon the next day. MEW also obtained testimony from Tunisian workers about bombing in the same area on or

---

[41] MEW interview, Azraq Evacuee Center, Azraq, Jordan, February 15, 1991.

about February 6 and 7. Both attacks of these attacks took place at about 10:30 am.

During the first raid, the market was full of people shopping for vegetables, food, clothing, jewelry. Although they insisted that there were no military installations near the market, the Tunisians had a theory: they thought that the planes were aiming at an unfinished construction site in the market whose columns might have appeared to be rockets. They had seen the site before it was bombed. The construction had commenced four years ago but was never completed. The vegetable market was across the street from this site. Other than this construction site there was no bridge, post office or other conceivable military target or governmental structure anywhere in the vicinity.

One of the Tunisians was about 500 meters away from the market when it was bombed on or about February 6. There was a very strong explosion and he saw the doors of several stores flying in the air. He heard the sound of the plane as it bombed the market and then ascended. A second Tunisian went to the scene shortly after the bombing and said that the people there were panicked, crazy, running around in utter confusion.

There was no one in the abandoned construction site itself when the attack took place. The columns at the site were destroyed and the foundations were heaved up. The damage to civilians was less than might be expected because the construction site was surrounded by a concrete wall, about two meters high, which contained some of the blast. But pieces of concrete and shrapnel flew into the market; the blast also blew off doors and the zinc roof of the structure. Vegetables, meat, and other products were scattered everywhere. Worst hit were the street vendors, according to the Tunisians, who saw blood on the sidewalk after the bombing. They heard there were injured and dead, but they did not see any casualties. The market cleared out and no one was there when bombs dropped the next day, at the same location, they told MEW.[42]

Yemeni students interviewed by Middle East Watch said that this market was bombed about four times before they left Basra on February

---

[42] MEW interview, Azraq Evacuee Center, Azraq, Jordan, February 28, 1991.

7.[43] One student remarked that some of the craters were as large as swimming pools; in a film made of his trip to Iraq from February 2 to 8, Ramsey Clark photographed a swimming-pool-sized crater half-filled with water in the market of Basra, where it was reported that eight were killed and 40 injured. The crater size suggests that the ordnance dropped may have been a 2,000-pound guided bomb: the GBU-14, one of the 2,000-pound "smart bombs" used during Operation Desert Storm, "can blast away more than 8,500 cubic feet of material, leaving a hole the size of a large suburban swimming pool."[44] Press reports also noted the bombing of vegetable markets in Basra. Dharm Paull, a 30-year-old accountant, was interviewed by *The Washington Post* after he evacuated to Jordan. He said that several bombs had hit Basra's vegetable market.[45] Indian evacuees interviewed by *The Guardian* said that a vegetable market and food warehouses had been bombed in Basra, in addition to Shu'aiba refinery, military sites, roads, the port and two television towers.[46]

Daytime Bombing of Bridges in Basra

MEW collected testimony about the daytime bombing of two bridges in Basra, both close to hospitals. At lunchtime on or about January 28, an Indian construction worker who lived in Basra was shopping and noticed three or four white aircraft coming in. He watched the planes dive and saw one of them bomb a 50-meter-long bridge near Basra Hospital. He told MEW he was standing about 50 meters from the bridge.[47]

Tunisian workers described an attack on a bridge that meets al-Kornash Street near the General Teaching Hospital in Basra at around

---

[43] MEW interview, Azraq Evacuee Center, Azraq, Jordan, February 13, 1991.

[44] James Schwartz, "Munitions Used in the Air War," *The Washington Post*, February 6, 1991.

[45] Nora Boustany, "'Sky Was Black--We Could Not Breathe,'" *The Washington Post*, January 30, 1991.

[46] *The Guardian*, February 5, 1991.

[47] MEW interview, Azraq Evacuee Center, Azraq, Jordan, February 15, 1991.

7:30 in the morning on or about January 26. Three bombs were dropped and none of them hit the bridge, according to the Tunisians. One of the off-target bombs, which left a crater five meters wide, landed near the back of the hospital, killing three patients. The next attack on the bridge was carried out the following night at 8:30; four bombs were dropped, and once again all of them missed the bridge (see Chapter Five for details of this account).

Scores of Civilians, Waiting for Cooking Gas, Killed and Injured During Daytime Attack

At 3:30 in the afternoon, in the middle of the third week after the start of the war, an area east of Hilla was bombed. The apparent military targets were large grey rectangular oil storage tanks, supported on concrete columns, according to testimony taken by MEW. The site also included a distribution point where civilians queued up to purchase gas for cooking and heating. At the time of the attack, many people were at the site and some 200 civilians were killed or injured, according to what witnesses told a Sudanese poultry yard worker who had lived in Hilla for nine months. One of the witnesses was a housemate of the Sudanese, who was nearby when the attacked occurred and rushed to the site, where he saw "many injured and dead." A nearby hospital also was damaged in the attack.

The Sudanese visited the site the next day and saw a large crater 30 meters from the storage tanks. "Everything in the vicinity was completely burned," he said, including all eight storage tanks. The windows in some cars about 30 meters outside the station were shattered from the blast. There were no houses nearby.[48]

In a separate interview, a 25-year-old Egyptian who worked at a cinderblock factory in Karbala confirmed aspects of the account provided by the Sudanese. He visited Hilla on or about February 17 and he, too, saw damage from bombing that had occurred, he was told, a few days before, at the gas distribution station at the entrance to the town. He said that the station had oil storage tanks on large columns. The bombs fell on the tanks, which exploded and burned, destroying much of the area.

---

[48] MEW interview, Azraq Evacuee Center, Azraq, Jordan, February 25, 1991.

He saw about 15 to 20 charred cars. The Egyptian was told that over 75 civilians were killed and 15 injured when the site was attacked.[49]

Both the Sudanese and the Egyptian noted that the site was about 500 meters from a public hospital. The Egyptian noted that the hospital's windows were shattered; the Sudanese believed that the name of the hospital was Marajan, the same name as the street that passed between the gas-distribution station and the hospital. The hospital is a three-story building with a detached one-story reception building of four rooms, each about four by four meters. The reception building was destroyed in the attack, according to the Sudanese, with just its beams remaining. He thought that the damage was caused by the explosion and shrapnel from the attack. The Sudanese remembered that the second and third stories of the hospital were "very damaged," and he heard that patients had been killed but did not know how many. He said there was a red and white flag in front of the yellow hospital building, near the gate and the reception building. About 600 to 700 meters from the hospital is a military college but it was not attacked, the Sudanese said. "There is no antiaircraft near the hospital."[50]

Civilian Factory in Southern City Bombed in Afternoon; Seven Killed
An allied attack on an underwear-manufacturing factory in Hilla at 2:00 in the afternoon, on the third day of the war, killed seven administrative workers. The casualty toll would have been higher, but the normal shift of 200 workers had been dismissed by management at noon on the day of the bombing and told to report back to work in five or six days.

A Sudanese worker who had lived in Hilla described the attack in an interview with MEW. He said that the government-owned, one-story plant, which manufactured cotton and polyester underwear, was bombed at 2:00 in the afternoon on the third day of the air war.[51] The factory

---

[49] MEW interview, Ruwayshid Evacuee Center, Ruwayshid, Jordan, February 24, 1991.

[50] MEW interview, Azraq Evacuee Center, Azraq, Jordan, February 25, 1991.

[51] MEW interview, Azraq Evacuee Center, Azraq, Jordan, February 25, 1991.

employed about 800 workers on successive shifts. The manager of the factory had told the workers at noon on the day of the bombing to leave and return in five or six days, so the normal shift of about 200 workers was away when the factory was attacked. The Sudanese said that he visited the factory the day after the bombing; he said that the roof and a corner of the building were destroyed from two bombs, killing seven administrative workers. A third bomb landed on six workers' shacks some 50 meters from the building, completely destroying them. There were no casualties because the shacks were not occupied at the time. The Sudanese said that there was nothing of military or strategic significance near the factory, and that the nearest post office was some 1.5 km distant.

Legal Standards, Conclusions and Unanswered Questions

To comply with customary law principles regarding precautionary steps to be taken to spare civilians, and their own often-stated policy about minimizing civilian casualties during Operation Desert Storm, Middle East Watch believes that coalition air forces should have refrained -- at least once their self-proclaimed air supremacy was achieved early in the air war -- from attacks during daytime hours on targets, such as bridges, and factories not being used in direct support of military operations, where civilians were likely to be present.[52]

By way of comparison, the ICRC *Commentary* to Article 57 of Protocol I notes that during World War II factories in occupied German territory were bombed on days or at times when the buildings were empty, in order to destroy the structures without killing the workers. It states: "It is clear that the precautions prescribed here will be of greatest

---

[52] Regarding factories directly involved in military production, civilians working there must assume the risk of possible attack. The *New Rules* states: "By being within, or in the vicinity of a military objective, these civilians assume the risk of collateral injury from the effects of attack. It is also doubtful that incidental injury to persons serving the armed forces within a military objective will weigh as heavily in the application of the rule of proportionality as that part of the civilian population which is not so closely linked to military operations." See *New Rules* at 295.

importance in urban areas because such areas are most densely populated."[53]

Allied air forces clearly had the capability to execute attacks with precision-guided weapons at night. In fact, it was announced in mid-February that U.S. fighter-bombers, equipped with "enhanced night-vision sensors," were dropping laser-guided bombs on Iraqi military targets such as armored and mechanized Republican Guard divisions.[54] The technique was reportedly new, and had been tested first with a few aircraft; the results reportedly were so successful -- 70 to 80 percent of the targets said to have been destroyed -- that additional sorties of this nature were flown.[55]

In its July 1991 report, the Pentagon noted that thousands of coalition sorties were flown at night and stressed the importance during the air war of this night-flying ability:

> The ability to operate at night deprived the Iraqis of the sanctuary of darkness. Iraqi doctrine emphasizes the movement and resupply of forces under the cover of darkness. Coalition air forces flew thousands of sorties at night using a variety of night capable systems to locate and destroy Iraqi forces.[56]

On the basis of the evidence presented above, Middle East Watch calls on the Pentagon and allied forces to answer the following questions about daytime attacks on targets in populated civilian areas of Iraq:

> • Who was responsible for decision making about *the time of day* to execute attacks against specific military targets

---

[53] *ICRC Commentary* at 679.

[54] Eric Schmitt, "High-Tech Night Raids Cost Iraq Many Tanks," *The New York Times*, February 18, 1991.

[55] *Id.*

[56] Pentagon Interim Report at 6-4.

in or near cities and towns in Iraq? Were civilian casualties foreseeable in such cases, and was the varying likelihood of civilian casualties taken into account in the decisionmaking process about the time of day to attack?

- In the cases of bridges used by civilian vehicular and pedestrian traffic, was consideration given to launching attacks at night? If not, why not?

- Why were the attacks on the bridges in Nasiriyya, Falluja and Samawa carried out in the afternoon, particularly when aerial reconnaissance would have indicated that the bridges in Falluja and Samawa had crowded public market areas nearby? Similarly, why were daytime attacks executed near crowded market areas in Basra and al-Kut? Were pilots ordered to examine the target area visually prior to releasing their munitions to determine whether civilians were present in large numbers? If not, why not?

- Why was the factory in Hilla attacked at approximately 2:00 in the afternoon? Was the likelihood of civilian casualties anticipated from this attack, given the time of day that the mission was executed? If so, were civilian casualties deemed acceptable and, if so, why?

- Regarding all daytime attacks launched by allied air forces against fixed targets in or near populated areas, did the circumstances permit prior warning of the attack in order to protect the civilian population? If not, what specific circumstances were prevailing that would have jeopardized the success of the attacks, had warnings been given?

"SMART" BOMBS, "DUMB" BOMBS, AND INACCURATE ATTACKS ON TARGETS IN CIVILIAN POPULATION CENTERS

The munitions used by the allies to attack targets in Iraq and Kuwait included precision bombs guided by infrared, electro-optics or laser systems -- "smart" bombs -- as well as conventional high-explosive bombs, known as "dumb" bombs because they are unguided.[57] However, numerous public statements and televised video footage released by U.S. spokespersons appeared designed to reinforce the public's perception that Operation Desert Storm was prosecuted exclusively with precision weapons, with minimal "collateral" civilian damage and casualties. The use of precision weapons, of course, reduces the level of civilian casualties because there is a greater likelihood of hitting the target, and because of this greater accuracy fewer bombs are needed to do the required level of damage. British Royal Air Force Group Captain David Henderson described the advantage of precision bombs this way: "The whole concept of precision-guided munitions means you can attack tight targets like bridges because the weapon is going specifically at these targets and not for a target area."[58]

In testimony before the Armed Services Committee of the U.S. House of Representatives in June, Gen. Schwarzkopf praised the "technological edge" enjoyed by the allied forces during Operation Desert Storm.[59] In an April 1991 report, the U.S. Air Force stated that during

---

[57] "Dumb" bombs -- or low-drag, general-purpose bombs -- are "the most common type of air-to-ground munition in service today. A general-purpose (GP) bomb is a medium-case weapon in which the explosive filler amounts to some 40-50 percent of total weight, as opposed to 60-75 percent in light-case 'demolition' bombs or as little as 20 percent in heavy-case armor-piercing bombs. Relying on a combination of blast and fragmentation, GP bombs are effective against most soft and 'semi-hardened' targets." Edward Luttwak and Stuart L. Koehl, *The Dictionary of Modern War* (Harper Collins:1991) at 350.

[58] David Sharrock, "Tornado crews defend inflicting injury on civilians," *The Guardian* (London), February 6, 1991.

[59] June 12, 1991.

the war precision weapons were used "with deadly effectiveness."[60] The report also noted that "not every target requires a precision weapon .... When it was important to avoid collateral damage, civilian casualties, or to directly hit a target, PGMs [precision-guided munitions] were the right choice. F-117 attacks over Baghdad demonstrated the ability to precisely kill military targets while minimizing civilian casualties."[61]

It was not until the war was over that the U.S. Air Force disclosed that coalition forces relied overwhelmingly on unguided general-purpose bombs to attack Iraqi targets. Air Force chief of staff Gen. Merrill A. McPeak released information at a briefing in Washington, D.C., that precision-guided bombs accounted for only 7,400 tons (or 8.8 percent of the approximately 84,200 tons of ordnance dropped by the allies during Operation Desert Storm.[62] Some of these precision munitions reportedly were used against Iraqi military targets in the Kuwaiti theater of operations, away from any civilian population, leaving an even smaller percentage for use in populated areas. MEW is unaware of any detailed information released by the Pentagon about the relative proportion of precision-guided and unguided munitions used on targets in or near populated areas of Iraq.

When asked the percentage of smart bombs that hit their targets, Gen. McPeak said: "I don't have any good data on that. If I had to give you a guess, I would say on the order of 90 percent."[63] He did not provide an evaluation of the performance of the unguided dumb bombs. But a senior Pentagon official told *The Washington Post* that dumb bombs

---

[60] U.S. Department of the Air Force, White Paper "Air Force Performance in Desert Storm," April 1991 at 6.

[61] *Id.* at 7.

[62] McPeak Briefing, Transcript at 6. General McPeak said: "Coalition air forces dropped about 84,200 tons of ordnance." Confusingly, a visual aide used at the briefing, titled "Tonnage Expended, US--Only," indicated that the tonnage figure referred to ordnance dropped by the U.S., not allied forces as a whole. Gen. McPeak, however, spoke in terms of allied forces.

[63] McPeak Briefing, Transcript at 11.

had an accuracy rate of about 25 percent.[64] During the war, the *Post* reported that several U.S. officials said the estimated accuracy rate of many unguided bombs was lower than 50 percent.[65] Former U.S. Army Col. David H. Hackworth wrote that the unguided bombs "were the same dumb iron bombs that fell on Berlin, Pyongyang and Hanoi."[66] Pentagon officials told the *Post* that unguided bombs were frequently missing their targets:

> Several Pentagon officials, speaking on condition they not be named, said unguided munitions frequently have missed such military targets as bridges or armored revetments, a circumstance that delayed successful prosecution of the air war against Republican Guard forces around the Iraqi-Kuwaiti border.[67]

According to *Aviation Week & Space Technology*, "conventional bombs were less effective than anticipated."[68] The Pentagon's director of tactical warfare programs, Frank Kendall, said: "Dumb bombs were not all that effective. One of the lessons that came out of this, and I'll quote the science adviser to the commander-in-chief, is that dumb bombs are just that."[69] Gen. John M. Loh, the head of the Tactical Air Command, acknowledged that dumb bombs were used with full knowledge that half would miss. According to *Aviation Week*, Gen. Loh "said planners never

---

[64] Barton Gellman, "U.S. Bombs Missed 70% of Time," *The Washington Post*, March 16, 1991.

[65] R. Jeffrey Smith and Eveyln Richards, "Many Bombs May Have Missed," *The Washington Post*, February 22, 1991.

[66] Col. David H. Hackworth, "The Lessons of the Gulf War," *Newsweek*, June 24, 1991.

[67] *See* R. Jeffrey Smith and Evelyn Richards, "Many Bombs May Have Missed," *The Washington Post*, February 22, 1991.

[68] John D. Morocco, "Looming Budget Cuts Threaten Future of Key High-Tech Weapons," April 22, 1991 at 66.

[69] *Id.*

expected more than one-half the unguided bombs to fall within the established circular error probable (CEP). So the fact that a large number missed was consistent with expectations."[70] Dumb bombs equipped with technological adaptations also were said to perform poorly: "Even with improvements in aircraft avionics and computerized continuous impact point (CIIP) systems, accuracy with conventional bombs was disappointing."[71]

Former Undersecretary of Defense for Research and Engineering William J. Perry noted that the accuracy of precision-guided munitions "is independent of the altitude of delivery," which is not the case for general-purpose bombs. According to Perry: "Because of the high density of antiaircraft guns in Iraq most of the bombs were released at medium or high altitudes, which decreased the accuracy of delivery of the 'dumb bombs.'"[72]

All these assertions stand in sharp contrast to public statements made throughout the war by Administration and Pentagon officials, particularly President Bush's reassuring words on February 6 that the bombing campaign was "fantastically accurate" and on February 11 that "this war is being fought with high technology."

In the section of the Pentagon's July 1991 report that addresses the use and performance of munitions during the war, there is not one mention of conventional unguided bombs, either in terms of their use or

---

[70] Id.

[71] Id.

[72] William J. Perry, "Desert Storm and Deterrence," *Foreign Affairs*, Fall 1991 at 79.

accuracy.[73] In fact, the report misleadingly reinforces the impression that much of the ordnance used was precision-guided bombs:

> Virtually every type of combat aircraft operated by the Army, Navy, Air Force, and Marine Corps took part in Operation Desert Storm. These aircraft -- both fixed and rotary wing -- delivered a wide variety of munitions, *many of which were precision guided*....According to the Air Force, over 80% of the precision guided bombs released were hits, limiting collateral damage.[74] (Emphasis added)

The post-war disclosure by the Pentagon of the amount of general-purpose high-explosive bombs used in the air campaign, combined with reports of the inaccuracy of these bombs, gives added weight to the accounts taken by Middle East Watch from former residents of Iraq who provided testimony about inaccurate bombing that caused civilian deaths and destroyed civilian property (see Chapter Five for these accounts).

The Need for a Definition: What Constituted a "Successful" Attack on a Target?

Complicating allied public statements about the accuracy of the munitions used to attack targets in Iraq is the absence of a clearly articulated definition from the Pentagon about what constituted a "miss" during the air war.

---

[73] The report notes that "an evaluation of the employment and performance of military equipment, weapons and munitions ... requires a thorough, systematic analysis of all available data....The data collection efforts and preliminary analyses are underway. When complete, this will provide a basis for continuing, more detailed analyses designed to allow the Department to draw conclusions about weapons' performance." (Pentagon Interim Report at 6-1.)

[74] Pentagon Interim Report at 6-1 to 6-2.

In the early days of the war, allied spokespersons consistently claimed an 80 percent "success rate" for combat sorties over Iraq.[75] "Success," however, was not necessarily a measure of the accuracy an aircraft achieved in destroying or even hitting an assigned target and -- importantly -- did not foreclose the possibility of civilian casualties and damage from such an attack. *The Independent* reported from Saudi Arabia that the 80 percent success rate was not an indication that a target had been destroyed:

> The 80 per cent is the statistic for the number of times aircraft unload their bombs *over* the target -- not the accuracy of the hit. Air force personnel in Saudi Arabia's Eastern Province...state this bluntly enough when they are certain of anonymity.[76]

And in a story the same day from Washington, *The Independent* noted that the use of the word "effective" did not mean that a target was destroyed, explaining that the terms used by military briefers were technical concepts, capable of creating false impressions for an uninformed public:

> They have been using military jargon, and in that case, words such as "performance" and "effective" are strictly technical terms. A different set of accounting words assess actual damage to the targets.
>
> For a missile, for example, good performance means it got off the ground, flew faultlessly to its target and landed on or around the target. Each missile has what is called "circular error probable" or CEP, a circle within which it is supposed to land. But, that does not mean it destroyed the target, or even disabled it.[77]

---

[75] R. Jeffrey Smith, "Official Accounts of Battle Leave Many Gaps," *The Washington Post*, January 22, 1991.

[76] Robert Fisk, "Searching for truth along the military's margin of error," *The Independent* (London), January 19, 1991.

[77] Peter Pringle, "Subtle military jargon obscures the target," *The Independent*, January 19, 1991.

Further, U.S. military officials interviewed by *The Washington Post* admitted that the "success rate" of bombing missions was a reflection of "the judgment of returning pilots that they correctly sighted their targets and released their munitions."[78] Several sources told the *Post* that the assessment of targets successfully destroyed was "much lower" than the reported success rates.[79]

The Pentagon should release information about the actual performance of the allies' bombs and missiles during the air war, including -- importantly -- a clear definition of the terms used to measure performance. Filling this information gap is an important step in assessing the claims of "success" in attacking targets, and in evaluating the accounts of inaccurate attacks on targets in proximity to civilian population centers in Iraq, such as those included in Chapter Five of this report.

Munitions Used to Attack Targets in Civilian Population Centers: The Need for Public Disclosure
Middle East Watch believes that the Pentagon, to permit an evaluation of its compliance with the duty to minimize civilian casualties, should disclose if and where unguided, general-purpose bombs were used in populated areas of Iraq, and on what basis such choices were made. The Pentagon also should release all relevant information about the type and size of such munitions used on targets located in or near cities, towns and villages. Such information, to be meaningful, must include specifications for the expected accuracy and lethality of each type of bomb (see below). This data is important for an independent assessment of the likelihood of civilian casualties from an attack -- both if the weapon hit the target accurately and, especially, if it misfired or missed the target completely due to technological malfunction, pilot error or evasive action to avoid Iraqi antiaircraft fire. The release of such data also may help explain the incidents of inaccurate bombing throughout Iraq included in this report.

---

[78] R. Jeffrey Smith, "Official Accounts of Battle Leave Many Gaps," *The Washington Post*, January 22, 1991.

[79] *Id.*

If munitions known to be inaccurate were used to attack military targets located in civilian population centers, then the resulting civilian casualties were potentially avoidable. That is, the civilian casualties and damage were likely to have been avoided or reduced had the allies made the choice of using the precision weapons in their arsenal instead of conventional ones. Middle East Watch believes that the United States and other allied forces should explain the reasons for their decision to use conventional bombs and to outline in greater detail how this choice squared with the allies' duty and often-stated goal of minimizing Iraqi civilian casualties.

The choice of weapons was the responsibility of personnel on Gen. Schwarzkopf's staff at Central Command. Once identified for attack, targets in Iraq and Kuwait were categorized into "target sets."[80] The target sets then were "weaponeered" by specialists working under Gen. Schwarzkopf, whose task was to match targets and ordnance, based on the type of damage that was sought.[81] For example, bombs or missiles selected to completely destroy a building would be different from those chosen if the goal was simply to damage a structure and disable its functions.[82] Similarly, targets such as hardened troop bunkers and command-and-control centers were matched with 1,000- or 2,000-pound bombs to produce one powerful explosion, while cluster bombs were chosen if many smaller explosions were needed over a wide area.[83]

Public statements by Bush Administration and Pentagon officials during the war suggested that the choice of weaponry took into account

---

[80] Christopher Bellamy, "Fine art of assessing the battle damage," *The Independent*, January 28, 1991.

[81] R. Jeffrey Smith, "Picking Right Weapon for a Target is Complex Decision," *The Washington Post*, February 6, 1991.

[82] Christopher Bellamy, "Fine art of assessing the battle damage," *The Independent*, January 28, 1991.

[83] R. Jeffrey Smith, "Air Bombardment: A Terrifying Prospect," *The Washington Post*, January 18, 1991. See Chapter Four, section D, for more information about the use of cluster bombs during the war.

the need to minimize civilian casualties. But this claim is yet to be squared with the Pentagon's public admission that less than nine percent of the total tonnage of ordnance dropped during the air war was precision-guided bombs. The critical question still unanswered is, of the total number of targets attacked in close proximity to the civilian population, what percentage of attacks were executed with dumb bombs as opposed to smart bombs?

It is not yet known, for example, the extent to which cost and availability were factors in the choice of weapons used in civilian areas. Precision munitions are costly, ranging from $50,000 to $100,000 each,[84] while each Tomahawk cruise missile has a price tag of $1.6 million.[85] In contrast, conventional high-explosive bombs are less expensive and available in "vast quantities."[86] One Pentagon official said a dumb bomb "costs less than $1 a pound--it's cheaper than hamburger."[87]

Whether precision-guided or conventional, high-explosive munitions of the type used in Operation Desert Storm have enormous destructive power at the point of impact. One-thousand-pound bombs can create craters 35 feet wide and blast shrapnel in a 600-foot radius.[88] Two-thousand-pound bombs are capable of blasting a crater 50 feet wide and 36 feet deep, and throwing deadly shrapnel within a

---

[84] R. Jeffrey Smith and Evelyn Richards, "Many Bombs May Have Missed," *The Washington Post*, February 22, 1991.

[85] *The Wall Street Journal*, January 21, 1991.

[86] Benjamin Weiser, "No Shortage of Bombs, Missiles Foreseen For U.S.," *The Washington Post*, January 25, 1991.

[87] *Id.*

[88] R. Jeffrey Smith, "Picking Right Weapon for a Target Is Complex Decision," *The Washington Post*, February 6, 1991.

1,200-foot radius.[89]   One precision bomb in use was the GBU-15, a 2000-pound bomb which can be guided by an infrared system or an electro-optical system that includes a television camera in its nose.[90] The bomb "can blast away more than 8,500 cubic feet of material, leaving a hole the size of a large suburban swimming pool."[91]   The reports of journalists in Iraq and the accounts of former residents of Iraq interviewed by Middle East Watch indicate that bombs with similar cratering power fell in populated areas of Basra, Iraq's second-largest city.

One factor in evaluating the likelihood of civilian casualties is a bomb's "lethal blast range," which varies with the weight of the bomb's explosive material. For example, a 200 kg bomb has a lethal range of 9.7 meters -- that is, 100 percent mortality can be expected for anyone within this range.[92]   Beyond the immediate lethal range, there is the additional danger of secondary injuries from shrapnel travelling at high velocity:

> Secondary blast injuries are those that result from projectiles set in motion by the blast. Many types of material may act as missiles, including stones, splinters of wood or glass, and pieces of metal. The pieces may range in size from fine dust to large chunks. These projectiles may or may not penetrate the body.[93]

---

[89] Rick Atkinson, "War's Course Depends on Air Power," *The Washington Post*, January 17, 1991.

[90] James Schwartz, "Munitions Used in the Air War," *The Washington Post*, February 5, 1991.

[91] James Schwartz, "Munitions Used in the Air War," *The Washington Post*, February 5, 1991.

[92] Stockholm International Peace Research Institute, *Antipersonnel Weapons* (Taylor & Francis, London: 1978) at 165 [hereinafter SIPRI].

[93] SIPRI at 168.

A Sudanese worker interviewed by Middle East Watch said that when a bomb fell on the evening of February 7 in the residential area where he lived 45 km north of Basra, neighbors told him that the shrapnel was "like knives." Another former resident of Basra who fled the city on February 9 told MEW that civilians feared injury from flying shrapnel as much as they feared the consequences of a direct attack.

Another factor that can be used to assess likely civilian casualties is the "effective casualty radius" -- ECR -- of a bomb or missile. The U.S. Army defines ECR as "the radius of a circle about the point of detonation in which it may normally be expected that 50 percent of the exposed personnel will become casualties."[94] Based on the ECR, a "safety zone" can be calculated for each type of munitions -- the area beyond the detonation point in which civilians or friendly forces can be considered safe from harm. The Stockholm International Peace Research Institute described the safety-zone range for a bomb of 250 kilograms as follows:

> [A] typical 250 kg bomb has an effective casualty radius of about 30 meters against troops in the open (i.e., it is expected to incapacitate 50% of persons within 30 meters of the explosion), but individual fragments may travel much further. To cope with the dispersion of fragments and aiming errors, a safety zone of about 1000 to 3000 meters is required, depending on bombing tactics (high or low level), type of aircraft and other factors."[95]

Although figures of this sort can vary depending on a host of operational factors, those selecting weapons during the allied bombing campaign would have had access to information of this sort. Allied commanders have given no indication of how such information was used to determine the likelihood of civilian casualties from the use of a particular weapon and the resulting appropriateness of using that weapon.

---

[94] SIPRI at 121.

[95] SIPRI at 145.

The Inaccurate Bombing of Bridges in Iraq: Avoidable Civilian Losses
    Iraqi civilians may have paid a high price for the allies' initial attempts to destroy bridges in Iraq with unguided, general-purpose bombs. During the air war, Middle East Watch obtained testimony from former residents of Iraq who described residential buildings and other civilian objects, including hospitals, destroyed or damaged by bombs that missed bridges by 200 to 400 meters or more, often resulting in civilian deaths and injuries. These accounts are included in Chapters Three and Five. Middle East Watch does not know the type of munitions that were used to attack each of these bridges. We believe that in each case the United States and other allied forces should disclose information about the type of bombs used to attack bridges that were located in proximity to civilian structures and the civilian population. If precision weapons were not used, MEW calls on the Pentagon and allied commands to explain why the choice of unguided munitions in a populated area was deemed compatible with the legal duty to take a feasible precautions to avoid civilian casualties.

    Iraq's bridges were attacked early in the air war: the bombing of the bridges, particularly across the Euphrates River, was a key tactic in the allies' effort to disrupt or sever supply lines to Iraqi troops massed in Kuwait and north of the Kuwait-Iraq border. In the war's first week, however, *The Washington Post* reported that "relatively few" precision bombs were used to attack bridges:

> Many Navy "dumb" bombs dropped by F/A-18 and A-6 bombers flying from the Persian Gulf to the Basra area missed their targets, a senior Pentagon official said, and as a result supplies continued to pour into Kuwait until early [February].[96]

    Gen. Schwarzkopf reported at a briefing on January 30 that 36 bridges in Iraq were targeted and 33 of them had been attacked with over 790 sorties. "Obviously," he said, "by shutting off the bridges, we shut off

---

[96] Rick Atkinson, "Iraqis Called Vulnerable to Land Attack," *The Washington Post*, February 15, 1991.

the supply lines that supply the forces in southern Iraq and Kuwait."[97] He then showed a video of an attack on a railroad bridge. "We try to hit right near the shore," he said, "because that's the most difficult to repair and does the most damage if you get in at that point."[98]

What Gen. Schwarzkopf failed to mention was that pilots' instructions to hit "right near the shore" must be balanced against the greater likelihood of civilian casualties in such attacks in the event that ordnance fell wide of the intended target. Since over 20 sorties were launched per bridge, it is obvious that a fair number of the bombs missed their targets. For example, in the daytime attack on a bridge near the bank of the Euphrates River in Samawa -- described in the previous section of this chapter -- over 100 women and children who were washing clothes and playing "right near the shore" are believed to have been killed.

Gen. Neal said on February 6 that at least 42 bridges in Iraq had been attacked and "apparently have suffered major damage."[99] Military officers interviewed by *The New York Times* provided more details. They said that F-15E, F-16 and F/A-18 fighter-bombers flew over 100 missions against 42 key bridges in Iraq, but the aircraft used unguided bombs which did not destroy the targets.[100] Military planners later directed F-117s and F-111s -- equipped with 500-pound laser-guided bombs -- to attack the bridges; seven bridges were reportedly destroyed or severely damaged during the first night in which precision-guided weapons were used.[101]

---

[97] Pyle at 211.

[98] Pyle at 211.

[99] Rick Atkinson, "Gulf Ground War Not Felt Imminent," *The Washington Post*, February 7, 1991.

[100] Michael R. Gordon with Eric Schmitt, "Radios and Mine Sweepers: Problems in the Gulf," *The New York Times*, March 28, 1991.

[101] *The New York Times*, March 28, 1991.

The evidence collected by Middle East Watch about the inaccurate bombing of bridges -- while not comprehensive -- indicates that the initial decision to use unguided, general-purpose bombs against these targets when they were in close proximity to Iraqi civilians caused avoidable casualties and damage. Given the U.S. Air Force's knowledge that "dumb" bombs lack the accuracy of precision weapons, the choice of this ordnance for attacking bridges in populated areas should be explained, particularly in view of the Air Force's own rules that requiring "all feasible precautions" to be undertaken in the choice of means and methods of attack to avoid or minimize the incidental loss of civilian life and damage to civilian objects.

Unanswered Questions

Chapter Five of this report provides additional accounts of allied attacks in cities and towns in Iraq which caused civilian casualties, and damage to or total destruction of civilian objects, typically one- and two-family homes. In numerous incidents, it appears that bombs or missiles may have been properly directed at specific military targets but fell wide of the mark, causing civilian losses.

The critical question is whether the allied air forces did everything feasible in choosing means and methods of attack to minimize civilian casualties and damage, as required by the laws of war. Given the well-publicized technologically advanced munitions available to the allied forces in this conflict, Middle East Watch believes that the most discriminating weapons should have been used in attacks against military targets in populated civilian areas. However, although U.S. military spokespersons fostered the public impression during the war that only precision bombing was being used in these cases, no hard facts have emerged from the Pentagon to substantiate this view.

A first step in understanding the civilian casualties that did result is for the allied forces to come forth with a public accounting of the types of weapons used in these cases and to explain its use of non-precision weapons in urban areas. The accounting should include information about the ordnance used by all branches of the allied air forces, since an accounting of weapons used only by the U.S. Air Force, for example, would obscure the fact that Navy aircraft -- which, together with Marine aircraft, flew 23 percent of the total number of sorties, according to Adm.

Frank B. Kelso, the U.S. chief of naval operations[102] -- used mostly conventional unguided bombs. As *The Washington Post* noted:

> The Navy...which dropped primarily "dumb bombs" and had only a limited number of the high-technology, precision-guided missiles, is now using the success of the Air Force's "smart" weapons in lobbying to expand its own arsenal.[103]

As noted above, during the war Gen. Schwarzkopf stated that the allied forces "deliberately determined" to use their technological capabilities to limit civilian damage. However, what is not yet known is the extent to which smart bombs were used against military targets located in or near civilian population centers in Iraq. It is important to know whether the allies' technological edge from precision weapons was fully employed to maximize the protection of Iraqi civilians, and if it was not, why it was not.

If unguided "dumb" bombs were used to attack military targets in cities and towns, Middle East Watch raises the following questions:

- Who was responsible for the selection of the munitions to be used against military targets in close proximity to the Iraqi civilian population?

- What factors were considered and weighed in the decisionmaking process? Was cost a factor in the choice of munitions, and, if so, how significant a factor?

- Was the relative inaccuracy of "dumb" bombs part of the decisionmaking calculus?

- If so, was it expected that there might be an incidental loss of civilian life or damage to civilian objects during

---

[102] Molly Moore, "War Exposed Rivalries, Weaknesses in Military," *The Washington Post*, June 10, 1991.

[103] *Id.*

attacks if such munitions were used? Was the civilian
loss judged acceptable, and, if so, what expected
military advantage guided such judgments? By what
criteria were expected civilian casualties balanced
against the reasons for using "dumb" bombs?

Middle East Watch also calls on the Pentagon to disclose whether
the rules of engagement for allied pilots who bombed targets in
proximity to civilian objects in occupied Kuwait differed from the rules
governing pilots who carried out similar missions in Iraq. A Kuwaiti Air
Force pilot told reporters that the Kuwaiti air force avoided any
possibility of civilian damage when targets in Kuwait were attacked: "If
there is a target near a house, we won't touch it," said Capt. Ayman al-
Muehaf, who flew a Mirage bomber during the war.[104] Based on the
testimony taken by MEW from former residents of Iraq, it is clear that
targets in proximity to residential buildings in Iraq were hit, indicating
that the restraint noted by the Kuwaiti pilot over occupied Kuwait clearly
did not apply to the bombing of military targets near populated areas of
Iraq. If such discrimination was reflected in the allies' rules of
engagement, the Pentagon should explain this apparent different regard
for Kuwaiti and Iraqi civilians.

THE LACK OF WARNING PRIOR TO ATTACK:
THE AMERIYYA AIR RAID SHELTER

The bombing of the air raid shelter in the residential Ameriyya
quarter of western Baghdad took place at approximately 4:30 am on
February 13, killing between 200 and 300 civilians, according to various
Iraqi reports -- the highest reported death toll from a single allied attack
during the entire air war. Under the principles established in
international humanitarian law, the U.S. should have taken steps to
ensure that what at least previously was known to be a civilian defense
shelter was no longer considered a safe haven by the civilian population.
Specifically, under the principles of the laws of war, the Ameriyya shelter
should have been protected from attack until such time as U.S. forces

---

[104] R.W. Apple, Jr., "Heaviest Shelling By the Allies Yet Rips South Kuwait,"
The New York Times, February 13, 1991.

gave a warning to the Iraqi civilian population that the facility was no longer considered a protected shelter and provided sufficient time to elapse so that warning could be heeded.

The attack on the shelter occurred in the course of what was described as some of the most intense bombardment of Baghdad since the war began, during a 12-hour period from the evening of February 12 to the early morning of February 13. The Associated Press reported from Baghdad that "dozens of other targets" were hit in the city during the nighttime raids, including the Conference Center, across the street from the Rashid Hotel.[105]

The air raid shelter was located in the Ameriyya district of western Baghdad, in what journalists have described as a middle-class neighborhood. A nursery school, a supermarket and a mosque were located in the immediate vicinity. The structure was built as a civilian bomb shelter in 1984 and, according to the U.S. military, later reinforced with a concrete and steel roof ten feet thick. Peter Arnett of CNN reported that at the building's entrance was a sign: Department of Civilian Defense Public Shelter No. 25.[106] Television footage also showed a sign marked "shelter" in Arabic and English.

The building was attacked with two 2,000-pound bombs from F-117A aircraft: the first reportedly hit the air vent of the facility, weakening the structure; the second tore through the roof and exploded inside. Dr. Fayek Amin Bakr, the director of the Baghdad Forensic Institute, put the death toll at 310, some 130 of whom were children.[107] In a report to the United Nations Human Rights

---

[105] Dilip Ganguly, "'I was asleep...Suddenly the blanket was burning,'" *The Independent*, February 14, 1991.

[106] Robert D. McFadden, "Iraqis Assail U.S. As Rescue Goes On," *The New York Times*, February 15, 1991.

[107] Alfonso Rojo, "Bombs rock capital as allies deliver terrible warning," *The Guardian*, February 20, 1991.

Committee in June 1991, Iraq stated that 204 citizens were killed in the attack.[108]

After the attack, Abdel Razzaq Hassan al-Janabi, who identified himself as a supervisor of the shelter, described how the building was used by civilians:

> Each evening since the start of the war, local people would come along with their food, blankets, pillows and their things to the bunker. Nothing had ever fallen on [al-Ameriyya], but people preferred to spend the night down there for safety's sake. Last night, there must have been at least 400 people inside....There are shelters like this in lots of parts of Baghdad. They have room for 2,000 people. We always thought they were the best civilian shelters in the city.[109]

Hassan Ali Hussein, a local resident, told the press about his 14-year-old son Ahmad who was in the building:

> The boy went to spend the night in the shelter. They'd linked up a television to the generator and used to show videos. Clint Eastwood, Bruce Lee. That sort of thing....We were sure nothing could have happened to him. It's a nuclear shelter with walls of cement three metres thick.[110]

It was suggested that the bombing of the shelter may have been an attempt to strike against Saddam Hussein or other top Iraqi leaders.

---

[108] Third Periodic Report submitted by Iraq under Article 40 of the International Covenant on Civil and Political Rights covering the period from January 1, 1986 to May 31, 1991; United Nations CCPR/C/64/Add.6, June 24, 1991 at 9.

[109] Alfonso Rojo, "Bodies shrunk by heat of fire," *The Guardian*, February 14, 1991.

[110] *Id.*

Senior U.S. officials interviewed by *The Washington Post* said that the structure was a "leadership bunker," thought by intelligence experts to be one of some 20 similar facilities in Baghdad residential neighborhoods reserved for senior Iraqi government officials and their families for use during air raids.[111] A U.S. official who had been stationed in Baghdad said: "We watched them build those things. Our understanding was that these were VIP shelters, built for government cadres and party people."[112] After the war, Dr. Baghos Paul Boghossian, director of Baghdad's Yarmuk Hospital which treated victims of the bombing, told a visiting U.S. delegation that the shelter "had been reserved for 'V.I.P.s' until two weeks before the bombing [January 30 or January 31], when the local population was admitted."[113]

One resident of the Ameriyya neighborhood interviewed by *The New York Times* in June said that the shelter initially was reserved for the elite when the war began:

> At the beginning of the war, only the elite with special badges could go there. Other things [not further identified in the article] went there as well. I don't know what. When the people nearby complained that they couldn't use it, the authorities let more people in. Then it was bombed. Maybe the allies thought only the leaders were there.[114]

Another resident told the *Times* that a friend had told him that there was communications equipment in the building: "It was not a main

---

[111] R. Jeffrey Smith, "Design Convinced U.S. Analysts Building Was a Bunker," *The Washington Post*, February 14, 1991.

[112] Patrick J. Sloyan, "Was Hussein Target of Bunker Bombing?" *Newsday*, February 15, 1991.

[113] Erika Munk, "The New Face of Techno-War," *The Nation*, May 6, 1991 at 584 [hereinafter Munk].

[114] Alan Cowell, "Baghdad Rebuilds But Has Far To Go," *The New York Times*, June 11, 1991.

communications center when the allies bombed it. There had been some kind of equipment there until a couple of days before. Then they scaled it down and let the civilians in." But, as the *Times* reported, this resident "had not personally seen communications equipment inside the building or being removed."

Civilian Use of the Shelter: Middle East Watch Accounts
     Middle East Watch interviewed former residents of Baghdad who provided testimony indicating that women and children used the facility since the war began, even prior to the end of January. Whether some of these individuals were family members of Baath party officials is not known, but at least one family that used the shelter had recently arrived in Baghdad from Kuwait. Of course, even if the users of the shelter were family members of Iraqi government officials, that would not change their status as civilians who are exempt from attack.

     Middle East Watch interviewed Fawzi Muhtasseb, whose entire immediate family -- his wife and five children, aged six to 15 years, four sons and a daughter -- perished in the attack.[115] Mr. Muhtasseb, a Jordanian of Palestinian origin, had lived in Kuwait for 16 years, where he owned a small retail textile business. He and his family relocated to Iraq on January 10 because his business was no longer profitable in Kuwait, and rented a house in the Ameriyya neighborhood. According to Mr. Muhtasseb, two or three days after the aerial bombardment of Baghdad began, he and his family began to spend the night in the Ameriyya shelter because the bombing was so intense.

     He told Middle East Watch that he spent the first few nights at the shelter with his family, but that he and other men soon stopped going, in order to afford greater privacy to the women and children. (It is uncomfortable for Muslim men and women to share, and sleep together in, close quarters with individuals who are not related to them by blood or marriage, particularly in a space where there are no partitions to separate families and to provide privacy.) Mr. Muhtasseb would take his family to the building at about 5 pm and they would return at about 7 am the next day. Mr. Muhtasseb said that the building was a public shelter, with a sign outside describing it as a shelter; other

------

[115] MEW interview, Amman, Jordan, February 23, 1991.

signs in the neighborhood gave directions to the building. He described the building as a three-story structure: one above ground and two underground. The top floor contained the sleeping area, configured as one large hall without partitions. There were triple bunkbeds for children, enclosed areas for bathrooms, a kitchen and a television. Food and water were kept on the middle floor; food was not prepared at the building, and families would eat at home during the day. They would, however, bring sandwiches in case the children became hungry.

The building's bottom level contained standby electrical generators and other building equipment. Mr. Muhtasseb insisted that although there were several technicians to manage the building and operate the generators, the building was only used for civilians and he never noticed any military use. He said that it looked like a simple large concrete building from the outside. From the street, he said, he never saw camouflage paint on the building.

Mr. Muhtasseb said that on the night of February 12, he stayed at home and his wife and children went to the shelter. When they did not return home the next morning, he went to the shelter, knowing that the neighborhood had been bombed the night before. He said that he was never able to identify his family members because the bodies of the victims were charred beyond recognition. (Members of at least one other Jordanian family were killed in the attack: Adibah Ahmad Amir, 45, and her four daughters, ranging in age from 14 to 21 years old.[116] Her husband was a university professor in Iraq.)

Middle East Watch also interviewed a 22-year-old Egyptian retail worker, who was a resident of Iraq for three years and lived near the shelter.[117] He arrived at the building before the police cordoned it off and assisted in the rescue effort. He said that it took 15 minutes to open one of the doors, because of the heat and smoke. Once inside the building, he said he saw three-tiered bunk beds that were melted from

---

[116] *Jordan Times*, February 19, 1991, as reported in FBIS, February 20, 1991 at 39.

[117] MEW interview, Ruwayshid Evacuee Center, Ruwayshid, Jordan, February 24, 1991.

the high temperatures; he also said he saw three children completely burned and another whose back was burning. He told Middle East Watch that he knew of one Egyptian and two Iraqi families who were killed inside the building. The sole survivor was the father of the Egyptian family, who did spend the night of February 12 at the shelter.

A Sudanese student of veterinary medicine at Baghdad University told Middle East Watch that he had lived in the Ameriyya neighborhood because it was close to his college, where he had studied since 1986.[118] He said that he had never been inside the building, but that "everyone knew it was a shelter." He said the sign outside, marking it as a civilian shelter, was very old; the same sign was there during the Iran-Iraq war. The building was concrete and square-shaped, and looked like a very large hall. He told Middle East Watch that the wife and six children of one of his neighbors were killed in the bombing, and that he visited the homes of other neighbors in mourning.

The U.S. Position on the Attack

In a briefing on February 13 in Washington, D.C., Lt. Gen. Thomas Kelly of the Joint Chiefs of Staff laid out the U.S. position on the attack:

> We knew this to be a military command-and-control facility and targeted it for that reason....We targeted it, we bombed it very accurately, we bombed a building that had barbed wire around it, not an indication of a bomb shelter. We bombed a building that had a camouflage roof painted on it for whatever reason, again, didn't look like a bomb shelter.[119]

Gen. Kelly further noted that the building was the only one in the Ameriyya neighborhood "that had the roof painted camouflage." Pentagon officials also said that the building was "EMP" -- electromagnetic

---

[118] MEW interview, Azraq Evacuee Center, Azraq, Jordan, February 26, 1991.

[119] *The New York Times*, February 14, 1991.

pulse -- hardened with special equipment, in order to protect communications in the event of nuclear attack.[120]

MEW interviewed a European journalist who had rushed to the shelter immediately after he learned of the attack. He disputed Gen. Kelly's contention that the building was camouflaged: "I immediately asked to go to the roof. There was no camouflage paint on the roof," he said, adding that he saw the evidence of the incoming bomb. He told MEW that there was "no barbed wire" around the building. "There was no doubt at all that it was a civilian shelter, and there were road signs showing directions to the shelter," he said.[121]

White House press secretary Marlin Fitzwater said in a statement on February 13 that "[t]he bunker that was attacked...was a military target....We don't know why civilians were at this location, but we do know that Saddam Hussein does not share our value in the sanctity of life." However, U.S. Brig. Gen. Richard Neal acknowledged at a briefing in Riyadh the same day that the U.S. knew that the shelter was originally built for civilians:

> As to air raid shelters, my understanding is that [the Iraqis] do have air raid shelters. In fact, this was an air raid shelter in 1985, but then was upgraded. We had talked to folks that had worked in the construction area that this one was upgraded to a hardened shelter used for command and control.[122]

Two reasons were offered by U.S. military spokesmen to justify placement of the building on the bombing target list: the interception of military communications from the building, and aerial and satellite

---

[120] R.Jeffrey Smith, "Design Convinced U.S. Analysts Building Was a Bunker," *The Washington Post*, February 14, 1991; William J. Broad, "Baghdad is Heart of Iraq's Complex Military Communications Structure," *The New York Times*, February 15, 1991.

[121] MEW interview, March 25, 1991.

[122] *The Guardian*, February 14, 1991.

photographic intelligence that revealed the presence of military vehicles and personnel. Gen. Neal described the activity that had been noticed there in previous weeks: "We are able to intercept an active communications mode. There [were] military folks in and around the facility on a routine and a continuous basis." He also explained why the shelter was not attacked earlier in the air war:

> It became an active command-and-control bunker. We knew it was a military target, a military bunker during the work-up to the actual execution of the air campaign. But we haven't really seen any activity out of this bunker until the last two or three weeks...and so it was added to the target list as a result of this analysis and assessment by our J2 (military intelligence) folks.

Senior military sources in Saudi Arabia also said that near al-Ameriyya was "a significant bunker in the series of bunker complexes that [Saddam Hussein] has. He moves frequently. He has a series of bunkers in the Baghdad suburbs."[123] Capt. David Herrington, deputy director of intelligence for the Joint Chiefs of Staff, said that "over a period of time, military vehicles...leadership vehicles...[and] a whole range of other equipment" were seen outside the building.[124] Military officials also said U.S. intelligence revealed that military trucks and limousines used by senior Iraqi leaders were seen entering and leaving the building in early February.[125]

Gen. Neal added: "[W]e have no explanation at this time really why there were civilians in this bunker." Nevertheless, he insisted that the facility was not attacked in error: "[W]e don't feel we attacked the wrong bunker or that we made a mistake."

---

[123] Christopher Bellamy et. al., "Shelter 'a military target,'" *The Independent*, February 14, 1991.

[124] R. Jeffrey Smith, "Design Convinced U.S. Analysts Building Was a Bunker," *The Washington Post*, February 14, 1991.

[125] Michael R. Gordon, "U.S. Calls Target a Command Center," *The New York Times*, February 14, 1991.

* * *

The videotape of the victims pulled out of the Ameriyya shelter was sanitized by television stations before it was aired. An American journalist who is a medical writer said that charred and severely burned bodies were evident in the unedited tapes:

> [T]hey showed scenes of incredible carnage. Nearly all the bodies were charred into blackness; in some cases the heat had been so great that entire limbs were burned off. Among the corpses were those of at least six babies and then children, most of them so severely burned that their gender could not be determined.[126]

Rabah Rousan, a Jordanian television anchor who also saw the unedited tapes, put it this way: "All my life I will remember these things in vivid detail. I was educated in the States -- I lived there seven years when my father was ambassador, in the sixties -- and I was expecting the American people to say, 'We made a mistake, we're so sorry.' But they didn't."[127]

Legal Standards and Conclusions

• A WARNING SHOULD HAVE BEEN GIVEN PRIOR TO THE ATTACK: Middle East Watch recognizes that civilian objects may lawfully lose their immunity from direct attack if they are used to make an effective contribution to enemy military action, although civilians in those objects are still protected. However, to strengthen the customary law principle of civilian immunity, Protocol I contains certain specific rules giving special protection to civilian defense shelters. As noted in Chapter One, the U.S. supports the principle in Protocol I that civilian defense organizations and their personnel should be respected and protected as part of the civilian population.

---

[126] Laurie Garrett, "The Dead," *Columbia Journalism Review*, May/June 1991 at 32.

[127] *Id.*

The United States also accepts as a matter of customary international law the principle that "all practicable precautions, taking into account military and humanitarian considerations, be taken in the conduct of military operations to minimize incidental death, injury, and damage to civilians and civilian objects, and that effective advance warning be given of attacks which may affect the civilian population, unless the circumstances do not permit."[128] Article 65 of Protocol I builds on these principles by providing that the special protection afforded civil defense structures ceases in the event that a shelter is used for military purposes "only after a warning has been given setting, whenever appropriate, a reasonable time-limit, and after such warning has remained unheeded."

Although the United States has not commented on whether it considers this rule set forth in Article 65 to be binding as a matter of customary international law, Middle East Watch believes that the rule is a fair interpretation in the context of civil defense shelters of the duties to which the United States has subscribed regarding the need to take "all practicable precautions" to avoid civilian injury, including, when possible, by giving "effective advance warning" of an attack. In our view, regardless of the possible military use of the facility at the time of the attack, the United States should have issued a public warning that it considered the one-time civil-defense shelter to be a military target and should have provided time for civilians to heed that warning. Because such a warning was not given in the case of the attack on the Ameriyya facility, despite conceded U.S. knowledge that the building had at least in the past been used as a civil defense shelter, between 200 and 300 civilian lives were needlessly lost.

• NEITHER IRAQ'S FAILURE PROPERLY TO MARK THE SHELTER, NOR THE PRESENCE PER SE OF MILITARY PERSONNEL AT THE SITE, DEPRIVED IT OF ITS PROTECTED STATUS: Protocol I recommends that civil defense facilities be clearly marked with an internationally recognized symbol. Article 66 instructs parties to the conflict to "endeavour to adopt and implement methods and procedures which will make it possible to recognize civilian shelters as well as civil defence personnel, buildings and *materiel* on which the international distinctive

---

[128] Matheson at 426-7. *See also* Protocol I, Arts. 57-60.

sign of civil defence is displayed." The international civil defense symbol is an equilateral blue triangle placed on an orange ground. Annex I of Protocol I recommends that the symbol "shall be as large as appropriate under the circumstances. The distinctive sign shall, whenever possible, be displayed on flat surfaces or on flags visible from as many directions and from as far away as possible....At night or when visibility is reduced, the sign may be lighted or illuminated; it may also be made of materials rendering it recognizable by technical means of detection."

Middle East Watch is not aware that Iraqi civilian shelters have been marked with the international blue-and-orange symbol; regarding the Ameriyya building in particular, one U.S. official said that three black circles, resembling bomb holes, had been painted on its roof, to suggest that it already had been attacked.[129] However, Iraq's failure properly to identify civilian civil defense buildings in itself did not relieve the U.S. military of its obligation to take appropriate precautions to avoid harming civilians who had taken refuge in the facility because the U.S. military admitted knowledge of the building's prior use as a strictly civilian shelter.

Article 65 of Protocol I states that the protection afforded to civilian civil defense buildings, shelters and personnel terminates if "they commit or are used to commit, outside their proper tasks, acts harmful to the enemy." However, the presence of military personnel at civil defense facilities -- which the U.S. claims was the case at al-Ameriyya -- does not *per se* lift the immunity of such buildings from attack unless the military personnel are engaged in military activity unrelated to civil defense. Article 65 states in pertinent part: "The following shall not be considered as acts harmful to the enemy: (a) that civil defence tasks are carried out under the direction or control of military authorities; (b) that civilian civil defence personnel co-operate with military personnel in the performance of civil defence tasks, or that some military personnel are attached to civilian civil defence organizations...."

• NO DEMONSTRATION THAT ADEQUATE PRECAUTIONS WERE TAKEN PRIOR TO ATTACK: In public statements, U.S. military officials

---

[129] William J. Broad, "Baghdad Is Heart of Iraq's Complex Military Communications Structure," *The New York Times*, February 15, 1991.

repeatedly emphasized the basis for their judgment that the Ameriyya building was used for military-related activity and therefore was a legitimate military target. Gen. Kelly said on February 13: "We didn't know that the Iraqis had civilians in there." He posited the notion that U.S. reconnaissance did not observe civilians using the building because they moved inside under the cover of darkness: "[W]e did see military people going in and out. Why didn't we see civilians going in and out? Maybe they didn't go in and out until after dark last night and we didn't have a picture of it....They could have gone in after dark last night when we weren't up there looking."[130]

Testimony taken by MEW provides evidence that civilians in fact used the shelter since the bombing of the Baghdad began. Even if they entered the building once darkness fell, what is left unexplained by U.S. military briefers is why aerial reconnaissance did not detect civilians leaving the building in the daylight of morning.

Gen. Kelly said on February 13 that "we did take all the precautions we could." He did not, however, spell out the specific nature of the precautions that were and were not taken -- including why morning photos were apparently not taken -- in sharp contrast to the disclosure of specific information to support the contention that the building was used for military purposes. The need for such disclosure is particularly important in view of the U.S. military's acknowledgment that the building originally served as a civilian shelter during the Iran-Iraq war and its contention that the building only recently "became" an active command-and-control bunker.

The need for such precautions is underscored by the doctrine that, in the case of any uncertainty that a civilian object is being used for military purposes, it should be presumed to be used by civilians. This principle is reaffirmed in Article 52 of Protocol I, which provides:

> In the case of doubt whether an object which is normally
> dedicated to civilian purposes, such as a place of worship,
> a house or other dwelling or a school, is being used to

---

[130] *The New York Times*, February 14, 1991.

make an effective contribution to military action, it shall be presumed not to be so used.

The accompanying official ICRC *Commentary* states:

> The presumption established here constitutes an important step forward in the protection of the civilian population, for in many conflicts the belligerents have "shot first and asked questions later."[131]

Importantly, the U.S. Air Force also expressly accepts this presumption. Air Force Pamphlet states that "location as well as prior uses are important factors in determining whether objects are military objectives."[132] The *Commentary* further describes the exacting nature of this presumption, which extends to front-line areas where armed forces are present:

> [E]ven in contact areas there is a presumption that civilian buildings located there are not used by the armed forces, and consequently it is prohibited to attack them unless it is certain that they accommodate enemy combatants or military objects. Strict compliance with the precautions laid down in Article 57 (*Precautions in attack*) will in most cases bring to light the doubt referred to in this provision or the certainty that it is a military objective.[133]

Article 57 of Protocol I codifies principles of pre-existing customary and conventional law concerning precautionary steps which an attacking party must take prior to launching an attack to avoid or minimize civilian casualties and damage to civilian objects. It states, in part, that those who plan or decide upon an attack must "do everything feasible to verify that the objectives to be attacked are neither civilians

---

[131] ICRC *Commentary* at 637.

[132] Air Force Pamphlet, Chapter 5 at 8.

[133] ICRC *Commentary* at 638.

nor civilian objects". The *Commentary* on Article 57 notes that "the identification of the objective, particularly when it is located at a great distance, should be carried out with great care."

Further, the *Commentary* states that "in case of doubt, even if there is only slight doubt," those who plan or decide on an attack "must call for additional information and if need be give orders for further reconnaissance....The evaluation of the information obtained must include a serious check of its accuracy, particularly as there is nothing to prevent the enemy from setting up fake military objectives or camouflaging the true ones."[134]

As clarifications and reaffirmations of existing customary law, these precautionary measures are binding on the United States, as the U.S. State Department has recognized:

> We support the principle that all practicable precautions, taking into account military and humanitarian considerations, be taken in the conduct of military operations to minimize incidental death, injury, and damage to civilians and civilian objects, and that effective advance warning be given of attacks which may affect the civilian population, unless circumstances do not permit.[135]

In addition, the Air Force Pamphlet expressly adapts and incorporates the precautionary measures specified in Article 57 (2)(a) through (c) of Protocol I and notes pointedly that "precautionary measures are not a substitute for the general immunity of the civilian population, but an attempt to give effect to the immunity of civilians and the requirements of military necessity."[136]

---

[134] *Id.* at 680-681.

[135] Matheson at 426-427.

[136] Air Force Pamphlet, Chapter 5 at 10.

Unfortunately, the U.S. military has remained silent on the steps it took to ensure that the Ameriyya facility was no longer being used as a shelter. The U.S. thus has not demonstrated that it acted in strict compliance with the standards set forth in Article 57 -- particularly the process used to verify that the building was not being used by civilians -- at the time when the Ameriyya building was placed on the target list, and at the time when the bombing attack was planned and then executed. The importance of such a showing is only heightened by the U.S. military's assertion that following the onset of the war Iraqi command-and-control facilities were decentralized and placed in civilian structures. MEW calls on the Pentagon to provide this information so an independent assessment can be made of U.S. compliance with the duty to take precautions to avoid civilian casualties.

• THE USE OF CIVILIANS TO SHIELD MILITARY TARGETS IS PROHIBITED: U.S. military and civilian spokesmen claimed that the shelter was a legitimate military target because they believed it was being used as a military command center. Iraqi military command-and-control facilities were targeted and attacked since the first days of the air war. Gen. Kelly said on February 13 that the Iraqis moved their command centers to alternative facilities as a result of the allied bombing campaign: "What you are seeing on TV today [the Ameriyya building] is one of those alternate command-and-control facilities that we knew was active."[137]

This implicitly raises the issue of shielding, a violation of the rules of war. In order to give effect to the principle of civilian immunity, Article 28 of the Fourth Geneva Convention, ratified by all parties to the Gulf conflict, effectively enjoins the parties from using civilians "to render certain points or areas immune from military operations." This means that civilians may not be used to shield a defensive position, to hide military objectives, or to screen an attack. These principles are reaffirmed and codified in Article 58 of Protocol I. By using foreign civilians and prisoners-of-war to shield military targets from attack, Iraq violated its obligations under the Third and Fourth Geneva Conventions. Iraq thus would have borne the primary responsibility for civilian casualties that might have resulted from legitimate attacks by coalition

---

[137] *The New York Times*, February 14, 1991.

forces against shielded military objectives. However, even if it were shown that the Ameriyya building was in part a military facility, civilians in the shelter still retained protection under the rule of proportionality.

• THE CONTINUING RELEVANCE OF THE RULE OF PROPORTIONALITY: A statement by Gen. Schwarzkopf in the context of the Ameriyya bombing raises concern about whether U.S. forces applied the rule of proportionality in selecting targets. On February 13, after the shelter bombing, he said in reference to Iraqi efforts to shield military forces behind civilians:

> [R]ight now they've dispersed their airplanes into residential areas, they've moved their headquarters into schools, they've moved their headquarters into hotel buildings, they've put guns and things like that on top of high-rise apartment buildings. *Under the Geneva Convention, that gives us a perfect right to go after those things if we want to do them.* We haven't done it.[138] (Emphasis added)

Gen. Schwarzkopf was correct when he stated that legitimate military targets, even when shielded by civilians, are subject to direct attack. However, he was incorrect when he suggested that the legitimacy of a target provides unlimited license to attack it. Individual civilians and civilian objects located within or near the target still retain the benefits of the rule of proportionality as it applies to collateral civilian casualties and damage to civilian objects. Article 51 (4) and (5)(b) of Protocol I, in codifying customary law, characterizes and prohibits as "indiscriminate" an attack that

> may be expected to cause incidental loss of civilian life, injury to civilians, damage to civilian objects, or a combination thereof which would be excessive in relation to the concrete and direct military advantage anticipated.

---

[138] Dan Balz and Edward Cody, "Third of Force In Kuwait Said To Be Depleted," *The Washington Post*, February 15, 1991.

Similarly, the customary principles embodied in Article 57 (2)(a)(iii) and (b) of Protocol I bound Gen. Schwarzkopf and his subordinates to refrain from launching, or to cancel, such a disproportionate or indiscriminate attack. In this respect, Gen. Schwarzkopf's February 13 comment was an erroneous interpretation of the principles of customary law.

In this context, Middle East Watch notes that the Air Force Pamphlet states, *inter alia*, the following regarding minimizing civilian casualties:

> ....Attacks are not prohibited against military objectives even though incidental injury or damage to civilians will occur, but such incidental injury to civilians or damage to civilian objects must not be excessive when compared to the concrete and direct military advantage anticipated. Careful balancing of interests is required between the potential military advantage and the degree of incidental injury or damage in order to preclude situations raising issues of indiscriminate attacks violating general civilian protections. An attack efficiently carried out in accordance with the principle of economy of force against a military airfield or other military installations would doubtless not raise the issue. On the other hand, attacks against objects used predominately by the civilian population in urban areas, even though they might also be military objectives, are likely to raise the issue.[139]

Unanswered Questions

The men, women and children who perished in the Ameriyya shelter represented the largest known single-incident civilian death toll from any allied attack in Iraq during the 43-day air war. Middle East Watch believes that the hasty, unilateral decision by the Bush Administration and the Pentagon to "close" the case was improper -- an unjustified effort to shut the door on holding the U.S. accountable for the hundreds of Iraqi lives lost in the attack.

---

[139] Air Force Pamphlet, Chapter 5 at 10.

The day after the bombing, White House spokesman Marlin Fitzwater refused to discuss the incident further: "We said yesterday that we didn't know there were civilians [in the building]. I don't see any reason to go through all this again. The data and the information have not changed, nor have our conclusions."[140] Pressed by reporters, Mr. Fitzwater remained firm: "The issue is settled." The same day, Pentagon spokesman Pete Williams indicated that he was barred from providing additional information: "We have gone as far as we can. It would be a lot easier for me to get you all off my back if I could just stand up here and lay it all out for you, but I can't do that."[141]

Regrettably, this official stonewalling brought any further examination of the incident to a premature dead end: there was no public pressure in the U.S. to investigate why the shelter was targeted and bombed without warning, and why adequate precautions were not taken to discern the continuing civilian use of the shelter.

Nor, to date, has the Bush Administration and the Department of Defense made public any evidence -- such as satellite photographs or electronic data -- to support their claim that the building functioned as a military command center. The Pentagon's July 1991 public report devotes a mere six lines to the Ameriyya bombing and does not provide any estimate of the number of civilians who were killed:

> The most notable incident of Iraqi civilian casualties occurred when a penetrating bomb destroyed a hardened shelter in Baghdad used for military command communications. Many civilians who had, unbeknownst to the Coalition, taken shelter inside, were killed or injured.[142]

---

[140] Patrick E. Tyler, "U.S. Stands Firm on Bomb Attack And Says Investigation is Closed," *The New York Times*, February 15, 1991.

[141] *Id.*

[142] Pentagon Interim Report at 4-4.

Since the war is now over, the rationale that the release of photographs and transcripts of intercepted Iraqi military communications would compromise military security in a manner advantageous to Iraq is no longer as pressing. Although MEW recognizes that the Pentagon has an interest in concealing the means and methods of intelligence acquisition, the tragedy of the Ameriyya bombing presents a compelling case for release of pertinent information. Middle East Watch calls on the U.S. government to investigate fully the targeting of the shelter and the surprise attack on it, and urges that the findings of the investigation, including any additional information to substantiate the U.S. position that the building was a legitimate military target, be publicly released.

4
OBJECTS ATTACKED:
THE NEED FOR FULL DISCLOSURE
AND ACCOUNTABILITY

In the months prior to the war, the attention of the Bush Administration and the media was focused on Iraq's brutal occupation of Kuwait, the formidable power of the Iraqi military, and the regime's abysmal human rights record. The public learned practically nothing else about the Republic of Iraq, a highly urbanized and developed nation of 168,000 square miles, slightly larger than the state of California, and thus had little appreciation of the damage to be wrought.

Iraq's population was estimated at almost 18.8 million as of July 1990.[1] Over 46 percent of the population is under the age of 16; some 5 million Iraqi children are under five years old.[2] Iraq's economy also absorbed over one million third-country nationals -- workers and their dependents -- prior to the outbreak of the Gulf crisis.[3] By January 1991, approximately 750,000 foreigners remained, including 80,000 Palestinians. Three cities had a population of over a half-million by 1980: Baghdad, Basra and Mosul. By 1987, seventy percent of Iraq's residents lived in urban areas, compared to 64 percent in 1977 and 44 percent in

---

[1] Central Intelligence Agency, *The World Factbook 1990* at 149.

[2] World Bank, *World Development Report 1990* at 229; Paul Lewis, "Allies Asked to Guarantee Safe Transit on Medical Aid," *The New York Times*, February 9, 1991.

[3] UNHCR, "Summary of Activities in the Persian Gulf," February 4, 1991. According to the International Labor Organization, there were about 2.6 million foreign workers, and 700,000 of their dependents, in Iraq and Kuwait prior to the August 2 invasion. Within two months, some 1.5 million workers and their families had fled. Countries of origin, beginning with the largest group, were as follows: Egypt, Jordan/Palestine, India, Sudan, Sri Lanka, Pakistan, Bangladesh, the Philippines and Thailand.

1965.[4] Even harsh critics of the Ba'athist regime acknowledge its accomplishments in transforming Iraq into a modern state:

> The Iraqi Baath not only built up the fifth largest army in the world and an enormous, pervasive secret police; it also transformed Iraq's physical infrastructure, its educational system, social relations, and its technology, industry, and science. The Baath regime provided free health and education for everyone, and it also revolutionized transport and electrified virtually every village in the country. Iraq has today a proportionately very large middle class; its intelligentsia is one of the best educated in the Arab world.[5]

The petroleum industry was the source of 95 percent of Iraq's export earnings. Oil fueled Iraq's economy, accounting for two-thirds of the gross domestic product prior to the disruptions of the Iran-Iraq war, which included the bombing of facilities in Basra in the south.[6] The largest and richest oil fields are located in northern Iraq, near Mosul and Kirkuk; smaller fields are near Basra. Before the Gulf war, Iraq's refineries and petrochemical plants met the country's domestic needs for refined petroleum products.[7]

After the cessation of hostilties with Iran in 1988, Iraq mounted a major reconstruction program to rebuild and expand its petroleum industry. By the beginning of 1990, Iraq was pumping three million barrels of crude oil daily, making it the second-largest oil producer in

---

[4] Helen Chapin Metz, Ed., *Iraq/A Country Study* (Federal Research Division, Library of Congress, U.S. Government as represented by the Secretary of the Army: 1990) at 79 [hereinafter *Country Study*].

[5] Samir al-Khalil, "Iraq and Its Future," *The New York Review of Books*, April 11, 1991 at 12.

[6] *Country Study* at 125.

[7] Congressional Quarterly, *The Middle East*, 7th Ed. (Washington, D.C.: 1990) at 159.

OPEC, next to Saudi Arabia.[8] Later that year, the London *Financial Times* noted Saudi nervousness at the post-war resurgence of Iraq's petroleum industry: "Saudi Arabia was almost bound to be irritated by the re-emergence of such a powerful rival. Riyadh well knows that Iraq -- with oil reserves second only to its own -- could threaten its pre-eminence in the Organisation of Petroleum Exporting Countries."[9] In the early months of 1990, Iraq supplied 675,000 barrels of oil to the U.S. daily.[10] Its capacity to export was growing faster than any other oil-producing state -- former Iraqi oil minister Issam Abdul Raheem al-Chalabi said that $2 billion a year was being invested in the oil industry.[11]

Iraq's oil exporting depended primarily on pipelines across Saudi Arabia -- to the Red Sea port of Yanbu -- and Turkey. The pipelines carried over 90 percent of the country's crude oil to markets abroad. The 820-mile twin pipelines that run from Iraq across southern Turkey to the Mediterranean port of Yumurtalik -- bypassing Syrian territory -- carried 1.5 million barrels daily from the Kirkuk oilfields in northern Iraq.[12] Half of Turkey's oil imports were from Iraq, and Turkey earned $300 million a year in pipeline transit fees.[13]

Iraq's pre-eminence as an oil producer earned it classification by the World Bank in 1990 as one of the world's 17 upper middle-income

---

[8] James Tanner, "Iraq Is Fast Rebuilding Its Ravaged Oil Trade Into a World Leader," *The Wall Street Journal*, January 8, 1990.

[9] Andrew Gowers, "Iraq elbows its way back in with its Gulf friends," *Financial Times*, April 12, 1990.

[10] John H. Kelly, "U.S. Relations with Iraq," April 26, 1990, Current Policy No. 1273, U.S. State Department Bureau of Public Affairs.

[11] *The Wall Street Journal*, January 8, 1990.

[12] Clyde Haberman, "Trade Sanctions Against Baghdad Imposed by European Community," *The New York Times*, August 5, 1990.

[13] Clyde Haberman, "Iraqi Official Urges Turkey Not to Shut Oil Pipeline," *The New York Times*, August 6, 1990.

economies, based on gross national product per capita.[14] Iraq ranked
above the 37 lower-middle-income states, which include Egypt, Syria and
Turkey.[15] Compared to other countries in the region, Iraq's labor
force includes a high proportion of skilled workers, administrators,
scientists and technocrats.[16] Educated women enjoyed high labor-force
participation rates; prior to the Iran-Iraq war, for example, women
comprised 46 percent of all teachers, 29 percent of all doctors, 46 percent
of all dentists and 70 percent of all pharmacists.[17]

The allies' air war wreaked major destruction on Iraq's oil
industry and modern infrastructure. For example, by the end of the war
only two of Iraq's 20 electricity-generating plants were functioning,
generating less than four percent of the pre-war output of 9,000
megawatts.[18] The report of the United Nations mission that visited
Iraq in March 1991 concluded:

> The recent conflict has wrought near-apocalyptic results
> upon the economic infrastructure of what had been, until
> January 1991, a rather highly urbanized and mechanized
> society. Now, most means of modern life support have
> been destroyed or rendered tenuous. Iraq has, for some
> time to come, been relegated to a pre-industrial age, but

---

[14] *See* World Bank, *World Development Report 1990*. In addition to Iraq,
other "upper middle income" states included Algeria, Argentina, Iran, Korea,
South Africa and Venezuela.

[15] The U.S., United Kingdom, Israel, Saudi Arabia, Kuwait, United Arab
Emirates and 19 other countries were classified as high income states.

[16] *The Middle East Review 1990* (Hunter Publishing Company, Edison, New
Jersey) at 74.

[17] Samir al-Khalil, "Iraq and Its Future," *The New York Review of Books*,
April 11, 1991 at 12.

[18] Harvard Study Team, "Public Health in Iraq After the Gulf War," May
1991 at 19 [hereinafter Harvard Study Team Report].

with all the disabilities of post-industrial dependency on an intensive use of energy and technology.[19]

Estimates about the extent of damage in Iraq vary wildly. Then-Iraqi Deputy Prime Minister Saadoun Hammadi in February put the cost of repairing the damage in Iraq from the air war -- to roads, bridges, electrical-generating plants, oil refineries and other facilities -- at $200 billion.[20] One U.S. official interviewed by Reuters indicated that such a figure was not off the mark:

> The Iraqis spent at least $160 billion on infrastructure projects in the 1980s. Assuming that most of them have been damaged or destroyed, reconstruction would cost considerably more in 1991 dollars.[21]

Others say the cost of repairing the damage will be lower. Ahmed Chalabi, an Iraqi expatriate banker "familiar with internal Iraqi data" estimated that $60 billion worth of infrastructure was destroyed in the allied bombing campaign.[22] And the U.S. Central Intelligence Agency believes that the cost of repairing the bomb damage could reach $30 billion.[23]

---

[19] Ahtisaari Report at 5.

[20] Glenn Frankel, "Allies Must Now Win the Peace," *The Washington Post*, February 27, 1991.

[21] Bernd Debusmann, "'$200 bn and an entire generation to bring Iraq out of the 19th century,'" *Mideast Mirror*, February 26, 1991 at 13.

[22] Glenn Frankel, "Iraq: A Devastated Nation," *The Washington Post*, April 9, 1991.

[23] Patrick E. Tyler, "U.S. Officials Believe Iraq Will Take Years to Rebuild," *The New York Times*, June 3, 1991.

TARGET SELECTION: THE NEED FOR PUBLIC DISCLOSURE

The bombardment of Iraqi targets was reportedly based on an "intricately detailed air-war plan," drafted six weeks after the invasion of Kuwait by Brig. Gen. Buster C. Glosson -- commander of the 14th Air Division -- and his associates at U.S. Central Command.[24]   Gen. Schwarzkopf introduced Gen. Glosson at a briefing on January 30 as the "principal Air Force target planner." Lt. Gen. Charles A. Horner, the head of air operations for Central Command, had overall responsibility for the air-war campaign.[25]

A retired U.S. Air Force officer described the "massive surveillance" effort over Iraq during the five months leading up to the war:

> For a full five months before the Jan. 15 deadline, the U.S. focused its intelligence gathering capabilities on Iraq's 170,000 square miles.   Using satellites, high-altitude aircraft, electronic eavesdropping equipment and state-of-the-art analysis techniques, the U.S. patiently examined nearly every square inch of Iraq and listened to the voice communications of its military and civilian leaders.[26]

Verification of objects as military targets apparently had to proceed without "human intelligence" on the ground in Iraq, a tightly controlled society, where the CIA reportedly lacked even one skilled agent:

---

[24] Eric Schmitt, "Clouds Reported To Delay Bombing," *The New York Times*, February 9, 1991.

[25] Barton Gellman, "Allied Air War Struck Broadly in Iraq," *The Washington Post*, June 23, 1991.

[26] Col. Michael R. Boldrick (Ret.), "The Message of the Scuds," *The Wall Street Journal*, February 7, 1991.

The wheels of power in Baghdad were controlled entirely by Saddam Hussein and members of his family, supported by an efficient and omnipresent secret police force. William Casey, director of the CIA under Reagan, had been forced to admit that the Agency did not have a single skilled agent in Iraq, and the situation had not changed since.[27]

During the war, the initial list of 400 strategic targets almost doubled to over 700, based on two factors: additional intelligence-gathering that identified targets, and an increased number of B-52 and F-117A bombers available in the military theater to attack targets.[28]

Information has not been disclosed by the Pentagon or the White House about the U.S. military and civilian officials involved in approving these target lists. *The New York Times* reported that target selection was the responsibility of Central Command headquarters, not the White House.[29] Journalist Bob Woodward reported that President Bush, Secretary of Defense Cheney, Secretary of State Baker and Joint Chiefs of Staff Chairman Gen. Powell all reviewed the target list, but "[t]o avoid a repeat of the military's Vietnam nightmare -- President Lyndon Johnson leaning over maps in the White House, circling specific targets -- Powell had kept as much air-targeting information as possible out of Washington."[30]

With the first strikes of the air war set to begin at 3 am Saudi time on January 17, Secretary Cheney went over the target list with the President on the night of January 13. According to Woodward:

---

[27] Pierre Salinger with Eric Laurent, *Secret Dossier* (Penguin Books, New York: 1991) at 8.

[28] Barton Gellman, "Allied Air War Struck Broadly in Iraq," *The Washington Post*, June 23, 1991.

[29] John H. Cushman, Jr., "Crucial Tests for Tools of Command," *The New York Times*, Section 4, January 20, 1991.

[30] Woodward at 368.

> The President was concerned about one set of targets
> and asked that it be dropped. It included statues of
> Saddam and triumphal arches thought to be of great
> psychological value to the Iraqi people as national
> symbols.[31]

The next day, Secretary of State Baker reviewed the targets at the
Pentagon. According to Woodward: "Cheney wanted Baker to apply his
political eye to the air campaign, to see if he spotted any unforeseen
consequences. No other changes were made in the target lists."[32]
Secretary Cheney told reporters in June that every target was "perfectly
legitimate" and that "If I had to do it over again, I would do exactly the
same thing."[33]

Gen. Horner, at a briefing on January 18 in Saudi Arabia, praised
the independence given to the military in developing the air war plan.
"If we have any success in this air campaign," he said, "I can attribute it
in large measure to the freedom with which we've been allowed to plan
the campaign."[34] Gen. Schwarzkopf said that he was responsible for
target selection and, according to *The Wall Street Journal*, "is overruled by
civilians only if they think he is doing something particularly 'dumb.'"[35]

However, after the bombing of the civilian air-raid shelter in
Baghdad's al-Ameriyya neighborhood on February 13, described in
Chapter Three of this report, U.S. Defense Secretary Cheney reportedly

---

[31] Woodward at 364.

[32] Woodward at 365.

[33] Barton Gellman, "Allied Air War Struck Broadly at Iraq," *The Washington
Post*, June 23, 1991.

[34] John H. Cushman, Jr., "Crucial Tests for Tools of Command, *The New
York Times*, Section 4, January 20, 1991.

[35] Gerald F. Seib, "Military Reform Has Given Field Commanders Decisive
Roles and Reduced Interservice Rivalry," *The Wall Street Journal*, January 24,
1991.

ordered that all targets in Baghdad be reviewed by the U.S. Joint Chiefs of Staff prior to the execution of bombing raids.[36]

Target Verification: Unanswered Questions

As we pointed out above, an object on the target list was not necessarily attacked in the opening days or weeks of Operation Desert Storm unless it had priority status. For example, the Ameriyya shelter was said to have been on the target list for months, but it was not classified as a priority target until early February, when U.S. military officials claimed that military messages were being transmitted from the building.[37]

The actual bombing raids were planned several days in advance, according to Lt. Gen. Thomas Kelly, operations director for the U.S. Joint Chiefs of Staff.[38] A few days prior to an attack, "strike packages" of aircraft and ordnance were prepared, and the targets were said to have been examined by photo-reconnaissance satellites.[39] But military officials admitted that it was difficult to check recent aerial photographs in a timely fashion, prior to each attack. "We get a lot more intelligence data than we have time to look at and there are literally thousands of targets worth looking at," a senior U.S. official said.[40] The apparent failure to carefully check intelligence data for the presence of civilians has been noted as one of the fatal flaws in the bombing of the Ameriyya shelter, which had long been on the allies' target list. Noting the overload of intelligence information, one senior U.S. official told *The Washington Post*: "It's not surprising that we didn't look at this the day

---

[36] Christopher Bellamy and Patrick Cockburn, "Allies assess precision of bomb raids," *The Independent*, March 19, 1991.

[37] R. Jeffrey Smith, "Design Convinced U.S. Analysts Building Was a Bunker," *The Washington Post*, February 14, 1991.

[38] *The Washington Post*, February 13, 1991.

[39] R. Jeffrey Smith, "Design Convinced U.S. Analysts Building Was a Bunker," *The Washington Post*, February 14, 1991.

[40] *Id.*

before the [Ameriyya] raid," assuming that intelligence photographs were available.

Witnesses interviewed by Middle East Watch, including witnesses from the neighborhood, stated that civilians consistently had been using the Ameriyya shelter since the first days of the air war (see Chapter Three), which suggests that the U.S. intelligence lapse was not merely of one day's duration. The tragedy at Ameriyya raised questions, first, about the criteria that were used to place objects on the target list and, second, about the procedures used to verify that these objects were indeed military objectives that could be attacked under the rules of war. These questions still remain unanswered.

The Need for Disclosure

As discussed in Chapter One of this report, it is not permissible to launch an attack which offers only potential or indeterminate advantages. A legitimate military target must meet two tests: it must effectively contribute to the enemy's military action *and* its destruction must offer a "definite military advantage" to the attacking party in the "circumstances ruling at the time." The military advantage to the attacker must be "concrete and perceptible," and not "a hypothetical or speculative one," in the words of one authoritative commentary on the laws of war.[41]

Allied military spokesmen have never publicly disclosed the specific criteria used to categorize Iraqi "strategic" targets as military objectives. Nor has a detailed list of targets -- over 700 by one report -- been revealed.

Only *some* of the targets attacked were mentioned by allied military briefers during the war, and most of these were indisputable military objectives such as Iraqi armed forces, military equipment, and military production facilities. In contrast, allied spokespersons were generally reluctant to provide information about other targets that were attacked. *The Washington Post* noted the refusal of the Pentagon to discuss this subject at a briefing on January 21:

---

[41] *New Rules* at 326.

Nor has the military said how many hits were made on economic targets such as Iraqi oil refineries and manufacturing plants, or explained the rationale for striking targets that could play a key role in Iraq's recovery after the war.

When asked if he would anwer some of these questions at the daily Pentagon briefing [on January 21], Army Lt. Gen. Thomas Kelly, senior operations officer for the Joint   Staff, said, "The short answer is no."[42]

This chapter contains information about attacks by coalition forces on targets that had civilian uses or supported Iraq's civilian population, including electricity-generating and water-treatment facilities, food-processing plants, food- and seed-storage warehouses, flour mills and a dairy-products plant. Allied damage to other objects with civilian uses is noted elsewhere in this report. Reports from northern Iraq during the war indicated that a sugar refinery, a textile factory and domestic heating-gas plant were bombed (see Chapter Five). A journalist who visited southern Iraq after the war saw a sugar factory and clay-baking kilns that had been bombed.[43]   Middle East Watch took testimony about the bombing of an underwear-manufacturing plant in southern Iraq (see Chapter Three).

The Iraqi government also complained during the war that a number of non-military industrial and manufacturing facilities had been attacked by coalition forces. For example, in a January 24 letter to the United Nations Secretary General, Iraqi Deputy Prime Minister and Minister for Foreign Affairs Tarek Aziz listed, among other objects, the following as being attacked between January 17 and January 21:

---

[42] R. Jeffrey Smith, "Official Accounts of Battle Leave Many Gaps," *The Washington Post,* January 22, 1991.

[43] In the area south of Amara, a city near the Iranian border in southern Iraq, "even the kilns that baked the clay for housing have been bombed, and new homes, built with straw, are being busily constructed. A sugar factory is reduced to a tangle of metal." *See* Ed Vulliamy, "Fear At the End of the Basra Road," *Weekend Guardian* (London), May 18-19, 1991.

pasteboard, plastic foam and vegetable oil factories in Baghdad governorate; a poultry farm in al-Anbar governorate; a sugar factory in Maysan governorate; and a textile plant in Hilla in southern Iraq.

Allied attacks on such targets generally were not mentioned by military briefers during the war. Since these factories do not appear to have been involved in military-related production, Middle East Watch believes that the burden is on the allies to explain why these facilities were attacked and how the attacks complied with the rules of war.

- On what basis were Iraqi factories -- whose purpose was not essentially military -- included on the target list?

- How did target planners verify that certain factories had a military purpose? What effective contribution were these factories thought to be making to Iraq's military action, and what definite military advantage, in the circumstances ruling at the time, was expected from a successful attack that resulted in their destruction?

REPORTS OF ATTACKS ON FOOD, AGRICULTURAL AND WATER-TREATMENT FACILITIES

Middle East Watch collected eyewitness testimony and other information about allied attacks on food and grain warehouses, flour mills, a dairy factory and several water-treatment facilities in Basra. In light of any evidence that these objects were being used solely by or in direct support of Iraq's military forces, these attacks appear to violate the rules of war, particularly in the context of the severe deprivations of food faced by the Iraqi civilian population due to the United Nations embargo.

U.N. Security Council Resolution 661 of August 6, 1990 imposed mandatory sanctions on Iraqi imports and exports. The embargo greatly affected the food supply in the country, which had been dependent on imports for about 70 percent of total consumption. The agricultural sector accounted for less than 10 percent of Iraq's gross national product but employed a third of the country's labor force.[44] About 20 percent of Iraq is cultivated agricultural land: half of it is located in the northeastern part of the country, and the balance in the valleys of the Tigris and Euphrates rivers, extending south to Basra governorate.[45] The government supported agricultural development with investment in dam-building, irrigation, drainage and land reclamation.[46] Iraqi farms produced enough dates and vegetables, including legumes, to make the country self-sufficient in these items.[47] But other major stapies, notably wheat and rice, were largely imported before the war, the United States being a major supplier.

So concerned was the Iraqi government about food shortages that, despite the impending military crisis, farmers were exempted from military and Popular Army reserve duty by order of the Iraqi Revolutionary Command Council (RCC), headed by Saddam Hussein.[48] The RCC also issued a decision on September 7, 1990, which allowed the government, as of November 1, to seize, without compensation, any privately owned agricultural land "not planted by their owners or others

---

[44] Central Intelligence Agency, *The World Factbook 1990* at 150.

[45] *Country Study* at 154. In 1989-90, the Basra governorate in southern Iraq had some 4,200 farms on 95,500 dunums [almost 24,000 acres] of cultivated agricultural land, up from 4,800 dunums [1,200 acres] in 1975. Almost ten percent of the total acreage was rice-producing marshlands. The areas in the south around Safwan and Zubeir had large-scale greenhouse production of tomatoes; other crops in the Basra governorate included dates, fruit, garlic, onions, cucumbers, pumpkins, wheat and barley. (Statement by Basra governor to *al-Jumhuriyah*, September 18, 1990, FBIS, September 26, 1990 at 37.)

[46] *The Middle East Review 1990* at 76.

[47] Susan B. Epstein, "Iraq's Food and Agricultural Situation During the Embargo and the War," Congressional Research Service, February 26, 1991.

[48] Baghdad INA in English, September 7, 1990, as reported in FBIS, September 11, 1990 at 42.

in accordance with the scheduled agricultural density".[49]   The land would revert to state ownership, to be used by the Ministry of Agriculture. The RCC decreed that leases of state-owned agricultural land not planted to established specifications would be canceled. It said that the state-owned land then would be leased rent-free for five years to citizens who planted wheat, maize and rice.[50]

Under the pressure of the embargo during the Gulf crisis, the Iraqi authorities took measures designed to increase domestic food production. The Ministry of Agriculture urged citizens in September 1990 to raise poultry and use their gardens to grow vegetables; it said that winter-vegetable seedlings would be made available at cost and that instructions would be provided about planting and care.[51]   Also in September, the price for crops purchased from farmers by the government was raised and prices of seeds and fertilizers reduced.[52]

Prior to the imposition of food rationing in September 1990, the Iraqi authorities had begun to limit the amount of food released to stores from government warehouses, according to U.S. government officials.[53] The population's monthly allocation of staples -- such as flour, sugar, rice, tea, vegetable oil and powdered milk -- dropped from 343,000 tons in September 1990 to 135,000 tons in January 1991, or 39 percent of the

---

[49] Baghdad Domestic Service, September 10, 1990, as reported in FBIS, September 11, 1990.

[50] Al-Thawrah, September 9, 1990, as reported in FBIS, September 14, 1990 at 21.

[51] Baghdad Al-'Iraq, September 19, 1990, as reported in FBIS, September 26, 1990 at 38.

[52] Al-Thawrah, September 7, 1990, as reported in FBIS, September 14, 1990 at 21.

[53] Keith Bradsher, "Stretching Food in Iraq: Rationing and Feed-Grain Bread," The New York Times, September 1, 1990.

pre-embargo level.[54] To ensure the continuing availability of bread, on August 29 the Minister of Trade banned the closure of any bakery in Iraq for any reason, and said that any request to close a bakery would be denied.[55] If a bakery stopped production for any reason, its allotment of flour would be transferred to another bakery in the neighborhood, and its license would be forfeited. Bakeries also were required to open to the public at 5:00 am each day and to maintain fixed prices. The Trade Minister also announced that equipment maintenance services would be available to bakery owners and that spare parts would be directly provided. In early September 1990, Iraqi authorities began to issue family ration cards for commodities such as rice, flour, cooking oil, tea, sugar, soap, detergent, milk for infants, potatoes and beans.[56]

It is within this context of growing scarcity that the allies' bombing of food and agricultural facilities must be viewed.

Middle East Watch interviewed former residents of Iraq who provided accounts of allied bombing of, among other objects, government food-storage warehouses and a dairy products factory. Seed warehouses, flour mills and a veterinary-vaccine manufacturing facility also were reported to have been destroyed in allied attacks.

Reports of Attacks on Civilian Food Warehouses

During the second week of the war, four government food warehouses in Diwaniyya, a city south of Baghdad, were bombed at about 9:30 in the evening, according to a Sudanese mechanic, 30, who had lived in the city for two years.[57] He told Middle East Watch that the warehouses were located in an isolated area about eight kilometers north

---

[54] Ahtisaari Report at 6.

[55] Announced by Minister of Trade Muhammed Mahdi Salih, as reported in FBIS, September 7, 1990 at 23-24.

[56] Agence France-Presse, September 2, 1990, as reported in FBIS, September 4, 1990 at 23.

[57] MEW interview, Azraq Evacuee Center, Azraq, Jordan, February 26, 1991

of the entrance to Diwaniyya. He said that there was no military installation or activity in the immediate area, or any obvious military targets such as a bridge, telecommunications tower or anti-aircraft artillery. The warehouses were steel-framed, zinc-covered buildings, the main storage area for Diwaniyya's food.

The Sudanese saw the warehouses three days after they were bombed. He said that two of the buildings had sustained direct hits, collapsing the walls and half of the roofs; bomb craters some 15 meters (50 feet) in diameter were inside each of the buildings, suggesting that the structures may have been hit with 2,000-pound bombs. He saw large quantities of sugar, rice, flour and milk in the rubble. Civilians were not killed or injured during this bombing, he said, but local food prices subsequently rose, presumably due to shortages.

Iraq reported on February 19 that a flour mill had been attacked in what it described as the heaviest allied bombing raids to date.[58] Journalists who visited Diwaniyya during the war were taken to a residential area of the city where "a large plant with a camouflaged roof had been reduced to wasted masonry and tangled steel."[59] Local Iraqi officials said that the building was a flour mill and grain warehouse; large sacks of grain and rice were visible in the rubble, some of which were labeled "Product of the United States."[60] (Across the street from the warehouse were craters where houses had been hit on the first day of the war, killing nine civilians.)

Two Pakistani workers who lived in Najaf in southern Iraq and regularly traveled on Fridays to nearby Hilla, told Middle East Watch that they saw a food warehouse in Hilla that had been completely destroyed.[61] They were traveling by bus with other Pakistanis on the

---

[58] *The Guardian*, February 20, 1991.

[59] Fred Bruning, "In Iraq, 'No Place to Hide,'" *Newsday*, February 4, 1991.

[60] *Id.*

[61] MEW interview, Azraq Evacuee Center, Azraq, Jordan, February 18, 1991.

road to Baghdad, and stopped to look at the building. They saw rice and other foodstuffs inside the collapsed structure, but they did not know the date it was bombed.

On the outskirts of Basra, Iraq's second-largest city, a large zinc-roofed government food- storage warehouse, the General Establishment for Food, was bombed on or about February 6, according to a 26-year-old Yemeni student who had lived in Basra for 18 months while studying at the Academy of Marine Sciences.[62] He said the building was located near Amar Mohatab Street and Amar Khattab Street, about four kilometers from the al-Moakal railroad station. He lived about four kilometers from the warehouse and visited it two days after it was bombed. He said the building had been completely burned; he saw charred food, cardboard food boxes and fork lifts inside the structure, which was surrounded by a fence. He said that Basra was usually bombed between 8 pm and 4 am and that the destruction was widespread. Rice and bread were scarce, food was rationed and there was little water in the city; he left for Baghdad on February 9. An Iraqi exile who arrived in Basra from Iran on March 1 told MEW that the tin-food (canned food) factory near the al-Ma'qil quarter had been bombed.[63]

Report of Attack on Dairy Products Plant
A Sudanese truck driver, 28, who had lived in Iraq for over two and a half years, told MEW that a new dairy factory,[64] some 30 kilometers north of Basra, had been bombed about two weeks after the

---

[62] MEW interview, Azraq Evacuee Center, Azraq, Jordan, February 16, 1991.

[63] MEW interview with Ali al-Basri, London, May 4 and May 6, 1991.

[64] Iraq produced dairy products. According to the director-general of the General Establishment of Dairy Products, the country's largest factory produced in September 1990 200 tons of pasteurized milk, 20 tons of cream, 16 tons of soft cheese, and 20 tons of processed cheese. (*Al-Jumhuriyah*, September 18, 1990, as reported in FBIS, September 26, 1990 at 38.)

war began.[65]   The factory, a two-story building constructed of steel beams and zinc, was about 50 meters off the road, located in an area of flat desert.   A poultry-raising farm with three medium-sized sheds was 500 meters to a kilometer away. The Sudanese was driving past the building at about 9 am and saw fire and smoke pouring from the structure.   However, he said he did not hear any explosions or see any dead or injured civilians near the site. All that remained of the building were the beams, which were still standing; delivery trucks parked nearby had not been damaged.   The Sudanese was familiar with the plant through other Sudanese who worked there as drivers. Iraqi army camps with anti-aircraft artillery emplacements, located about a kilometer away, were the nearest unambiguous military target known to be in the vicinity.

Reports of Attacks on Water-Treatment Facilities

During a visit to Basra in May, journalist Ed Vulliamy reported that water-treatment plants in Iraq's second-largest city had been bombed, and that the allies targeted both the transformers and the turbines of these facilities. "It was not merely the transformers in the water plants that were bombed," he wrote, "but the giant Japanese-built turbines themselves, which cannot be repaired under the embargo."[66]

An Iraqi exile who arrived in Basra from Iran on March 1 told MEW that the main water-supply facility in the densely populated Bratha'iyya quarter of the city had been damaged beyond repair.[67] He said that the system in nearby Tenuma "was only hit by machine guns from the planes, so we were able to repair it." British journalist Patrick Cockburn told MEW that the water facilities near the al-Khalij Hotel were partially destroyed.[68]

---

[65] MEW interview, Azraq Evacuee Center, Azraq, Jordan, February 26, 1991.

[66] Ed Vulliamy, "Fear At the End of the Basra Road," *Weekend Guardian*, May 18-19, 1991.

[67] MEW interview with Ali al-Basri, London, May 4 and May 6, 1991.

[68] MEW interview, London, May 7, 1991.

Agricultural Sector Facilities: Reports of Attacks and Effects

Despite Iraq's dependence on both imported wheat and rice for 82 percent of total consumption, these and other grains, such as barley and corn, were also planted and harvested locally. Wheat is planted from November to mid-December and harvested from May to mid-June.[69] Wheat seeds are distributed to farmers by the Ministry of Agriculture at seed distribution centers through the Iraqi Company for Seed Production. For the winter wheat planting, farmers were asked to submit their applications for seeds to local Agriculture Ministry offices beginning in mid-September.[70]

The Congressional Research Service (CRS) reported that flour milling facilities and grain storage warehouses were destroyed during the air war, and predicted that the 1991 grain harvest would suffer from the effects of the war:

> Even if the wheat yield is substantially increased, Iraq will have trouble harvesting and delivering it....[W]ith limited fuel available commercially, farmers will have difficulty operating the farm tractors, combines, and trucks to get the grain out of the fields and to the mills.

> Moreover, if Iraq does manage to harvest the crop, the country could face problems in milling and storing it because of the incidental bombings of flour milling facilities and grain storage warehouses.[71]

United Nations representatives who visited Iraq in March reached a similar conclusion:

---

[69] Susan B. Epstein, "Iraq's Food and Agricultural Situation During the Embargo and War," Congressional Research Service, February 26, 1991 at 3-5 [hereinafter Epstein].

[70] *Al-Thawrah*, September 14, 1990, as reported in FBIS, September 19, 1990.

[71] Epstein at 10.

> This year's grain harvest in June is seriously
> compromised for a number of reasons, including failure
> of irrigation/drainage (no power for pumps, lack of spare
> parts); lack of pesticides and fertilizers (previously
> imported); and lack of fuel and spare parts for the
> highly-mechanized and fuel-dependent harvesting
> machines.[72]

The team warned that if the 1991 grain harvest fails or falls short, "widespread starvation conditions become a real possibility."

Iraq's agricultural sector relied on imported vegetable seeds. During the March visit, the U.N. representatives inspected seed warehouses that were destroyed during the air war,[73] and Iraqi agricultural authorities told them that all stocks of potato and vegetable seeds in the country were depleted. The U.N. team also reported that Iraq's only laboratory that produced veterinary vaccines -- an FAO-funded facility -- was destroyed during the war. The team inspected the center and said that the bombing had destroyed all stocks of vaccines at the complex. By March 1991, Iraq was judged to be in urgent need of imported seeds, fertilizers, pesticides, veterinary drugs, and agricultural machinery, equipment and spare parts.[74] The United Nations Food and Agriculture Organization reported in July that Iraq required some $500 million to rebuild or replace damaged or destroyed agricultural sector facilities and supplies, including machinery, irrigation systems, fertilizers and animal feed.[75]

One physician who participated in the Arab American Medical Association delegation to Iraq in May recorded in her notes that there was "a shortage of essential food items throughout Iraq." The food that

---

[72] Ahtisaari Report at 6.

[73] Ahtisaari Report at 6.

[74] Ahtisaari Report at 7.

[75] Jerry Gray, "5 Powers At U.N. Decide To Allow Iraqis To Sell Oil," *The New York Times*, August 8, 1991.

was available was high-priced and beyond the reach of the average family.[76] Rationed food items, distributed by the government, "are not enough for the average family and are of inferior quality." In Saddam City, the densely packed Shiite quarter of Baghdad, "malnutrition is rampant," the doctor wrote.[77]

Legal Standards and Unanswered Questions
        Civilian objects may not be attacked. Allied attacks on food- and agriculture-related facilities in Iraq raise serious questions about whether the destruction of these objects was a legitimate military objective under the rules of war or whether the objects were entitled to special protection deriving from the customary law principle that starvation of civilians as a method of warfare is prohibited, a principle which the United States accepts (see Chapter One).

        In the first instance, since these appear to have been civilian facilities, they were improper targets for attack. In addition, Article 54 of Protocol I states that attacks on such objects are prohibited if the purpose of the attacks is to deny the "sustenance value" of these objects "to the civilian population ...whether in order to starve out civilians, to cause them to move away, or for any other motive." The ICRC *Commentary* states that the objects listed in Article 54 -- foodstuffs, crops, livestock, drinking water installations and supplies --are illustrative and not exhaustive; the *Commentary* cautions that protected objects under Article 54 "should be interpreted in the widest sense, in order to cover the infinite variety of needs of populations in all geographic areas."[78]

---

[76] The average income for an Iraqi family is 120 dinars. During the AAMA mission, one kilogram of meat with bones cost 14 dinars, a three-day supply of baby milk was priced at 7 dinars and a tray of 30 eggs cost 14 dinars. One Iraqi dinar is the equivalent of $3.70.

[77] The AAMA conducted this mission jointly with the International Physicians for Prevention of Nuclear War (Germany). The report of the delegation, "Medical Conditions in Iraq," was published in July 1991. Information from this report is cited in the next section of this chapter.

[78] ICRC *Commentary* at 655.

The only exception to the rule set forth in Article 54 is if the objects are used "as sustenance *solely* for the members of [an adverse Party's] armed forces" or "*in direct support* of military action."[79] Even if this is the case, attacks are prohibited if they "may be expected to leave the civilian population with such inadequate food or water as to cause its starvation or force its movement."

Before the war, U.N. Security Council sanctions dramatically reduced the supply of imported food staples in Iraq and led to government-imposed rationing. There is a heavy burden on the allied military forces in respect to the bombing of food warehouses and other food- and agriculture-related facilities under these circumstances. In each case, the allies should demonstrate that these objects served exclusively the Iraqi military or, alternatively, that they directly supported military action. If this is claimed, what was the information supporting such conclusions, and what steps were taken, as required, to ensure the accuracy of the information?

Moreover, even if true, the allies would need to demonstrate that the destruction of these facilities could not be expected to leave the civilian population with "such inadequate food...as to cause its starvation or force its movement." Did the allied military forces make such a determination? What information supported any conclusions reached?

If allied planners knowingly targeted civilian food production, processing and supply facilities with the specific purpose of denying their use to the civilian population, such an attack would violate the specific protections accorded to such objects by customary law. Particularly in light of the humanitarian principles underlying this rule, Middle East Watch believes that the allied military forces should explain their attacks on these objects.

Regarding reports of attacks on water-treatment facilities, the questions that must be answered by the allied forces are the following:

- Were water-treatment plants in Basra or elsewhere in Iraq placed on the target list? If so, what information

---

[79] Emphasis added.

was available to allied planners that such facilities were serving a military purpose and that their destruction would yield a definite military advantage? More to the point, what information was available that these facilities were used either solely by the Iraqi armed forces or directly in support of Iraqi military action?

• What assessments were made to determine that the destruction of water-treatment plants, even if they were used solely by or in direct support of Iraqi military forces, would not leave the civilian population with inadequate potable water? What alternative sources of potable drinking water were believed to be available to Iraqi civilians at the time?

THE CRIPPLING OF THE ELECTRICAL SYSTEM

The targeting and destruction of Iraq's electricity-generating plants, including four of the country's five hydro-electric facilities, was little-discussed and never questioned during the war. To Middle East Watch's knowledge, Pentagon and Bush Administration officials never publicly offered a justification during the war for attacking and crippling most of Iraq's electrical power system -- destruction which continues to have devastating consequences for the civilian population.

After the war, in its July 1991 report, the Pentagon states that attacks on "electricity production facilities that power military and military-related industrial systems" were related to the goal of isolating and incapacitating the Iraqi regime.[80] The report's only mention of the impact of these attacks on the civilian population is as follows:

It was recognized at the outset that this campaign would cause some unavoidable hardships for the Iraqi populace. It was impossible, for example, to destroy the electrical power supply for Iraqi command and control facilities or chemical weapons factories, yet leave untouched that

---

[80] Pentagon Interim Report at 2-6.

portion of the electricity supplied to the general populace.[81]

Still, the report asserts that the bombing campaign was intended to "leave most of the basic economic infrastructure of the country intact"[82] and does not reveal beyond the above brief statement any weighing of the military advantage of these attacks against the cost to the Iraqi civilian population of the near-total crippling of the country's electrical power system.

*   *   *

As a modern, electricity-dependent country, Iraq was reliant on electrical power for essential services such as water purification and distribution, sewage removal and treatment, the operation of hospitals and medical laboratories, and agricultural production. Iraq's electricity consumption had quadrupled between 1968 and 1988, and rural electrification projects brought electricity to 7,000 villages throughout the country during this 20-year period.[83] In 1981, Iraq contracted $2 billion worth of construction work to foreign companies to build hydroelectric and thermal electricity generating plants and transmission facilities.[84] Some 30 percent of Iraq's electric power was generated by hydroelectric facilities.[85] By 1983, Iraq produced more electricity than it consumed, and in December 1987 it became the first country in the region to export electric power.[86] Newly constructed power lines to Turkey were expected to generate initial electricity sales of $15 million

---

[81] Pentagon Interim Report at 2-6.

[82] Pentagon Interim Report at 2-6.

[83] *Country Study* at 167.

[84] *Country Study* at 167.

[85] Ahtisaari Report at 12.

[86] *Country Study* at 167-168.

annually; plans called for expanded transmission to Turkey and the eventual sale of electricity to Kuwait.[87]

The report of a U.N. mission to Iraq in March stated that the allied bombing "has paralysed oil and electricity sectors almost entirely. Power output and refineries' production is negligible".[88] The Iraqi government acknowledged in April that the al-Shu'aybah and the al-Nujaybiyah power plants in Basra had been heavily damaged by allied bombing during the war.[89] The thermal power-generating plant at Bayji, north of Baghdad, was reportedly the largest in the Middle East; each of the plant's six units produced 220 megawatts.[90] It was "heavily damaged" during the air war, according to the Iraqi authorities, who announced on April 18 that a team of 500 engineers and technicians had repaired four of the facility's six units.[91]

A Harvard University group that visited Iraq for nine days in April and May found that electricity was supplied at only 23 percent of the pre-war level, up from a mere 3 percent to 4 percent immediately after the war.[92] By the end of June, the figure apparently had not changed; in an interview with *The New York Times*, Iraq's Minister of Industry, Amer Asadi, said that the level of electricity generated at that time was about 20 percent of the pre-war level, with repairs hampered by a lack of spare parts.[93]

---

[87] *Country Study* at 168.

[88] Ahtisaari Report at 12.

[89] Baghdad INA, April 13, 1991, as reported in FBIS, April 16, 1991 at 15.

[90] Baghdad INA, April 18, 1991, FBIS, April 19, 1991 at 14.

[91] *Id.*

[92] Harvard Study Team Report at 19.

[93] Patrick E. Tyler, "Iraq Tells of Constant Electricity Crisis," *The New York Times*, June 25, 1991.

One member of a delegation from the Arab American Medical Association who traveled to Iraq in May reported to Middle East Watch that while "electricity runs in most of the major cities for approximately 18-20 hours a day," the situation remained "dismal" in the provinces. The group traveled to southern Iraq on May 11 and found that in Karbala, electricity had been restored for only several hours daily; in Najaf, electricity also had not been restored and Saddam Hospital was operating with a generator that provided electricity for two hours in the morning and one hour in the evening, due to severe shortages of kerosene for the generator.[94]

Hydro-electric generating plants were attacked by the allies. Investigators from Harvard University reported that four of the country's five dams were attacked; two in the first days of the war and two others in early February, with the level of damage at each facility ranging from 75 to 100 percent.[95] Middle East Watch interviewed a filmmaker who visited northern Iraq in March and saw bomb damage to the 400-megawatt Dukan Dam on the Zab River, north of Suleimaniyya and east of Arbil in northern Iraq, which was bombed in early February. Looking up at the dam from the south, he saw a three- to four-foot wide hole on the left part of the dam's main wall. Located beneath this section of the wall are the electricity-supplying generators.[96]

U.S. Public Statements

Information released by the U.S. Air Force after the war indicates that electrical power facilities in Baghdad and northern Iraq were targets identified for attack on the first day of the war. The electricity-generating system in occupied Kuwait, in contrast, was spared the broad attacks executed by the allies in Iraq, despite the apparent use of electricity there to support Iraq's military efforts. In fact, despite reports of some damaged electrical-generating facilities, electricity generally was

---

[94] Arab American Medical Association/Emergency and Disaster Committee, "Medical Conditions in Iraq," July 1991 at 9-11 [hereinafter AAMA Report].

[95] Harvard Study Team Report, Table 6, "Electrical System's Prewar, Postwar and Current Outputs."

[96] MEW interview with Gwynne Roberts, May 19, 1991, London.

available in Kuwait throughout Operation Desert Storm until 3 am (Kuwait time) on February 24, the opening hours of the ground war.[97]

Gen. Schwarzkopf reported at a briefing on January 30 that in less than two weeks of bombardment that allies had rendered 25 percent of Iraq's electrical-generating facilities "completely inoperative" and an additional 50 percent "degraded."[98]   In the same briefing, Gen. Schwarzkopf stated that civilian needs were a consideration in limiting the scope of the destruction:

> I think I should point out right here that we never had any intention of destroying all of Iraqi electrical power. Because of our interest in making sure that civilians did not suffer unduly, we felt we had to leave some of the electrical power in effect, and we've done that.[99]

---

[97] A United Nations mission, led by Abdulrahim A. Farah, former Under-Secretary-General, visited Kuwait from March 16 to April 4, 1991 to report on infrastructure and economic damage during Iraq's occupation. According to the mission's report, five power stations supplied electricity in Kuwait and "[c]ritical parts of the electrical generating capacity and also part of the distribution grid were destroyed during the occupation." (at 21)   Two stations, Doha East and Doha West, "were blown up and totally destroyed." (at 71) The small Shuwaikh station inside Kuwait City sustained severe damage (at 71). The U.N. report, while assessing the extent and cost of the damage, does not describe how the damage was sustained. (See Annex to Letter Dated 26 April 1991 from the Secretary-General Addressed to the President of the Security Council, S/22535, 29 April 1991.)

Middle East Watch obtained conflicting information during a fact-finding mission to Kuwait in March 1991 about the cause of the damage to electrical-generating facilities; some Kuwaitis, mostly members of the military, told MEW investigators that the damage was caused by the Iraqis; other Kuwaitis said the facilities had been attacked from the air.

[98] Pyle at 208.

[99] Pyle at 208.

When asked if the balance of Iraq's power stations would be attacked, Gen. Schwarzkopf replied: "That's a decision that lies in the hands of the President of the United States."[100]

But, contrary to Gen. Schwarzkopf's words, civilians did suffer unduly as electrical power to most of the country was severed during the early allied attacks. Middle East Watch interviewed former residents of Iraq who described the lack of electricity throughout Iraq, from north to south, soon after the war began:

- Sudanese laborers who lived in al-Qayyara, an agricultural village 60 kilometers south of Mosul in northern Iraq, told Middle East Watch that the electricity and water supplies in their village were severed after the bombing started.[101] They said that their village began to use diesel-powered back-up generators to pump water, but even then, water was available only every three days.

- MEW interviewed a Mauritanian woman who left Baghdad with her family two days after the bombing started for the safety of Dawaya, a small village in southern Iraq, near Nasiriyya on the Euphrates River. The family stayed with the relatives of Iraqi neighbors in a small house in Dawaya. But, the woman reported, the villagers had no electricity because of the bombing and carried water from the river to their homes, boiling it before drinking it.[102]

- Kashmiri workers who lived in a compound in Kifl, a village near Najaf in southern Iraq, recounted that the electricity cut-off severed the village's water supply. They

---

[100] Pyle at 231.

[101] MEW interview, Azraq Evacuee Center, Azraq, Jordan, February 15, 1991.

[102] MEW interview, Azraq Evacuee Center, Azraq, Jordan, March 1, 1991.

said they helped bring water to civilians in the village from a water-purification plant they had built six months previously for their own use.[103]

• A resident of Najaf in southern Iraq told MEW that the city's power station was attacked in the early days of the war, severing the civilians' water supply and sewage-removal facilities as well as electricity.[104]

• In Basra, Iraq's second-largest city, there was no electricity after the first two or three days of the air war, according to a former resident.[105] He said that the government brought water trucks into neighborhoods, and women and children lined up with buckets. He also saw people collecting water from puddles in the roads, and others drawing water from the river running through the city.

Effects of Allied Attacks on the Electrical System
The immediate and longer-term consequences of denying almost the entire civilian population of an energy-dependent country an essential service such as electricity are grave indeed and should have been readily anticipated by the U.S. military planners of the air war. Almost a half-century ago, the consequences for civilian health of bomb damage of water, sewer and refuse disposal facilities in Germany and Japan during World War II was documented in meticulous detail in the United States Strategic Bombing Survey.[106] The Survey -- a comprehensive study

---

[103] MEW interview, Azraq Evacuee Center, Azraq, Jordan, February 18, 1991.

[104] MEW interview, London, May 7, 1991.

[105] MEW interview, Azraq Evacuee Center, Azraq, Jordan, February 12, 1991.

[106] See, for example, U.S. Strategic Bombing Survey, *The Effect of Bombing on Health and Medical Care in Germany* (First Edition, 30 October 1945; Second Edition, January 1947). Chapter Ten, which discusses environmental

by U.S. military and civilian experts of the effects of the air war on Germany -- was ordered by President Roosevelt and established by the U.S. Secretary of War on November 3, 1944.[107]

Among its numerous conclusions, the Survey found that there was a "reliable and striking" correlation between the disruption of public utilities and the willingness of the German population to accept unconditional surrender.[108] The allied bombing of Germany during

---

sanitation, states: "Sanitation facilities, consisting essentially of an adequate supply of potable water and a system of sewage and refuse disposal, are the principle planks in the platform supporting good health and a high standard of living. Most people in the civilized cities of the world are accustomed to such facilities in the course of every-day life. They take them for granted. Take them away suddenly and there is cause for immediate concern, not particularly with their origin an disposition, but with the dread of disease and the hardships involved.

"Aerial bombing of German cities had a devastating effect upon water supplies and waste disposal facilities. Much damage resulted from direct hits; additional damage resulted indirectly from the destruction of supplies and equipment necessary for maintenance and operation." (at 229)

[107] The study of Germany resulted in a summary report and some 200 supporting reports. The mission of the German study was to examine "the effects of our aerial attack on Germany, to be used in connection with air attacks on Japan and to establish a basis for evaluating the importance and potentialities of air power as an instrument of military strategy for planning and future development of the United States armed forces and for determining future economic policies with respect to the national defense." (The United States Strategic Bombing Survey, *The Effects of Bombing on Health and Medical Services in Japan*, June 1947 at iii.) On August 15, 1945, President Truman directed that the Survey conduct a similar study of the effects of all types of air attack in the war against Japan; headquartered in Tokyo in September 1945, Survey staff questioned over 700 Japanese military and other officials and reported on a wide range of issues, including "the course of health and morale among the civilian population" and "the effects of the atomic bombs." (*Id.*)

[108] The United States Strategic Bombing Survey, *The Effects of Strategic Bombing on German Morale*, Volume II (December 1946) at 3. Based on data from 18 German cities, the survey found that the highest correlation was

World War II deprived over one-third of the German pre-war population of utilities: 20 million of 69.8 million.[109] Of this number, almost 5.8 million Germans were subjected to severe electricity deprivation, and 14.5 million to moderate deprivation.[110] The Survey noted, for example, that damage to the environmental sanitation system in Germany created a situation that "was ripe for the development of disease into epidemic proportions....disease would have become rampant had not the Germans been forced to surrender when they did. In any event, *the dread of disease*

---

between disruption of transportation services and a willingness to surrender, following by the disruption of electricity; disruption of gas and water ranked lower. (*Id.*)

[109] *Id.* at 7.

[110] **Table 4 Deprivation of utilities and services**

Electricity deprivation:	Persons affected
Severe	5,766,000
Moderate	14,520,000
Total	20,286,000
==============	
Gas deprivation:	
Severe	12,402,000
Moderate	6,018,000
Total	18,420,000
==============	
Water deprivation:	
Severe	7,692,000
Moderate	10,254,000
Total	17,946,000
==============	

United States Strategic Bombing Survey, *The Effects of Strategic Bombing on German Morale*, Vol. I (US Government Printing Office, Washington, D.C.: May 1947) at 10.

and the hardships imposed by the lack of sanitary facilities were bound to have a demoralizing effect upon the civilian population."[111]

Similar effects have been documented following the allied bombardment of Iraq. The United Nations reported that with the destruction of electricity-generating facilities and oil refining and storage plants, "all electrically operated installations have ceased to function."[112] Predictably, the effects of this massive destruction on Iraq's water supply, sewage-treatment system, agricultural production and food distribution systems, and public-health system were severe and continue to be felt.

• WATER SUPPLY: All of Iraq's urban population had enjoyed access to safe water, although only 54 percent of the rural population was similarly served.[113] All of Iraq's water treatment plants -- seven in Baghdad, another 238 central stations in other parts of the country, and some 1,134 smaller facilities -- operated on electricity.[114] Some 75 percent had back-up diesel generators. The destruction of the electrical power generating plants rendered water treatment plants inoperable, except if diesel generators were available.[115] Back-up generators had limited utility because of the lack of fuel, spare parts and maintenance workers able to travel to their jobs.[116] The World Health Organization

---

[111] The United States Strategic Bombing Survey, *The Effect of Bombing on Health and Medical Care in Germany* (First Edition, 30 October 1945; Second Edition, January 1947) at 263. (Emphasis added.)

[112] Ahtisaari Report at 8.

[113] UNICEF, *The State of the World's Children 1991* at 106.

[114] Ahtisaari Report at 8.

[115] WHO/UNICEF Special Mission to Iraq, February 1991, U.N. Security Council S/22328, 4 March 1991 at 17 [hereinafter WHO/ UNICEF Report].

[116] Ahtisaari Report at 8

estimated in March 1991 that Baghdad's water supply was at five percent of its pre-war level.[117]

A WHO/UNICEF team that visited Iraq from February 16 to 21 described the water and sanitation situation in Baghdad as "grim." Ninety-five percent of the city's daily water needs were supplied by Tigris River water. The water was first treated at seven plants operated by electricity, then each plant would pump water into a 6,000 kilometer system of pipes. The team noted that conditions in Baghdad were similar to those in other areas of the country, but that the worst conditions were in Basra, Iraq's second-largest city.

The impediments to water treatment created by the destruction of the electrical system were compounded by the destruction of the factories that had produced the chemicals used to purify water, including chlorine. The WHO/UNICEF team noted "detailed reports that the whole of the Iraqi drinking water system is in or near collapse" and that the chemical supplies needed to treat the water were dwindling: "The chemical plants which used to supply the main treatment elements, aluminum sulphate (alum) and chlorine, have been destroyed by bombing."[118] Iraq's Ministry of Industry told *The New York Times* in an interview in June that six chlorine-manufacturing plants were damaged during the war.[119] He said that one of the plants was under repair and expected to be operational in June but that it would meet only 20 percent of the 50 tons of chlorine Iraq needed daily.

• SEWAGE TREATMENT: The lack of electricity also brought all sewage treatment and pumping stations "to a virtual standstill," the March U.N. mission found. The WHO/UNICEF team that had visited earlier described the sanitary system in Baghdad as "critically deteriorating" and "dangerous." The sewer system operated by the movement of waste to treatment plants by 252 electrically operated pumping stations, of which

---

[117] *Financial Times*, March 13, 1991.

[118] WHO/ UNICEF Report at 18.

[119] Patrick E. Tyler, "Iraq Tells of Constant Electricity Crisis," *The New York Times*, June 25, 1991.

192 had stand-by generators. The lack of fuel and spare parts for the generators caused the pipes to back up, flooding houses with raw sewage; sewage also overflowed at the pumping stations in large pools.

An Indian civil engineer who had been working in Basra on the construction of a new sewage treatment facility told Middle East Watch that the city's sewage system was not functioning because of the lack of electricity. He explained that sewage pipes in Basra are located 1.5 to seven meters below ground, and that they operated by the higher pipes draining to lower pipes, where pumping stations then moved the sewage to higher levels again, until the waste reached the treatment facility. The engineer, who was evacuated from Basra on February 4, said that sewage was seeping out of houses and accumulating in the streets.[120]

Noting that warm weather was approaching, the WHO/UNICEF team warned: "If nothing is done to remedy water supply and improve sanitation, a catastrophe could beset Iraq." On March 12 two mobile water purification and packaging units and equipment were brought to Baghdad by the International Committee of the Red Cross (ICRC).[121] It said that the Iraqi civilian population's priority needs were sanitation and medical care.

An ICRC team of medical and sanitation specialists visited the southern cities of Nasiriyah, Basra, Amarah, Karbala and Najaf beginning on March 21, as part of an assessment of humanitarian needs in Iraqi cities. The ICRC reported that the most urgent problem was inadequate and unsafe water supplies.[122] The ICRC said that the situation was especially critical in Basra and Nasiriyya, and that it planned to send water purification equipment there "to combat the risk of water-borne diseases -- a threat which will grow with the start of the warmer weather."

---

[120] MEW interview, Azraq Evacuee Center, Azraq, Jordan, February 12, 1991.

[121] ICRC Press Release No. 91/21, March 12, 1991.

[122] ICRC Press Release No. 91/25, March 28, 1991.

• AGRICULTURAL PRODUCTION AND FOOD DISTRIBUTION: The allied attacks on electricity-generating plants countrywide also inevitably disrupted Iraq's domestic food production and distribution systems, upon which the country increasingly relied since the international embargo imposed after the invasion of Kuwait (*see* previous section of this chapter for additional information). Iraq's agricultural sector, which was highly mechanized and relied on pumped-water irrigation, felt the impact of the lack of electricity and fuel. The attacks also disabled irrigation, as well as harvesting and food distribution systems. Food, grain and seed warehouses and flour mills were reportedly bombed by allied forces, creating additional disruptions. And, without electricity, food requiring refrigeration could no longer be stored.

• HEALTH-CARE SYSTEM: Hospitals and clinics in Iraq were gravely affected by the destruction of the electrical system. Two physicians from Doctors Without Borders, a private voluntary organization based in France, visited Iraq for six days in March and reported that the "lack of energy is paralyzing the whole health care system."[123] They visited six hospitals in Baghdad, and one hospital and five clinics in Falluja, west of Baghdad. They found the facilities operating at 5 to 10 percent of capacity, treating only emergency case; vaccines had deteriorated from lack of refrigeration, medication and other supplies were scant, and medical laboratories could not function. The ICRC also identified the need to provide support and medical supplies for hospital and dispensaries in southern Iraq as another priority.[124]

A delegation of 15 physicians representing the Arab American Medical Association and International Physicians for Prevention of Nuclear War (Germany) traveled to Iraq for six days in May and found similar conditions in the hospitals they visited in nine cities throughout the country. The director of al-Qadisiyya Hospital in Baghdad, a 325-bed facility serving the low-income Saddam City suburb, reported that at the time of the group's visit an average of 20 children were dying a day from

---

[123] Lee Hockstader, "Power Outages Said to Burden Iraqi Hospitals," *The Washington Post*, March 16, 1991.

[124] ICRC Press Release No. 91.25, March 28, 1991.

severe gastroenteritis.[125]   During the air war, premature infant
mortality at the hospital was 100 percent because the pediatric intensive
care unit could not function due to the lack of electricity. At al-Husseini
Hospital in Karbala, in southern Iraq, the group saw many children with
severe malnutrition; doctors at the hospital reported that the number of
gastroenteritis cases "increased by three to four times the numbers usually
encountered in the summer."[126]

The group found that the the effects of the war, exacerbated by
shortages attributable to the U.N.-mandated embargo, "produced a
signficantly deteriorated public health system in Iraq, characterized by
unavailability or extreme shortages of medicines and medical supplies,
absence of electricity, water supply, and sewage disposal in many regions
of the country, prevalence of infections, particularly gastrointestinal, and
extreme malnutrition."[127]   The delegation noted a marked increase
in illness, particularly among children:

> Interviewed physicians in the various hospitals conveyed a clear
> impression of a significantly increased morbidity for their
> patients, both in terms of severity of illness and length of stay in
> the hospital.   Further, there was a clear negative impact of
> malnutrition   on   the   morbidity   of   children   with
> gastroenteritis.[128]

Investigators from Harvard University visited hospitals and other
health facilities in major cities throughout Iraq from April 28 to May 6.
Based on their research, the group projected that a minimum of 170,000
children under the age of five would die in the coming year -- from
gastroenteritis, cholera, typhoid and malnutrition -- as a result of the

---

[125] AAMA Report at 7.

[126] AAMA Report at 11.

[127] AAMA Report at 19.

[128] Id.

delayed effects of the Gulf crisis and war.[129] The figure represents a 100 percent increase in infant and child mortality since August 1990:

> These projections are conservative. In all probability, the actual number of deaths of children under five will be much higher. While children under five were the focus of this study, a large increase in deaths among the rest of the population is also likely.
>
> The immediate cause of death in most cases will be water-borne infectious disease in combination with severe malnutrition....The incidence of water-borne diseases increased suddenly and strikingly during the early months of 1991 as a result of the destruction of electrical generating plants in the Gulf War and the consequent failure of water purification and sewage treatment systems.[130]

The Harvard team found that the public-health crisis was exacerbated by the lack of public utilities and medical supplies at health facilities around the country:

> Hospitals and community health centers also lack reliable clean water, sewage disposal, and electrical power. Of the 16 functioning hospitals and community health centers that the study team surveyed, 69% have inadequate sanitation because of the damage to water purification and sewage treatment plants. There is not enough electricity for operating theaters, diagnostic facilities, sterile procedures, and laboratory equipment.
>
> Staff at every health facility visited reported severe shortages of anesthestic agents, antibiotics, intravenous fluids, infant formula, needles, syringes, and bandages.

---

[129] The report discusses the methodology used to derive this figure; *see* Harvard Study Team Report at 12-13.

[130] *Id.* at 1-2.

186 • PART II: THE AIR WAR AGAINST IRAQ

Existing stores of heat-sensitive vaccines and medicines have been depleted by the loss of electrical power for refrigeration.[131]

Legal Standards and Unanswered Questions

In less than two weeks of bombardment, 25 percent of Iraq's electrical-generating capacity was destroyed by the allies and an additional 50 percent "degraded." Still -- despite Gen. Schwarzkopf's comment at that time that "we never had any intention of destroying all of Iraqi electrical power" so that "civilians did not suffer unduly"[132] -- the bombing of the electrical system continued. But Dominique Dufour, the head of a team of 90 specialists sent to Iraq by the ICRC, said in June: "I am absolutely sure that no Pentagon planner calculated the impact bombing the electrical system would have on pure drinking water supplies for weeks to come, and the snowball effect of this on public health."[133]

By the time the air war was over, Iraq was left with less than five percent of its pre-war electrical-generating capacity. This resulted in severe deprivation of clean water and sewage removal for the civilian population and paralyzed the country's entire health care system, exceeding the deprivations experienced by German civilians as a result of allied bombing during World War II.

Middle East Watch recognizes that the injunction against starvation of the civilian population as a method of warfare does not prohibit incidental distress to civilians as a result of attacks against legitimate military targets. Yet, it is difficult to reconcile the devastation of Iraq's electrical-generating facilities with the humanitarian concerns underlying this legal injunction.

---

[131] Harvard Study Team Report at 15.

[132] January 30, 1991.

[133] Patrick E. Tyler, "Disease Stalks Iraq as Trade Ban Saps Its Strength," *The New York Times*, June 24, 1991.

Insofar as the civilian population is concerned, it makes little or no difference whether a drinking water facility is attacked and destroyed, or is made inoperable by the destruction of the electrical plan supplying it power. In either case, civilians suffer the same effects -- they are denied the use of a public utility indispensable for their survival.

This destruction is all the more problematic given the allied air forces' supremacy and control of the skies,[134] which enabled them to attack with virtual impunity any production or communication facility supporting Iraq's military effort. The apparent justification for attacking almost the entire electrical system in Iraq was that the system functioned as an integrated grid, meaning that power could be shifted countrywide, including to military functions such as command-and-control centers and weapons-manufacturing facilities. But these key military targets were attacked in the opening days of the war. The direct attacks by the allies on these military targets should have obviated the need simultaneously to destroy the fixed power sources thought to have formerly supplied them. If these and other purely military targets could be attacked at will, then arguably the principle of humanity would make the wholesale destruction of Iraq's electrical-generating capability superfluous to the accomplishment of legitimate military purposes.

---

[134] Gen. Norman Schwarzkopf stated publicly on January 30 that the allied forces had control of the skies. (Edward Cody, "Iraqi Targets Bombed at Will, General Says," *The Washington Post*, January 31, 1991.) U.S. Air Force Chief of Staff Gen. Merrill A. McPeak described at a Defense Department briefing on March 15, 1991 the plan for the first phase of the air campaign: "Phase I, lasting about seven to ten days, would be the air superiority phase aimed at destroying Iraqi intergrated air defenses and their offensive capability, and disrupting their command and control setup -- attacking the brains and nervous system of the Iraqi ability to control their own forces." (McPeak Briefing, Transcript at 3.) Discussing the first allied attacks in the early morning hours of January 17 in Baghdad, Gen. McPeak said that coalition forces "achieved tactical surprise....the Iraqi Air Force never recovered from this opening attack. We took the initiative at the beginning and we held it throughout the rest of the war period." (McPeak Briefing, Transcript at 4.) Gen. McPeak added: "Once we had achieved air superiority, our next goal was to cut off the deployed field army." (McPeak Briefing, Transcript at 8.)

There is also reason to question whether the attacks on the electrical system ever affected Iraq's key military command-and-control facilities. During the eight-year Iran-Iraq war, Iraq's power stations were "a special target of the Iranian air force from the outset of the war, and severe shortages of electricity became common."[135] To overcome such difficulties, Iraq developed military communications systems placed in secure bunker-like facilities or in mobile units,[136] powered by stand-by diesel-supplied generators independent of the national electric grid. Long after electricity was no longer available in Baghdad, the location of the Iraqi military's functioning command-and-control facilities continued to elude the allies.[137] One of the justifications offered for the bombing of the Ameriyya shelter on February 13, for example, was that the building served as a command-and-control center.

As early as January 23, Gen. Colin Powell acknowledged that the Iraqi military was "very good" at command-and-control systems:

> They have redundant systems, resilient systems, they have work-arounds, they have alternatives, and they are still able to command their forces....they're doing it, for the most part, on generator power, because we have taken care of the central power system within the city.

The Pentagon's July 1991 report provided additional information about the redundancy and dispersal of Iraq's military communications system:

---

[135] Economist Intelligence Unit, *1986/87 Yearbook, Energy, Middle East* (London: 1986) at 42.

[136] One of the priority targets during the war was a U.S.-made Wanderlodge luxury mobile home thought to be used by Saddam Hussein as a mobile command center. Newsday reported that one Air Forces officer said "the search at one point rivaled allied efforts to destroy Scud missiles sites in Iraq." Patrick J. Sloyan, "Air Force Tracked Motor Home In War's 'Get Saddam' Mission," *The Washington Post*, June 23, 1991.

[137] Earl Lane and Knut Royce, "War's 'Biggest Surprise,'" *Newsday*, February 15, 1991.

> Iraq ... placed significant emphasis on developing a secure, redundant communications system. This multilayered system included many built-in backups. If one layer were disrupted, other layers would theoretically take up the slack. In addition to a "civil" telephone system which carried more than half of the military's telecommunications, there was a microwave system, and a high-capacity fiber-optics network. Much of this system was buried or dispersed.[138]

During the war, it was reported that the Pentagon had apparent knowledge that Iraq's military communications system relied on special underground cables or radio transmissions using sophisticated "spread spectrum" technology, making jamming and interception difficult.[139] As the fifth week of the air war began, senior Pentagon officials conceded that Iraqi military commanders were able to maintain their operational security (and were not forced to give orders by radio) because of an underground fiber optic cable than ran from Baghdad to Basra and on to Kuwait.[140] These officials indicated that microwave communications towers had been bombed, including some in remote villages, but that the fiber optic line continued to function.

Gen. Powell's admission that Iraq's military command used redundant systems and alternative generators to supply power to these sophisticated command-and-control systems, coupled with the Pentagon's release of additional information after the war, gives less significance that would ordinarily be the case to the military advantages for destroying virtually the entire electrical system when weighed against the predictably severe consequences for Iraq's civilian population.

---

[138] Pentagon Interim Report at 2-4.

[139] Earl Lane and Knut Royce, "War's 'Biggest Surprise,'" *Newsday*, February 15, 1991.

[140] Rick Atkinson, "Iraqis Called Vulnerable to Land Attack," *The Washington Post*, February 15, 1991.

The U.S. Air Force acknowledges that a legitimate military target may not be attacked if its destruction is expected to cause excessive injury or damage to civilians and civilian objects:

> Attacks are not prohibited against military objectives even though incidental injury or damage to civilians will occur, but *such incidental injury to civilians or damage to civilian objects must not be excessive when compared to the concrete and direct military advantage anticipated.* Careful balancing of interests is required between the potential military advantage and the degree of incidental injury or damage in order to preclude situations raising issues of indiscriminate attacks violating general civilian protections.[141] (Emphasis added)

The term "concrete and direct military advantage" -- the measure of what should be weighed against civilian cost -- sets a high standard, higher than the term "definite military advantage" used to define a military objective.[142] The Air Force Pamphlet specifically requires that, when "a choice is possible between several military objectives for obtaining a similar military advantage, the objective to be selected shall be that which may be expected to cause the least danger to civilian lives and to civilian objects."[143]

Middle East Watch believes the allies should explain, under the rule of proportionality and the principle of humanity, the continuing attacks on and near-destruction of Iraq's electric power system, particularly as attacks on the system grew increasingly redundant in light of the allies' targeting of indisputable military targets such as fixed command-and-control centers and weapons manufacturing and research facilities, in view of the crippling impact the destruction of the electrical

---

[141] Air Force Pamphlet 110-31 at para.5-3 (c) (2) (b).

[142] *New Rules* at 365. The ICRC *Commentary* at 685 makes the same point: the words "concrete and direct" impost stricter conditions on the attacker than those implied by the criteria defining military objectives.

[143] Air Force Pamphlet 110-31, para. 5-3 (c) (1) (c).

power system immediately had and continues to have on the health of Iraqi civilians. The allies also should offer a public explanation for certain attacks on hydroelectric facilities in Iraq. The U.S. does not consider the prohibition against attacks on dams, dykes and nuclear electric-generating stations contained in Article 56 of Protocol I to be customary law.[144] Even accepting this, questions remain about the need for continuing attacks on Iraq's hydro-electric facilities as the war progressed.

According to the Harvard University team that visited Iraq after the war, two hydro-electric facilities -- Saddam Dam and Haditha Dam -- were attacked in the first days of the air war. But two other installations -- Samarra Dam (a small facility with only a 60 megawatt output) and Dokhan Dam -- were not attacked until early February. MEW believes that the allies should justify the attacks against the Samarra and Dokhan Dams in the circumstances that prevailed in early February, when 75 percent of Iraq's electrical-generating facilities had been degraded or destroyed. In particular, Middle East Watch calls on the allies to outline the concrete and direct military advantages expected from the destruction of these facilities, and how these advantages were deemed to outweigh the obvious cost to the civilian population.

The burden on the allies to disclose additional information about the destruction of Iraq's electrical system is heightened by subsequent public statements from U.S. Air Force officers involved in planning the air war which indicate that the purpose of destroying the electrical system was to harm civilians and thus encourage them to overthrow Saddam Hussein. As we noted in the Introduction to Part II of this report, Air Force officers in June indicated that the targeting of Iraq's infrastructure was related to an effort "to accelerate the effect of the sanctions."[145] Col. John A. Warden III, the deputy director of strategy, doctrine and plans for the Air Force, acknowledged that the crippling of Iraq's

---

[144] *See* Matheson at 427.

[145] Barton Gellman, "Allied Air War Struck Broadly in Iraq," *The Washington Post*, June 23, 1991.

electricity-generating system "gives us long-term leverage."[146] He
explained it this way:

> Saddam Hussein cannot restore his own electricity. He
> needs help. If there are political objectives that the U.N.
> coalition has, it can say, "Saddam, when you agree to do
> these things, we will allow people to come in and fix
> your electricity."

Another Air Force planner admitted that the attacks also were designed
to put pressure on the Iraqi people to oust Saddam Hussein:

> Big picture, we wanted to let people know, "Get rid of
> this guy and we'll be more than happy to assist in
> rebuilding. We're not going to tolerate Saddam Hussein
> or his regime.   Fix that, and we'll fix your
> electricity."[147]

Insofar as Iraq's electrical-generating facilities were targeted not
because the electricity directly supported the military effort but for the
purpose of harming the civilian population as part of a strategy for using
this civilian suffering to further military or political goals, the attacks
were in clear violation of the most basic principles of the laws of war
designed to exempt the civilian population from military attack.

Among the unanswered questions in regard to the allies'
destruction of the electrical system are the following:

- Gen. Schwarzkopf stated on January 30 that the U.S.
  "never had any intention of destroying all of Iraqi
  electrical power." He further stated that "some" of the
  electrical power would be left functional so that civilians
  would not suffer unduly. Who made the calculations
  about the level of destruction that was warranted, given
  the stated concern that Iraqi civilians not suffer unduly?

---

[146] Id.

[147] Id.

On what basis were such calculations made? Who was charged with investigating the potential secondary effects on the civilian population of various levels of deprivation of the supply of electricity? Who reviewed such investigations? Who determined the threshold of civilian suffering that was considered appropriate? What indicators of suffering were used to calculate the harm caused by relative levels of deprivation?

• Toward the end of the second week of the air war, the Pentagon disclosed that about 25 percent of Iraq's electrical-generating capacity was "completely inoperative" and that another 50 percent was "degraded." Who made the decision to continue with the attacks at this stage of the war? Was President Bush involved in this decisionmaking process, as Gen. Schwarzkopf implied he would be? What effective contribution to Iraqi military action were the remaining electricity-generating plants making at this time? Given the reported successful destruction by the allies at this stage of the war of Iraqi military production facilities -- coupled with the allies' total control of the skies over Iraq -- what concrete and direct military advantage was expected from the continued crippling of the country's remaining electrical-generating system?

• To what extent did the goal of harming or demoralizing the civilian population, to prompt it to overthrow Saddam Hussein or for any other purpose, enter into the decision to destroy Iraq's electrical system?

CIVILIAN VEHICLES ON HIGHWAYS

Middle East Watch obtained eyewitness testimony about apparently indiscriminate attacks on civilian vehicles on highways in Iraq. With the exception of one attack on a bus traveling from Kuwait to Iraq, in which 31 civilians were killed, these accounts described incidents that took place on the Baghdad-Amman international highway in western Iraq, the area from which missiles were being launched into Israel.

Civilian vehicles on other highways in Iraq also were destroyed in allied attacks. In a visit to southern Iraq in May, a journalist saw the bombed-out wreckage of 29 Soviet fighter-bombers on either side of the six-lane highway that runs from Basra northwest to Nassariya: "They apparently had been parked there, far from any airfield, and protected by nothing except a few berms."[148] But civilians were not spared in the allies' attempt to destroy the aircraft: "Hundreds of burned-out trucks, cars and taxis destroyed by allied aircraft litter the road."[149] These accounts call into question whether the allies were taking all feasible precautions to distinguish civilian objects and military targets along Iraqi highways and, if not, why public warning of this policy was not given so that civilian victims could be spared.

Middle East Watch also interviewed three eyewitnesses to cluster-bomb[150] attacks; in one case, a cluster bomb exploded three to six

---

[148] Jonathan C. Randal, "Battle-Scarred Basra Struggled Toward Recovery," *The Washington Post*, May 23, 1991.

[149] Id.

[150] A cluster bomb is an "air-delivered, free-fall weapon...that contains numerous small submunitions, or bomblets. A time of proximity fuze in the nose of the cluster bomb activates a burster charge, which splits open the canister after release to disperse the bomblets over a wide area. That compensates for the inherent inaccuracy of low-altitude bombing, and increases the probability of multiple target kills with a single weapon....Some submunitions are fitted with delay or pressure fuzes, to act as mines." Edward Luttwak and Stuart L. Koehl, *The Dictionary of Modern War* (Harper Collins:1991) at 123.
    Cluster bombs, including cluster bombs that released bomblets with delayed-action or contact fuses, were used by allied forces during Operation Desert Storm. The ordnance was employed against Iraqi troops and military emplacements in the Kuwaiti military theater and dropped on or near roads and highways inside Iraq. Middle East Watch interviewed two former residents of Samawa who described civilian casualties and damage from cluster bombs used in the area (see Chapter Five).
    An Iraqi health minister announced in August that 608 civilians had been killed or injured from exploding cluster bombs that had been dropped in residential districts of Iraq during the air war. Dr. Shawqi Sabri Murqus,

meters from the car in which a Jordanian doctor was traveling. The U.S. military publicly confirmed that cluster bombs were dropped on highways during the war. Gen. Buster Glosson was asked at a briefing in Riyadh on January 30 if cluster bombs were being dropped on the Baghdad-Amman highway, the major evacuation route for foreign-worker residents of Iraq fleeing the war to the safety of Jordan. He replied: "Yes, we use the cluster munition to cover a wider area when the military situation dictates that."[151] However, Gen. Glosson did not reply to the second part of the reporter's question: "How do you reconcile that with your efforts to minimize civilian casualties along this...refugee route?"

In a letter to U.S. Secretary of Defense Richard Cheney dated February 1, Middle East Watch raised concerns about reports of the bombing of civilian cars and commercial transport vehicles on the Baghdad-Amman desert highway. MEW asked if cluster-bombs and delayed-action bombs were being used to attack major highways in Iraq, and urged that the U.S. military take all practical steps to ensure that civilians were not harmed by attacks on military targets. The Pentagon's reply to Middle East Watch's letter did not include an answer to this or other questions raised.

U.S. Public Statements
The civilian vehicles in western Iraq -- as well as Bedouin tents located there (see next section of this chapter) -- came under fire during what the U.S. Air Force termed "the great Scud chase" for Iraqi fixed and mobile missile launchers. Allied efforts to find and eliminate Iraq's surface-to-surface ballistic missile sites and equipment became a major focus of the air war. Maj. Gen. Martin Brandtner, the Joint Chiefs of Staff deputy for operations, said on January 26 that the allies were "undertaking every conceivable course we can" to detect and destroy the

---

the first under secretary of the Health Ministry, said this number included three Jordanians killed and four injured. The official Iraqi news service reported that Dr. Murqus had said in May that dozens of civilians, especially children, had been hit by exploding cluster bombs. (Baghdad Iraqi News Agency, August 6, 1991, as reported in FBIS, August 7, 1991 at 28.)

[151] *The New York Times*, January 31, 1991.

missile launchers, particularly the mobile launchers.[152]   Air Force Chief of Staff McPeak admitted after the war that "we had to improvise and figure out how to handle the SCUD problem....What surprised us was that we put about three times the effort that we thought we would on this job."[153] Iraq's mobile missile launchers confounded and frustrated the allies -- locating them was "like finding a needle in a haystack," according to Gen. Schwarzkopf.[154]   The Pentagon provided the following assessment in its July report:

> Decoy Scud missile launchers, some incorporating heat producers to simulate active generators, complicated the Coalition effort to eradicate the Iraqi ballistic missile threat.   Finding and destroying Iraq's mobile Scud launchers proved a difficult and vexing problem, diverting resources from other aspects of the air campaign and prolonging the threat to Israeli, Saudi and other civil and military targets throughout the region.[155]

The missile launchers were developed from Saab Scania tractors.[156] These massive vehicles bear little resemblance to civilian buses or cars loaded with luggage on their roofs. The mobile missile units were organized in convoys of five or six vehicles using "one set of command and support vehicles, including equipment to test the missiles

---

[152] Molly Moore, "Arms Caches, Supply Lines Targeted; Marines Direct Artillery at Kuwait," *The Washington Post*, January 27, 1991.

[153] McPeak Briefing, Transcript at 5.

[154] Martin Fletcher, "Hunt for Scuds as 80% of strikes succeed," *The Times*, January 19, 1991.

[155] Pentagon Interim Report at 24-1.

[156] Duncan Lennox, "Iraq -- Ballistic Missiles," Jane's Soviet Intelligence Review, October 1990 at 440.

and a crane to place them on the truck launchers."[157]   Military experts told *The Washington Post* that "fueling and preparing a Scud missile for launch can take hours, but would still be difficult to detect if rudimentary efforts are made to keep the missile and launcher hidden."[158]   What could be observed was the safety precautions taken to handle the missile's fuel, a volatile liquid. After launching, the detection possibilities were not any easier. According to *The Post*:

> Once the Scuds are fired, the trucks move after the launcher cools. During launch preparations, the trucks and launchers emit few telltale electronic signals. It is often difficult to intercept launch orders, because they can be issued by telephone, rather than radio.[159]

The Pentagon notes that the task of destroying the mobile launchers was difficult because the missile units would "emerge from hiding places, fire, and hide again."[160]   Many aircraft, the equivalent of three squadrons, were employed in daytime and nighttime missions:

> F-16s in the west and A-10s in the east were placed on constant airborne alert during daylight hours, with F-15Es, F-16s and A-6Es on constant airborne alert at night. RF-4C and F-14A reconnaissance aircraft flew daily flights against suspected Scud sites. However, once a suspected Scud site was found through intelligence or following a launch, aircraft would proceed to the target area to search for and destroy the launch complex.[161]

---

[157] R. Jeffrey Smith, "Compactness, Simplicity of Iraq's Scuds Complicate U.S. Search," *The Washington Post*, January 20, 1991.

[158] *Id.*

[159] R. Jeffrey Smith, "Compactness, Simplicity of Iraq's Scuds Complicate U.S. Search," *The Washington Post*, January 20, 1991.

[160] Pentagon Interim Report at 4-4.

[161] Pentagon Interim Report at 4-4.

198 • PART II: THE AIR WAR AGAINST IRAQ

The allies offered various public and background explanations for the reports of attacks on civilian vehicles on the highway. At night, civilian fuel tankers could be mistaken for the vehicles that carried fuel for the missiles, according to a senior U.S. military official.[162] As for other civilian vehicles, the closest to an explanation came from U.S. Brig. Gen. Buster Glosson, who stated on January 30 that only military targets along the highway had been attacked. He added, however, that the Iraqis hid missiles "in culverts and other things along the highway...When we see those type of vehicles go into those facilities, we bomb them. We make every attempt to minimize any possibility of civilian casualties."[163]

Air Force Chief of Staff Gen. Mc Peak said: "Mobile SCUD-launchers operated at night, drove into [launch locations] and launched, so we had to do a lot of road [reconnaissance], even with the A-10s. An old, slow aircraft was used to go out and run up and down the road and try to find these mobile launchers."[164] Gen. Thomas Kelly, director of operations for the U.S. Joint Chiefs of Staff, also stated that many of the attacks took place at night, suggesting that darkness could mar pilots' vision.[165]

In its July 1991 report, the Pentagon does not acknowledge that civilian buses and cars were attacked on highways -- only Jordanian oil tankers are mentioned:

> Some oil trucks were mistaken for Scud launchers and other military vehicles during night attacks; others were struck collaterally during daytime attacks on nearby

---

[162] Susan Sachs and Patrick J. Sloyan, "Allied Raids Taking Massive Toll on Iraq," *Newsday*, February 6, 1991.

[163] Excerpts from military briefing in Riyadh, Saudi Arabia, *The New York Times*, January 31, 1991.

[164] McPeak Briefing, Transcript at 5.

[165] R. Jeffrey Smith, "U.S. Military Pressed About Civilian Casualties," *The Washington Post*, February 3, 1991.

military targets. The destruction, which occurred despite extraordinary Coalition efforts to avoid collateral damage to civilian targets, was largely attributable to Jordan's failure to ensure adherence to [United Nations Security Council] sanctions and to warn its nationals of the combat zone's peril.[166]

The Pentagon also states that measures taken to minimize civilian casualties and damage affected the allies' ability to target military objects on the roads in western Iraq:

Coalition forces took additional measures to avoid collateral damage to civilian vehicles and incidental injury to noncombatants. As a result, the ability to target Iraqi military vehicles and convoys, including mobile Scud missile launchers and support equipment, was affected.[167]

An Inquiry by Middle East Watch

In a February 1 letter to U.S. Secretary of Defense Richard Cheney, Middle East Watch requested information and assurances about the precautions taken by the allied air forces to avoid injury and damage to civilians and civilian objects on the Baghdad-Amman highway. Among the questions raised in the letter were the following:

- Is it technologically feasible to distinguish between civilian automobiles and buses, the roofs of which were often loaded with personal effects, and single and distinct military objectives, such as missile launchers or other military vehicles?

---

[166] Pentagon Interim Report at 12-7 to 12-8. Jordan claimed that its receipt of oil from Iraq, as repayment for debt owed, was conducted with notice to and without objection from the United Nations Sanctions Committee. See below for additional information.

[167] Pentagon Interim Report at 12-8.

- Were any Jordanian and other commercial vehicles considered military targets?

- Did the rules of engagement regarding attacks on the Baghdad-Amman highway clearly specify that civilian objects were not to be attacked?

- Were supplemental rules of engagement provided to military personnel involved in aerial bombardment of the Baghdad-Amman highway to take account of the fact that this route was used by fleeing civilians and commercial truckers?

- Prior to each air attack on the highway, what was done to ascertain that the targets were military and not civilian objects?

- Was it feasible to provide effective advance warning to civilians in vehicles prior to an attack on the highway when civilian objects were identified?

Middle East Watch also requested the Defense Department to make available specific information about the nature and extent of the aerial bombardment of the Baghdad-Amman highway, and asked whether reports were available about civilian objects damaged in the raids.

Gen. Kelly replied to Middle East Watch in a letter dated February 12. He stated that the U.S. forces "recognize our obligation to do everything feasible to minimize civilian casualties and collateral damage to civilian property when we engage military targets." Gen. Kelly expressed confidence that civilian targets were not being intentionally attacked on the Baghdad-Amman highway:

> I am absolutely certain . . . that any coalition forces capable of conducting air to ground missions in the vicinity of the highway would not knowingly attack innocent civilians. Coalition forces are doing everything within their capabilities to distinguish between military targets and innocent civilians, and to attack only the military targets.

But Gen. Kelly declined to provide Middle East Watch with specific information about the bombing of civilian vehicles on the highway: "At this point we do not have sufficient factual detail in our possession to either confirm or rebut the alleged attacks by coalition forces."

Eyewitness Accounts: Attacks on Civilian Vehicles Carrying Evacuees to Jordan

The 915 km Baghdad-Amman highway, running east-west, is the sole international highway in western Iraq. The only official border crossing point to leave Iraq for Jordan is along the highway at Trebil, Iraq. From Trebil, the highway continues to the official Jordanian entry point at Ruwayshid, about 80 km west of Trebil.[168] This highway was the primary escape route for foreign nationals living in Iraq and Kuwait after August 1990.[169] Most were "evacuees" -- foreign nationals who entered Jordan and departed to their country of origin between September 3 and January 15, 1991.

After the air war started, the highway continued to serve as the primary evacuation route from Iraq.[170] From that date until February 27, some 37,970 persons entered Jordan through the border

---

[168] The Jordan-Iraq border crossing used to be at Ruwayshid and was moved several years ago. The Jordanian official entry point was simply left in Ruwayshid. There is no other town in the desert between Ruwayshid and Trebil.

[169] IOM, Geneva, Gulf Emergency Programme: Updated Plan of Action, dated January 17, 1991. From September 3, 1990 to January 15, 1991, 13,176 evacuees left directly from Iraq to their countries of origin, by air; from Turkey, 7,889; and from other areas, IOM-coordinated departures totalled 1,410.

[170] There also was civilian traffic from Jordan through Ruwayshid into Iraq during the air-war period: 6,320 people of all nationalities traveled from Jordan to Iraq, according to information provided by the Jordanian authorities to MEW during an interview on February 28, 1991 in Amman. Some of those who entered Iraq were Jordanians who assisted their relatives in leaving Kuwait and Iraq, as well as enterprising truckers hired to transport Jordanian citizens and their possessions back to Jordan.

post at Ruwayshid, according to the Jordanian Ministry of Interior.[171] Of this number, 22,008 were evacuees -- including 11,900 Egyptians, 4,400 Sudanese and over 1,100 Yemenis[172] -- and the balance were Jordanians.

In a letter dated February 7, Jordan's permanent ambassador to the United Nations informed the U.N. Secretary General that 14 civilians had been killed on the Baghdad-Amman international highway from January 29 through February 5, and an additional 26 injured.[173] The letter stated that the casualties resulted from "the bombing by United States and allied aircraft of trucks and tankers belonging to Jordanian companies" and that 52 vehicles had been completely destroyed or damaged during the eight-day period. British journalist Patrick Cockburn, who traveled the Baghdad-Amman highway in February, told MEW that he counted 28 vehicles damaged by bombing on the road and that "at least" half of them were civilian.[174]

Middle East Watch interviewed evacuees and truckers for Jordanian companies who saw or were traveling in cars and buses that were attacked by allied aircraft on the highway.

• TWO CARS DIRECTLY HIT BY DIVING AIRCRAFT IN DAYTIME ATTACK, KILLING TWO FAMILIES: MEW interviewed a group of Yemeni students who were eyewitnesses to attacks in broad daylight on two civilian cars between Rutba and Trebil on the Baghdad-Amman

---

[171] MEW interview, Amman, Jordan, February 28, 1991.

[172] There were many fewer evacuees legally crossing the Iraqi border to countries other than Jordan from January 17 to February 28: IOM reported that 7,700 fled to Iran; 400 to Turkey; and 31 to Syria.

[173] Letter dated 7 February 1991 from the Permanent Representative of Jordan to the United Nations Addressed to the Secretary-General, S/22205, February 7, 1991. Jordan asked that the letter be circulated as a document of the Security Council.

[174] MEW interview, London, May 7, 1991.

highway. According to the witnesses, it was unlikely that the occupants of the vehicles survived these direct hits.

The students had left Basra on February 7 because their university was closed when the war started. They traveled in two buses with Sudanese and Iraqis to Baghdad, and then continued on to Jordan with a group of 53 people -- Yemenis, Sudanese, Egyptians and an Ethiopian -- in two "Super" Mercedes buses. Each bus held about 28 passengers. The buses, pained light green with the company name on the side, were carrying only civilians. Luggage was piled on the roofs of the vehicles. As reports spread of the danger from the bombing on the highway, drivers and passengers began to develop their own theories about the safest way to travel. This group and the drivers had decided to drive only during the day and to avoid traveling convoy-style, so as not to be mistaken for Iraqi military vehicles.

The students saw a white sedan attacked at about 9:30 am that day, on or about February 8. They noticed a family in the car when it passed their bus. The sedan rode low from the suitcases piled on top. A few minutes later, when the white sedan was about 400 meters in front of them, they saw four planes, flying low and very fast, swoop down. One struck the sedan with a rocket, a direct hit. The other planes also fired rockets but they did not see where the rockets landed; as soon as this happened, the driver stopped the bus and the passengers ran into the desert, ducking for cover.

The planes were small black planes -- "so close we could have thrown a stone at them." The planes dived to about 30 meters from the ground, the students said. There were other civilian cars on the road in front and in back of them when the attack occurred, but no military vehicles and no military emplacements were in sight. The only installation or structure they saw was a gas station that had been blown up.

About an hour after the first attack, they saw, at a distance, two or three planes flying very low. The planes dove down in the same manner as before and hit a red Brazilian Volkswagen with a family inside and luggage on top. The bus driver did not stop to look at the remains of either car out of fear, but the students said it appeared highly unlikely that there were any survivors.[175]

Three times during the trip from Baghdad to the Jordanian border, between Rutba and Trebil, the passengers had to jump out of the buses and run into the desert because of air strikes nearby. The students saw and heard several rocketing attacks; every time they heard planes, they heard rockets falling afterwards. They did not know where all the rockets hit: sometimes it was on the highway, sometimes not. They saw black smoke rising from areas on and off the road. In this stretch of the highway, the students said they saw many vehicles that had been destroyed. They told MEW that they were convinced that if the planes had wanted to target their bus "we would all be dead." At the time, they were not sure that they would survive the journey.

• 30 KILLED IN ATTACK ON BUS: MEW interviewed Sudanese evacuees who told of three buses that loaded up with Sudanese evacuees and left Baghdad on February 13 at about noon. They said that each of the public carriers waited until it was filled before departing. The first bus reached the border crossing at Trebil that night. A second bus stayed the night in Rutba. The third bus was bombed on the road before reaching Rutba and reportedly there were no survivors. Some drivers arriving at Trebil told the Sudanese in the first two buses that the third bus was destroyed and all of the passengers, some 30 to 35 Sudanese, were killed.[176]

MEW separately interviewed another group of Sudanese workers who arrived in Jordan on two different buses a few days later, on February 18 and 19. They saw a destroyed Costa Nissan bus at km 160 between Rutba and Ramadi: the bus, they were told, had carried 30 Sudanese passengers. They heard that all the passengers were killed

---

[175] MEW interview, Azraq Evacuation Center, Azraq, Jordan, February 13, 1991.

[176] MEW interview, Azraq Evacuee Center, Azraq, Jordan, February 16, 18 and 22, 1991.

except one, who reportedly returned to Baghdad under severe mental stress.[177]

• CLUSTER BOMB FALLS METERS FROM TWO CARS IN DAWN ATTACK: A Jordanian doctor interviewed by MEW was injured when a cluster bomb was dropped three to six feet from his car on the Baghdad-Amman highway. Dr. Samir A. Qawasmi, an ophthalmic surgeon, was part of a medical team of 13 doctors and nurses sent to Baghdad by the Arab Medical Committee for Emergencies. The team departed from Jordan in late January to provide emergency medical services in hospitals in Baghdad. After working around-the-clock treating civilian bombing casualties for four or five days, four members of the exhausted team set out for Jordan at 11pm on the night of January 27. They traveled in two cars: a white Mercedes sedan with a Red Crescent on the hood and a four-wheel-drive gray vehicle with a Red Crescent on the front.

Dr. Qawasmi told MEW that after driving through the night without incident, they pulled to the side of the road at a parking area at about 5:15 am for dawn prayers. They were about 400 km from Baghdad and had not yet reached Rutba. They prayed in the desert cold and then got back in their vehicles. At that moment, Dr. Qawasmi said he heard "a huge noise, with lightning," and they were tossed around inside the cars. They were totally startled, he said, because they did not hear or see planes. The windows of the car were closed because it was cold.

Dr. Qawasmi, who was in the driver's seat of the white Mercedes sedan, was injured with lacerations on his face, nose, cheek, and hands. Tossed against the side of the car, he was still suffering pain in his left shoulder when he was interviewed by MEW. The driver of the other car suffered similar injuries but the two passengers were not physically injured.

The bomb hit the side of the road, about three to six feet from the car, creating a crater about a half-meter deep and one and a half meters wide. It divided into two parts, apparently a cluster bomb.

---

[177] MEW interview, Azraq Evacuee Center, Azraq, Jordan, February 22, 1991.

There were many small bombs inside the canister and other bomblets scattered outside. They left as quickly as they could, before any of the small bombs exploded. The badly damaged Mercedes was towed behind the four-wheel-drive vehicle which had a broken windshield and windows and damage to its left side. They passed many burned cars, and passenger vans of the type used by Kuwaiti families.

About a half-hour later, before reaching Rutba, Dr. Qawasmi through the rear view mirror saw a 40-foot refrigerator truck with a 12-foot rig hit by a rocket, and turned around to get a better look. They heard the explosion but did not stop. They later learned that the driver of the truck had been killed.[178]

• STRAFING OF BUSES ON HIGHWAYS DURING DAYTIME: MEW also took testimony about the strafing of buses on highways that left evacuees scared for their lives. Pakistani construction workers, evacuated by their company from Najaf in southern Iraq on three buses on February 15, told MEW of a strafing incident involving one of their buses. The last of the three buses was strafed 10 km west of Rutba on February 15 at about 4:10 pm. There were 36 Pakistani workers in the white bus, which had luggage piled on the top. According to several workers interviewed by MEW, there were four attacks on the bus at two- to three-minute intervals. They heard machine-gun fire and were quite sure that rockets or bombs had not been used. Bullets were fired close to the bus, but it was not hit.

One Pakistani thought that there was one plane; another said he saw four planes. A third said he did not see a plane because he ducked down to avoid danger, but he heard bursts of machine-gun fire. A fourth said he saw four planes that were the color of smoke. The bullets hit the road near them, he said.

The bus did not stop. It was the only vehicle on the road; there were trucks in the distance, they said. There was "only desert" around

---

[178] MEW interview, Amman, Jordan, February 15, 1991.

them -- "no military trucks, no buildings, no gas station, no tents, nothing."[179]

Later in the air war, bus drivers seemed to believe that traveling the Baghdad-Amman highway at night afforded more protection. A young Egyptian furniture finisher told Middle East Watch that he left Baghdad on the evening of February 19 with a cousin and some friends. They were in a bus with 50 Egyptians and three Sudanese. The two buses drove together, his bus in front. It was night, and both buses had their headlights on. A few kilometers outside of Ramadi, a plane fired bullets at the bus, hitting to the right and left side. The driver kept going, but turned off the headlights. No one was hurt and the bus was not damaged.[180]

An Egyptian couple interviewed by MEW told of strafing of their bus, a white Coaster which left Baghdad on February 23 with luggage piled on top. There were 28 Egyptians on the bus: 22 adults and six babies. Theirs was the only bus, indeed the only vehicle, on the road. The journey was very difficult because the planes were shooting at the bus while it traveled the road: "It sounded like bombs were falling almost over our heads," the husband said. The strafing occurred after the bus left Rutba, between 7 and 10 pm. The bus stopped several times; the driver was travelling without lights for greater safety. The family said they were very afraid. The father told MEW how he dashed out of the bus several times carrying his daughter. The bus was not hit, and they arrived safely in Trebil at about 11 pm.[181]

Similar stories of strafed civilian vehicles appeared in the press. *The New York Times* reported that a Jordanian Red Crescent official had

---

[179] MEW interview, Azraq Evacuee Center, Azraq, Jordan, February 18, 1991.

[180] MEW interview, Aqaba Transit Camp, Aqaba, Jordan, February 21, 1991.

[181] MEW interview, Ruwayshid Evacuee Center, Ruwayshid, Jordan, February 24, 1991.

seen a Jordanian family whose two infants were killed in a strafing
attack.[182] A group of evacuees told journalists that on February 3 an
Egyptian worker running toward his bus was machine-gunned and killed
instantly on the road to Trebil.[183]

• SOUTHERN IRAQ: 31 DEAD IN DAYTIME ATTACK ON CIVILIAN
VEHICLES: A Jordanian bus carrying civilians fleeing Kuwait was
attacked by allied planes near the Kuwaiti border on February 9 at 2 pm,
killing 27 in the bus and another four in two cars traveling with the bus.
MEW interviewed the driver of the bus, Shawqi Naji, 32, a Palestinian
who lives in Jordan. A bus driver for 10 years, he had made several
round trips in his 1983 Mercedes model 303 luxury passenger bus from
Jordan to Kuwait to pick up Palestinians, Jordanians and others
evacuating Kuwait.

He told MEW that his bus left Kuwait on February 9, at 1 pm.
Orange in color, with a six-inch blue stripe around the side and Jordanian
plates, the vehicle had capacity for 51 passengers but was carrying 61
because some of them were children. There was baggage underneath
and on the roof of the bus. Two cars drove in front of the bus: a white
Chevrolet and a dark blue Chevrolet. The passengers in the white car
were newlyweds, and a family was riding in the blue car.

The highway from Kuwait City to southern Iraq traverses desert
terrain, the driver told MEW. "There is nothing else there, just a
highway ... no bridges, river, military fortifications ... nothing." The
attack took place when the bus was an hour outside of Kuwait City, some
20 km beyond al-Metla'. The driver said he did not hear any aircraft.
He was confident that the bus was identifiable as civilian because of its
size, color and the baggage piled on top.

He said that he passed another bus parked on the side of the
road. Some 500 meters beyond the parked bus, he heard a rocket

---

[182] Alan Cowell, "More Air Attacks on Road to Jordan," *The New York
Times*, February 1, 1991.

[183] Wafa Amr, "Ruined Basra lacks food and water," *The Guardian*,
February 4, 1991.

explode behind his bus, hitting it with shrapnel. He slammed on the brakes, quickly opened the two doors, and he and the passengers began to run off the bus. The rear of the bus was in flames. Before all of the passengers could get off, about two minutes after the first rocket, a second rocket struck, piercing the roof of the bus. The whole bus was engulfed in fire: 27 men, women and children were incinerated.

As he ran out of the bus, the driver helped drag an acquaintance from the bus, holding her on one arm and her young daughter on the other. While the passengers were running away from the bus into the desert, a third rocket struck at the place where some of them had gathered about 200 meters off the road. It left a crater five meters in diameter and three meters deep. This rocket hit about two to three minutes after the second rocket. Because of the confusion, the driver did not know if any passengers in this location were injured or killed.

When they were outside the bus, the woman he had helped was hit with shrapnel. Cut almost in two, she died immediately. Her daughter, injured with shrapnel in her heel, clung to the driver, crying, "Please, I don't want to die!" Of this family of six, three were dead: the mother, grandmother and a daughter, 9, who was hit by shrapnel in the chest.

After the third rocket, Naji heard other explosions. He told MEW that he heard about six rockets in all during that short period of time but only saw where the first three had landed. The area was covered with smoke and debris. He believed a plane strafed them with machine-gun fire. He was hit with a bullet at about this time; he was numb and did not feel anything. He did not see any planes, but he heard their roar. Two pieces of shrapnel were lodged in his right side, which were removed at Sabah Hospital in Kuwait. He also sustained a bullet wound on his right thigh; the doctors told him it was a bullet after it was removed.

The driver took the survivors to Sabah Hospital in Kuwait, using a car that was being driven by someone behind the bus but belonged to a family which had been riding in the bus because they thought it was safer. At the hospital, he met the man and woman who were riding in the blue Chevrolet. They said that their two daughters were killed in the attack but the rest of the family survived. They did not have much time to talk or exchange more information, the driver said.

The next day, he returned with the Palestinian Red Crescent to assess the damage. They counted 25 charred bodies on the seats of the bus; another two bodies were partially burned. The bus had a large hole in the roof from the rocket and the interior of the vehicle had been badly burned. There were holes on the outside of the bus, like machine-gun fire, he thought. The Red Crescent took photos of the bus and the human remains.[184] The newlywed passengers in the white car were dead. The driver saw their charred bodies, still inside the car, in front of the bus.

A MEW fact-finding team that visited Kuwait in April was able independently to corroborate some aspects of the account provided by the bus driver. In interviews with the supervisor and two assistants at the Selaibekhat Cemetery, 15 km west of Kuwait City, MEW investigators learned that eight victims of the bus attack were buried at the cemetery on February 10. The cemetery supervisor, Abdel Razzaq al-Karraf, told MEW that the bodies of five Jordanian women, two Jordanian men and one Kuwaiti woman were brought in while he and his assistants were on duty on February 10. He said that they were told that the total number of fatalities from the rocket attack on a civilian bus traveling north totaled 18, but that 10 other victims were buried elsewhere. The cemetery workers told MEW that the attack occurred north of al-Metla', next to the Kuwait satellite station.

Legal Standards and Conclusions

It is legitimate under the laws of war to attack an enemy's transportation system, including by destroying roads and highways, if they are making an effective contribution to military action and the total or partial destruction of which would offer a definite military advantage. The use of highways and roads by Iraqi military vehicles and missile launchers made it legitimate to attempt to stop that traffic by, for example, destroying bridges or strategic passes. In addition, individual military vehicles traveling the Baghdad-Amman highway and other roads

---

[184] MEW interview, Amman, Jordan, February 19, 1991.

were legitimate military targets, as were aircraft, military vehicles or missile launchers parked or hidden along the roadside.

Civilian buses and cars traveling the road, however, were not legitimate military targets. Coalition pilots therefore could not directly target them and had a duty to take precautions to avoid hitting them when attacking military targets. At a military briefing in Saudi Arabia on January 30, U.S. Brig. Gen. Buster Glosson acknowledged this, stating that only military targets along the Baghdad-Amman highway were under attack. The attacks on civilian vehicles, including in some cases strafing by low-flying aircraft, indicates that something clearly went wrong on the part of the allied air forces, who had consistently reiterated their intent to avoid civilian casualties. In the strafing incidents in particular, pilots presumably were close enough to have visual contact with the target. Eyewitnesses reported to MEW that aircraft dived once before opening fire; others were reported to be quite close to the vehicles when opening fire.

Given the known use of highways and roads by the civilian population -- there were repeated press reports of such use, and the Jordanian government filed a formal complaint with the U.S. ambassador in Amman on January 30 that Jordanian civilian vehicles on the highway had been wrongly attacked by allied aircraft -- allied pilots were under a duty to distinguish military objectives on these roads from civilian objects, such as cars and buses, and prohibited from striking military objectives and civilian objects indiscriminately (*see* Chapter One). Pilots also were obliged to take "constant care" to "spare the civilian population, civilians, and civilian objects" on highways in Iraq. They were required under the laws of war to "do everything feasible to verify that the objectives to be attacked are neither civilians nor civilian objects." They further were obliged to "take all reasonable precautions to avoid losses of civilian lives and damage to civilian objects." (*see* Chapter One)

Accordingly, allied forces should have taken care before firing to ensure that each target was military, especially since no warning was given to civilian vehicles to stay off the road. The legal burden is on the allies to demonstrate how they could have mistaken the civilian buses and cars for military targets, and to disclose the rules of engagement or other guidelines that they were following in these circumstances to avoid civilian casualties. If for technological or other reasons, coalition pilots could not distinguish civilian objects from military targets, then this should have been publicly stated, so that potential civilian victims of these attacks would have had notice to avoid public highways.

One possible cause of the civilian casualties is that allied bombers were not required to make visual contact with their targets but relied only on radar. According to U.S. Air Force Chief of Staff Gen. McPeak, the "most effective" tactic devised for the great Scud chase was the use of the Joint Surveillance Target Attack Radar System (JSTARS) -- which he described as "an airborne radar system now under development" -- to locate moving targets on the ground.[185] Gen. McPeak described how this system of "*ad lib* attacks" worked:

> This radar finds and tracks moving targets on the ground. So with it, we could track all of these vehicles, and when we found one that looked suspicious, then these JSTARS aircraft were able to divert the airborne [combat air patrol planes] and perform on-the-spot ad lib attacks.[186]

After the war, Gen. McPeak was queried about the precise ability of JSTARS to distinguish between moving objects on the ground. "These JSTARS that can identify mobile targets, could they identify them well enough to distinguish between a truck that might have a SCUD and a Jordanian oil tanker? Or are they just identifying large moving targets?"

---

[185] McPeak Briefing, Transcript at 5. The Pentagon's July 1991 report acknowledges that JSTARS aircraft were prototypes, "not scheduled to be operational until 1997." Despite this, the Pentagon states that JSTARS performed well, in 49 combat support missions: "Although still a prototype, the JSTARS aircraft proved effective in detecting and rapidly targeting tactical air assets against enemy ground units. Of particular importance, JSTARS offers both wide area coverage and more focused imagery of moving or fixed items of interest....JSTARS was an integral part of the system used to locate and track the movements of Scud launchers and to direct aircraft into position to search for and attack Scuds." (Pentagon Interim Report at 6-10.)

[186] McPeak Briefing, Transcript at 5.

a reporter asked. Gen. McPeak's reply to this critical question: "I can't answer the question. I'm not sure."[187]

According to *Aviation Week*, a typical U.S. "Scud patrol" was approximately six hours; the aircraft in the patrol were equipped with 2,000-pound laser-guided bombs, and others carried cluster bombs or conventional high-explosive bombs.[188]   If the laser-guided bombs missed the target, other aircraft in the formation would drop cluster bombs or dumb bombs; the precision bombs were dropped from altitudes of over 15,000 feet and some four miles from the target.[189] "We'd set up a pattern where we would weave back and forth across a road and perform [reconnaissance] by looking though the targeting pod," Lt. Col. Steve Pingel, commander of the 335th Tactical Fighter Squadron, said. "It was like looking through a soda straw."[190]

The allies should explain how such targeting techniques against vehicles on a road that was known to carry civilians comports with the requirement to take all feasible precautions to verify that the objects to be attacked are military and not civilian. Moreover, such long-distance reconnaissance does not explain the apparently deliberate strafing of cars and buses recounted by eyewitnesses interviewed by Middle East Watch.

Attacks on Jordanian Civilian Oil Tankers
In addition to the widely publicized evacuee traffic before and during the air war, Jordanian oil tankers traveled a portion of the Amman-Baghdad highway from Jordan through Rutba to a turnoff 120 km from the Jordanian border. From there, the drivers proceeded north to al-Qa'im, near the Syrian border, where they loaded up with oil and brought it back to Jordan. Gen. Kelly of the Joint Chiefs of Staff

---

[187] McPeak Briefing, Transcript at 13.

[188] Jeffrey M. Lenorovitz, "Air Crew Training, Avionics Credited for F-15E's High Target Hit Rates," *Aviation Week & Space Technology*, April 22, 1991 at 55.

[189] *Id.*

[190] *Id.*

suggested on February 2 that distinguishing civilian oil tankers from
military-supply vehicles was a problem for the allies: "It's difficult to look
at the ground and tell what a civilian target is and what a military target
is, because, for example, oil trucks out in that area could be carrying fuel
for Iraqi [military] aircraft," or for other military purposes.[191] A
senior U.S. military officer confirmed to *The New York Times* in early
February that oil tankers on the road were being attacked, "arguing that
it was impossible to tell which trucks were carrying civilian cargoes and
which were carrying military material."[192]

Despite these admissions, at no time during the air war did the
allied forces publicly warn Jordanian truckers that *all* civilian vehicles
hauling oil from Iraq to Jordan would be subject to attack. To the
contrary, U.S. Maj. Gen. Robert Johnston said at a briefing on February
5 that "we are not specifically targeting Jordanian civilian tankers."[193]
Gen. Kelly sent the same message, while noting that civilian-tanker
drivers assumed some risk: "If a truck chooses to operate in that
environment, there is some risk. We're not purposely going after civilian
vehicles. [But] if one got hit, it was certainly by mistake."[194]

Jordan's Dilemma: Dependence on Imported Oil

The Gulf crisis had wreaked havoc on Jordan's already shaky
economy: remittances from its citizens working in the Gulf states were
lost, and the substantial revenues generated by Iraqi shipping through the
port of Aqaba and Jordanian trucking of goods to Iraq disappeared.
Jordan had imported about half its oil from Saudi Arabia, via the Trans-
Arabian Pipeline (Tapline) from eastern Saudi Arabia to the Zarka

---

[191] R. Jeffrey Smith, "U.S. Military Pressed About Civilian Casualties," *The Washington Post*, February 3, 1991.

[192] R.W. Apple, Jr., "U.S. Hits Hussein's Town, As War Hits Home in Iraq," *The New York Times*, February 6, 1991.

[193] R.W. Apple, Jr., "U.S. Hits Hussein's Town, As War Hits Home in Iraq," *The New York Times*, February 6, 1991.

[194] R. Jeffrey Smith, "U.S. Military Pressed About Civilian Casualties," *The Washington Post*, February 3, 1991.

refinery in Jordan. The balance of Jordanian oil arrived by tanker truck from Iraq, at below-market rates.

On September 20, the Saudi government abruptly cut off the Tapline supply, citing a financial dispute over Jordanian payments due for previously imported oil.[195] By October 1990, Jordan's oil reserves were perilously low and the government ordered conservation measures aimed at reducing fuel consumption by 20 percent or more.[196] An appeal by the Jordanian Energy Ministry in October for the resumption of Saudi oil shipments, pending settlement of the dispute, was turned down by the Tapline company.[197] Since the Saudi cutoff, it was reported that Jordan imported about 60,000 barrels of oil from Iraq daily, but that, with the allied attacks on the highways once the air war began, only 5,000 to 6,000 barrels per day were being imported, against the country's normal oil consumption of about 70,000 barrels daily.[198]

The Jordanian Minister of Finance, in a letter dated 15 October 1990, notified the Special Representative of the United Nations Secretary-General of the measures taken by Jordan to implement Security Council Resolution 661 which imposed trade sanctions on Iraq. A memorandum appended to the letter, dated October 13, stated that Jordan "will continue to import certain petroleum products from Iraq...because of the lack of any immediate or foreseeable alternative and in view of Jordan's total dependence on it for the production of energy. Jordan will consider

---

[195] Youssef M. Ibrahim, "Citing a Default, Saudis Stop Sending Jordan Oil," *The New York Times*, September 21, 1990.

[196] Joel Brinkley, "Short of Oil and Supporters, Jordan Orders Fuel Savings," *The New York Times*, October 8, 1990.

[197] *Mideast Mirror*, October 25, 1990 at 20.

[198] Youssef M. Ibrahim, "Citing a Default, Saudis Stop Sending Jordan Oil," *The New York Times*, September 21, 1990.

halting such imports if an alternative becomes available."[199] The memorandum also pointed out that Jordan was receiving the oil at "concessionary prices" and that Iraq was generating no income from the supply of oil to Jordan, as the transfer was in satisfaction of a debt.

On January 30, then-Jordanian Foreign Minister (and now Prime Minister) Taher al-Masri summoned U.S. Ambassador Roger Harrison and presented him with an official protest that four Jordanians had been killed and several others injured in allied bombing on the highway. The Foreign Minister said the bombing took place on January 29 and January 30, in Iraqi territory, and that nine Jordanian oil tankers and numerous civilian cars were destroyed.[200] In a statement later that day to the Jordanian Parliament, al-Masri said:

> It was obvious the cars were carrying evacuees and the Jordanian trucks were oil tankers and not military vehicles that were driving on an international highway during daytime. These brutal planes knew exactly what they were doing. Because of that I called the American ambassador and the ambassadors of the four other members of the Security Council.[201]

U.S. State Department spokeswoman Margaret Tutwiler said on February 4 that the allies had "credible information that war materiel, including some related to Scud missiles, has been transported in convoy with civilian oil trucks." She further cautioned: "While we seek to

---

[199] *See* Letter dated October 22, 1990 from the Secretary-General Addressed to the President of the Security Council, S/21938, November 13, 1991.

[200] "Masri: Jordan reserves right to respond if attack is repeated," *Jordan Times*, January 31, 1991.

[201] David Hirst, "Jordan protests at 'deliberate' civilian deaths," *The Guardian*, January 31, 1991.

minimize coalition damage in all our operations, this is made difficult by Iraq's policy of co-locating military and civilian targets."[202]

Tutwiler also stated on February 4 that although Iraq's oil exports to Jordan "do violate the sanctions, it is not coalition policy to attacks civilian trucks exporting petroleum to Jordan." She also stated that "there is not exemption at the United Nations Sanctions Committee and ...there is no document specifically dealing with this at the UN." In its July 1991 public report, the Pentagon also stated that Jordan obtained oil from Iraq by truck and that "such purchases were technically in violation of the UN Security Council sanctions."[203]

Then-Jordanian Prime Minister Mudar Badran challenged the U.S. view in a statement released on February 4. He said that after the October memorandum, noted above, was sent to the Security Council, Jordan received verbal assurances from the Council that the import of Iraqi oil would be allowed to continue until an alternative source was found.[204] On February 5, Badran accused the Security Council of bad faith:

> Our trucks are being bombarded en route because they are carrying oil. Now they say: You are violating the UN resolution. No, we did not violate it. We asked and told them that we did not have any oil route other than this one and that we would continue to use it to transport oil until you, the Security Council, found an alternative, in accordance with your charter of conditions. We were told to continue until we secured oil for you. To date, nothing has been secured. Now, it is up to the Security Council to secure oil for us. Do you think I like to send trucks, approximately 700 or 800 tankers, and risk

---

[202] State Department Regular Briefing, Washington, D.C., February 4, 1991.

[203] Pentagon Interim Report at 12-7.

[204] *Mideast Mirror*, February 5, 1991 at 21.

Jordanian citizens to this bombardment, death, and destruction? No, I do not.[205]

Ms. Tutwiler also charged in the February 4 briefing that Iraqi war material was transported with the Jordanian tankers:

> [W]e have credible information that war material, including some related to Scud missiles, has been transported in convoy with civilian oil trucks. Such material contributes to Iraq's occupation of Kuwait and is a legitimate military target.

Pressed for additional specific information about the charge, Tutwiler referred journalists to the Pentagon because "that gets into their operations in targeting and ... I don't do that." The Pentagon's preliminary report provides additional details about this charge:

> There have been reports that Jordan may have supplied materials, including munitions to Iraq, during the course of hostilities....As the United States became aware of specific cases, they were raised with the Government of Jordan. Some of these cases were without foundation but some were substantiated. Regarding the latter, the Government of Jordan took action to terminate and reassured the United States that these instances had been the result of individual initiative and not as a result of governmental policy. In any event, it seems fair to say that such logistical assistance as Jordan may have provided Iraq did not substantially improve Iraq's ability to conduct operations, nor did it have an appreciable effect on the operational capabilities of the Coalition forces.[206]

---

[205] Amman Domestic Service, February 5, 1991, as reported in FBIS, February 6, 1991 at 35.

[206] Pentagon Interim Report at 12-7.

Civilian Trucker Casualties: Eyewitness Testimony
In a February 7 letter to the U.N. Secretary-General circulated to the Security Council, Jordan stated that from January 29 to February 4, seven Jordanians and one Indian had been killed in allied attacks on trucks and tankers and another 21 injured; 42 vehicles had been partially or completely destroyed.[207] On February 5 alone, another six had been killed, five wounded and eight vehicles destroyed. Despite these public reports about the attacks,[208] Jordanian government high-level protests and the letter to the Security Council, the attacks continued. MEW interviewed five wounded truckers in a hospital in Amman about allied attacks involving their vehicles in Iraq, and took testimony from two evacuees who were eyewitnesses to other attacks on civilian trucks. These accounts follow.

• CONVOY OF FOUR TANKERS ATTACKED: One Jordanian oil-tanker driver, 52, did not recall the date in late January when he was injured. As far as he knew, his convoy was the first to be attacked on the road. They did not notice any other vehicles wrecked on the road, or any destruction to the road. He had been a driver for 30 years. At the time of the attack, he was in a convoy of four tankers which had filled up with oil in al-Qa'im and were on their way back to Jordan. About 30 km east of Trebil, the Iraqi border crossing point, they stopped by the road for afternoon prayers. After prayers, he was checking the air in the tires of his red-cabined 44-ton truck when he heard planes. He did not become alarmed because he did not expect the planes to attack civilians. There were no military facilities or installations nearby, he said emphatically.

He said that suddenly he heard an explosion and a "cloud" hit him. He was on the ground and the next thing he knew he woke up in a hospital in Amman. He did not know what happened to the other three truck drivers who were driving with him. At the time of his interview

---

[207] Letter dated February 7, 1991 from the Permanent Representative of Jordan to the United Nations Addressed to the Secretary-General, S/22205, February 7, 1991.

[208] See, for example, Laurie Garrett, "At Jordan-Iraq Border, Refugees Tell of Suffering," *Newsday*, January 29, 1991, and Nora Boustany, "'Sky Was Black--We Could Not Breathe,'" *The Washington Post*, January 30, 1991.

with MEW, the man was blind. One of his eyes had been removed in the hospital. He had no vision in the other eye but the doctors hoped that with surgery they would be able to restore his vision. The driver had multiple wounds: his first and second left toes, and part of his third and fourth left toes had been amputated. He had multiple shrapnel wounds in his pelvis, lower abdomen, and both thighs, a metatarsal fracture on his right foot, and a fractured right hand. His right arm was broken.[209]

• 28-TRUCK CONVOY HIT IN NIGHTTIME ATTACK: Another Jordanian truck driver was in a tanker truck that was part of a convoy of 28 tankers on their way to pick up oil at al-Qa'im. At 9 pm on the night of January 28, at the intersection for the turnoff to al-Qa'im, the convoy was attacked by planes, which this driver did not see. Everything was ablaze; he had many burn injuries on his bald head and elsewhere on his body. He told MEW that the planes returned and hit the truckers with machine-gun fire, killing two drivers. "I never thought I would live through it," he said weakly from his hospital bed.[210]

• ONE DRIVER KILLED, OTHERS INJURED, WHEN AIRCRAFT MACHINE-GUNNED FIVE-TRUCK CONVOY: A 57-year-old driver was traveling in a convoy of five tanker trucks, all with yellow Mercedes cabins, to the intersection at al-Qa'im. It was 1 pm on the afternoon of February 2, 1991 when he reached the intersection, where there were only Bedouin tents -- "there is nothing else around," the trucker told MEW. "There were no military objects or installations. It is empty, except for the tents." When he reached the intersection, his truck -- a German-built M.A.N. with a red cabin -- was hit with a rocket, which landed between the trailer and the cabin. "Everything burst into flames," he said. Only his truck was hit.

He threw himself out of the truck. He sustained burns and had shrapnel in his thighs. His face and eye area were scarred from the fire

---

[209] MEW interview, Farrah Centre, King Hussein Medical City, Amman, Jordan, February 17, 1991.

[210] MEW interview, Farrah Centre, King Hussein Medical City, Amman, Jordan, February 17, 1991.

and his left hand badly burned. He crawled away from the truck and, as he was lying on his back, he saw two planes circle back, flying low, and machine gun the other trucks. He said that the planes aimed at him as well but did not hit him. The aircraft made three runs over the trucks, gunning them each time, he told MEW. One of the drivers, in the tanker in front of him, was killed when he jumped out of his truck. The other three drivers were injured.[211]

• CLUSTER BOMB DROPPED AT TRUCK STOP IN AFTERNOON ATTACK: A Turkish tanker-truck driver, 34, who had been driving for 10 years, was injured by a cluster bomb 30 km east of Rutba. He was on his way to the intersection near Rutba in a red German-made M.A.N. truck on a sunny but cold day, either February 9 or 10. He was traveling with a Turkish friend who was driving another tanker truck. On the road, he saw about 50 or 60 tankers that were damaged, in addition to other automobiles.

At 3 pm in the afternoon they stopped their trucks about 400 meters from a corrugated zinc stand where truckers stop for coffee and tea. He started walking over to the stand, telling his friend he was going to get a blanket for a nap in the truck. About 100 meters from the stand, he heard but did not see aircraft. Then a bomb hit near the shed, scattering many small bombs over a few hundred meters. The bombs exploded at the same time, injuring the driver and two Iraqis. There were no military installations or objects nearby. Except for the shed and some Bedouin tents, it was a deserted area; there was not even a gas station. The closest military object was antiaircraft artillery off the highway about one and a half km from the place where the bomb fell. His left leg was fractured and in a cast. His right arm was in a cast. He had shrapnel up and down his right leg.[212]

• TWO TANKERS DESTROYED AT INTERSECTION: A Circassian tanker-truck driver, 38, interviewed by MEW in King Hussein Medical City hospital, had been driving a white Scania tanker truck and his cousin, 39,

---

[211] MEW interview, Farrah Centre, King Hussein Medical City, Amman, Jordan, February 17, 1991.

[212] MEW interview, Farrah Centre, King Hussein Medical City, Amman, Jordan, February 17, 1991.

recuperating in the next hospital bed, had been driving a green Styer. They arrived at the intersection for al-Qa'im at about 7:30 pm on February 10. The crossroads has a water pump and a few Bedouin tents. The driver knew the place well since he passed there many times. There was nothing there of a military or even a civilian nature, except for the tents: "It was totally deserted," he said. Drivers sometimes stop there to buy bread from the Bedouin. They pulled over to the side of the road because it was night and they could not go further because it was too dangerous to use their headlights. They took out a portable stove and boiled water for tea. They were drinking tea when they heard the noise of planes in the distance. Suddenly there was a "big explosion" and both men were knocked down, unconscious. The explosion was "like compression," he remembered.

He does not know how long they remained unconscious. When he awoke, his head was next to his cousin's, but he did not see the bottom of his cousin's body and thought he was dead. He touched his cousin's hand and found he was alive. A fender that had been blown off the truck covered the cousin's body. Both of the tanker trucks were destroyed, with everything "in a shambles." The cabins had been blown off the trucks. The driver said he was wearing a leather jacket and jeans that were totally shredded. His nose was bleeding. He had and still has difficulty breathing. He had shrapnel all over his body, as did his cousin. A pickup truck stopped and took them to Rutba hospital. He thinks the Bedouin may have seen the explosion and got them help.[213]

• CLUSTER BOMB DROPPED IN DAYTIME ATTACK, TWO INJURED: Middle East Watch took testimony from a 19-year-old student at the school of art in Kirkuk who was on his way with his brother, also a student, to stay with an uncle in Jordan. Their parents lived in Kuwait and the brothers had lost touch with them. One brother hitched a ride in a refrigerator trailer with a yellow cabin, and the other rode in a vehicle behind. They left Baghdad at 5 pm on February 9. About 10 km from the border with Jordan, at about 8 am the next day, they saw planes coming. When the driver of the refrigerator truck heard the planes, he pulled off the road and told the student to get out of the truck and run

---

[213] MEW interview, Farrah Centre, King Hussein Medical City, Amman, Jordan, February 17, 1991.

away. The student heard numerous explosions and saw lots of debris and dust from a bomb that fell close to the truck. He saw many cylindrical yellow canisters on the ground, with a parachute-like cone of cloth, military green color, on the end. The area was "full of canisters," he said.

He told MEW that when he hit the ground he felt a canister close to his body. He got up on his knees, tossed the canister away, and it exploded in the air. Then: "I saw myself flying off the ground and there was blood all over the place." He tried to get up, but could not. He had multiple fractures in his left leg, among other injuries.

The student and the driver of the truck, injured with shrapnel in his chest, were taken by a passing pickup truck to the Rutba hospital. While riding in the pickup, they heard another plane coming. The pickup stopped and the passengers jumped out and ran from the road. The student could not leave the pickup because he could not move. The plane went away and they continued on to the hospital.[214]

• REFRIGERATOR TRUCK ATTACKED NEAR BORDER: Middle East Watch interviewed a Sudanese carpenter, 28, a resident of Baghdad since 1984, who left the city on February 15 in a green Nissan bus with 36 Sudanese and Jordanian passengers. He said that during the trip the bus stopped twice and passengers ran out for safety because of nearby attacks.

Toward the end of the journey, at about 8 pm on February 15 when the bus was 30 kilometers out of Rutba, the Sudanese heard approaching planes. The driver pulled off the road and turned off the lights; the passengers stayed in the bus. There was one explosion. When it was over, the driver proceeded. One kilometer down the highway, they passed a yellow refrigerator truck that appeared to have been hit in the raid: in the headlights of the bus the carpenter saw that the truck's cabin was on fire. The bus drove on and the carpenter did not see if anyone

---

[214] MEW interview, Farrah Centre, King Hussein Medical City, Amman, Jordan, February 17, 1991.

was killed or injured. He saw many other vehicles along the road that had been destroyed in earlier attacks.[215]

• OTHER ACCOUNTS OF STRAFING OF TRUCKS BY ALLIED AIRCRAFT: The Amman trucking company, Odeh Nabr and Sons, has a fleet of 750 trucks, including oil tankers. About 95 percent of the company's transport business was based on hauls between Iraq and Jordan.[216] Samir Nabr, the owner, told the *Financial Times* that seven of his trucks were destroyed on the Baghdad-Amman highway from direct attacks by allied bombers.[217] He said that two of his drivers were hospitalized with severe burns and the cost of each destroyed vehicle was $110,000. He showed a reporter one oil tanker with eight bullet holes in the window of the cab.

A Filipino driver, Ramon Agila, said that he had been attacked twice in two weeks; during one raid he said his oil-tanker truck was sprayed with machine-gun fire. The driver also said he witnessed other strafing attacks: "They were bombing every three hours, all along the road. When some of the drivers fled, they were shot by the planes' machine guns."[218]

Samir Nabr said that in some cases pilots flew over the convoys of trucks before bombing, allowing time for drivers to escape. But in other cases, the attacks occurred without warning: "It depends if the pilot has any ethics," he said.

Legal Standards and Conclusions
    To be legitimate military targets, the Jordanian oil tankers would have had to satisfy the two-pronged test of military objectives: by their

---

[215] MEW interview, Azraq Evacuee Center, Azraq, Jordan, February 18, 1991.

[216] Mark Nicholson, "Jordanian truck drivers vow to defy air raids," *Financial Times*, February 7, 1991.

[217] Id.

[218] Id.

nature, location, purpose or use the vehicles must have been making an effective contribution to Iraq's military action, and their total or partial destruction, in the circumstances ruling at the time, must have offered a definite military advantage to the allies (*see* Chapter One). Under these standards, the tankers in and of themselves were not legitimate military targets. The vehicles were owned by private citizens of a state that was not a party to the conflict. The tankers were driven not by Iraqi military personnel but by civilian truckers from Jordan. With isolated exceptions, the tankers are not alleged to have been transporting fuel destined for military or any other use by Iraq; all evidence indicates that they were carrying fuel to Jordan, for consumption there. The "nature, location, purpose or use" of the tankers made no contribution whatsoever to Iraqi military action.

Nor is there any evidence that Iraq generated any immediate revenue from the export of this product, since the unrefuted statement by Jordan was that the oil was taken as repayment of loans; the oil shipments did not produce currency that could be used by Iraq to further its war effort. Accordingly, the destruction of the oil tankers, in the circumstances ruling at the time, did not offer a "definite military advantage" to the allies.

Indeed, the allies, to MEW's knowledge, never asserted that Jordanian oil tankers were legitimate military targets, but instead justified or excused these attacks on the grounds that it was difficult to distinguish these civilian vehicles from trucks carrying materiel for military purposes or the volatile fuel for mobile missile units. This defense, however, is undercut by the failure of the coalition forces to issue a specific warning to civilian drivers to stay off the highways because pilots were unable to distinguish civilian tankers from military vehicles.

Given that the Jordanian government had placed the allies on notice at the very latest as of January 30 that Jordanian oil tankers were on the road and had been improperly attacked by allied planes, Middle East Watch believes that the allies were under a duty to take effective steps to distinguish these tankers from Iraqi military vehicles, or to issue an unequivocal warning to civilian-tanker drivers to stay off the highways. The allies are at fault for failing to take one or the other precaution.

The U.S. Air Force Pamphlet requires that "constant care must be taken to spare the civilian populations, civilians, and civilian objects." It further states that those who plan or decide upon an attack have the duty to "[d]o everything feasible to verify that the objectives to be attacked are neither civilians nor civilian objects" (*see* Chapter One).

Objects used for civilian purposes, such as civilian trucks hauling oil, gas and other fuels, may be subject to direct attack "whenever a commander or other person responsible for planning, deciding upon or executing an attack honestly concludes, on the basis of information reasonably known to him at the time,"[219] that the object satisfies the test of a military objective.

Whether the numerous attacks on these tankers were reasonable under the circumstances and based on the information available to the planners and pilots at the time is an issue on which the allied air forces have the burden of proof. It is particularly important to know what "credible information" the allies had that "war material, including some related to Scud missiles, has been transported in convoy with civilian oil trucks," as claimed by the U.S. State Department on February 4.[220]

It is a matter of concern to Middle East Watch that allied military spokesmen conceded that it is "difficult to look at the ground and tell what a civilian target is and what a military target is, because, for example, oil trucks out in that area could be carrying fuel for Iraqi aircraft." It was also noted that many of the operations were taking place at night, which could mar pilots' vision. Taken together, these comments -- and the eyewitness testimony taken by MEW -- suggest that the allied air forces did not exercise the required duty of care in the circumstances to distinguish between civilian and military objects on highways.

When they were in doubt, pilots apparently chose to believe that the object was military rather than civilian, in violation of the opposite presumption dictated by the laws of war. The duty to discriminate

---

[219] *New Rules* at 326.

[220] Margaret Tutwiler, State Department regular briefing, February 4, 1991.

between civilian and military objects and to "do everything feasible to verify that the objectives to be attacked" are not civilians or civilian objects is not lessened because of the political importance attached to the elimination of Iraq's capability to launch missiles at Israel.

In MEW's view, if there was doubt about whether the oil tankers were Jordanian civilian vehicles or Iraqi vehicles carrying fuel for missile launchers or other military purposes, allied aircraft should have refrained from attacking. If, on the other hand, U.S. military planners regarded *all* vehicles transporting fuel within Iraq as legitimate military targets, they should have given, at the very least, effective advance warning of their intention to attack these vehicles. To have issued such a warning would not have jeopardized the security of allied aircraft and their crews, given their total control of the skies, and could possibly have averted death and injury to civilians driving such vehicles, as well as to civilians traveling in proximity to these fuel trucks.

To resolve these troubling issues, Middle East Watch calls on the allies to disclose fully the means and methods used to distinguish between civilian and military vehicles on highways and roads in Iraq, and the rules of engagement governing the attacks on military vehicles on those highways.

ATTACKS ON BEDOUIN TENTS

Bedouin civilian casualties in Iraq -- sustained during "the great Scud chase" -- were barely noted by the Western media during the air war. Desert-dwelling Bedouin families who reside in the Iraq-Jordan-Saudi Arabia border areas typically camp at sites with their sheep and goats for months or years at a time. They live in distinctive long, black, goat-hair tents (*beit al-sh'ar*, in Arabic), familiar to travelers in the region. The Bedouin have long disregarded national boundaries, and move freely throughout the desert. Approximately 95,000 nomadic or seminomadic Bedouin were identified in the 1977 Iraqi census, comprising less than one percent of the population.[221]

---

[221] *Country Study* at 80.

Middle East Watch obtained information about several Bedouin encampments in western Iraq -- located far from towns and main roads -- that were bombed by the allies, leaving at least 46 dead civilians, including infants and children. Mkhelf Dayes, a Bedouin who lived with his family in the desert on the Iraq-Jordan border, was the only survivor of a daytime attack on his three tents on January 22 which killed 12 members of his family and two others. He was interviewed by MEW in his hospital bed in Amman, Jordan, on February 17.

Mr. Dayes told MEW that he had established his compound 12 years ago. The site was isolated: the nearest military installation was 120 km away and the nearest town, Rutba, the largest town in western Iraq, was 160 km away. His tents were 100 km from the nearest highway, to which Mr. Dayes drove over the desert in his four-wheel-drive vehicle.

On January 22 at about 4:30 pm, Mr. Dayes saw four planes circle over his compound of three tents. Each black tent was about 30 meters long. Outside the compound were many sheep and goats, he said. The planes dove and attacked, firing 12 rockets. He was standing at the entrance to the compound watching, transfixed, when one of the rockets landed next to him. Rockets hit two of the tents, killing all 14 people inside. Mr. Dayes told MEW that his family members who were killed included two daughters, ages four and six, and nieces and nephews, among them a 19-year-old woman and her 18-month-old son and four-month-old daughter. The woman was the wife of his 17-year-old nephew, Adnan Dayes, who was in the hospital room taking care of his uncle at the time of the MEW interview. A father and daughter, unrelated to the family, also were killed in the attack.

Mr. Dayes said that after the attack some of his Bedouin friends just happened to come to his camp to visit; if they had not, he would have bled to death. They rushed him across the desert to the nearest clinic, in Ruwayshid at the Jordanian border; from there he was brought to the hospital in Amman for surgery. He already had undergone five operations for 36 injuries. He had a fractured scapula, 20 stitches on his left hip, five on his right thigh, a fractured ankle and a badly fractured and dislocated shoulder, among other injuries. He said that the attack destroyed blankets worth JD 6-7,000[222], four-wheel drive vehicles, sheep and other property, including cash.[223]

Mr. Dayes told MEW that he knew of only one other Bedouin encampment that had been attacked before the attack on his compound: 20 members of the family of Karim Khamar were killed inside their tents when they were bombed. He had since heard from relatives who came to visit him in the hospital that other Bedouin compounds had been attacked by allied aircraft. Some four or five days after the attack on his site, 18 rockets hit the tents of the Flayeh family who lived not far from him, killing 12 to 16 people. There were only two survivors: a four-year-old girl and her father. The tents of Ayed Mraydi also were attacked -- the man lost his wife, daughter, and 900 sheep with a market value of about $50,000.

The Bedouin herdsman, quoted above, told *The Guardian* that attacks on Bedouin camps near the Iraq-Saudi border had taken place near Zamlat Houran, Kalabat and Makar al-Na'am.[224]

Legal Standards and Conclusions

Bedouin tents fall into the category of objects to which a presumption of civilian use attaches under the customary principle codified in Article 57(3) of Protocol I.[225] The presumption requires that, in the case of doubt, pilots should have refrained from attacking.

---

[222] Jordanian dinars. One US dollar was then equal to 0.64 Jordanian dinars. The blankets, held for sale, were worth about US $9-10,000.

[223] He estimated the value of all the property lost at US $117,000.

[224] Wafa Amr, "Bedouins claim allied jets attacked camps in Iraq," *The Guardian*, January 25, 1991.

[225] Article 57(3) states: "In case of doubt whether an object which is normally dedicated to civilian purposes, such as . . . a house or other dwelling . . . , is being used to make an effective contribution to military action, it shall be presumed not to be so used."

Middle East Watch assumes that the aircraft that attacked Mr. Dayes' camp were seeking to destroy concealed Iraqi mobile missile-launchers and accompanying support vehicles, although it is difficult to understand how it reasonably could be expected that these large vehicles could travel easily over desert roads so distant from major highways. The attack on Mr. Dayes' camp took place during the afternoon. The planes did not attack from a high altitude, but dove down. Three long black tents, a herd of animals and four-wheel drive vehicles were in plain view. Even assuming that pilots thought that the 30-meter-long black tents could be hiding places for mobile missile launchers and other equipment, it is reasonable to assume that the signs of civilian life at the encampment also were visible.

Since the tents were relatively fixed objects, and since there were no antiaircraft artillery batteries nearby, there was no apparent need to strike quickly or lose the military advantage. There should have been time, therefore, to examine the site more closely and establish with greater certainty that it was a legitimate military target, or to provide some form of effective advance warning, given the evidence of civilian life.

From the perspective of the military planner, it is difficult to see how a commander or other person responsible for planning, deciding upon or executing the attack could "honestly conclude, on the basis of information reasonable known to him at the time,"[226] that these Bedouin tents satisfied the test of a military objective set forth in U.S. military manuals and Article 57(2) of Protocol I. Although the U.S. Air Force target planners perhaps never visited the Middle East and perhaps never saw Bedouin tents, the Arab members of the coalition who participated in the air war campaign had ample experience in the air and on the ground in the region and knew well the configuration of typical Bedouin encampments -- information which should have been communicated to pilots responsible for bombing missions in isolated desert areas of Iraq.

---

[226] *New Rules* at 326.

5
THE VIEW FROM THE GROUND: EYEWITNESS ACCOUNTS OF CIVILIAN CASUALTIES AND DAMAGE

This chapter contains testimony about civilian casualties and damage taken by Middle East Watch from former residents of Iraq who fled during the war. The accounts are organized geographically, beginning with Baghdad and Basra, Iraq's largest cities. Journalists' reports and information from post-war visitors to Iraq are cited when they corroborate accounts of eyewitnesses interviewed by Middle East Watch or provide supplemental information.

Most of the testimony included here was collected in February 1991 by Middle East Watch in random interviews with evacuees and others in Jordan. Additional accounts were obtained after the war from interviews Middle East Watch conducted in New York, London, Saudi Arabia and Kuwait.

We must emphasize that this testimony provides only a partial view -- not a comprehensive accounting -- of civilian casualties and damage in Iraq during the air war. Moreover, as is true throughout this report, the accounts in this chapter represent only *some* of the testimonies obtained by Middle East Watch; accounts were omitted if details were sketchy or information was contradictory. Other testimonies were excluded because the civilian damage described by witnesses appeared to be truly collateral to allied attacks on legitimate military targets, a tragic but inescapable consequence of warfare.

We must further emphasize that while some of the testimonies in this chapter provide graphic descriptions of the total destruction of civilian objects -- most notably residential buildings -- it was not possible in many cases for Middle East Watch to ascribe with absolute certainty direct responsibility to the allied forces for this damage and the resulting civilian deaths and injuries. While we present these accounts for the documentary record, their inclusion here should not be taken to indicate that each attack was a violation of the rules of war by coalition forces. In some cases, it appears that damage to civilian objects was caused by inaccurate bomb or missile attacks. But inaccurate attacks -- or "misses" -- are not in and of themselves violations of the rules of war. And, as we note below, the inaccurate delivery of munitions can be due to a variety of actions by the attackers or the defender.

Other accounts in this chapter suggest that attacks may have been indiscriminate -- based on eyewitnesses' claims that there were no military targets in the immediate vicinity of the civilian object attacked. However, in the absence of an on-site investigation and additional factual information about military targets near the areas where bombs fell and missiles landed that might not have been known to the witnesses, Middle East Watch cannot conclude definitively that the attacks were indiscriminate and hence clearcut violations of the rules of war.

As we pointed out in the introduction to this report, the subject of Iraqi civilian casualties and damage during the air war remains one of the major unanswered questions of Operation Desert Storm. Middle East Watch believes that the accounts in this chapter are sufficient to draw certain preliminary conclusions about the bombing campaign and, we hope, to focus attention on the need for more information from the allied forces to break the silence surrounding this issue.

SUMMARY OF FINDINGS

- Although, as described below, the allied air campaign raises troublesome issues, not one witness interviewed by Middle East Watch described seeing widespread destruction and damage in residential areas that would be suggestive of indiscriminate bombing on a systematic basis during the air war.

- Nevertheless, among the civilian objects in Iraq documented in this report that were destroyed or damaged were over 400 one- and two-story homes, 19 apartment buildings and several hotels; two hospitals and two medical clinics; two schools and one mosque; various commercial buildings; and public market areas in four cities -- Basra, Falluja, Samawa and al-Kut.

- Numerous witnesses described incidents in which civilian structures, most typically houses in residential areas they lived in or knew well, were destroyed or damaged in areas where they believed there were no conceivable military installations or facilities nearby, including antiaircraft artillery. Despite additional questioning and substantial probing by Middle East Watch, these interviewees insisted that there were no legitimate military targets located in these areas. These accounts, taken separately over a series of days -- and, in some cases, months -- from individuals of different nationalities, suggest that some civilian casualties during the war were not the product of inaccurate bombing -- mere misses -- but of attacks that, pending convincing justification from the allies, appear to have been indiscriminate.

- Additional witnesses provided accounts of bombs and missiles that fell wide of their targets, most often bridges and telecommunications towers,[1] by 200 or 300 meters or more, causing death and injury -- often substantial -- to civilians, and total destruction or substantial damage to civilian objects, most often residential buildings.

These accounts contrast sharply with the picture of pinpoint accuracy portrayed by allied military spokespersons during the war. For example, Gen. Robert Johnston, chief of staff to Gen. Schwarzkopf, stated in early February that "I quite truthfully cannot tell you of any reports that I know of that would show inaccurate bombing, particularly north of

---

[1] One journalist who was in Iraq during the air war told MEW that telecommunications centers were "visible and distinctive targets." He said that the buildings, typically two stories, "are all marked by triangular red and white masts about 15 meters high; many had satellite dishes on top." In many cases, the centers were located in tightly packed residential districts. "In one incident in Diwaniyya, an entire street and a hotel was wiped out. The telecommunications tower was wedged in between two streets," he said. (MEW interview, July 19, 1991.) See Chapter Five for a description of this incident, in which 11 civilians reportedly were killed and another 49 injured.

the Saudi-Kuwaiti border....I cannot tell you of any that I know of that have grossly missed their targets." Although, as we point out below, inaccurate attacks might be attributable to a variety of factors involving the attackers or the defender, the number of these accounts, particularly in light of the pinpoint targeting known to have been possible with the aircraft and munitions available to the allies, suggests a failure to use all possible means to limit collateral civilian casualties.

> • The Iraqi authorities told United Nations representatives who visited the country in March 1991 that about 9,000 homes -- housing some 72,000 people -- had been destroyed or badly damaged during the air war. Some 2,500 of the buildings were in Baghdad and another 1,900 in Basra.[2] However, one member of a U.S. delegation who visited Baghdad for four days after the war did not find physical evidence in the city to support the Iraqi government figures. After traveling around Baghdad, she concluded that the Iraqi figures were "not credible."[3]

Particularly because of our inability to obtain permission to visit Iraq after the war, Middle East Watch lacks sufficient information to assess the overall accuracy of Iraqi statistics about damage to civilian houses during the air war or to attempt to quantify the destruction nationwide. However, this chapter alone includes testimony from former residents of Iraq indicating that hundreds of homes and other civilian buildings throughout the country were destroyed or damaged when allied bombs and other ordnance missed apparent military targets by hundreds of feet or more.

British journalist Patrick Cockburn, who was based in Baghdad during part of the war, wrote about the inaccuracy of some attacks even in that city, where post-war visitors generally have noted that the bombing appeared quite precise:

----

[2] Ahtaasari Report at 11.

[3] Munk at 584.

From the beginning, the allies' bombs and missiles were never as accurate as might have appeared from the spectacular destruction of a number of prominent targets. Allied intelligence about buildings and other facilities to be destroyed has also been at fault. In Baghdad, opposite the Mansour Melia hotel, a telecommunications tower had been neatly gutted by a single bomb. But elsewhere there were craters where missiles had hit houses or waste ground, or were far from any obvious targets.[4]

Another journalist who was in Iraq during the air war told MEW: "I had the impression that the precision of the bombing diminished day after day. When I returned to Baghdad with the first group of journalists, the pinpoint bombing was not as pinpoint."[5] He speculated that decreasing availability of precision-guided bombs or their high cost were possible reasons for the change as the war dragged on. Regarding incidents in which bombs fell wide of intended military targets, he added that in these cases it was possible that "pilots flew into a wall of antiaircraft artillery and just let the bombs drop."

- The various incidents of civilian damage and resulting casualties in Iraq warrant explanation from the allied forces, and in particular the United States, given its lead role in directing the international military coalition and planning and coordinating the air war. It is not enough to dismiss these incidents as inevitable instances of inaccuracy: too many bombs reportedly fell nowhere near any apparent military target. The U.S. and its allies should explain why this happened. In other cases, pilots missed their apparent targets by wide margins. Here, allied commanders should explain whether the precautions required to avoid civilian casualties, detailed in Chapter One of this report, were taken in all cases.

---

[4] Patrick Cockburn, "Myth of pinpoint bombing," *The Independent*, February 14, 1991.

[5] MEW interview, July 19, 1991.

Allied commanders should also explain how the likelihood of collateral civilian damage was taken into account in selecting targets. This is made more urgent by the disclosure before the Commons Defence Select Committee by British Air Vice-Marshal Wratten that "the RAF twice refused to bomb targets given to it by US military commanders because the risk of civilian casualties was too high."[6]

• As discussed in Chapter Three, allied commanders should also facilitate an assessment of allied compliance with the rules of war by disclosing the kinds of munitions that were used in populated civilian areas of Iraq, including data about the expected accuracy of these munitions, particularly the unguided "dumb" bombs.

• Middle East Watch also calls on the U.S. to disclose whether an effort was made, during routine bomb damage assessments, continuously to monitor and document the extent of civilian casualties and damage as the war proceeded. If such analysis did not take place, the allies have a duty to explain why it did not, particularly given the numerous public assurances from allied spokespersons during the war about the care taken to spare Iraqi civilian lives.

POSSIBLE CAUSES OF DAMAGE
TO CIVILIANS AND CIVILIAN OBJECTS

As noted above, Middle East Watch cannot draw definitive conclusions from the information included in this chapter about the actual causes of the destruction of civilian objects in Iraq. We present here some of the possible factors that may have been responsible for inaccurate bombing or for what, in the absence of additional information, appear to have been indiscriminate attacks.

---

[6] *New Statesman and Society,* June 21, 1991 at 27.

Damage Caused by Allied Pilots who did not Follow the "Positive-identification" Rule

The Pentagon's July 1991 report notes some of the precautions that were taken to minimize civilian casualties, including instructions that pilots positively identify their targets:

> To the degree possible and consistent with risk to aircraft and aircrews, aircraft and munitions were carefully selected so that attacks on targets within populated areas ... could provide the greatest degree of accuracy and the least risk to civilian objects and the civilian population. Where required, attacking aircraft were accompanied by a high number of support mission aircraft in order to minimize aircrew distraction from their assigned missions.[7]

The report states that pilots "attacking targets located in populated areas were directed to return to base with their munitions if they lacked positive identification of their target; a significant percentage of the sorties by attack aircraft did so."[8]

The Pentagon should provide additional information on this important point, as it can help clarify some of the damage on the ground reported by eyewitnesses. The Pentagon should disclose the number of attack sorties that did not comply with the positive-identification rule, and the extent to which damage to civilians and civilian objects can be attributed to this factor. In addition, the Pentagon should disclose whether targets were assigned to aircrews in which positive identification might not have been possible, and, if so, the provisions of the rules of engagement in these cases.

Damage Caused by Ordnance from Iraq's Crippled Air-Defense System

The U.S. Air Force described Iraq's pre-war air defenses as an integrated "state of the art" system, which included as many as 17,000 surface-to-air missiles and some 9,000 to 10,000 antiaircraft artillery

---

[7] Pentagon Interim Report at 12-2 to 12-3.

[8] Pentagon Interim Report at 12-3.

pieces.[9] The Pentagon stated that the system included over 700 non-shoulder-launched surface-to-air missile launchers and 6,000 antiaircraft artillery pieces of 23 mm and larger.[10]

The allied forces quickly crippled the system when Iraq's early-warning radar sites along the country's southern border were attacked in the opening hours of the war.[11] Continued electronic jamming of Iraqi radar and attacks on radar antennae by HARM missiles caused the Iraqis to fire their defensive surface-to-air missiles blind, or unguided.[12] Jamming by the allies of Iraq's command-and-control system's frequencies "disrupted the radio communication links, severing Baghdad's ability to communicate with its radars, missiles and artillery batteries."[13] It is not yet known why the Iraqis fired so many defensive surface-to-air missiles during the war and, according to *Aviation Week*, "[i]ntelligence units interviewed Iraqi prisoners of war trying to learn the reasons for the

---

[9] McPeak Briefing, Transcript at 2. *Aviation Week* reported: "In addition to the radar and command and control systems, the Iraqi air defense system contained several hundred Soviet SAMs and more than 100 French Roland command-guided SAMs as well as antiaircraft artillery (AAA)." (Bruce D. Nordwall, "Electronic Warfare Played Greater Role In Desert Storm Than Any Conflict," *Aviation Week & Space Technology*, April 22, 1991 at 68.)

[10] Pentagon Interim Report at 2-4.

[11] According to the Pentagon: "The air defense system, partially blinded by the first attacks, was overwhelmed by the sheer number of attacking aircraft. Nothing approaching the depth, breadth, magnitude, and simultaneity of this coordinated attack had been previously achieved. The Iraqi air defense system could not coordinate a defense." (Pentagon Interim Report at 4-3.)

[12] *See*, for example, Guy Gugliotta, "High-Tech Weapons Earn Rave Reviews in Wartime Debuts," *The Washington Post*, February 3, 1991.

[13] Bruce D. Nordwall, "Electronic Warfare Played Greater Role in Desert Storm Than Any Conflict," *Aviation Week & Space Technology*, April 22, 1991 at 68.

seemingly bizarre unguided launches," which could have included a simple attempt to frighten allied pilots.[14]

This "blind fire" by the Iraqis has been mentioned as one cause of the reported damage on the ground. During the war, Gen. Schwarzkopf stated that Iraqi defensive surface-to-air missiles could have caused some of the damage: "Knowing the way they are now indiscriminately firing their missiles, and before, it's highly probable that what goes up must come down."[15]

Damage Caused When Allied Pilots Took Evasive Action to Avoid Iraqi Air Defenses

The Pentagon's report acknowledges that, despite allied air supremacy, Iraqi defensive systems remained a threat to allied air crews:

> Although Coalition aircraft were able to fly virtually unopposed in Iraqi airspace, the surface-to-air missile (SAM) and antiaircraft artillery (AAA) threats were at times very heavy and sometimes lethal.[16]

For example, one nuclear-research site outside Baghdad, a quarter-mile square, "was surrounded by an earthen berm, many calibers of antiaircraft artillery (AAA) and numerous SAM sites."[17] F-16 pilots reported heavy defensive fire, were forced to bomb "from a fairly great distance and did little damage with a large number of aircraft," according to the commander of a U.S. tactical fighter squadron.[18] *Aviation Week* reported: "The level of defensive fire varied each night, and [Lt. Col.

---

[14] *Id*. at 69.

[15] *The Independent*, February 5, 1991.

[16] Pentagon Interim Report at 6-4.

[17] Michael A. Dornheim, "F-117A Pilots Conduct Precision Bombing in High Threat Environment," *Aviation Week & Space Technology*, April 22, 1991 at 53.

[18] *Id*.

Ralph] Getchell, [commander of the 415th tactical fighter squadron], surmised this may have been linked to the health of the [Iraqi air-defense system], the amount of ammunition available, and gunners' morale."[19]

According to *Aviation Week*, "coalition aircraft operating low-level missions reported encountering 'enormous' Iraqi anti-aircraft artillery (AAA) and surface-to-air missiles (SAM) and, in the first week, the RAF lost four aircraft on such low-level operations."[20]

To avoid enemy fire in such circumstances, pilots would "jink and dive" -- zigzag -- which decreases the accuracy of an attack. Pilots also flew above the range of defensive systems: "As with most other allied aircraft, the F-15Es went to higher altitudes for their attacks to escape heavy enemy SAMs and AAA encountered early in the war."[21] Higher-altitude bombing, however, decreases the accuracy of both smart and dumb munitions.[22]

Damage Caused by Allied Munitions that Malfunctioned, Were Known to be Inaccurate, or were Untested in Actual Warfare
As discussed in Chapter Three, the unguided general-purpose bombs used by the allies to attack targets during the war had a low level

---

[19] *Id.*

[20] Carole A. Shifrin, "Britain's Gulf Role Highlights Value of Flexible Tactics, New Technology," *Aviation Week & Space Technology*, April 22, 1991 at 107.

[21] M. Lenorovitz, "Air Crew Training, Avionics Credited for F-15Es High Target Rate Hits," *Aviation Week & Space Technology*, April 22, 1991 at 107.

[22] "Preliminary reports indicate the allies' tactic of dropping precision munitions from higher altitudes -- 15,000-20,000 ft. -- diminished their lethality." (John D. Morocco, "Looming Budget Cuts Threaten Future of Key High-Tech Weapons," *Aviation Week & Space Technology*, April 22, 1991 at 66.) "The problem with bombing from higher altitudes is the loss of accuracy when using unguided weapons. Early analysis indicates dumb bombs dropped by attack aircraft were not all that effective, according to a Pentagon official." ("Flexibility of Attack Aircraft Crucial to Crushing Iraq's Military Machine," *Aviation Week & Space Technology*, April 22, 1991 at 46.)

of accuracy and their use in populated urban areas should be explained. In addition, some of the reported damage on the ground may have been caused by the more advanced weaponry used by coalition forces. For example, the one-thousand-pound precision bombs dropped by British Tornado aircraft reportedly missed their targets as much as 25 percent of the time, defense officials told the London *Financial Times*, which noted that the accuracy of the laser system could be marred by clouds or smoke.[23]

Similarly, *The Washington Post* reported that not only "dumb" bombs were inaccurate, but some precision munitions as well:

> Independent analysts also note that the allied coalition has been using several types of munitions with poor accuracy records in past conflicts and poor operational test results, including at least one type of guided bomb found to be so inaccurate that its production was halted abruptly six years ago.[24]

In stating that precision-guided weapons may have been responsible for some of the civilian damage in Iraq, Middle East Watch in no way suggests that it would have been preferable to use unguided weapons in populated areas. To the contrary, as we explain in greater detail in Chapter Three. Rather, we note that civilian damage caused by precision-guided weapons should be investigated both to determine why these weapons at times went astray and to avoid such errors in the future.

The Pentagon's July 1991 report provides no conclusions about the performance of weapon systems and munitions, in sharp contrast to the public claims of spectacular accuracy from U.S. military and civilian officials. Nor does the report indicate which weapons systems may have been responsible for civilian casualties and damage to civilian objects. The report contains only one sentence about the performance of

---

[23] David White, "Britain admits bombs missed target and hit town," *Financial Times*, February 18, 1991.

[24] R. Jeffrey Smith and Evelyn Richards, "Many Bombs May Have Missed," *The Washington Post*, February 22, 1991.

precision-guided bombs: "According to the Air Force, over 80% of the precision guided bombs released were hits, limiting collateral damage."[25] The report states that any conclusions about the performance of weapons systems must be based on comprehensive data collection and analysis, which was only in the earliest stages as of the report's publication.

The report also highlights an often-neglected aspect of the war, namely the use of new weapons systems and munitions:

> While some equipment, weapons and munitions had been in the inventory for some time, others were new. In fact, some were still in the developmental stages when the war began and were fielded prior to completion of normal test and evaluation schedules. A few systems had been used in combat prior to the Gulf War, but many were not combat proven. Therefore, an evaluation of the employment and performance of military equipment, weapons and munitions takes on a special significance and requires a thorough, systematic analysis of all available data.[26]

For example, Operation Desert Storm was the first time that Tomahawk cruise missiles[27] were used in warfare. Middle East Watch

---

[25] Pentagon Interim Report at 6-2.

[26] Pentagon Interim Report at 6-1.

[27] The missile is designed to carry a conventional 1,000-pound high-explosive warhead, or "a cluster of 166 soda-can-size 'bomblets' that can be dropped over three targets en route to a fourth." ("The Mind of a Missile," *Newsweek*, February 18, 1991.) Each of the 166 bomblets from the cluster-bomb unit carries a half-pound of explosives. (Francis Tusa, "Pinpoint strikes vindicate 40 years of planning," *The Guardian*, January 18, 1991.) The circular error probable (CEP) of the Tomahawk BGM-109A is 280 meters, according to the International Institute for Strategic Studies. (The Military Balance 1990-1991, Brassey's: 1990 at 217.) This CEP notwithstanding, the Tomahawk has been heralded for its pinpoint accuracy because of its ability at times to land within less than 100 feet of a target. (Will Bennett, *The Guardian*, January 18,

collected information about Tomahawks that crashed into civilian areas
where no obvious military targets were in plain sight (see Chapter Five).
The Pentagon has not released information about the accuracy of the 288
Tomahawks launched at Iraqi targets during the war, nor has data been
disclosed about inaccurate Tomahawk attacks that caused civilian
casualties and damage, even though the U.S. Navy admits that in 15
percent of all launches the missiles did not hit their intended targets.[28]
During the war, according to former U.S. Secretary of the Navy John
Lehman, Pentagon officials acknowledged that the overall success rate of
individual Tomahawks was closer to 66 percent.[29]

      The Pentagon's July 1991 report provides little information about
the Tomahawk's performance, although it does state that "initial
indications" point to the fact that the missiles were "highly successful."[30]
The report contains no specific information about the missile's success in
hitting its assigned targets; the only hard data provided is about the
success of the missile's launch phase: of the 288 fired, "282 are assessed
to have successfully transitioned to a cruise profile for a 98 percent
launch success rate."[31]   Nothing is said about the extent to which
Tomahawk misses caused civilian casualties and damage. Gen. Sir Peter
de la Billiere, the British joint forces commander, claimed that civilian
damage attributed to cruise missiles occurred because the missiles were

---

1991.)

[28] Molly Moore, "War Exposed Rivalries, Weaknesses in Military," *The
Washington Post*, June 10, 1991. "When the Navy...got the sea-launched missiles
included in the war plan, the Air Force remained so skeptical of their accuracy
that in one case it assigned as many as 30 missiles to hit a Scud missile
assembly plant, according to a senior Navy official. The Navy now reports the
missiles struck 85 percent of their targets, and naval authorities say initial
uncertainty over the Tomahawk forced them to fire up to twice as many of the
$1.75 million weapons as they needed--costing taxpayers an extra $245
million." (*Id.*)

[29] "The Mind of a Missile," *Newsweek*, February 18, 1991.

[30] Pentagon Interim Report at 6-8.

[31] Pentagon Interim Report at 6-8.

"intercepted and shot down [by the Iraqis] over areas occupied by civilians."[32]   During the war, *The Washington Post* interviewed U.S. officials about reports of Tomahawks hitting residential areas around Baghdad:

> U.S. officials said the weapons were aimed at airfields, and may have gone off course by themselves or been deflected by Iraqi antiaircraft fire. More than 280 of the cruise missiles have been fired to date, and at least a few can be expected to malfunction, several officials said.[33]

Middle East Watch understands that the specific U.S. Department of Defense instructions require that all new weapons and their effects undergo a legal review to ensure compliance with international law.[34] The office of the Judge Advocate General of the U.S. Air Force, for example, must review all new weapons for legality and state whether the weapon is consistent with restrictions imposed by international law. Permanent files of opinions in implementation of the Defense Department instruction must be kept. To our knowledge, the Defense Department directive is still in effect. The Pentagon's July report did not indicate whether munitions used in Iraq that were not "combat proven" -- such as the Tomahawk cruise missile -- had been approved for legality prior to their use in the conflict. The Defense Department should clarify this point.

THE NEED FOR ANSWERS

Given the numerous specific accounts of civilian casualties and damage to civilian objects in Iraq, Middle East Watch believes that the

---

[32] David Fairhall, "No absolute way to measure damage," *The Guardian*, February 4, 1991.

[33] R. Jeffrey Smith, "U.S. Military Pressed About Civilian Casualties," February 3, 1991.

[34] Air Force Regulation 110-20, dated September 10, 1981, implements Department of Defense Instructions 5500.15.

Pentagon should provide information in each of these cases that could shed light on the eyewitnesses' claims. Answers to the following questions would help clarify the circumstances surrounding reports of attacks that caused often-substantial damage to civilian objects in Iraq:

- Is there evidence of the damage described in the testimonies in this chapter from U.S. bomb damage assessment photographs and other reports?

- If there is evidence of damage, was there a legitimate military target in the immediate vicinity that was the intended object of attack? What was the target in each case?   Is there documentation that this target was successfully attacked? What are the possible explanations for the reported damage to civilian objects in each case?

- Of the cases in which there is evidence of civilian damage but no legitimate military target in the vicinity, what are the suspected factors that caused the reported civilian damage?

- What further steps can be taken to ensure that in future conflicts civilian casualties are minimized?

BAGHDAD

Allied statements, reflecting a concern over adverse publicity for civilian targets hit in Baghdad, suggest that greater-than-usual care was taken to avoid civilian casualties in the Iraqi capital.   Even there, however, testimony taken by Middle East Watch reveals that the allied bombing campaign came at a considerable civilian cost.

The city of Baghdad, on the Tigris River, has four million residents. By 1989, 55 percent of Iraq's urban population lived in Baghdad, up from 35 percent in 1960.[35] However, this population was substantially reduced during the air war. Reuters reported on February

---

[35] World Bank, *World Development Report 1990* at 239.

3 that as many as one million Baghdad residents may have evacuated the city by the time the war began.[36] One journalist told MEW: "There were huge queues of cars going north and going south beginning around January 13. People were driving out of Baghdad like crazy; it was a tremendous exodus."[37] Most took shelter with friends or relatives in towns and cities they assumed would be spared the worst of allied bombing, particularly in the Kurdish north and the southern cities of Najaf and Karbala, where holy Shiite shrines are located.

Reports both during and after the war attested to the overall accuracy of the allied air forces' bomb and missile attacks in Baghdad. In the war's opening days, most eyewitness accounts, including those of journalists themselves based in Baghdad, noted the precision of the bombing. On the first full day of the air war, the Iraqi Defense Ministry was bombed; one BBC correspondent said he saw three bombs hit the building: "It seems it was hit very, very accurately and it appears that there was extraordinarily little damage around it."

Eyewitnesses reported that civilian casualties and damage most frequently occurred in areas near Iraqi military targets. For example, most evacuees at the Jordanian border interviewed by *The New York Times* on January 22 said that civilian casualties were "concentrated in areas near military targets."[38] *The Washington Post* obtained similar accounts from evacuees in Jordan who "spoke of serious damage to civilian neighborhoods adjacent to military, political and industrial sites."[39] An

---

[36] Bernd Debusmann, "No Havens, Says Resident of Baghdad," *The Washington Post*, February 4, 1991.

[37] MEW interview, July 19, 1991.

[38] Alan Cowell, "Refugees From Baghdad Report Some Casualties Among Civilians," *The New York Times*, January 23, 1991.

[39] Nora Boustany, "Iraq, Arabs Dispute U.S. on Raids," *The Washington Post*, January 23, 1991.

Indian electrical engineer said the bombing in Baghdad was "perfect."[40]

The bombing of Baghdad, however, was not without civilian casualties and damage to civilian objects. Some early evacuees in Jordan reported incidents of inaccurate bombing in the city. A white collar worker interviewed at a Jordanian camp recounted an explosion 200 yards from his home in Baghdad on January 19. He said four houses had been hit and collapsed into rubble, leaving five or six civilians dead.[41] A *Financial Times* reporter who was in Baghdad for seven days after the bombing began "saw two apartment blocks near the center of the capital that had been bombed."[42] She also reported that residents of areas near military installations or communications centers said some of the bombing had been off-target.

Middle East Watch obtained additional accounts from former residents of Baghdad, included below, who described incidents of inaccurate bombing of military targets. For example, in an incident in the first week of February, described in detail below, allied aircraft twice attacked Jumhouriyya Bridge, one of five major bridges linking downtown Baghdad with the other bank of the city across the Tigris River. The first strike did not destroy the bridge but the second strike on or about February 5, with two rockets, did. Iraqi officials reported that two other rockets landed off-target and destroyed two movie theaters and 200 shops.[43] Testimony taken by Middle East Watch from three former residents of Baghdad about this incident, corroborated in part by a journalist, indicates that the allied strike on the bridge in fact was messy and not precise -- one rocket created a 15-by-8 meter elliptical crater in a civilian neighborhood at least 300 meters from the bridge.

---

[40] Phil Reeves, "Refugees from Baghdad say city 'a complete mess,'" *The Independent*, January 25, 1991.

[41] *Id.*

[42] Lamis Andoni, "Defiance and sadness as allied bombing raids envelop Baghdad in a dreadful beauty," *Financial Times*, January 25, 1991.

[43] "Iraqis Sever Ties With Six Nations," *The New York Times*, February 7, 1991.

Two British journalists, one of whom was in Baghdad for part of the air war, noted that the precision of the bombing varied with the size and characteristics of the target. The larger the "point target," the more successful was the strike:

> Successes in the city centre were primarily against telecommunications centres and ministries which were large and standing apart from other buildings .... Where the targets were smaller buildings -- generally intelligence centers -- little different from the buildings nearby, accuracy was less impressive, bombs or missiles being several hundred yards off target.[44]

The Use of U.S. "Stealth" Bombers to Attack Targets in Downtown Baghdad

One explanation cited for the low level of civilian damage and casualties in Baghdad is the aircraft and ordnance used to attack targets in the city, as well as the rules of engagement for the pilots. At the beginning of the fourth week of the bombing campaign, a Pentagon official said that more than 80 percent of the raids on Baghdad were flown by F-117 "Stealth" aircraft.[45] At a Defense Department briefing on March 15, U.S. Air Force Chief of Staff Gen. Merrill A. McPeak said that F-117 bombers were used to do "all the work in the heavily defended downtown Baghdad area."[46] Gen. McPeak said that if there was any doubt about the accuracy of the target, crews were instructed to return to their bases:

> Air crews were informed to bring home the ordnance if they weren't sure they were locked to the right target. We made very few mistakes. I'm quite proud of the fact

---

[44] Christopher Bellamy and Patrick Cockburn, "Allies assess precision of bomb raids," *The Independent*, March 19, 1991.

[45] Rick Atkinson, "Allies to Intensify Bombing To Prepare for Ground War," *The Washington Post*, February 8, 1991.

[46] McPeak Briefing, Transcript at 4.

that we achieved high levels of destruction against military targets with minimum collateral damage.[47]

Gen. McPeak said that the F-117s hit their targets with precision and caused minimal collateral damage:

> We did not carpet bomb downtown Baghdad. As a matter of fact, it's obvious to anyone who's been watching on television, the pictures of Baghdad neighborhoods untouched, people driving around, walking around on the sidewalks and so forth. We took special care to make sure that we attacked only military targets, and we attacked them quite precisely.

The Pentagon's July 1991 report makes a similar point:

> Coalition targeting policy and aircrews made every effort to minimize civilian casualties and collateral damage. Coalition rules of engagement directed pilots to withhold their weapons if the target could not be positively identified or if other factors were likely to degrade weapons performance (for example, cloud cover, weather, or other constraints). Because of these restrictive policies, only the use of precision guided munitions enabled the destruction of key targets in the heart of downtown Baghdad while leaving untouched civilian buildings virtually next door.[48]

The Pentagon's public claim of near-perfect attacks on downtown Baghdad that left civilian buildings "untouched" is contradicted by reports of the attack in February on the Ministry of Local Government in downtown Baghdad left six civilians dead amd others injured. The Ministry reportedly was first bombed on January 22 but little damage was

---

[47] McPeak Briefing , Transcript at 5.

[48] Pentagon Interim Report at 2-7.

caused.[49]   It was headed at the time by Ali Hassan al-Majid,[50] a cousin and confidant of Saddam Hussein, who for a short time after the Iraqi invasion served as the "governor" of the "province" of Kuwait.[51] On February 12, one day before the bombing of the Ameriyya shelter in Baghdad, the Ministry of Justice and the Ministry of Local Government - - housed in two five-story buildings on the west bank of the Tigris -- were hit in an early morning raid. An Associated Press account, cleared by Iraqi censors, described the attack:

> Two fireballs rose in the city after raids scored direct hits on the two ministries near densely populated Haifa Street, a business and residential route in the city center. Witnesses said at least 6 people were killed on Haifa Street and 17 were wounded, many seriously....Residential neighborhoods adjacent to the buildings also were damaged. So powerful were the bombardments that part of the Local Government Ministry crumbled to the ground.[52]

* * *

---

[49] "2 Government Ministries Hit in Raids on Baghdad," *The New York Times*, February 13, 1991.

[50] Ali Hassan al-Majid, now Iraq's Minister of Interior, was appointed in 1987 to head Ba'ath Party operations in northern Iraq, presided over the repression of the Kurds and is widely considered responsible for ordering chemical weapons attacks in 1988 against Kurdish civilians and rebels. He became Minister of Local Government in June 1989. In March 1991, the Ministry of Local Government was dissolved, pursuant to a decision of the ruling Revolution Command Council; its departments were absorbed into the Ministry of Interior and Ali Hassan al-Majid was appointed Minister of Interior by Saddam Hussein.

[51] Simon Henderson, *Instant Empire/Saddam Hussein's Ambition for Iraq* (Mercury House, San Francisco: 1991) at 88 [hereinafter Henderson].

[52] "2 Government Ministries Hit in Raids on Baghdad," *The New York Times*, February 13, 1991.

Despite the unrelenting bombing of targets in Baghdad during the air war, journalists and others who visited the city after the war generally have not disputed Gen. McPeak's assessment of the low level of "collateral damage" in the city. An American journalist who left Baghdad on March 6, pursuant to an Iraqi government order that all foreign journalists depart by 4 a.m. on March 8, wrote in an uncensored report from Jordan:

> Baghdad is not a ruined city. It is possible to drive through many neighborhoods and even down main avenues without seeing a trace of bomb damage. There are some shops and homes that were destroyed by wayward bombs and missiles, as well as by Iraqi antiaircraft fire returning to earth. But the most spectacular damage is to big targets such as postal and telecommunications buildings, government ministries, bridges and power plants.[53]

A correspondent who visited the city in April reported that damage "appeared remarkably limited. Baghdad's skyline has been preserved, and most high-rise buildings emerged unscathed." He noted that government buildings were still standing but "their interiors have been gutted" and that targets such as the Baath Party headquarters and telephone exchanges were "destroyed with precision."[54] One post-war American visitor, the member of a four-person U.S. delegation that visited for four days to document civilian casualties and damage, wrote: "We expected to find enormous unreported destruction....Instead we found a city whose homes and offices were almost entirely intact....I think the reason we didn't see more destruction was that it wasn't there."[55] (The group did not visit the outskirts of Baghdad, Basra or other cities in southern Iraq.)

---

[53] Lee Hockstader, "Death, Defeat Come Home to Baghdad," *The Washington Post*, March 7, 1991.

[54] William Drozdiak, "Saddam's Presence Remains Pervasive After Gulf Defeat," *The Washington Post*, April 29, 1991.

[55] Erika Munk, "The New Face of Techno-war," *The Nation*, May 6, 1991 at 583.

Several journalists have noted that the urban form of Baghdad helped minimize civilian casualties: Baghdad is a low-rise city, not densely packed like New York or Cairo. A French journalist based in Baghdad during the war told Middle East Watch that Baghdad reminded him of Los Angeles. Two British journalists made a similar observation: "Civilian casualties could have been higher, but Baghdad is very spread out, with low population density compared to Tehran or Damascus. The typical inhabitant of Baghdad lives in a sprawling suburb."[56]

Also significant in minimizing casualties was the fact that the residents of Baghdad were prepared for war because of the recent experience during the bombardment of the capital during the Iran-Iraq war, several phases of which were known as "The War of the Cities" because both countries launched surface-to-surface missiles at each other's major urban areas (*see* introduction to Part Three). The Iraqi government constructed air raid shelters, civil defense personnel gained experience coping with casualties and damage, and buildings were camouflaged. In Febuary 1988 the Iraqi authorities carried out an experimental evacuation of Baghdad.[57] Air raid shelters were put to use during the Desert Storm bombing campaign. Ironically, the highest reported casualty toll in any incident during the air war occurred on February 13 when the Ameriyya civilian shelter in Baghdad was targeted and destroyed with two precision bombs dropped by U.S. aircraft, killing 200 to 300 civilians. (The attack on the shelter is discussed in Chapter Three.)

The Unrelenting Bombing of Baghdad: Unanswered Questions
Gen. Colin Powell said on January 16 that "militarily oriented targets" in Baghdad were the object of attack:

> The purpose of our bombing facilities in the vicinity of Baghdad is essentially to go after the command and control system of the Iraqi armed forces. We're looking at principally military targets, command and control

---

[56] Christopher Bellamy and Patrick Cockburn, "Allies assess precision of bomb raids," *The Independent*, March 19, 1991.

[57] Dilip *Hiro, The Longest War/The Iran-Iraq Military Conflict (Routledge, New York: 1991)* at 200 [hereinafter Hiro].

installations, air-defense sites that could put our planes at
risk, but they are militarily oriented targets.

Given this clear statement, the allies have yet to explain the factors
leading to the civilian casualties and damage that did occur in Baghdad,
some of which are detailed below. The Pentagon has stated that some of
the damage in the city was caused by Iraqi defensive fire: "Some damage
in downtown Baghdad, blamed by Iraq on US planes, was in fact caused
by Iraqi antiaircraft fire and [surface-to-air missiles] fired without
guidance."[58]

But other factors also may account for some of the damage.
First, regarding the Stealth bomber, these aircraft are not infallible in
their targeting, as a Pentagon official conceded in February.[59] Their
accuracy during the bombing campaign has not been revealed. Second,
the Stealth used ordnance that was not battle-tested. Gen. McPeak stated
in his briefing that the Stealth were equipped with case-hardened 2,000-
pound bombs "that we have not used before"[60] but the Pentagon has
not revealed how accurately this new ordnance functioned. Third, the
Stealth bomber was not the only aircraft to attack targets in Baghdad. It
is not yet known how the Pentagon defined the boundaries of "downtown"
reserved for the Stealth, nor is it known what other aircraft and ordnance
were used to attack targets in the sprawling city outside the downtown
area, or how accurate that weaponry was. Last, the accuracy of sea-
launched Tomahawk cruise missiles -- reportedly used to attack "high-
value" targets in Baghdad -- has not been publicly disclosed by the
Pentagon.

Another lingering issue is the Pentagon's reluctance to identify
the military targets in Baghdad that were the objects of continuing allied
bombardment after the successful strategic strikes in the first days and
weeks. For example, well into the air war on February 12, journalists in

---

[58] Pentagon Interim Report at 24-1.

[59] Rick Atkinson, "Allies to Intensify Bombing to Prepare for Ground
War," *The Washington Post*, February 8, 1991.

[60] McPeak Briefing, Transcript at 15.

Baghdad reported more than 25 explosions in central Baghdad: the result, at least in part, was that the five-story Ministry for Municipal Affairs on Haifa Street was totally destroyed and the Ministry of Justice, nearby, was damaged. As noted above, witnesses reported six dead and 17 wounded.[61]

When asked about the intense bombing of the city that day, Lt. Gen. Thomas Kelly, director of operations for the Joint Chiefs of Staff, provided little information: "We are going after hard targets in Baghdad. Therefore, it takes more bombs on each target in order to be successful."[62] But in a statement the same day in Washington, Rear Adm. Mike McConnell, intelligence director for the Joint Chiefs, said: "Virtually everything militarily that Saddam Hussein has to bring to bear . . . is either destroyed or combat ineffective. The only effective fighting force left is the army dug in in the field."[63] If Adm. McConnell's statement was accurate, it suggests that there was little justification for the bombing that continued in Baghdad after February 12. MEW thus calls on the Pentagon to demonstrate that further destruction in Baghdad and elsewhere, particularly of civilian or dual-use objects, offered a definite military advantage under the circumstances ruling at the time, as required by the rules of war.

The issue is pressing in light of the significant bombardment of Baghdad after February 12. Most tragic was the attack on the Ameriyya civilian air raid shelter on February 13, killing 200 to 300 civilians, as discussed in Chapter Three. Three days later, according to a Pentagon report, the Pentagon decided to limit bombing in downtown Baghdad: "Concerns about negative publicity...contributed to a decision to curtail bombing in downtown Baghdad after 16 February."[64] The report included no additional information on the extent to which bombing was limited or curtailed. But two days after the decision reportedly went into

---

[61] *The Washington Post*, February 13, 1991.

[62] *The Washington Post*, February 13, 1991.

[63] *The Washington Post*, February 13, 1991.

[64] Pentagon Interim Report at 24-1.

effect, in the late evening of February 18, it was reported that "the allies launched one of their most ferocious attacks in the center of Baghdad".[65] According to a journalist, the bombing began at 11 pm:

> [M]issiles began skimming past the windows of the al-Rashid hotel. Against a background roar of high-flying aircraft, the hum of a cruise missile was heard every 10 minutes or so, followed by a terrific explosion that shook the entire hotel. The attack continued until 1:30 am. . . .[I]t was difficult to estimate how many missiles had fallen. But the consensus among correspondents was between 10 and 20.[66]

Perhaps because of Adm. McConnell's admission on February 12, the Pentagon publicly would not confirm that these intense missile attacks had occurred. Gen. Kelly described the bombing of the city during this period as "not exceptionally heavy," despite journalists' reports of the powerful explosions felt in the Rashid Hotel.[67] Gen. Kelly responded to a German television correspondent's claimed sighting of several Tomahawk missiles flying past the hotel by stating that "we haven't fired a Tomahawk missile in a number of days."[68]

At 1:35 a.m. on February 27, Radio Baghdad announced that Iraqi troops had been ordered to leave Kuwait and move to the positions they occupied prior to August 1, 1990. But that night Baghdad was

---

[65] Alfonso Rojo, "Bombs rock capital as allies deliver terrible warning," *The Guardian*, February 20, 1991.

[66] *Id.*

[67] Rick Atkinson and Ann Devroy, "Soviet Proposal 'Falls Well Short,' Bush Says," *The Washington Post*, February 20, 1991.

[68] *Id.*

bombed for the 39th consecutive night, according to *The Washington Post*; one resident described the raids as "a sleepless night of horror."[69]

The issue of the continued bombing of Baghdad was raised at Gen. McPeak's press conference on March 15 when a reporter asked about the bombing of Baghdad late in the war. "You were continuing to strike targets in Baghdad," the reporter said. "You drew the map. It looked like 900 to 1,000 sorties a day against strategic targets. Can you give us some sense of breaking down those strategic targets and what kinds of things were you still hitting in Baghdad weeks into the war?" Gen. McPeak refused to answer: "We were not flying 900 sorties a day late in the war against strategic targets. Beyond that, I think I'll duck the rest of the question."[70] Middle East Watch believes the Pentagon and its allies now have a duty to answer these troubling questions.

Middle East Watch collected no evidence that civilian areas of Baghdad were the object of systematic indiscriminate attacks by allied air forces that might lead us to suspect that such attacks were a matter of policy. Nevertheless, former residents of Iraq and Western journalists reported attacks in residential quarters that appear not to have been directed at specific military targets, according to their accounts. Other eyewitness accounts suggest that the claims by U.S. military and Bush Administration spokesmen of pinpoint accuracy in the bombing attacks were incorrect. Middle East Watch thus calls on the Pentagon and other allied commands to explain why the civilian damage described in this chapter occurred, including an assessment of the choice of targets, the selection of the means and methods of attack, and the manner in which attacks were executed.

Middle East Watch collected testimony from former residents of Iraq, as well as additional information, about the following incidents of civilian casualties and damage in Baghdad:

---

[69] Rick Atkinson and William Claiborne, "Baghdad Announces Retreat; Allies Encircling Iraqi Forces," *The Washington Post*, February 26, 1991.

[70] McPeak Briefing, Transcript at 11.

• BOMBING IN THE BATAWEEN QUARTER: WHAT WERE THE TARGETS?: Middle East Watch took six separate accounts -- in interviews in New York, Jordan and Saudi Arabia -- of civilian casualties and damage in Bataween, a residential quarter of one- and two-story buildings on the east bank of the Tigris River in downtown Baghdad. An Iraqi doctor who was in Baghdad during the war and later fled to Saudi Arabia told MEW that 30 to 40 civilians were killed when bombs fell on a few houses on Saddoun Street in Bataween. He said that the only possible military targets in the neighborhood were places where it was rumored Saddam Hussein may have been hiding.[71]

A European journalist, who was based in Baghdad for 12 weeks prior to and after the start of the war, told MEW that Bataween's old one- and two-story homes are constructed of ochre-colored clay tile, which leaves a lot of dust in the air when they collapse. He saw the aftermath of an attack in Bataween that occurred in mid-February: "The bombing was in the second block. Thirty houses were completely destroyed." He had been told that one or two residents were killed and 20 injured. "I don't see why this area was hit, there is nothing military there," he said.[72]

An Egyptian driver told MEW of an attack in Bataween on or about the night of February 11 which destroyed seven buildings. The one- or two-story houses, for low-income families, were located on or near Saddoun Street, close to a market. He had seen them before the bombing. The houses collapsed and the crater was full of rubble. The driver lived one km away in the Karada district and went to see the damage the next morning. He was told that civilians had been killed but he did not see any bodies. He said that there was nothing of military significance near the houses. The closest government building was the six-story Ministry of Higher Education, about two km away.[73]

---

[71] MEW interview, Rafha Refugee Camp, Saudi Arabia, May 28, 1991.

[72] MEW interview, March 25, 1991, New York.

[73] MEW interview, Aqaba Transit Center, Aqaba, Jordan, February 21, 1991.

Middle East Watch interviewed a Sudanese employee of the Sheraton Hotel, located about one km from the site of the bombing, who went to see the damage. He estimated that about 20 homes, two to three stories high, had been destroyed or damaged. They were not far from a vegetable market. He saw no military objects nearby, not even antiaircraft guns. Although he slept in the hotel shelter after the air war started, he was worried enough about safety to leave Baghdad the day after the bombing in Bathween.[74]

In a separate interview, an Egyptian printing company employee provided an account possibly of the same attack. He told MEW that he saw five to six residential buildings damaged by bombing in a low-income residential neighborhood behind Nasr Park at approximately 5 am on or about February 13. Nasr Park is in front of and opposite Tahrir Square, near Batween. The houses were on a branch of Tunis Street close to offices for doctors and import/export businesses, and about 500 meters from the Nasr bus station, which he said is between Saddoun and Nidhal Streets. The Egyptian, who had lived in Iraq for five years, worked in this area. He saw the damage at about 10 am on the the morning it occurred. He said the buildings were old two-story single-family houses. There was "considerable destruction," he said. He did not see a crater. He heard that many civilians were killed, but did not know the number. He told MEW that there was no bridge or military target near the houses, not even antiaircraft guns. The tallest structures nearby were five-story private buildings -- there were no government buildings in the area, "absolutely nothing."[75]

Middle East Watch also took an account of an earlier nighttime attack in Batween on or about January 20 or 21, when two residential duplexes in the neighborhood were completely destroyed. A Sudanese worker saw the damage to the buildings, which he said were on al-Mushajar Street, the next day. The cinderblock buildings, which he had seen many times, were adjacent two-story duplexes, where a total of four

---

[74] MEW interview, Azraq Evacuee Center, Azraq, Jordan, February 15, 1991.

[75] MEW interview, Ruwayshed Transit Center, Ruwayshed, Jordan, February 24, 1991.

families lived. The Sudanese lived a half-kilometer from the buildings. There was one water-filled bomb crater; the houses were completely destroyed, he told MEW -- nothing was left of them but metal. He said there was no military building nearby or anything of military significance.[76]

• CRUISE MISSILES IN THE KARADA AND MASBAH QUARTERS: WHAT WERE THE TARGETS?: The Karada and Masbah neighborhoods of Baghdad each were attacked on the same day with Tomahawk cruise missiles. Reuters reported that at least 11 people were injured in the two attacks, including six children.[77] Masbah is an exclusive enclave of expensive marble-facaded houses enclosed within high walls, according to a journalist interviewed by MEW. The neighborhood is located on the Tigris River south of downtown. He said that Taha Yasin Ramadan, Iraq's then-First Deputy Prime Minister (and now Vice President), was believed to live there. He also noted that in the nearby Karada quarter were "a lot of houses of security people" as well as a five- to six-story building known as "The Ship" among diplomats and Iraqi intellectuals. The building was believed to be the headquarters of the Iraqi security apparatus; CBS journalist Bob Simon and three others who vanished with him for almost six weeks were thought to have been detained there.[78] According to the journalist, Saddam Hussein's eldest son Udai was believed to live in the area between Masbah and Karada.

Several journalists reported that five or six Tomahawk cruise missiles hit Baghdad on February 1. One of the missiles landed in Karada and one other in Masbah. One journalist told MEW: "I saw six missiles flying by. We were only allowed to see two of the sites that were hit," in Masbah and Karada.[79] The Pentagon said on February 1 that

---

[76] MEW interview, Azraq Evacuee Center, Azraq, Jordan, February 22, 1991.

[77] From News Services, "Cruise Missles Level Houses In Baghdad," *The Washington Post*, February 2, 1991.

[78] MEW interview, March 25, 1991, New York.

[79] MEW interview, March 25, 1991, New York.

the Tomahawks were fired at Baghdad toward airfields but, according to *The Washington Post*, "U.S. officials declined to say more about the volley of missiles fired at Baghdad [on February 1]".[80]

The first missile landed in Masbah, leveled the home of an Iraqi merchant, Razzak Salman, and started a fire. Reporters saw four victims from the blast, including a boy six to eight years old, being put into ambulances. Journalist Patrick Cockburn, who visted both neighborhoods, wrote that he saw "no sign of military facilities nearby . . . There was no question of the explosions being caused by anything other than Tomahawks. I saw the missiles go over, was at the sites where they exploded an hour later and, at Karada, handled a piece of the missile."[81] A resident of Karada, Hashem Jassem, said: "This is just bombing. There are no government buildings around here."[82] *The Washington Post* reported that in the second missile attack several houses were destroyed in the Masbah quarter; the missile landed less than 1,500 feet from the U.S. Embassy compound. One journalist told Middle East Watch that this missile landed 150 feet from the house of Saddam Hussein's son Qusai; he said the crater from the missile was approximately 15 meters wide and 10 meters deep.[83] Reuters described the attack in a report:

> Correspondents were taken to the blackened ruins of a house near the U.S. Embassy. According to a diplomat, the missile appeared to have been aimed at the house of Saddam's second son, Qusai, and overshot it by 50 yards.[84]

---

[80] *The Washington Post*, February 2, 1991.

[81] *The Independent*, February 2, 1991.

[82] From News Services, "Cruise Missile Level Houses in Baghdad," *The Washington Post*, February 2, 1991.

[83] MEW interview, July 19, 1991.

[84] Bernd Debusmann, "Dazed Disbelief in Iraq," *The Washington Post*, February 15, 1991.

Saddam Hussein's sons have clearly enjoyed privileges and stature because of their powerful father, and British journalist and Mideast expert Simon Henderson, in a recently published book about Saddam Hussein, states that both sons "are believed to hold senior positions in different security organizations."[85] However, Middle East Watch is aware of no evidence that either man had any substantial role in Iraq's military effort that could justify missile attacks directly against them, much less on their private residences, if in fact these were the targets in Masbah and Karada. (Udai, the oldest, had been editor-in-chief of a local sports newspaper and head of the Iraqi Olympic Committee and the Iraq Football Federation; he was also rector of Baghdad's Saddam University for Science and Technology.[86] He reportedly was relieved of these positions after the death in October 1988 of one of Saddam's bodyguards, in which he was implicated but never formally charged. According to Henderson: "Udai was partially rehabilitated in 1989, when he wrote the foreword to a local Arabic-language biography of his father, and he fully reemerged in public in February 1990, when he was reappointed head of the Olympic Committee and the Iraq Football Federation."[87] Qusai in 1988 became the second deputy of the Olympic Committee; according to Henderson, he "later was said to have a senior position in one of the intelligence organizations."[88]

Middle East Watch learned of a subsequent attack on the Karada quarter from a Sudanese worker, who said that a dermatologist -- whose first name was Basil and had a difficult-to-pronounce Persian surname -- was killed when a bomb directly hit his house at 52 Nen Khamsen street on or about the evening of February 11. The doctor's wife and children were in a shelter and were not injured. The Sudani saw the house four or five hours after the bombing but did not see a crater; he thought the "rocket" fell inside the house -- its walls and the rest of the structure collapsed, and two adjacent houses were badly damaged. He said there

---

[85] Henderson at 193.

[86] Henderson at 82.

[87] Henderson at 89-90.

[88] Henderson at 90.

was nothing of military significance or importance that he could see in the neighborhood, and that this was the only part of the neighborhood attacked that night.[89]

• DESTRUCTION OF THE CENTRAL BANK: The Central Bank of Iraq, located on the east bank of the Tigris in the city center south of Martyrs Bridge and west of Rashid Street, was attacked by allied aircraft. MEW interviewed a journalist who saw the exterior damage but did not go inside the building. "It was a very big modern building, five or six stories," he said. "It was cracked open at the top...it looked as if it had been destroyed from the inside."[90] *The Washington Post* reported that the bank was "ruined...its roof collapsed, its pillars buckled inside their masonry lining."[91]

Middle East Watch is not aware of any allied briefer's acknowledgement that the Bank was attacked or release of information about the reasons for the attack. The financial institutions of an enemy are not listed in the U.S. Air Force, Navy or Army operations manuals as undisputed or per se military targets (see Chapter One). For the attack on the Bank to be justified under the rules of war, the Bank had to be making an effective contribution to Iraq's military action and its destruction had to have offered a definite military advantage to the allies in the circumstances ruling at the time. The allies' justification of this attack must particularly address the prevailing circumstances: Iraq's inability, given the effective international embargo and blockade, to use its currency or foreign reserves to import arms or other military-related supplies and materiel in support of its war effort.

• CIVILIANS KILLED IN ATTACK ON MAJOR BUS STATION: A Sudanese worker interviewed by *The Independent* claimed that central Baghdad's bus

---

[89] MEW interview, Azraq Evacuee Center, Azraq, Jordan, February 22, 1991.

[90] MEW interview, New York, March 25, 1991.

[91] Lee Hockstader, "Iraqis in Devastated Capital Worry," *The Washington Post*, February 28, 1991.

station had been attacked, injuring dozens of people and killing two.[92] MEW interviewed Iranian ex-combatants against the Khomeni government who left their camp near Hilla and went to Baghdad on about January 30, en route to Jordan. They arrived in the city at the bus station at al-Lauwi and saw a large crater in the middle of the yard. They were told that perhaps 40 to 50 people waiting for buses had been killed and injured in the open station when the bombing occurred on or about January 25. The Iranians said that the station is 15 minutes by car from the center of the city and is a departure point for buses that travel inside Iraq.

They told MEW that the station's building and buses parked nearby were burned. The crater in the yard was about five meters in diameter, filled with asphalt and debris. The stores in the one-story zinc buildings with iron beams nearby, some 20-30 meters from the crater, sold bus tickets, cigarettes and other items. There were no military targets near the bus station -- no bridge, tower, antiaircraft guns, they said. About 300 meters away was an intelligence building, which had been bombed before the bus station was hit. No other buildings were damaged in this attack.[93]

• FIVE TO SIX HOUSES TOTALLY DESTROYED IN THE WORKING-CLASS QUARTER: MEW took three separate accounts of an attack in the working-class Nahda quarter on the east bank of the Tigris River which totally destroyed at least five residential buildings. A European journalist saw a 300-meter row of five to six flattened buildings on a street off Rashid Street, which runs parallel to the Tigris in the city center, near the al-Shawi mosque. The street houses locksmiths, mechanics and artisans, he said, adding that no military targets were visible.[94]

Several Sudanese interviewed by MEW also saw the damage to six houses near the mosque in Nahda; they described the houses as two-

---

[92] Phil Reeves, "Fugitives tell of civilian suffering," *The Independent,* January 30, 1991.

[93] MEW interview, Azraq Evacuee Center, Azraq, Jordan, March 1, 1991.

[94] MEW interview, New York, March 25, 1991.

story cinderblock buildings. They saw a crater, approximately six meters wide, in the midst of the houses. "There was nothing there but civilians," one told MEW. "There was no military installation or operation in that area and the closest government office was about one and a half km away, a post office. The bridges were very far away. The tallest buildings were four stories, all residential."[95]

An Egyptian furniture finisher, separately interviewed by MEW, said that on or about February 11 six buildings on Kifah Street in Nahda were destroyed in nighttime bombing. The man, who lived 200 meters away and worked in the area, saw the damage the next morning. There were four craters about 3 to 4 meters apart near the destroyed buildings, he said. The attached two-story buildings had stores on the first floor. One crater, filled with water, was five meters in diameter; it was near a bakery. The doors had been blown off nearby stores. The only government office nearby was a small post office that distributes mail, the Egyptian said. There were no factories, tall buildings or military emplacements nearby: "It is all civilian." He heard from neighbors that civilians had been killed in this attack but did not know the number.[96]

• SIX HOUSES IN RESIDENTIAL NEIGHBORHOOD SUSTAIN DIRECT HIT: Six houses in the Mansour quarter in western Baghdad were hit in a bombing raid on February 10 or 11, leaving several civilians dead and substantial damage. A Sudanese employee of the Melia Mansour Hotel, who lived in the neighborhood not far from the International Exhibition and Trade Fair building on Mansour Street, said that his house was damaged and two of his friends injured in this attack. Some of the houses that were directly hit had three floors, some five floors. The buildings were not located on a main street. He went to look at the houses the next morning but civil defense personnel prevented anyone from entering. He saw ambulances removing many dead and injured from these damaged houses. He saw two bomb craters inside the cluster of six houses; the craters, each four meters in diameter, were filled with water. The houses

---

[95] MEW interview, Azraq Evacuee Center, Azraq, Jordan, February 22, 1991.

[96] MEW interview, Aqaba Transit Center, Aqaba, Jordan, February 21, 1991.

were about four kms from a broadcasting station, which he believed was the closest target. As far as he knew, there was nothing of military significance closer than that, he told MEW.[97]

He said that the attack began with an initial explosion at around midnight but not much in his house was damaged, then the planes returned after four or five minutes and bombed again. This time, there were two explosions and his house was damaged, mainly on the second floor. Part of the side of the building and a corner were knocked off, but the roof did not collapse. His two injured housemates, a Sudanese and an Egyptian, had been sleeping on the second floor. One had shrapnel in his lower right leg and the other in his calf, and they were taken to the hospital. He said that they heard the air raid siren go off but did not go to the shelter because they were afraid of being trapped inside, he said.

• COMMERCIAL AREA IN RESIDENTIAL NEIGHBORHOOD BOMBED; FOUR HOMES DAMAGED: On or about February 13 or 14, bombs fell in the Kadhimiyya quarter in northwestern Baghdad, according to two former residents interviewed by MEW. Some stores were hit and four nearby one-story homes damaged, according to an Egyptian truck driver who saw the damage the next day. There were no antiaircraft guns or other military targets near the buildings: "There was not even any government office nearby." The driver saw a crater five meters in diameter and two meters deep in front of the stores.[98] The Egyptian may have been referring to the attack described by the Associated Press in a February 15 dispatch from Baghdad: "In one poor neighborhood...a dozen shops were wrecked during an allied bombing raid two nights ago".[99]

---

[97] MEW interview, Azraq Evacuee Center, Azraq, Jordan, February 15, 1991.

[98] MEW interview, Aqaba Transit Center, Aqaba, Jordan, February 21, 1991.

[99] "Jubilation in Baghdad, and Then Bombing," *The New York Times*, February 16, 1991.

An Egyptian hotel employee, interviewed separately, said he saw the damage to four homes in Kadhimiyya on the same day they were bombed in mid-February. He heard that all the civilians inside were killed. He too knew of no military targets nearby.[100] After the war, a U.S. visitor to Baghdad was taken to a site in Kadhimiyya where nine houses were bombed; local residents said that 40 people had been killed in the incident.[101]

• FIVE HOMES COLLAPSE, KILLING FAMILY OF SIX: On February 18 in the Saddoun quarter of downtown Baghdad, five houses on Rasafi Street collapsed from nighttime bombing and the windows of surrounding houses were shattered. A family of six in one house was killed, according to an Egyptian interviewed by MEW who saw the damage the next day. The family had just returned 10 to 15 minutes earlier from the shelter, he was told, thinking the air raid was over; the authorities do not let people leave the shelter if they think the air raid is in progress, he said. The houses were part of a row of one- and two-story homes. The post office, the nearest object of military significance, was a half kilometer away and was not hit that night.[102]

• FIVE RESIDENTIAL BUILDINGS IN VICINITY OF DOURA OIL REFINERY COMPLETELY DESTROYED: MEW interviewed a Sudanese family who reported seeing on or about January 20 five or six residential buildings that they were told were damaged in bombing on the second day of the war. The houses were on Saja Street, about 1.5 to 2 km from the Doura oil refinery south of Baghdad, the closest military target to their knowledge. *The Times* of London reported that the Doura refinery was destroyed on January 19.[103]

---

[100] MEW interview, Aqaba Transit Center, Aqaba, Jordan, February 21, 1991.

[101] Erika Munck, "The New Face of Techno-war," *The Nation*, May 6, 1991.

[102] MEW interview, Aqaba Transit Center, Aqaba, Jordan, February 21, 1991.

[103] Richard Beeston, "'We could lose a million,'" *The Times*, January 21, 1991.

The family, including two adult sisters and a brother, got out of their bus to look at the damaged buildings. The concrete houses were completely destroyed; nearby on the street was a crater three meters in diameter and very deep, filled with rubble. Other bombs also had fallen on the street in front of the houses, leaving many craters of the same size and some unexploded rockets. They heard that many civilians were killed and injured.[104] This attack confirmed the family's decision to move in with relatives hundreds of kilometers west of Baghdad.

Journalists took similar accounts from evacuees in Jordan about civilian areas that were hit during the attack on the refinery. *The Wall Street Journal* interviewed a Sudanese factory technician who lived in the Doura suburb and saw many civilian casualties during the attacks on the oil refinery near his home. "The whole area was hit," he said. "You didn't know what was happening. You couldn't tell who was helping or who was injured."[105]

The Washington Post obtained similar testimony from evacuees:

> The residential neighborhoods of Jadriyyah and Qadissiyya, and the Doura central bus station, were also hit, according to a group of refugees who reached here from Baghdad today....
>
> "On the first morning after the raid, a bus full of people at Doura was hit, when the planes came in the daytime," one man said. Half a dozen others interviewed separately confirmed the report.

---

[104] MEW interview, Azraq Evacuee Center, Azraq, Jordan, February 25, 1991.

[105] Tony Horwitz and Geraldine Brooks, "Baghdad Portrait: The City Becomes Grim Ghost Town," *The Wall Street Journal*, January 30, 1991.

"Last night [January 20], some kind of rocket fell near our home in Jadriyyah. The bombing is not precise," he continued.[106]

Reports of Damage near Bridges

During the air war there were press reports that some of the allies' attacks on bridges in Baghdad were flawed. In the bombing of the city for a 12-hour period on the night of February 6-7, for example, the Associated Press reported that a missile hit houses in the Adhamiyya neighborhood northwest of the city center during a midnite raid, killing six; the missile may have been intended for the nearby Adhamiyya bridge over the Tigris River, some 200 yards away.[107] One of the houses, burned to the ground in the attack, was owned by a Kurdish family. "They left Baghdad before the war began and came back yesterday, convinced nothing would happen," a man whose sister lived in one of the houses told AP. "Two hours later, five of them were dead. They were burnt alive. All the people who lived in the area around the bridge have collected their belongings and left for the countryside." [108]

Middle East Watch collected testimony from former residents of Baghdad about inaccurate attacks on two other bridges in the city -- Sarafiya Bridge and Jumhouriyya Bridge -- which caused the loss of civilian life and damage, sometimes considerable, to civilian objects. These accounts follow.

• RESTAURANT DESTROYED, CIVILIANS KILLED, NEAR SARAFIYA BRIDGE: Several two-story buildings with stores on the first floor and residences above were damaged or destroyed on the first night of the war in the Waziriyya neighborhood just north of the city center, according to a Mauritanian student interviewed by MEW. He went to the

---

[106] Nora Boustany, "Refugees Describe Air Raid Horrors," *The Washington Post*, January 21, 1991.

[107] "Allies Bomb Baghdad," *The New York Times*, February 8, 1991.

[108] Alfonso Rojo, "A bridge too near for civilians as bombers strike," *The Guardian*, February 8, 1991.

neighborhood the morning after, when he saw smoke rising, fearful for his schoolmates who lived there.

His friends survived, but near their house, on a street he thinks was Abi Taleb, a main thoroughfare, he saw damage to a restaurant that was owned by Egyptians. It was a concrete detached building of two stories, with a residence on top. A bomb had landed in the corner on the street directly in front of the restaurant. The crater was about one to one and a half meters in diameter and the same depth. The roof fell down into the first floor and the walls were "tilting open," damaged but not completely collapsed.

Next to the restaurant was a photo studio and next to that a barbershop; both businesses were damaged. The roof of the studio had fallen in. The restaurant was on a 60 degree corner; on the other side of the 60 degree angle was a food store and next to it a metalworking shop, also damaged. The outer door of the food store was completely damaged and food and vegetables had been strewn in the street. The metalworking shop was slightly damaged on the outside but collapsed on the inside. Neighbors told him that members of three families were injured and killed.

The student said there was a bridge about 200 meters away that was not hit. (MEW maps of Baghdad indicate that the only bridge across the Tigris River in the vicinity of Waziriyya is the Sarafiya Bridge; the distance from Abi Taleb Street to the bridge is over 750 meters.) The student noted that on the top of a building 300 meters away was an antiaircraft emplacement dating from the Iran-Iraq war, closer to the bridge than to the restaurant.[109]

• FIVE HOUSES DAMAGED, CIVILIANS INJURED AND KILLED, NEAR SARAFIYA BRIDGE: Five houses on both sides of Jami'at Ali Khatum Street in the Medical City area north of the city center were badly damaged on January 21, according to what an Egyptian couple learned when they emerged from an air raid shelter with their two children. They heard that several Iraqis had been killed and injured in the attack, but

---

[109] MEW interview, Azraq Evacuee Center, Azraq, Jordan, March 1, 1991.

they did not see the bodies because civil defense personnel had already removed them.

The buildings were attached single-family houses of good construction, which they knew because they had lived in the neighborhood for three years. Four were one-story houses and the fifth was two stories. "This was not a poor area," they said. Shops in the area were damaged as well. The rocket directly hit one of the houses, the roof of which fell in, although some walls were still standing. The planes tried several times to hit the nearby Sarafiya Bridge, but the antiaircraft fire drove them away so they dropped the bombs on the houses, the couple guessed.

The houses were about 200 to 300 meters from Sarafiya Bridge, which the planes never hit to this family's knowledge, although there were two attacks. The damaged houses were located on a street perpendicular to the bridge. This Egyptian couple, who owned a small store and lived in a six-story building next to the bridge, promptly moved to the countryside for safety. When their food ran out, they left for Jordan.[110]

This censored account by a Baghdad-based foreign journalist may refer to the same attack:

> The effect of the missile is devastating. The roof of the
> building and the thick layer of cement of the first story
> have collapsed like a sugar lump. Of the little restaurant
> below, nothing is left. Just a few plates, still carrying the
> remains of a meal, and a few twisted pots and pans....
>
> On the other side of the street, some of the locals of Al
> Sarafia suburb watch us in silence. The blast has blown
> out the windows of the little hospital on the corner and

---

[110] MEW interview, Ruwayshed Transit Center, Ruwayshed, Jordan, February 24, 1991.

scattered glass shards over the carpets in the Adila Jatun mosque.[111]

• SHOPS AND TWO CINEMAS DAMAGED NEAR JUMHOURIYYA BRIDGE: On or about February 5 at 2:30 am, a rocket fell in a bus yard adjoining a market and two cinemas in downtown Baghdad, according to an Egyptian, 28, interviewed by MEW. The *Cinema Rasafi* was totally damaged and the *Cinema Fardoz*, next to it, was partially damaged. The crater, 15 by eight meters in elliptical size, was five or six meters from the cinemas. The crater filled with water. There was damage to some 10 to 15 buildings, with doors blown out and glass shattered. All the windows of the Afrah al-Nasr hotel, about 100 meters from the site, were broken. The Egyptian lived in this hotel, but on the night of the attack had been in a shelter.

He said that the area was at the crossroads between the entrance to Saddoun and Rashid Streets in the Souk al-Haraj neighborhood in downtown Baghdad. (Other former residents interviewed by MEW regard this as part of the Batawcen quarter.) The bus yard is for local buses in Baghdad. There is no military post nearby; Jumhouriya Bridge is 300 meters to one km away -- it was damaged by bombing the day before. In this attack the bridge was attacked again, the Egyptian told MEW. The tallest building nearby was the seven- to eight-story old Cultural Ministry, now used for artists' exhibits. Located about 100 meters from the cinema, its windows were shattered from the explosion. There was no antiaircraft or other military on top of this building.[112]

Middle East Watch also interviewed two Jordanians who saw the damage to the bus yard and two cinemas. They said they heard that six Egyptians were killed who had been sleeping in the cinema.[113] A press report, co-authored by a journalist who spent part of the war in

---

[111] Alfonso Rojo, "Dining out can be deadly in Baghdad," *The Guardian*, January 28, 1991.

[112] MEW interview, Ruwayshed Transit Center, Ruwayshed, Jordan, February 18, 1991.

[113] MEW interview, Amman, Jordan, February 23, 1991.

Baghdad, corroborated aspects of the testimony taken by MEW: "al-Jumhuriya bridge across the Tigris was hit twice, but one bomb landed 400 yards away in Tahrir Square, demolishing part of an empty cinema."[114] Associated Press reported from Baghdad on February 6 that two rockets hit Jumhouriyya Bridge and destroyed it, in the second attack on the bridge during that week.

• RESTAURANT DESTROYED NEAR JUMHOURIYYA BRIDGE: A two-story cement building, with a restaurant on the first floor and an apartment above, was destroyed in a nighttime attack on a Monday in the middle of February (probably February 11). A Yemeni married to an Iraqi woman told MEW that he had just completed construction of the building, with an apartment above for his family, 10 days after the invasion of Kuwait. It was located on Saddoun Street in al-Mushejar quarter of the city center on the east bank of the Tigris; several high-rise hotels were located close by.

The restaurant owner said that fortunately he, his pregnant wife and their child were in an air raid shelter at the time of the attack and no one was killed. The bomb caused the bottled cooking gas in the restaurant to explode. The family lost the contents of the restaurant and all their personal and household possessions in the ensuing fire. The roof of the building fell in and only about a meter and a half of the walls were left standing.

He told MEW that this was the third civilian building in the neighborhood to be damaged; the others were damaged on different nights. He thought about 25 rockets hit in a 100-meter or so radius of his restaurant. He speculated that perhaps the target was a vehicular tunnel about 50 meters away. The nearest antiaircraft guns were 100 meters away but they were not hit. The planes usually flew very high because of the antiaircraft, he said.

The Yemeni's building was located about 300 meters from a bridge over the Tigris. He said that the bridge has been hit about three times, at both ends and in the middle. Half of it fell in the river and the

---

[114] Christopher Bellamy and Patrick Cockburn, "Allies assess precision of bomb raids," *The Independent*, March 19, 1991.

other half was suspended, with one end in the air. It was a large bridge, used by trucks, with a walkway on either side for pedestrians, leading to government and military buildings on the other bank of the river. (Based on this description, and the location of the restaurant on Saddoun Street, MEW believes the bridge is Jumhouriyya Bridge.)

The Yemeni said that he had two smaller restaurants: one in the Karada neighborhood, two km away, and the other in Baghdad al-Jedida, 14 km away. These buildings' windows and doors were slightly damaged in other attacks; the restaurant in al-Jedida was damaged when a nearby gas station was hit.[115]

BASRA

During the war, little first-hand information reached the public about allied bombing in and around Basra, Iraq's second-largest city. Basra had been home to 1.5 million people in 1977, but by 1988 almost half the city's population was estimated to have fled the shelling during the Iran-Iraq war which killed thousands of civilians.[116] Iraqi health officials in Basra told a representative of the U.S.-based Physicians for Human Rights, who visited on March 31 and April 1, that about 10 to 15 percent of the city's residents fled during the Gulf air war.

A former resident of Basra, who lived in exile for 16 years, drove into the city on March 1 from Iran with a convoy of trucks carrying food. He told MEW that the densely populated areas of Ashshar, Bratha'iyya and Old Basra were "badly hit" during the air war, while other areas were not touched.[117] He visited Ashshar and found his family's house "totally destroyed," as were many houses nearby. He said the nearest military target was a bridge at least two miles away. Patrick Cockburn, a journalist for *The Independent* who was in Iraq during the war, told MEW

---

[115] MEW interview, Azraq Evacuee Center, Azraq, Jordan, March 1, 1991.

[116] *Country Study* at 106.

[117] MEW interview with Ali al-Basri, London, May 4 and May 6, 1991.

MEW that there was much more extensive damage from allied bombing in Basra than in Baghdad.[118]

A detailed report of the allied bomb damage in Basra was filed by journalist Ed Vulliamy in May.[119] In contrast to the low level of bomb damage journalists and others saw in post-war visits to Baghdad, Vulliamy found, from walking around Basra, that the bombing had not always been precise:

> The destruction meted out by the "precision" bombing of Al-Basra was merciless, ruinous and all-consuming, not always that "precise", and not always "strategic." Walking in Al-Basra, it is easy to work out which buildings were flattened from the air and which were shelled during the rebellion and counter-rebellion: the allied bombers struck at civilian homes, schools, hospitals, mosques and a host of buildings in the city centre.

He also noted that "offices that manage the oil industry were gutted; the port was knocked flat, factories obliterated. Most important, the electricity power stations and the water treatment centers, water tanks and towers were done away with. It was not merely the transformers in the water plants that were bombed, but the giant Japanese-built turbines themselves, which cannot be repaired under the embargo." MEW obtained information from two other witnesses about damage to water-supply facilities in Basra (see Chapter Four).

Despite reports of damage to civilian objects in Basra, some key targets apparently were untouched by allied bombs. A journalist who traveled to Basra in early February from Baghdad reported that near Basra "barracks seen from the road are still standing, albeit empty."[120]

---

[118] MEW interview, London, May 7, 1991.

[119] Ed Vulliamy, "Fear At the End of the Basra Road," *Weekend Guardian*, May 18-19, 1991.

[120] Bernard Estrade, Paris Agence France-Presse, February 19, 1991, as reported in FBIS, February 21, 1991 at 27.

An Iraqi exile who entered Basra on March 1 told MEW that a Republic Guard garrison just outside the city was intact, as was the Muhammad al-Qasim army camp near al-Jumhouriyya.[121]

Civilian Casualties and Damage in Basra

Basra had sustained extensive damage during the Iran-Iraq war. Although parts of the city were reconstructed after the war ended in 1988, "acres of shattered brick and stone are all that remain of what had been homes and businesses and thriving factories," wrote a journalist who visited Basra in November 1990.[122] Basra served as a major center for Iraqi military communications and as a staging point for supply lines to Iraqi troops in Kuwait, some 30 miles south. One U.S. intelligence official described the city as "a target-rich environment."[123]

U.S. Brig. Gen. Richard Neal discussed at a briefing in Riyadh on February 11 the daily bombing of Basra and "collateral damage." He noted that the city "is a military town in the true sense. It is astride a major naval base and port facility. The infrastructure, military infrastructure, is closely interwoven within the city of Basra itself."[124] Gen. Neal cited chemical and oil storage facilities, port installations, warehouses and a naval base as some of the military targets.[125] He added: "Our pilots, I would stress, go to extraordinary lengths to try to avoid...civilian damage. In most cases they've been very, very successful."[126]

---

[121] MEW interview with Ali al-Basri, London, May 4 and May 6, 1991.

[122] Philip Shenon, *The New York Times*, November 22, 1990.

[123] *The New York Times, January 25, 1991.*

[124] Rick Atkinson and Ann Devroy, "'Bush: No Immediate Plan to Start Ground War," *The Washington Post*, February 12, 1991.

[125] R.W. Apple, Jr., "Allies Step Up Gulf Air Offensive; Strikes Focus on Iraqis in Kuwait," *The New York Times*, February 12, 1991.

[126] Ron Howell, "A War of Words Over Civilian Toll," *Newsday*, February 12, 1991.

Middle East Watch obtained accounts from former residents of Basra which indicate that attacks were not always as "successful" as Gen. Neal claimed. Bombs and missiles landed off-target, often by hundreds of meters, causing civilian casualties and damage in the city proper and in outlying residential areas. In addition to the attacks described below, other incidents in Basra are described elsewhere in this report. These include the bombing of a food storage warehouse (see Chapter Four) and the daytime bombing of two bridges and an area near the Ashshar market (see Chapter Three).

Middle East Watch collected testimony from former residents of Basra, as well as additional information, about the following incidents of civilian casualties and damage:

• TWO MISSILES CRASH INTO CROWDED MARKET IN DAYTIME ATTACK: An Indian plumbing foreman, who had lived and worked in Basra for one year, told Middle East Watch of a missile attack that he saw at about 11 am on January 24 or January 25.[127] He said he was on his way to a market to buy fish for his crew when he saw two missiles fly by, 30 seconds apart. He saw no fighter-bombers in the sky. He watched the missiles crash into the market building, which was some 100 meters from where he was standing; he said his hair was blackened from the explosions.

When the missiles hit, "everything blew up and fell down," he told Middle East Watch. He ran to the scene and saw about ten to fifteen dead men, women and children. One small child, next to a dead woman, was crying: "Where is my mother?" Inside the market, which contained stands for food, clothing and shoes, he saw a crater filling with water and rubble. The market was near a television tower, about a three-minute walk away. The tower was destroyed in a bombing raid two days later.

• ASHSHAR MARKET AREA IN DOWNTOWN BASRA SUSTAINS DAMAGE FROM TWO MISSILES: According to former residents of Iraq, at least 15 stores were badly damaged when two cruise missiles landed in a vegetable market near downtown Basra. MEW interviewed Yemeni students who

---

[127] MEW interview, Azraq Evacuee Center, Azraq, Jordan, February 15, 1991.

attended university in Basra and lived about a half-kilometer from the wholesale vegetable market in Ashshar. The market stretches for one kilometer along both sides of a large street, they said. The market is adjacent to the Ashshar business district where the tallest buildings are hotels about six stories high. There are office buildings and shops in the district, but no military installations there, according to the students.

On or about January 20, at night, the students' house was shaken by a strong blast that broke the glass in the windows. Before the blast, they heard the whistle of a missile. They did not hear any planes and there was no air raid warning siren as there usually is when the planes attack. They did not leave their house. The next morning there was another blast of the same huge impact, preceded by the noise of a whistle. This occurred just before noon. This time, some of the students went out to look at the damage.

They saw that the vegetable market had been hit -- at the entrance and the stores at that end of the market. About 15 to 20 stores on both sides of the street, zinc-roofed of cinderblock construction, were badly damaged. There was a large crater in the street that had filled up with water, about six meters in diameter and maybe two and a half meters deep. Vegetables were scattered all over the rubble, the students said. Nearby buildings also had some damage, but it seemed to the students that the vegetable market had been directly hit twice.

Merchants told the students that the second missile fell 10 meters from the first, with the same type of damage to nearby stores and another crater of the same size in the street. When the students visited the market, there were people milling about, cleaning up the rubble. Some merchants were opening their shops as usual; Iraqis are used to it, one student said. The students did not know the number of civilian casualties from the two attacks.[128] Chapter Three of this report contains additional testimony about damage sustained in two daytime attacks in this crowded shopping area in February.

---

[128] MEW interview, Azraq Evacuee Center, Azraq, Jordan, February 13, 1991.

• 25 HOUSES DESTROYED IN MIDDLE-CLASS NEIGHBORHOOD DURING NIGHTTIME ATTACK; AT LEAST 11 KILLED: An Indian civil engineer told MEW about an incident in a residential neighborhood on February 3, the night before he left Basra for Jordan, that destroyed about 25 houses and damaged many others, killing at least four civilians.[129] His company's translator, an Iraqi, usually spent the night with the company's workers. But on the night of February 3 the translator wanted to return home to be with his wife and seven children. His home was in al-Hakimiyya, which he described as a one-kilometer-square residential neighborhood in the heart of Basra.

During the night, the translator's house was hit with a bomb. Half of the building collapsed, killing three grown sons and a daughter who was a schoolteacher. When the Indians heard what happened, they went to find their colleague. The engineer told MEW that he saw about 25 houses "collapsed" by the bombing and many others damaged. The homes in the neighborhood were middle-class, single-family buildings, multi-storied, of solid brick and stone construction with reinforced concrete roofs. The engineer said that the damage was so extensive that he believed more than one bomb had been dropped in this area.

He said he had no way of knowing the total number of civilian casualties from the attack because the authorities were quick to remove the injured and the dead. Sometimes, he said, they cordoned off an area for safety, fearful that if a site was bombed once it might be bombed again. The engineer found the translator, who was in his house when the bomb fell, but could not learn much from him because the man was dazed and in grief.

According to the engineer, the neighborhood itself had no visible military targets. He speculated that only two possible targets were nearby. The closest was an office building of the state-run South Oil Company (see below for descriptions of attacks on two South Oil Company office buildings in Basra). The other, an area of diesel storage tanks, was about a kilometer away.

---

[129] MEW interview, Azraq Evacuee Center, Azraq, Jordan, February 12, 1991.

In a separate interview with a group of Tunisian workers, MEW obtained a second brief account of a house in al-Hakimiyya neighborhood that was destroyed. The Tunisians found a woman in tears who worked in their hotel. When they asked her what was wrong she told them that her aunt, who lived in al-Hakimiyya, had been killed, along with six other members of the family, when their house was hit by a bomb while the aunt was baking bread in a wood stove. Her body was buried in the rubble and not removed; the army put dirt over the rubble the next day. The woman said that other houses were damaged in the attack but that her aunt's house sustained a direct hit. The Tunisians were not certain about the date of the incident, but it occurred prior to February 10, based on the date of their interview with MEW in Jordan.[130]

• ABOUT 60 HOMES DAMAGED IN SEVERAL ATTACKS IN AL-MA'QIL NEIGHBORHOOD: Some 60 single-family residential buildings were destroyed or damaged in al-Ma'qil neighborhood during bombing raids that occurred on several different days in late January, according to three Yemeni students interviewed by MEW.

The Yemeni students had lived in Basra and often traveled on the bus to school past al-Ma'qil. They described the area as a low-income community, its attached single-family houses constructed of cinderblock with zinc roofs. A major road traverses the perimeter of the neighborhood but its interior alleys are too small for cars. According to the students, there are no office buildings, TV towers, petrol fixtures or industrial plants in the vicinity.

The earlier bombing in January resulted in the destruction of about 10 houses. One of the students said he saw a woman, still bleeding in the left arm and chest, the next morning. The second bombing, on or about January 22, resulted in damage to about 40 houses and about 18 wounded men, women and children, according to another student who saw them. When they heard about this bombing, they went to see what happened; classes had been suspended when the air war started.

---

[130] MEW interview, Azraq Evacuee Center, Azraq, Jordan, February 28, 1991.

One student saw the aftermath of a bombing in the neighborhood on or about January 25. That night was cloudy, he remembered, because of the black smoke in the sky from distant fires. He passed by the next morning at 8 am and saw a group of 20 houses "flattened" -- the walls were not standing, there was only rubble. He said that the buildings were not of strong construction. The student saw a crater near the houses that was filled with water. People were crying, saying that "12 were killed in this house" and "all but two children were killed in this house." They were in a bus that slowed down but the driver would not stop because he was afraid that the site would be hit again. The following day, when the student passed the area again, people were still digging out the bodies with a front end loader. He did not know the total number of dead and injured.[131]

A Physicians for Human Rights representative who visited Basra on March 31 and April 1, saw five sites in al-Ma'qil where homes had been destroyed by allied bombing. In an attack on January 23 at 4:30 am, local residents said that 50 people were killed; seven others died when bombs fell on another section of the neighborhood the same night.

• EIGHT ADOBE HOUSES DESTROYED IN AL-ZUBAYR, SOUTH OF BASRA: A Sudanese truck driver, 28, who had lived in Iraq for two and a half years, told MEW that he saw eight houses completely destroyed and nearby houses damaged in al-Zubayr, a city about ten miles southeast of Basra. He put the date of the incident at 12 to 15 days after the war began. It occurred at about 3 am and he saw the damage the same morning.

He said the houses were rubble: "no walls, roofs, nothing." They were old adobe buildings -- attached single-family dwellings with zinc roofs, wood beams, most of them two stories high. The buildings were located on the main road; this driver had seen them many times before.

He saw four craters, each about three meters in diameter and two meters deep -- the craters were inside the houses and on the street in

---

[131] MEW interview, Azraq Evacuee Center, Azraq, Jordan, February 13, 1991.

front of the houses. He did not see any casualties but was told by others that eight civilians were killed and about 16 injured in the attack.

He said that there were no bridges or office buildings nearby and the houses were one to two km from the antiaircraft guns. He noted that a communications tower was about a kilometer away, and the post office was one to two km away. The same night the post office was bombed and destroyed; the tower next to the post office was also bombed but was still standing after the attack. The post office had been bombed before the houses were hit, and was attacked again after the bombs fell in al-Zubayr.[132]

After the war, a Physicians for Human Rights representative visited an old residential section in the center of al-Zubayr. He saw several completely destroyed homes around a large bomb crater. Residents reported that the attack occurred at 10:30 pm on January 18; 17 were killed and another 15 injured in ten houses, they said. Doctors in the town told PHR that approximately 200 civilians were killed and 300 to 400 injured during the air war.

• ONLY HOSPITAL IN AL-ZUBAYR DESTROYED: At least two journalists who visited al-Zubayr after the war noted that the 400-bed General Hospital was destroyed during the course of allied bombing. One noted that the small al-Baten clinic was the only medical facility currently serving the city of 150,000.[133] Another wrote that the clinic's "frail concrete structure is already teeming with people....500 mothers beseige the centre every day," bringing babies and children "for treatment of diarrhoea, typhoid and gastroenteritis -- the precursors of cholera."[134] A representative of PHR visited the clinic on April 1 and said it was the only one of five health centers in al-Zubayr that was functioning and the General Hospital was almost completely destroyed. A *New York Times*

---

[132] MEW interview, Azraq Evacuee Center, Azraq, Jordan, February 26, 1991.

[133] Saeeda Khanum, "Inside Iraq," *The New Statesman*, May 24, 1991.

[134] Ed Vulliamy, "Fear At The End of the Basra Road," *Weekend Guardian*, May 18-19, 1991.

correspondent, during a visit to Basra in July, wrote: "Ten miles away in Zubair, allied bombs struck the city's only hospital, medical officials here said, making it unusable."[135]

• MOSQUE DAMAGED: A journalist who traveled from Baghdad to Basra and spent the night of February 9 in the city. He told Middle East Watch that Basra that night "took a big pounding."[136] The next day he saw damage to an old mosque outside the city. He did not know when the mosque was damaged. The mosque, a clay-tile structure surrounded by a palm tree grove, is located about 200 meters from the warehouses at the edge of the Shatt al-'Arab waterway, which has been unusable since the beginning of the Iran-Iraq war in 1980 due to mines and sunken vessels. Part of the front wall of the mosque, and an inside wall, had been blown out by the blast from bombs that landed 50 to 100 meters from the building. The minaret was not damaged. Both bombs left craters four meters wide.

The mosque was 500 meters from the Pepsi Cola factory located in an industrial park -- see below for a description of this attack -- and the bomb craters were between the mosque and the Pepsi plant. The journalist said that there were no visible military targets in the vicinity of the mosque. A *Washington Post* correspondent who visited Basra in May wrote that the plant was "located close to a military fuel depot."[137]

• BOMBS MISS SMALL BRIDGE; HOSPITAL SUSTAINS DAMAGE AND SIX PATIENTS KILLED: Indian construction workers who had evacuated to Jordan told *The New York Times* before January 30 that bombs had hit a hospital in Basra.[138] Middle East Watch took an account of bombs

---

[135] Patrick E. Tyler, "Iraqi Hospitals Struggle With Wounds of War," *The New York Times*, July 5, 1991.

[136] MEW interview, New York, March 25, 1991.

[137] Jonathan C. Randal, "Battle-Scarred Basra Struggles Toward Recovery," *The Washington Post*, May 23, 1991.

[138] Alan Cowell, "War Refugees Flood Jordan, Telling of Raids and Extortion," *The New York Times*, Jan. 30, 1991.

that hit the General Teaching Hospital in Basra on or about January 26 from a group of eight Tunisian construction workers who lived together in a five-story hotel about 100 meters from the hospital. They left Basra on February 23; they had been living in the city for seven months.

The 435-bed hospital is a U-shaped yellow cement building of several stories, with an elongated bottom line. It backs on and is about 25 meters from al-Kornash street which runs along the Shatt al-Arab waterway. A bridge, perpendicular to al-Kornash street, is about 35 meters from the hospital. The bridge, for small cars and pedestrians, goes to Tenuma, a small town about 17 km from the Iranian border.

The Tunisians said that the hospital had a Red Crescent flag on top, on a pole, and a second banner about 30 meters square, white with a red crescent, on the side of the building facing some restaurants and bars perpendicular to the bridge. They had been inside the hospital before the bombing: "It was a general hospital, used by everyone." They said that there were no targets of a military nature other than the bridge nearby. There were no antiaircraft guns near the bridge because of the presence of the hospital.

Three bombs fell near the hospital at about 7:30 am on or about the tenth day of the war, the Tunisians told MEW. The first and the third bombs fell in the waterway near the hospital. The second bomb fell only a few meters from the rear of the hospital. The crater from this bomb was about five meters in diameter and was filled with water.[139]

One of the Tunisian workers went to the hospital from the hotel at about 8:30 am and helped move the injured from the second floor. (None of the other Tunisians interviewed went inside but they all saw the damage from the outside.) Several patients in the hospital were injured from shrapnel and broken glass. The blast had turned over some of the hospital beds and a few of the patients were on the floor. All the injured had been in the rear of the hospital. The Tunisian said that the nurses would go to a patient, see if he was still alive, then ask the volunteers to carefully push the hospital bed, with the patient in it, to another location.

---

[139] MEW interview, Azraq Evacuee Center, Azraq, Jordan, February 28, 1991.

They had to be careful with patients on intravenous, he said, and carefully hold the solution above the patients' heads. If the patient was dead, the nurse would cover the body with a blanket and leave it where it was.

He did not remember how many injured or dead he saw on the second floor. It was a hectic scene; there was blood on the floors and walls; when he finished working his clothes were covered with blood. He said he moved mechanically most of the time, and worked for several hours, until about noon.

The elevator was not working because of the lack of electricity but a generator was soon hooked up. There were so many patients to be moved that the elevator was very busy and sometimes they used the staircase to move people, a hard job, the Tunisian said. Patients were moved to the unaffected wings of the hospital, and some were taken to other facilities in Basra.

MEW was able to confirm part of the Tunisians' account with a British journalist who visited Basra and learned from the hospital's director that in late January a bomb hit the hospital and several patients were killed.[140]   Similar information was also provided by Physicians for Human Rights (PHR). In a meeting with a PHR representative on April 1, the hospital director said that the facility was damaged by a bomb on January 26 at 7:30 in the morning. The bomb left a large crater right next to one of the hospital's walls, according to PHR. Glass in the windows had shattered and parts of the ceiling in the intensive care unit (ICU) had collapsed. The hospital director told PHR that three patients in the ICU died when the ceiling fell on them and three others, including a young child, were killed from shrapnel and flying glass in other parts of the hospital. At the time of PHR's visit, the ICU was still not functioning and badly damaged equipment had not been removed. The hospital director said he assumed that the target was the nearby bridge over the Shatt al'Arab because this was not the first time that allied aircraft tried to bomb this bridge.

---

[140] MEW interview, London, May 7, 1991.

• SMALL BRIDGE MISSED AGAIN; RESTAURANTS AND BARS SUSTAIN DAMAGE: The day after the bombs fell near the hospital, the Tunisians said that a row of nearby restaurants and bars suffered damage in another failed attack on the bridge at approximately 8:30 at night. The restaurant row was about 150-200 meters long, consisting of about seven attached one-story buildings. The farthest building was about 200 meters from the bridge and the closest some 50 meters from the bridge, perpendicular to al-Shuhada street, which backed on an esplanade along the waterway.

Four bombs were dropped on the area, damaging the restaurants and bars. There were some Egyptian workers who used to sleep in the stores and the Tunisians did not know what happened to them. They heard that some civilians were injured and killed in the attack, but they did not know the numbers and did not see any of the bodies. They saw no craters and believe that the bombs landed directly on the buildings.[141]

The Tunisians told MEW that the following day -- at about 7:30 am and again at 6:30 pm -- the bridge was finally hit. One of the Tunisians was outdoors during the morning raid. He heard the planes coming and ran toward the door of his hotel, but the bridge was hit before he got inside. The power of the blast pushed him through the door and tore his leather jacket on the shoulder. (He showed the MEW representative the tear on the jacket, which he was wearing.) The next day they heard from soldiers that there had been three families on the bridge trying to leave Basra for the safer haven of Tenuma. When the bomb destroyed the bridge, the cars sank into the river and the passengers drowned, according to the soldiers.[142]

• 50 HOMES DAMAGED, TEN KILLED, AS BOMBS MISS TELECOMMUNICATIONS TOWER IN DAYTIME ATTACK: MEW took testimony about the inaccurate bombing of a telecommunications tower

---

[141] MEW interview, Azraq Evacuee Center, Azraq, Jordan, February 28, 1991.

[142] MEW interview, Azraq Evacuee Center, Azraq, Jordan, February 28, 1991.

that damaged dozens of houses in the Khamsamil residential area, a low-income quarter of one- and two-story houses about two to three km from downtown Basra. Several Indians live in the neighborhood and sell clothing and shoes. One of the Indian residents of Khamsamil saw planes come on January 18 or 19 after lunch; at least 10 people were found dead in the rubble of the houses. The Indians from the neighborhood told their Indian friends elsewhere in Basra of the raid, and an Indian plumber interviewed by MEW went to see the damage for himself several hours later.

He said that he saw over 50 houses damaged: "broken, all the concrete walls down, all glass in the houses broken."[143] He did not see any dead or injured since they had already been removed by the authorities. He told MEW that the area contains no military objects or army posts, but said that about 200 meters away was a TV or communications tower.

The plumber was employed by an Indian labor supply company to work as a foreman in the construction of large "palaces" -- as he described them -- for Iraqi government officials. These projects, numbering about a dozen, were halted when the war began. The plumber and other Indians employed by the company lived in the Snobar Hotel in Ashshar, the city center of Basra, four km from the TV tower and distant from the bridge and post office, all of which were bombed, he said. The city's electric plant had also been destroyed, stopping the flow of drinking water; Basra residents were drinking water from and bathing in the river, which was not clean, he said with a look of disgust. He left Basra for Jordan on January 28 with 19 other Indian employees of the company.

• CIVILIAN CASUALTIES AND DAMAGE FROM NIGHTTIME BOMBING OF RAILROAD STATION: There is a railroad station in the al-Moaka neighborhood of Basra, five km from the city center. Middle East Watch interviewed a former resident of Basra who lived several hundred meters from the station. He said that on the first day of the war, it was attacked and partially damaged. About 10 days later, the station was bombed again

---

[143] MEW interview, Azraq Evacuee Center, Azraq, Jordan, February 15, 1991.

and a nearby bank and four homes were damaged. The bank and the homes were on one side of Mahta Street and the railroad station was on the other side. The homes were one-story single-family buildings, each with a small yard around it.

On or about January 27, the witness heard an explosion at about 8 pm, followed by antiaircraft fire. The planes returned again after 10 or 15 minutes: there were two more explosions. After it seemed there was no more danger, the witness and his housemates went with their flashlights to see what happened, since the explosions had been so close by.

At the railroad station they saw a crater. Five ambulances were at the scene, and they saw medics removing the bodies of a woman and two children from a one-story house that had been reduced to rubble across the road from the station. The roof of the house had fallen in. Civil defense personnel came and moved the bystanders away -- they do not allow people to get too close to the rubble when there is a bombing, the witness said. He did not see a crater, only rubble of what had been the house. When he went to pay his condolences to the grieving families of the neighborhood, he learned that there had been 36 dead and injured.[144]

• SODA-BOTTLING PLANT DESTROYED: Tunisian construction workers who had lived in Basra for eight months told Middle East Watch that the city's Pepsi Cola bottling plant was bombed.[145] A journalist who visited Basra on February 9 and February 10 confirmed to Middle East Watch that the Pepsi plant -- located in an industrial park near the harbor area -- had been "completely destroyed."[146] He said that the building was made of metal sheeting, painted blue and white, and that the walls were "blown out, perhaps from the blast of the explosion." A

---

[144] MEW interview, Azraq Evacuee Center, Azraq, Jordan, February 16, 1991.

[145] MEW interview, Azraq Evacuee Center, Azraq, Jordan, February 28, 1991.

[146] MEW interview, New York, March 25, 1991.

Washington Post correspondent who visited Basra in May wrote that the plant was "located close to a military fuel depot."[147]

• REPORTS OF ATTACKS ON OIL-INDUSTRY ADMINISTRATIVE BUILDINGS: Middle East Watch took two separate accounts about the apparently inaccurate bombing of office buildings of the South Oil Company in Basra. The company operates the southern oilfields of Iraq that account for two of every three barrels that Iraq produced, according to *The Wall Street Journal.*[148] A Yemeni student, 26, who left Basra on February 9, told MEW of the bombing of an administrative office of the South Oil Company located on Malek Ben Dinar Street, on the road going to Ashshar in downtown.[149] He said that a sign outside the three-story building read: General Management, South Oil Company. The building is surrounded by a fence one meter high and there is a gatehouse for a guard at the entrance. The gatehouse was totally destroyed in the attack but the main building was not directly hit. The student said that the building only had offices -- there was no equipment or operating stations on the site. He said the windows of the homes across the street from the building were shattered from the blast.

In a separate interview, MEW learned of a nighttime attack on the Hakimiyya neighborhood in the heart of Basra on February 3, which collapsed about 25 houses and killed at least four civilians (see above). An Indian civil engineer who saw the damage from the attack thought that the target might have been an administrative office of the South Oil Company, which was located about 60 meters across the road from the houses that were destroyed. He said that he had passed the building often -- it was large, four stories, situated in an open compound without a fence. There were no oil facilities on the site. The engineer said that the building was not marked in a military fashion and had a sign with the

---

[147] Jonathan C. Randal, "Battle-Scarred Basra Struggles Toward Recovery," *The Washington Post*, May 23, 1991.

[148] James Tanner, "Iraq is Fast Rebuilding Its Ravaged Oil Trade Into a World Leader," January 8, 1990.

[149] MEW interview, Azraq Evacuee Center, Azraq, Jordan, February 16, 1991.

name: South Oil Company. "From the outside, it looked like just another office building," he told MEW. He said that the building did have guards, but added that every state building in Iraq is guarded, from banks on down. The building had no checkpost -- anyone visiting could go inside to the reception area without being stopped. He said he thought that this building was the likely target when the houses across the street were attacked because he knew that another South Oil Company office building -- several kilometers away -- had been attacked on January 28 or January 29.

During the war, coalition forces attacked Iraqi oil refineries and major oil storage facilities. At a briefing on January 18, Gen. Schwarzkopf was asked to confirm that Iraqi oil refineries and petroleum storage depots were military targets as such. He did not directly answer the question, but replied as follows:

> Let me tell you that we have consistently, all along, made it a point of not going against targets that were not of a military nature or would not contribute to the military effort. So any targets that we hit along those lines would be targets that we feel would contribute to the military effort, and not just simply done for the sake of destroying something.[150]

Gen. Schwarzkopf was equally evasive at a briefing on January 27 when a reporter noted reports that between 50 and 60 percent of Iraq's refinery and oil storage capacity had been destroyed and asked if these were priority targets. The general's brief reply was: "If it's a military target, it's very high on our list of priorities."[151] Several days later on January 30, a journalist asked Gen. Schwarzkopf to comment on oil-industry reports that 50 to 90 percent of Iraq's refined petroleum located near oil refineries and electrical generating plants had been destroyed. The general again refused to provide detailed information, limiting his response to the following:

---

[150] Pyle at 178.

[151] Pyle at 205.

> I told you, we went after militarily significant targets.
> We didn't want to destroy their oil industry, but we
> certainly wanted to make sure they didn't have a lot of
> gasoline for their military vehicles.[152]

The allied attacks on the two South Oil Company office buildings in Basra raise questions about the appropriateness of these buildings as military objectives in the circumstances prevailing at the time of the attacks. Although theoretically in a position to contribute to military action as management operations for Iraq's oil industry, allied attacks on refineries and other production and storage facilities -- combined with the crippling of sources of electrical power and all communications -- would appear to have left oil-industry managers with little to administer and no effective means of administration. Thus the role of these administrative facilities and their personnel in assisting Iraq's military effort would not seem to make the "effective contribution to military action" required by the U.S. Air Force rules and customary international law. In addition, it must be noted that although it is permissible to attack the production of export items whose earnings are vital to finance an enemy's war effort, Iraq was not able to generate export earnings from its petroleum industry since August due to the Security Council-imposed sanctions on all trade with Iraq and occupied Kuwait.

* * *

It is not yet known how many civilians were killed or injured in the allied attacks on Basra. The Iraqi government daily newspaper *Al-Thawra* reported on February 6 that 349 people had been killed in the city.[153] Middle East Watch is unaware of additional statistics released since that time.

---

[152] Pyle at 225.

[153] Rick Atkinson, "Gulf Ground War Not Felt Imminent," February 7, 1991.

OTHER CITIES AND TOWNS IN SOUTHERN IRAQ

Continuing the pattern that Middle East Watch found in Iraq's two largest cities, former residents of communities that stretch south along the Euphrates River from Baghdad did not report widespread or systematic destruction of civilian areas that would be suggestive of a policy of indiscriminate bombing. But civilians living between Baghdad and Basra paid a price during the allies' not-so-perfect air war.

A Shi'a cleric who witnessed some of the allied bombing in the holy city of Najaf told MEW that the city was first bombed on the night of January 21. He said that the allies aimed at, but missed, a telecommunications tower (see below). He also described a sequence of events that would not be unfamiliar to residents of other cities of Iraq during the air war. The power station was attacked during the same week, depriving civilians of electricity, water and sewage removal facilities. Civilians "had to manage without electricity," while government buildings were supplied with standby generators, he said. Sanctions had affected food supplies four months before the air war started, and "the people were not prepared -- there were no stockpiles of food."[154]

Civilian Casualties and Damage

Middle East Watch collected testimony from former residents of Iraq, as well as additional information, about incidents of civilian casualties and damage in southern Iraq, described below; two of these accounts concern civilian casualties and damage from cluster bombs dropped by allied forces. Additional testimony is included in Chapter Three, concerning civilian casualties and damage in southern Iraq from daytime attacks on bridges in Nasiriyya and Samawa, an apparel factory and a cooking-gas distribution site in Hilla, and a market area in al-Kut.

• 20 HOUSES DESTROYED IN AN AGRICULTURAL VILLAGE: An Egyptian interviewed by MEW said that a group of about 20 attached single-family homes had been bombed in al-Haswa, a village 3 km east of Iskanderiyya, south of Baghdad on the Baghdad-Hilla highway. The man, an employee of the Iraqi Ministry of Health who lived in Iskanderiyya, saw the craters after the bombing, which he said took place

---

[154] MEW interview, May 7, 1991, London.

in late January or early February. He was familiar with these houses and said they were simple residential buildings. The area itself was agricultural, he said, about 10 km from the Euphrates River; most of al-Haswa's residents were farmers.

There was no bridge in the village, no tower, no high buildings -- nothing. "This is indiscriminate bombing, they have no [military] targets. They just want to unload their bombs," the Egyptian charged.[155] What impressed him most was the sight of civil defense personnel removing the dead from the rubble, including a woman with a baby in her arms. "It was a scene I will never forget," he said.

Journalists who visited al-Haswa and interviewed residents provided additional details about the attack. One correspondent speculated that the target may have been a road some 150 yards from the houses:

> The next stop is in al-Haswa. . . The attack took place on the night of January 23 and has left in the mud three craters, each more than 30 yards in diameter and 10 yards deep. The bombs, which have damaged houses, were presumably aimed at the motorway 150 yards away.
>
> "Under there," murmurs Faisa Ibrahim, gesturing towards the dirty water, "there are still people buried."[156]

A 31-year-old teacher from al-Haswa personally saw five people killed from bombing in the village; her own house had been heavily damaged and several family members injured.[157]

---

[155] MEW interview, Aqaba Transit Center, Azraq, Jordan, February 21, 1991.

[156] Alfonso Rojo, "Press corps stocks up for guided tour of death and destruction," *The Guardian*, February 4, 1991.

[157] Fred Bruning, "In Iraq, 'No Place to Hide,'" *Newsday*, February 4, 1991.

Another journalist reported that several dozen residents of al-Haswa had been killed:

> In the nearby village of Haswa, a crater about 50 yards in diameter marked the impact of what appeared to have been 1,000 pound bombs in an area of one-story houses surrounded by low walls....residents gave varying casualty figures, with 35 to 40 dead frequently mentioned....[158]

• 36 HOUSES DESTROYED OR DAMAGED IN NIGHTTIME ATTACK: The Egyptian who provided MEW with the account of the bombing in al-Haswa, noted above, also saw damage to a group of 36 houses in Iskanderiyya during nighttime bombing of the area. The Egyptian had lived for 10 years in Musayyeb, a city about 12 km southwest of Iskanderiyya. He said the bombing, which occurred between 11:20 pm and 5 am on February 16 or 17, was "very savage."

The Egyptian visited the site the next morning. Some of the houses were damaged but still standing; others, where the rockets fell, were destroyed. He knew this area well, and emphasized that it was a residential area of one- and two-story detached single family homes.[159] He was told that about 50 civilians had been killed. He saw limbs of some of the dead that had not yet been removed: arms and heads. He also saw four or five craters filled with water -- the craters were about 10 meters apart and about five meters in diameter.

He told MEW that Iskanderiyya was about 10 km from the nearest military site he knew of. That military site was also hit and soldiers killed, he heard, but he did not know if the military site was hit on that night or another, since there were raids almost every night. (A conventional weapons plant was located near Iskandariyya, according to

---

[158] Bernd Debusmann, Reuters, "No Havens, Says Resident Of Baghdad," *The Washington Post*, February 4, 1991.

[159] MEW interview, Aqaba Transit Center, Aqaba, Jordan, February 21, 1991.

The New York Times; this may have been the "military site" to which the Egyptian referred.[160])

The Egyptian left Iraq for safety reasons on February 19 with his wife, daughter and two sons. "The bombing was getting too close," he said.

• THREE HOUSES DESTROYED IN AN AGRICULTURAL VILLAGE: Three one-story one-family houses on the main road in Hamya, a residential village, were destroyed in a nighttime attack on or about February 10. MEW learned of the incident from an Egyptian who rebuilds electric motors and lived since 1981 in Musayyeb. Hamya is located about three km from Musayyeb. The Egyptian saw the damage the next morning. Three homes on the main road of the village had been hit; the Egyptian had seen these buildings before.

He saw a crater in the middle of one house; the houses on either side had some walls still standing. The crater was about three meters across and two meters deep. He did not know the total number of casualties, but he saw four bodies being removed from the debris.[161] One was an old man with a beard; the others were badly burned, he said. The village was located in an agricultural area and had "nothing important" -- not even an office building or a factory, according to the Egyptian.

• TWO-STORY MEDICAL CLINIC DESTROYED: A Sudanese resident of Hilla told Middle East Watch of the damage he saw to a small yellow two-story clinic in the Bakari neighborhood in the center of Hilla the day after it was bombed. The columns and foundations of the clinic were still standing, but not much else. He said he did not see any craters and did not know if anyone was killed or injured in the attack, adding that the clinic did not keep patients overnight.

---

[160] "Iraq: Targets for U.S.," *The New York Times*, November 19, 1990.

[161] MEW interview, Aqaba Transit Center, Aqaba, Jordan, February 21, 1991.

He said that the windows and doors of nearby houses also were damaged in the attack. There were only residential buildings in this area, he said -- no military structures, no post office, no bridge, nothing. A tower, located about three km away, also was bombed that night, he told Middle East Watch.[162]

In a separate interview, two Pakistanis, an electrician and a welder, told MEW of seeing damage to a "hospital" in Hilla that was for "delivery cases, ladies and children." The men lived in Najaf and they said they frequently visited Hilla on the day of rest, Friday. They saw the damage two or three days after the bombing. The building, which they had seen many times during their visits to Hilla, was about three stories, located in the center of the city, near a shopping center. There were no military installations, bridges, factories or communications towers nearby. They said that the post office, the nearest government building, was about two km away, and an army training base was located outside the city. They also noted that a school near the "hospital" also was damaged.[163]

Journalists brought to the site by the Iraqi authorities wrote about the attack on the clinic, confirming aspects of the account taken by Middle East Watch. One dispatch appeared in *The Washington Post*:

> In Hillah, correspondents were taken to a residential area hard hit by allied bombs as well as a secondary school and a clinic in the city center. Blackboards in the school and sheets of medical reports in the clinic left no doubt for this reporter that these buildings were as billed.[164]

---

[162] MEW interview, Azraq Evacuee Center, Azraq, Jordan, February 25, 1991.

[163] MEW interview, Azraq Evacuee Center, Azraq, Jordan, February 18, 1991.

[164] Bernd Debusmann, Reuters, "No Havens, Says Resident Of Baghdad," *The Washington Post*, February 4, 1991.

Another report appeared in *The Guardian*:

> Here [in Hilla] they show us a clinic and a secondary
> school, both hit by a missile in the early hours of January
> 18. "No one died because the attack was at night and
> both places were empty," explains Hassan Rasac, a 35-
> year-old teacher. "Bush wants to frighten us."[165]

• THREE RESIDENTIAL BUILDINGS DESTROYED: Three three-story
residential buildings were destroyed in al-Kufa, according to a 42-year-old
Kashmiri carpenter. He was one of 10 Kashmiris interviewed by MEW in
a group of 113 Pakistani construction workers who lived in a workers'
compound in nearby Kifl. The carpenter said the incident took place five
or six days after the start of the war, on or about January 23; al-Kufa is
located about 12-15 km northeast of Najaf and 20 to 25 km south of Kifl.

The Kashmiri was helping a driver take water from their
purification plant to civilians. He saw three residential buildings, each
three stories high, that had been totally destroyed by a bomb:
"Everything is going to out, there is no wall stay on the buildings," he
said in broken English.

Three families lived in one of the houses. He could not get closer
because the police had cordoned off the area. He saw an ambulance, and
said that many "ladies and small children" were killed. He said bystanders
told him that 104 people were killed in the three buildings. The houses
were located one kilometer from a bridge and the post office, which were
not damaged in the attack.[166]

• TWO-STORY HOUSE DESTROYED AS BOMB MISSES BRIDGE BY 500
METERS: A Pakistani worker interviewed by MEW saw a house in Kifl
hit by a bomb as he was traveling at about 2 pm on or about January 20

---

[165] Alfonso Rojo, "Press corps stocks up for guided tour of death and
destruction," *The Guardian*, February 4, 1991.

[166] MEW interview, Azraq Evacuee Center, Azraq, Jordan, February 18,
1991.

on a company road that leads north to Karbala. Kifl, a town on the east bank of the Euphrates River, is south of Hilla. The Pakistani heard one explosion but did not see a plane. He stopped his truck and ran to the house.

The house, a two-story building that the Pakistani had passed often, was located about 100 meters from a primary school. The school was not damaged, but the house was totally destroyed -- "all finished," the Pakistani said. The parents were working in the fields but two children were inside when the bomb hit the building. Only pieces of one child could be found after the attack; the other, 12 years old, was injured. "All people crying," the worker said of the scene as the relatives ran to the house, which caught fire after the bombing. The fire brigade and police arrived to put out the fire while he was there.

The eyewitness was one of a group of 113 Pakistanis who had been working in Iraq for two years on the construction of a tire-production factory near Najaf, 130 km southwest of Baghdad. The workers lived in a compound close to Kifl, a village about 35 km from Najaf.

The house was about 500 meters from the water purification plant built on the Euphrates in Kifl about six months before by the Pakistani workers for their own use; the house was about 250-300 meters from a minor road built for their construction company. Near the plant was a bridge over the river which could be used by large trucks. Other than the bridge, there were no military objects near the house, which was separated by 20 meters from the other houses whose windows were shattered. The bridge was not damaged in the attack and was still standing when the Pakistanis left for Jordan on February 15.[167]

• BOMB MISSES BRIDGE BY 500 METERS, FALLS IN RESIDENTIAL QUARTER, SIX KILLED: A Sudanese driver, 31, who lived in southern Iraq for five years and hauled gravel, told MEW of a bomb that fell at 8 pm on or about February 7, killing six of his neighbors. He lived in a

---

[167] MEW interview, Azraq Evacuee Center, Azraq, Jordan, February 18, 1991.

small community about 45 kilometers north of Basra on the Basra-Baghdad highway.

The explosion was so close it "damaged my ears" -- he said he could not hear immediately after but that his hearing shortly returned. The one-story concrete house he lived in with seven other Sudanese drivers had shrapnel all over it, including on the roof. The glass in the windows shattered. He and his housemates went out as soon as it was clear, and saw that their Iraqi neighbor's home had been totally destroyed. The house was 50 meters from their own, and about 150 meters from the river.

The Sudanese saw the bodies of his neighbors, whom he knew personally. There were 10 people in the house. Six were killed outright, two were injured, and two escaped injury. One of the two injured lost a leg and died two days later in the hospital. The other lost a hand. The house was totally destroyed. He did not see a crater.

Other houses in the neighborhood were damaged but he did not hear of other civilians injured or killed. Close to another house, a cow was killed. He did not see a crater. He said that a bridge was about 500 meters away, but that there were no factories, government buildings, offices or towers in this community of about 150 houses.

• BRIDGE MISSED AGAIN, ONE KILLED: The next night there were two more raids in the area, the Sudanese driver who provided the testimony above told MEW. In the first, some cows were killed, he was told. In the second, a few hundred meters away from where the cows were killed and immediately after the first attack, a young man was killed when a rocket fell close to his family's house. Six family members were sleeping inside the house, but only the son was killed, according to the father, to whom the Sudanese talked the next day when they saw the damage to the side of the house and to a pickup truck that was parked nearby. The house was next to the road. This man said he no longer felt safe and left with friends for Baghdad the same day, en route to Jordan and then home.[168]

---

[168] MEW interview, Azraq Evacuee Center, Azraq, Jordan, February 18, 1991.

• HEALTH CLINIC AND SEVERAL HOUSES DESTROYED IN BOMBING OF BRIDGES: A journalist who visited Nasiriyya, on the Euphrates River, during the uprising there in early March reported that several houses and a health clinic near two of the city's bridges "were reduced to rubble".[169] He said that two of the three bridges in the city were destroyed, and a third modern concrete bridge was damaged (see Chapter Three). He also reported that toward the end of the war ("eight days ago" -- the story had no dateline) "bombs fell in the market, killing 20 and injuring 57."

• BOMB MISSES TELECOMMUNICATIONS TOWER; AT LEAST 20 KILLED IN TWO-STORY HOUSE: Middle East Watch obtained three accounts of the inaccurate bombing of a telecommunications tower in the city of Najaf in the first week of the war that resulted in the destruction of residential buildings and the loss of civilian life. A Pakistani construction worker who lived near Najaf told MEW that several days after the start of the war civilians were killed during a nighttime attack. He and his housemates heard two explosions and they went out together to look at what had been hit. They saw a two-story house with the top story severely damaged and collapsed on the lower story. Najaf is a very old city, he said, and people build attached houses, on their neighbors' walls. He was told that 20 people asleep in the house were killed, all members of the same family. Others were injured. The windows of nearby houses had shattered.

They did not see the inside of the house because the police and fire brigade had arrived and did not permit civilians to help or get in the way. The worker told MEW that the bombs fell 10 km from Kufa, where there is a bridge that was bombed after this attack. He noted that Najaf and Karbala are holy places for Shia Muslims and that no military encampments are located in these cities. The house where the family was killed was two km from the holy shrines, he said.[170]

---

[169] Richard Dowden, "Iraqi revolution in chaos," *The Independent*, March 7, 1991.

[170] MEW interview, Azraq Evacuee Center, Azraq, Jordan, February 18, 1991.

Reuters reported from Iraq that local residents said 12 bombs were dropped in a residential area of the city, apparently aimed at but missing a telecommunications tower.[171] The residents said the attack took place on January 20 and that 50 houses were hit, killing at least 20 civilians. The Reuters correspondent who visited the site saw "several houses that had received direct hits."   A U.S. visitor to Iraq in May saw evidence that bombs fell in this residential area. "I saw four big craters next to each other, in a line, each about eight feet by 12 feet," she said.[172] It was difficult to tell how many houses had been destroyed in the attack, because rebuilding was in progress during her visit. One resident told her he was "the luckiest man in Iraq." He showed her where one bomb had landed in the front of his house and a second in the back yard; the house itself remained standing.

Middle East Watch interviewed an Iraqi Shi'a cleric who was in Najaf on the night the allies first bombed the city. He said he believed that the attack on the residential area described above was not deliberate, but that a telephone exchange tower was the likely military objective. He said that the attack occurred at approximately 9 pm, and residents were in their houses because there were no shelters in Najaf. Bombs fell in the al-Amir residential district of the city, aiming for the telephone exchange tower and the power station. The power station was hit later the same week, he told MEW. There were no Iraqi military units stationed in Najaf and no military industries, according to the cleric, but there were cement, brick and tire factories in the area.[173]

A resident of Najaf who fled to Iran told MEW that there was extensive damage from allied bombing in two civilian areas of the city: al-Amir and Mutanabi, killing 60 and injuring 200. "We think they were hit either by mistake or by Saddam for propaganda value," he said.[174]

---

[171] "Baghdad Jolted by Waves of B-52 Attacks," *The New York Times*, February 5, 1991.

[172] MEW interview with Frances Farenthold, New York, June 6, 1991.

[173] MEW interview, London, May 7, 1991.

[174] MEW interview, Qom, Iran, May 3, 1991.

• TELECOMMUNICATIONS TOWER MISSED; 11 KILLED WHEN HOTEL IS DESTROYED: On February 2, CNN aired footage from Diwaniyya of what appeared to be bombed apartment houses and shops, with no apparent signs of any military targets.[175] A journalist who visited the city with Iraqi officials indicated in his dispatch that the civilian objects were near a telecommunications center:

> "Why did they do that?" asked Saeed Haber, a middle-aged trader, near the ruins of the al-Yarmuk Hotel in Diwaniyeh, 110 miles south of Baghdad.
>
> "This hotel had no military people in it," said Haber, who ... spoke to reporters taking government tours of hard-hit civilian areas. "Neither had my shop next to it. Bush says his planes are hitting only military targets. He is lying."
>
> Local officials say the al-Yarmuk was among many non-military facilities -- small shops and kebab restaurants -- ravaged during three recent bombing raids. All were near a telecommunications center, ostensibly the focus of allied attacks.
>
> In the al-Yarmuk bombing, 11 people died and 49 were hurt, according to manager Saeed Ahmed Mohammed, a 46-year-old Egyptian.[176]

• CIVILIAN CASUALTIES IN BOMBING OF BUS STATION IN HILLA: About three weeks after the beginning of the war, on or about February 7, a bus station in the center of Hilla was bombed at night. A former resident interviewed by MEW saw six cars in the garage that were badly damaged as well as stalls in a nearby market. He heard that civilians were killed and injured in the attack but did not personally see any casualties. He said that there were electric generators 600 km from the garage but

---

[175] R. Jeffrey Smith, "U.S. Military Pressed About Civilian Casualties," *The Washington Post*, February 3, 1991.

[176] Fred Bruning, "In Iraq, 'No Place to Hide,'" *Newsday*, February 4, 1991.

that these were not the principal ones for the city and were not bombed. He also said there was an army service office about 70-75 meters from the station. The post office and tower were one km from the bus station.[177] Iranian refugees interviewed separately by MEW confirmed aspects of this account. They had lived nearby in Shomeli camp and saw the Hilla bus station two to three days after it was bombed. They saw many damaged and burned cars, as well as some damaged stores.[178]

• CIVILIAN CASUALTIES AND DAMAGE IN SAMAWA FROM CLUSTER BOMBS[179]: A Sudanese truck driver told MEW about what he thought were delayed-action bombs that were dropped in his neighborhood, Ashudhada, on or about February 7, at 4:00 in the afternoon. He said that a rocket landed in the yard of a home and that the blast reduced the cinderblock structure to rubble. The house was about one kilometer away from where he lived with seven other Sudanese.[180]

He said that first he heard an air raid siren, followed by the explosion. Then, after 20 minutes, he heard a series of small explosions, like gunfire, that lasted for a half-hour. He stayed indoors until the explosions stopped. When he and his housemates went outside, they saw a small green metal device in the yard, about 10 meters from the house. It was the size of a metal Spam can (the Sudanese reached for a nearby Spam can to indicate the size of the device). The device had no wires or protrusions on it: "When you looked at it, you would not think it was an explosive." Suddenly it detonated in a small explosion similar to those he had heard while indoors, and created a small crater one foot wide and about 18 inches deep.

---

[177] MEW interview, Azraq Evacuee Center, Azraq, Jordan, February 25, 1991.

[178] MEW interview, Azraq Evacuee Center, Azraq, Jordan, March 1, 1991.

[179] See footnote 149 in Chapter Four.

[180] MEW interview, Azraq Evacuee Center, Azraq, Jordan, February 15, 1991.

The neighborhood is totally residential, the witness said. Its cinderblock single-family homes are one or two stories high. It has no government buildings, military installations or communications facilities. He added that this was not the first time that the residents of Samawa saw this type of bomb. Other bombs fell in the Ashuhada neighborhood and other residential areas since the start of the war. Some of the small bombs were yellow and some green. "They exploded near houses, even if no one approached," he told MEW, indicating that the bomblets were on delayed-action fuses. He was unaware of any civilian casualties from these devices.

In a separate interview, another former resident of Samawa said that on or about February 14 two rockets fell on either side of a crossroads about 15 kilometers north of the city.[181] The crossroads, known as Takata al-Warqar, is where the main road north to Diwaniyya intersects other small roads, including one that leads to historic ruins.

The witness told MEW that he had traveled to the crossroads to pick up his car, which he had left there the day before. He said he found that the area had been bombed -- he saw many small army-green-colored bombs, perhaps 50, in different places alongside the road. He said the bombs were circular on top, but that the bottom halves were not visible because they were buried in the mud. He did not realize these were bomblets, however, until he saw a rocket of the same green color -- with the letter "F" in black and "danger" in English -- that had opened in two parts. The second part of the rocket was far from where he was, on the other side of the crossroads. He saw no crater from the rocket itself. After he noticed the rocket casing, he did not move closer than two meters to the bombs because he was afraid. He carefully left the area -- he had been told that people had been killed by small bombs like these that exploded after one or two hours or after one or two days. He told MEW that the devices did not explode while he was at the crossroads.

A Bedouin family of his acquaintance lived in an adobe house near the crossroads and he believed they were killed or injured by the bomblets. He saw their pick-up truck, its exterior damaged from

---

[181] MEW interview, Azraq Evacuee Center, Azraq, Jordan, February 25, 1991.

shrapnel. The inside of the truck was destroyed; he saw blood on the inside walls; shoes and clothes were scattered around the vehicle. He did not see any bodies. The pickup was about five meters away from where he saw one of the rocket casings. He insisted that there was nothing of military significance near the site. Two to three meters from the crossroads was a small area where vans and other vehicles picked up passengers. There were no buildings at the pick-up point.

He also heard from a fellow worker that a family from the al-Baath neighborhood in Samawa, which is near a high steel bridge, said that similar small bombs had fallen in the garden of their home. The family, fearful that the bombs might explode, warned the worker away from the garden. He told Middle East Watch that the steel bridge -- the largest of three in Samawa -- had been bombed four times and had not collapsed, but a large crater in the middle of the span prevented vehicles from using it.

CITIES AND TOWNS IN WESTERN AND NORTHERN IRAQ

This section contains accounts of incidents that caused civilian casualties and damage in cities, villages and towns to the west and north of Baghdad. Middle East Watch collected eyewitness testimony about the inaccurate bombing on February 14 of the bridge in Falluja, west of Baghdad, which the Iraqi authorities initially said killed 130 civilians and injured 78; these accounts are included in Chapter Three. MEW also obtained testimony about a series of attacks in Rutba, the largest town in the far west of Iraq near the sites from which missiles were launched into Israel. In one incident in Rutbah, civilians were strafed and killed in the early evening by a low-flying airplane.

Civilian Casualties and Damage in Rutba

Middle East Watch collected testimony about civilian casualties and damage on four different occasions in February in Rutba, a town in western Iraq. The objects damaged included three residential buildings, a one-story school and a seven-story hotel. In addition, eyewitnesses interviewed by MEW claimed that allied aircraft machine-gunned civilians in the early evening on February 14, killing a bride and other members of her wedding party.

• BOMB HITS HOUSE IN EARLY EVENING, KILLING FIVE: On February 20, at about 7:00 in the evening, a bomb fell on a residential building in Rutba, killing four Iraqi civilians, according to a Sudanese family interviewed by MEW. The family was in their home when a bomb fell on their neighbor's house, located 75 meters from their own. There was no air raid shelter in Rutba, so residents stayed in their homes at night.

After they felt the danger had passed, they went to see what had happened to their neighbors, who were friends. They saw two houses, both of concrete construction, that were damaged. In the first house, a one-story residence, a woman and her three daughters, one of them married and pregnant, had been killed -- "all that remained of the house was the gate." They did not see the bodies of the dead women because they were covered with black plastic. The father was injured. In the second house, shrapnel from the bomb hit the water tank over the three-story structure, causing it to collapse on the building, killing the father who was on the third floor at the time. Four cars parked outside the first house were totally destroyed. There was one bomb crater next to the house, about three to four meters across and nine meters deep.

Antiaircraft guns were about two to three km away, they told MEW. There were no government buildings, bridges or military installations in the vicinity of the houses. There was a gas station about a half-kilometer away. "This is a civilian area for poor people," one of them told MEW. Two days after this attack, the family left for Jordan.[182]

• AIRPLANE OPENS FIRE, KILLING MEMBERS OF WEDDING PARTY: On February 14 at about 6:00 pm, two Sudanese sisters were on the roof of their relative's one-story house in Rutba watching a wedding party in progress a block away. As the bride arrived in a car with her female relatives, the men, who were outside the house in the garden, shot off their guns in the air in traditional celebration. The women watched as a plane, black with yellow on the front, dove down and began to shoot.

---

[182] MEW interview, Azraq Evacuee Center, Azraq, Jordan, February 25, 1991.

They hit the ground. They heard the plane return several times, shooting at the wedding party each time.

The next day, the women took a sick child to the hospital and saw many wounded people from the wedding party. They saw some children who had been injured in the stomach; the nurses had put gauze over the wounds to stop the bleeding. They were told by the injured that the bride and her female relatives were killed and that others who were inside the house were injured. The men outside in the garden also were killed.[183]

• BOMB HITS HOUSE IN MIDNIGHT ATTACK, INJURED FAMILY OF 14 SURVIVES: The Sudanese mother of five children and her 13-year-old son told MEW of the bombing of a three-story house next door and seven meters from theirs in Rutba, where they had lived for five years. The neighbor's home, which housed a family of 14 people, was completely destroyed in an attack that took place on or about February 13, at midnight. The Sudanese family's house was damaged in the raid, and three cars parked in front of the neighbor's house were badly damaged. The houses were in a residential area of Rutba, close to the main road.

Three planes flew over the houses and dropped a bomb which landed on the neighbor's house. The Sudanese boy saw the crater inside the rubble of the house, which he said was "very big" -- he estimated it was 20 meters across. "Even water came to the surface of the ground," filling the crater, he said. His mother said she had been too scared to go look.

At the time of the bombing, the family had been on the first floor. The bomb fell on the roof, and the second and third floors collapsed onto the first floor. Since the walls fell on many family members, debris had to be removed to find them. No one was killed, but eight family members were injured, some severely. A son, 22, lost both arms. The 13 year old son, a schoolmate of the Sudanese witness, lost a leg. Some of the girls, ages eight, 15, 17 and 18, were burned in the faces and heads. The father was injured in his left arm; the mother was injured

---

[183] MEW interview, Azraq Evacuee Center, Azraq, Jordan, February 25, 1991.

in her legs and arms. The police came and took the injured to the hospital.

The witnesses were not certain about the possible military targets in the area. They said that they could see a radio tower from their home, at a distance. It was bombed several times, before and after the night of the attack, but was not hit that night. The tower was finally knocked down two days after the house was bombed. They told MEW that they had heard that there was "something military" in the area to protect it, but they never saw it and did not know where it was.

The woman said that she did not venture out much during the war. She had seen "many, many people" being carried in traditional fashion on the shoulders of their relatives in numerous funeral processions. She said there were "too many" civilians killed and injured in Rutba. She had heard that some civilians were killed near the radio tower but she did not know where others had been killed.[184]

• SCHOOL COMPLETELY DESTROYED, HOTEL DAMAGED, AT LEAST THREE CIVILIANS KILLED: A Sudanese family told MEW that on February 17 the tower on top of the four-story post office in Rutba was bombed and collapsed. The next day, it was hit again and completely destroyed. This Sudanese family saw it burning the next day. When the post office was hit, the windows and doors of nearby houses were damaged.

The post office and the hospital were on one side of the main street about 20 meters apart. On the other side of the main street was the market, a school (one of five in the city), and a hotel. The market, post office and hospital were the only ones in Rutba; there is also a small clinic.

The school, a one-story cinderblock building, had about six classrooms and three offices. The school was attacked by allied aircraft on February 19: one rocket exploded and three did not. The school was completely damaged in the attack, its roof and most of the walls

---

[184] MEW interview, Azraq Evacuee Center, Azraq, Jordan, February 28, 1991.

collapsed. The army detonated the unexploded bombs in the school. After two to three days, there was still smoke and fire in the school, and a bad smell, causing residents headaches and watery eyes.

The seven-story cinderblock hotel was between the school and the main street; people of many nationalities lived there, including Sudanese and Egyptians. The hotel was damaged on the same night as the school; "it looked collapsed," one Sudanese told MEW. They believed that a bomb fell on the roof of the hotel at 2 am when it was full of people. One of their relatives was injured in this hotel; his leg was amputated below the knee and he was badly burned on one side. At the time the Sudanese left for Jordan, their relative was still in a hospital in Baghdad. They knew of three other Sudanese who were killed in the hotel, but they did not know how many others. They were told there were "many dead" from this attack.[185]

23 Houses in Agricultural Area Hit with Bombs in Two Separate Attacks, No Survivors

A Sudanese man who lived in Ramadi, a city west of Baghdad, told MEW that in early February a group of eight one-story homes in an agricultural area about 3 km from his own home were bombed at night. He heard "lots of explosions" and saw the damage the next morning. He saw several craters, including one in the middle of one of the houses. He was told that everyone in the houses was killed. He said that there was nothing military anywhere in the area, and that antiaircraft guns were far away.

The same man said that about 15 attached, two-story cinderblock houses were hit at 4:00 in the afternoon on a clear day in early February. He was in the market when the bombs fell. He did not see the planes but heard them after the bombing. He went to look at the damage immediately after the attack. The area was two km from the market in the al-Malab neighborhood, on al-Eskan Street. He saw an ambulance taking the bodies of 15 men, women and children. People at the scene said there were no survivors and that 17 people had been killed. There was no military emplacement in the area, no antiaircraft. There were

---

[185] MEW interview, Azraq Evacuee Center, Azraq, Jordan, February 25, 1991.

railroad tracks some two km away, which were bombed four days later. Nothing else was bombed on this afternoon.[186]

Reports from Northern Iraq

The area of northern Iraq south of the city of Mosul and southwest of Kirkuk and Tikrit, the hometown of Saddam Hussein, is one of the two heartlands of Iraq's military-industrial complex, the other being the suburbs of Baghdad.[187] Middle East Watch obtained one account about a bombing incident in northern Iraq: Sudanese laborers who lived in an agricultural village 70 km south of Mosul, outside al-Qayyara, described how their house was bombed at 12:30 am on January 29, leaving four dead and seven injured. MEW interviewed two of the injured and other survivors of the attack. They described their house as a three-room, single-story cinderblock building with a concrete roof. The blast of the bombs knocked down the walls of the house. The four men who were killed -- all of them in their twenties -- were sleeping in two different bedrooms. Three were killed in one bedroom, where the second interviewee also was sleeping. All four men died from shrapnel injuries.

At the time of the bombing the workers were asleep and did not hear the noise of any planes. After the attack, one man ran outside and saw three planes flying away; it was a clear night, and he could see the stars. The bombs fell on open ground next to the house. There were two large craters about three to four meters from the side of the house; each crater was about five meters in diameter and three meters deep. The four adjacent homes, of similar construction to theirs, were badly damaged but no one in the other houses was injured or killed. The bombs fell closer to their house than to any other house.

There were about 150 houses in the village, which was surrounded by flat farmland. Most of the residents were farmers. The Sudanese had lived there for two years, earning money from free-lance construction work. The village is two km from the river; a railroad

---

[186] MEW interview, Azraq Evacuee Center, Azraq, Jordan, February 22, 1991.

[187] Interview with Hoshiar Zibari, representative of the Iraqi Kurdistan Democratic Party (KDP) on National Public Radio, January 22, 1991, London.

station is about 10 km away. The only other objects attacked in the immediate area, that they know of, were the railroad tracks, located about 2 to 3 km from their home. The railroad tracks were hit three nights after the bombs fell next to their house. They did not know if there were any houses damaged when the tracks were hit although there are houses nearby. The Sudanese insisted that there was no military base or installation even close to their village or nearby factories, government buildings, communications towers or post offices.

One survivor still had shrapnel in his left leg, which he showed to the MEW representative. Another was wearing sunglasses; he removed them to show he had sustained still-visible injuries in the area around his eyes, eyebrows and nose. He said that he was not able to see at all for some time after the blast; his vision had since returned but was weak. He was treated for nine days at Mosul Hospital. The workers told MEW that seven others were injured in the bombing; four were still in the Republican Hospital in Mosul in serious condition when their housemates departed for Jordan. Three had head injuries and one had surgery to remove a kidney. The workers told MEW that they decided to leave Iraq because the war had become "too much."[188]

Peter Arnett of CNN traveled with Iraqi officials to al-Dour, north of Baghdad, and reported on January 25 that some two dozen homes were destroyed in an allied attack. The town, on the east bank of the Tigris River, is south of Saddam Hussein's home town of Tikrit and about 25-30 km north of Samarra. Arnett said that 23 houses had been "flattened" in bombing raids and that residents said 24 civilians had been killed. He said he was told that the town had no military installations. Gen. Kelly, director of operations for the Joint Chief of Staff, did not deny that the houses had been destroyed but said: "In the vicinity of that town there was a military munitions depot, a chemical warfare production and storage facility, and a military communications site," in an obvious reference to nearby Samarra.[189]

---

[188] MEW interview, Azraq Evacuee Center, Azraq, Jordan, February 15, 1991.

[189] Michael Wines, "CNN Reports Allied Bombs Killed 24 Civilians in Iraqi Neighborhood," *The New York Times*, January 26, 1991.

* * *

Iraqi Kurdish opposition groups provided some information to the press about the allies' bombing in the north. They noted military targets that had been attacked in the early days of the war, and also stated straightforwardly that civilian areas themselves did not appear to be targets for allied aircraft.

Hoshiar Zibari of the Iraqi Kurdistan Democratic Party (KDP) said that from sources in Iraq "we know for sure no civilian or residential areas have been targeted," although when pressed he said that some civilians have been affected, but only those located in residential areas adjacent to military targets. He reiterated that most targets had been hit directly, adding that it was impossible to assess the extent of damage inside installations because these facilities were heavily guarded. Zibari did not have estimates of civilian casualties.[190]

The KDP list of targets attacked that was presented to the press in London on January 22 included major airfields at al-Qayyara in the north, major oil refineries at Bajii and al-Qayyara, a chemical plant at al-Qa'im near the Syrian border in western Iraq, and the Fifth Army corps headquarters in Arbil.[191]

In the second week of February, Masoud Barzani, another Iraqi Kurdish leader, identified sites in northern Iraq that had been bombed by allied aircraft. He said that most of the targets attacked were airfields and bridges, military barracks, and oil fields, refineries and petroleum storage facilities, noting: "Up to now we have definitive information that the allies have not targeted civilian objectives of residential areas."[192]

---

[190] National Public Radio interview, January 22, 1991.

[191] Glenn Frankel, "Iraqi Rebels Say Air Raids Hit Iraqi Industry Hard," *The Washington Post*, January 22, 1991.

[192] Barzani was interviewed in Iran, near the Iraqi border, by journalist Jonathan C. Randal. *See* "Kurd Region Casualties Put at 3,000," *The Washington Post*, February 11, 1991.

312 • PART II: THE AIR WAR AGAINST IRAQ

Barzani described some of the bombing as "very accurate," but added that civilians were injured or killed in cases of inaccurate bombing or where military targets had been located in civilian areas. He cited the bombing of a helicopter base in Harir, a town east of Arbil, that resulted in an estimated 300 Kurdish civilian casualties. He said that the base was "deliberately" located within a detention center where thousands of Kurds were interned.

Barzani also provided information about non-military targets that he said had been bombed in northern Iraq, including a sugar refinery in Suleimaniyya, and -- in Mosul, Iraq's third largest city -- a textile plant, Ibn Betar hospital and a domestic heating-gas plant. He also said that the Iraqi security headquarters and the central prison in Mosul had been bombed. Barzani estimated the number of civilian casualties in the Kurdish areas of northern Iraq at 3,000.

A KDP statement released in Cyprus on January 25 said that 60 civilians had been killed, and hundreds wounded, in the areas of the north around Mosul and Kirkuk.[193] The KDP said the bombing of military and industrial facilities was 50 percent successful, and mentioned that the following targets had been attacked: Saddam Dam north of Mosul, the Debis power station, television stations in Kirkuk and Mosul, and a uranium mine near Serseng. The statement also noted:

> Life has been paralysed in the country because of the destruction of power stations, oil refineries, communications centres and bridges. Electricity and telephone exchange lines have been cut off in the northern towns. Land transport is minimal due to the knocking down of several vital bridges and petrol shortages.[194]

The statements by Kurdish leaders about the overall accuracy of allied bombing in northern Iraq were echoed by residents of the north who fled to Iran during the post-war uprisings and were interviewed

---

[193] *The Independent*, January 26, 1991.

[194] *Id.*

there during a fact-finding mission by representatives of Middle East Watch and the U.S. Committee for Refugees. Civilian areas of Kirkuk, a major city in the north, were not attacked during the air war, according to a resident. He said that Iraqi soldiers during the war told residents that "the U.S. attacked Falluja but not Kirkuk, so we are going to get you."[195] A teacher who fled Kirkuk in early April told the U.S. Committee for Refugees that no houses in Kirkuk were bombed, only "military places and police stations -- they shot in the exact places they wanted to shoot."[196] The teacher also said that helicopters were placed "in between houses to make it so that if the American planes attacked the helicopters they might hit civilian targets. Rockets and airplanes were kept in schools to prevent them from being hit or if they were hit to make it a propaganda point."

A resident of Suleimaniyya who fled the city in early April said that it was called "Bush City" because allied aircraft were "playing" in the sky but never bombed the city; residents waved at allied planes.[197] A former Iraqi soldier who was a student in Suleimaniyya told a representative of the U.S. Committee for Refugees: "The bombing was very precise. It did not hit any of the houses in Suleimaniyya."[198]

---

[195]MEW interview, April 19, 1991, outside Saryaz Camp, Bakhtaran Province, Iran.

[196]Interview in Dolenav Refugee Camp, Kurdestan Province, Iran, April 24, 1991.

[197]MEW interview, Hirwe Camp, Iran, April 20, 1991.

[198]Interview in Quds Refugee Camp, Kurdestan Province, Iran, April 23, 1991.

PART III

IRAQ'S MISSILE ATTACKS AGAINST ISRAEL
AND THE GULF STATES

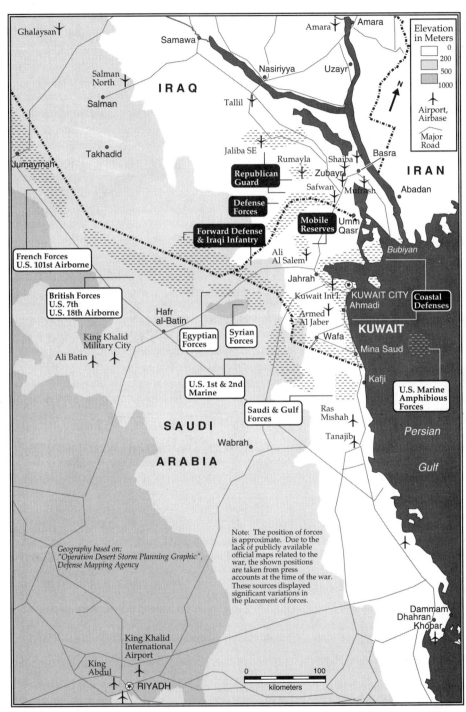

The Disposition of Military Forces at the Commencement of the Ground War

OVERVIEW

In contrast to the military role of Saudi Arabia and other Gulf states,[1] the State of Israel was not a member of the international military coalition to oust Iraq from Kuwait. Nevertheless, beginning with an initial attack at 2 am on January 18, Iraq reportedly launched 39 ground-to-ground ballistic missiles into Israel and the occupied West Bank, killing a total of 13 people, according to official Israeli government statistics. A majority of the missiles were aimed in the vicinity of Israel's largest city, Tel Aviv.

Saddam Hussein was asked during a CNN interview on January 28 about the missile attacks and he commented: "We said that if Baghdad were hit, we would strike Tel Aviv." Iraq's attacks were widely regarded as designed to provoke Israel into joining the war and thus precipitating a split in the Arab participants in the allied military coalition. On January 18, Middle East Watch condemned the Iraqi missile attacks on residential neighborhoods in Israel as a "blatant violation of humanitarian law, which prohibits the targeting of civilians."[2]

At dawn on January 18, Iraq also fired a missile at the allied air base in Dhahran in eastern Saudi Arabia, the first of the 37 missiles launched at that country during the war. In late February, Iraq also launched one missile at Bahrain and and one at Qatar, two Gulf states that participated in the war against Iraq and whose territory served as bases for allied air force units. According to statistics from the official Saudi Press Agency, there was only one civilian fatality from these attacks

---

[1] The air forces of the following Gulf states, for example, flew sorties against Iraq during the war: Saudi Arabia, Kuwait, Bahrain, Qatar and the United Arab Emirates. (Saudi Press Agency Daily English Service, February 25, 1991, citing information from a military spokesman at the Joint Forces Command.)

[2] *See* "Middle East Watch Urges All Parties To Obey Rules of War Protecting Civilians," January 18, 1991.

-- in Riyadh on January 25 -- and some 77 civilians injured, most of them slightly.

The possibility of the use of deadly chemical warheads on the Iraqi missiles generated fear among the Israeli and Saudi civilian populations and extensive civil defense preparations for the eventuality of such attacks. Saddam Hussein refused, in the CNN interview on January 28, to rule out the use of chemical weapons during the war. Asked about Iraq's possible use of chemical weapons against the allied forces, he replied evasively : "I said that we will use weapons that are equivalent to those used against us." In answer to a further query about the use of chemical warheads on the missiles launched at Israel, Saddam offered the same reply: "I have said that we use weapons that match those used by the opposite side." Despite the fact that the chemical attacks never materialized, the uncertainty and fear about Iraq's capabilities and intentions lingered throughout the war.

Lingering, too, and a cause for deep concern, were Saddam's comments in a lengthy speech on April 1, 1990: "We do not need an atomic bomb. We have the binary chemical. Let them take note of this. We have the binary chemical. According to our information, only the United States and the Soviet Union have it."[3]   Later in the speech, Saddam proclaimed that Iraq would not be intimidated and should not fear an attack by the West: "They will be deluded if they imagine that they can give Israel a cover in order to come and strike at some industrial metalworks. By God, we will make fire eat up half of Israel if it tried against Iraq."[4] These comments, taken together, were widely regarded as a threat to use chemical weapons in the event of an Israeli attack on Iraq.

Numerous public Iraqi military communiques issued during the war used very explicit language to indicate that the missile attacks were intended to terrorize the civilian populations of both Israel and Saudi Arabia (see Chapter Six).   Following a missile attack on Israel on February 12, for example, a communique stated that the attack was "to

---

[3] As reported in FBIS, April 3, 1990 at 34.

[4] As reported in FBIS, April 3, 1990 at 35.

spread death and terror among those who terrorized our nation."[5] On January 23, Iraq stated that a missile attack on Israel the previous night was "to disturb the sleep of the Zionists and blacken their night." In a similar vein, the object of the missile launched at Riyadh on February 8 was "to disturb the sleep of the tyrants."[6]

THE TARGETS OF IRAQ'S MISSILES

Although Iraqi statements often left the impression of wholly indiscriminate attacks, in fact not all of Iraq's missiles were indiscriminately fired at urban population centers. U.S. Air Force Chief of Staff Gen. Merrill A. McPeak acknowledged this at a press briefing in March:

---

[5] Armed Forces General Command Communique No. 45 stated: "First, to punish the Zionists whose base methods and conspiracies sparked off this war, and who were behind it and participated in it, who occupy Jerusalem, who seek the assassination of the existence of our Palestinian Arab people, who deal death and oppression to our kinfolk in the occupied lands, and who have participated in the air raids on our cities and villages, our heroic missile force yesterday evening pounded the city of Tel Aviv, the capital of the Zionist entity, with al-Husayn missiles to spread death and terror among those who terrorized our nation, defied its will, and descrated its holy shrines. Second, after midnight last night, our missiles forces once again pounded the city of Tel Aviv with al-Husayn missiles." (Baghdad Domestic Service, February 12, 1991, as reported in FBIS, February 13, 1991 at 18.)

[6] "To punish the traitor Al Sa'ud family...our heroic missile force after midnight last night directed a destructive missile strike at the city of Riyadh, the capital of the atheist Al Sa'ud family, to disturb the sleep of the tyrants." (Armed Forces General Command Communique No. 41, February 8, 1991, Baghdad Domestic Service, February 8, 1991, as reported in FBIS, February 11, 1991 at 34.)

Some of these were actually launched against military targets. For instance, King Khalid Military City was attacked in the northern part of Saudi Arabia.[7]

The majority of the missiles directed at Riyadh also were aimed at military targets, according to a U.S. Army official:

> One Army official said most of the Scuds fired at Riyadh, Saudi Arabia's capital, would have hit an airbase or other high-value target -- possibly destroying U.S. aircraft on the ground -- if they had not been intercepted.[8]

The Defense Department's July 1991 report confirmed that "a number" of the 41 Iraqi missile attacks on Saudi Arabia were against military targets. More precise information was not provided:

> There were a number of Scud missile attacks on Coalition forces within the Kuwait Theater of Operations during Operation Desert Storm. We do not know the number of casualties caused by particular weapon systems. However, the largest single cause of American losses was the 25 February Scud missile attack that hit a US barracks in Dhahran, Saudi Arabia, killing 28 US military personnel and injuring 97.[9]

But during the war allied military spokesmen appeared reluctant to acknowledge that Iraq might be launching *any* missiles at legitimate military targets. The direct hit on the U.S. military barracks was discounted at the time as a fluke. Brig. Gen. Richard Neal of the U.S. Central Command, explaining why the missile had not been intercepted by Patriots, stated at the time that the missile had disintegrated when it

---

[7] McPeak Briefing, Transcript at 6.

[8] David Hughes, "Success of Patriot System Shapes Debate on Future Antimissile Weapons," *Aviation Week & Space Technology*, April 22, 1991 at 90.

[9] Pentagon Interim Report at 27-1.

entered the atmosphere.[10] Gen. Neal said: "Our investigation looks like this missile broke apart in flight. On this particular missile it wasn't in the parameters of where it could be attacked."[11]

Subsequent investigations by the U.S. Army revealed that, contrary to Gen. Neal's initial public assertions, the Iraqi missile did not disintegrate. It was intact when it slammed into the U.S. barracks -- Patriots had not been fired at the missile because the radar system's computer had been shut down at the time of the attack.[12] *The New York Times* reported that the Army learned about the malfunction quickly: "Army experts said in interviews that they knew within days that the Scud was intact when it hit, and that a technical flaw in the radar system was probably to blame." Nevertheless, this information was not publicly reported. The *Times* aptly commented:

> The Army investigations raise questions why the Pentagon and Central Command perpetuated the explanation that the Scud broke up....During the war, American military officers were reluctant to discuss any weapon failings. But even after the cease-fire, many officers were averse to say anything that might tarnish the one-sided allied victory over Baghdad's forces.[13]

In contrast to the post-war public acknowledgments by the U.S. military that Iraq fired missiles at military targets in Saudi Arabia, Middle East Watch is aware of no public statements by U.S. military briefers or Israeli government spokespersons that described possible military targets in Israel that may have been the object of attack. On January 25, President Bush said in a news conference that the missiles launched at

---

[10] Donatella Lorch, "Twisted Hulk of Warehouse Tells a Grim Story of Death," *The New York Times*, February 27, 1991.

[11] *Id.*

[12] Eric Schmitt, "Army Is Blaming Patriot's Computer For Failure to Stop the Dhahran Scud," *The New York Times*, May 20, 1991.

[13] *Id.*

Israel constituted "brutal, senseless, non-military-value attacks on civilian populations." As discussed in Chapter Eight, given Iraq's choice of targets and the limited accuracy of its missiles, most of the attacks on Israel support the President's conclusion.

LEGAL STANDARDS

The Iraqi missile attacks against Israel and Saudi Arabia must be analyzed under legal standards prohibiting the targeting of civilians, the use of indiscriminate weapons and the issuance of threats of violence intended to cause terror among civilians.

As noted in Chapter One, customary international law enjoins attacks against the civilian population and requires that parties to the conflict at all times distinguish between military targets and civilian objects. The prohibition of indiscriminate attacks, as codified in Article 51(4)(b) of Protocol I, includes, *inter alia*, "method[s] or means of combat which cannot be directed at a specific military objective" and thus "are of a nature to strike military objectives and civilians or civilian objects without distinction." The provision was designed to forbid, among other things, long-range missiles with rudimentary guidance systems that cannot with any reasonable assurance be directed against a military objective,[14] such as the V2 rockets used at the end of the Second World War.[15]

Whether the use of a particular missile is indiscriminate, assuming the object selected for attack is a military target, depends in part on the accuracy of the weapon, the size and location of the military objectives and the target's proximity to civilians and civilian objects. As one commentator observed, "Those methods and means of combat which would be indiscriminate in a densely populated city, might be lawful in an unpopulated area such as a forest or a desert."[16]

---

[14] *New Rules* at 305.

[15] ICRC *Commentary* at 621.

[16] *New Rules* at 306.

Iraq's statements accompanying its missile attacks must be examined in light of the customary law prohibition codified in Article 51(2) of Protocol I, which enjoins "[a]cts or threats of violence the primary purpose of which is to spread terror among the civilian population."[17] While customary law does not immunize civilians against fear and anxiety as a consequence of legitimate attacks against military targets, the principle affirmed in Article 51(2) "is intended to prohibit acts of violence the primary purpose of which is to spread terror among the civilian population without offering substantial military advantage."[18]

Although Iraq might claim that it sought a military advantage from its missile attacks -- splitting the military coalition, either by prompting Israel to attack Iraq or by encouraging Saudi civilians under attack to rise against their leaders -- those objectives do not justify targeted or indiscriminate attacks on civilians or efforts to terrorize civilians. Just as it would be illegal for allied forces intentionally to target Iraqi civilians with the aim of encouraging them to overthrow Saddam, so it was illegal for Iraq to target civilians in Israel and Saudi Arabia with the aim of furthering Iraq's military or political objectives. Acts violative of the laws and customs of war cannot be justified or made lawful by a military necessity argument.

As described in the next chapter, some Iraqi statements accompanying the missile attacks might be taken to justify the attacks as reprisals for alleged allied violations of the laws of war. The lack of validity in this possible justification is explained in that chapter.

---

[17]The ICRC *Commentary* recognizes that acts of violence during a war "almost always give rise to some degree of terror among the population..." (ICRC *Commentary* at 618.)

[18] *Id.*

BACKGROUND:
THE USE OF MISSILES BY BOTH SIDES
DURING THE IRAN-IRAQ WAR

During the eight-year Iran-Iraq war, surface-to-surface ballistic missiles were used by both sides, although a greater number of missiles were launched by Iraq. The missiles used by both Iraq and Iran "had severe limitations in accuracy/range payload, and neither side had any abilities to target the weapons accurately," according to military experts.[19] Some 750 to 900 long-range rockets and missiles were used by both sides during the conflict, although these weapons "did not play a major role until the end of the war."[20] Despite the rhetorical bravado used by both sides, the missiles had indiscriminate effects rather than distinct military advantages:

> [T]he net impact of using Scud missiles against urban targets was roughly similar to randomly lobbing a 500-pound bomb into a city every few days or weeks. The Scud strikes usually did little more than produce a loud bang, smash windows, and kill a few innocent civilians. The most lethal attacks on both sides seem to have occurred when missiles hit targets like a school or a large funeral by sheer accident.[21]

The number of Scud missiles fired by Iraq during the Iran-Iraq war is a matter of dispute among military experts, as is the year the first Scuds were launched into Iranian territory (some say 1982, while others put the date at 1980).[22] Experts do agree, however, that commencing in 1987 the tempo of attacks picked up rapidly. Although Iraq fired no Scuds in

---

[19] Anthony H. Cordesman and Abraham R. Wagner, *The Lessons of Modern War, Volume II: The Iran-Iraq War* (Westview Press:1990) at 495 [hereinafter Cordesman].

[20] Cordesman at 495.

[21] Cordesman at 497-98.

[22] Cordesman at 497.

1986, it launched at least 15 in 1987 and at least 189 in 1988, the last year of the war. Iraq's initial attacks were mostly directed at Iranian urban areas, particularly cities along the border, since the missile's limited range at this time prevented attacks on major cities in the interior, including Tehran:

> Iraq began to use Scud largely to conduct sporadic terror attacks on urban areas or military concentrations, and its strikes seem to have been designed largely to try to put political pressure on Iran. Most of the time, Iraq used its Scud missiles against Iranian populations centers to the rear of the battlefield.[23]

It was not until May 1985 that Iraq began to attack Tehran and other major cities with aircraft, long-range artillery and surface-to-surface missiles.[24] Iraq noted publicly that civilian morale was an objective of its missile attacks on Iranian urban areas. The commander of Iraq's Fourth Corps, Major-General Thabit Sultan, stated in April 1985 that Iraq wanted to bring the war home to the Iranian people:

> We want to bring the Iranian people into the front lines of the war. We hope this will encourage the Iranian people to rebel against their government and bring the war to an end.[25]

Iran did not use surface-to-surface missiles until 1985, when up to 14 Soviet Scud-Bs were launched.[26] The Iranians launched eight Scuds in 1986, 18 in 1987 and 77 in 1988.[27] Iran's advantage in use of the

---

[23] Cordesman at 497.

[24] *Country Study* at 237.

[25] Dilip Hiro, *The Longest War/The Iran-Iraq Military Conflict* (Routledge, New York: 1991) at 135 [hereinafter Hiro].

[26] Cordesman at 497.

[27] Cordesman at 497.

missiles was geographic, since the weapons could reach Iraq's largest cities. During the 52-day "War of the Cities" in 1988, Iran fired 61 Scuds at Baghdad, nine at Mosul in the north, Iraq's third-largest city, and five at Kirkuk, the center of the northern oil-producing region.[28]   Like Iraq's missile attacks, the missiles launched by Iran were militarily insignificant:

> [M]any of the Iranian Scuds fired at Baghdad hit in the outskirts of the city. Further, even the missiles that did hit inside the city often hit in open spaces, while hits on buildings rarely produced high casualties. Iran never hit any of its proclaimed major targets, which included the Iraqi Ministry of Defense and Iraqi oil facilities.[29]

Iraq began to use its own modified longer-range missiles in 1988, when 16 al-Husayn missiles[30] were fired at Tehran between February 29 and March 1.[31] Between the initial attacks and April 20, a total of 200 missiles were fired at Tehran and other cities, resulting in 2,000 civilian deaths, according to one count.[32]   In a 40-day period during this time, the Iraqis "would normally fire their ballistic missiles in salvoes of three, and averaged just under two salvoes a day."[33]

---

[28] Cordesman at 499.

[29] Cordesman at 497

[30] For information about this modified version of the Soviet Scud, *see* Chapter Seven.

[31] Hiro at 200.

[32] Hiro at 200.

[33] Duncan Lennox, "Iraq--Ballistic Missiles," *Jane's Soviet Intelligence Review*, October 1990 at 438.

6
TARGETS IN ISRAEL AND THE GULF STATES:
IRAQI PUBLIC STATEMENTS

Iraq's Armed Forces General Command issued military communiques throughout the war, and among the subjects of these communiques were Iraq's missile attacks against Israel and Saudi Arabia. The communiques typically described the missile attacks in political and propagandistic terms. Iraq never specified any military targets in Tel Aviv that were the objects of attack, in contrast to the communiques that claimed missiles were directed at the port of Haifa and at Israel's nuclear facility at Dimona in the northern Negev desert.[34] Similarly, in announcing missile attacks against Riyadh, Saudi Arabia's capital city, there was no mention of military targets, as discussed below.

After the first attack on Israel on January 18, an Iraqi military communique stated that missiles had "pounded political, economic and scientific targets in Tel Aviv, Haifa and elsewhere in Israel." Subsequent statements were equally vague, mentioning "blows against selected targets in occupied Palestine" and "selected targets in Haifa port." A communique issued by the Iraqi Armed Forces General Command on January 23, after the third attack, stated that "our missiles slammed against the city of Tel Aviv."

---

[34] For example, Communique No. 52 on February 17 stated in part: "[O]ur heroic missile forces directed the following strikes [sic] missiles at the Zionist entity: A) Three destructive strikes on Dimona, in the south of occupied Palestine, where the Israeli reactor dedicated to war purposes is located, yesterday evening....B) One strike on the port of Haifa, on the Mediterranean, in occupied Palestine, yesterday evening, with al-Husayn missiles." (Baghdad Domestic Service, February 17, 1991, as reported in FBIS, February 19, 1991 at 46.)

TARGETING ISRAEL'S CIVILIAN POPULATION

Rather than stressing possible legitimate military objectives of the missile strikes, Iraqi statements throughout the war made clear in many cases that the civilian population in Israel was the target of attack -- a clear violation of the customary law principle codified in Article 51(2) of Protocol I. Many of the statements appear to have been made deliberately to spread terror among Israeli civilians -- again a violation of the customary-law principle codified in Article 51(2) of Protocol I -- regardless of the actual object of the attack (see Chapter One, xx-xx).

An official Iraqi military communique on January 19 used utterly ghoulish language -- clearly suggestive of deliberate attacks on the civilian population -- to describe a missile attack: "These missiles poured out of the sky, making Tel Aviv and other targets a crematorium last night, the night of January 18."[35] (A similar image was created by Saddam Hussein in his April 1, 1990 speech, when he threatened to "make fire eat up half of Israel" if it attacked Iraq.) A military communique issued on January 23 stated that a purpose of an attack the previous night was "to disturb the sleep of the Zionists and blacken their night." Following a missile launching on February 11, Radio Baghdad said that the strike was intended "to sow death and alarm in the hearts of those who have isolated our women and children in the occupied land." The Iraqi Armed Forces General Command stated that the missiles launched against Israel on February 12 were intended "to spread death and terror among those who terrorized our nation."

OTHER THEMES: REVENGE, PUNISHMENT AND PALESTINE

Much of the bombast from Baghdad clearly was designed for propaganda purposes among the Arab masses. Revenge against "Zionists" also figured prominently in the language of Iraqi statements about the attacks, as did mention of Palestine. On January 22, missiles were launched at Israel "in revenge for the crimes of Zionism." In describing two missile attacks against Tel Aviv on January 25, the Iraqi Armed Forces General Command said the intent was to "pour fire on the heads

---

[35] Communique No. 7, Armed Forces General Command, January 19, 1991, as reported in FBIS, January 22, 1991 at 45.

of the arrogant Zionists to avenge what their hands have committed."
Radio Baghdad said that the ninth attack on Israel, on February 2, was
"to avenge the Arab blood in Iraq and Palestine." Similarly, the eleventh
attack, on February 8, was "to avenge the intifadah and Iraqi martyrs,"
according to an Iraqi military spokesman. On February 23, after the
16th attack on Israel, Iraq said that missiles were launched "with the aim
of punishing the Zionist scoundrels."

Other official Iraqi statements noted that missiles were fired at
Israel "for the sake of Palestine" and "in implementation of the will of
the children of the intifadah and the will of their brothers in Iraq." A
military communique on January 24 stated: "If they insist on denying the
rights of our people in Iraq and Palestine...we will continue to strike until
they stop their aggression."

TARGETS IN THE GULF: MILITARY AND CIVILIAN

Iraqi military communiques about the missiles fired at Saudi
Arabia included progagandistic language and statements about both
civilian and specific military targets that were the objects of attack.[36]
The most frequently mentioned military target was the allied forces' base
at Dhahran, the largest in the region, described by the Iraqis as "one of
the staging posts for the aggression on our country." Other targets noted
in Iraqi communiques included the huge oil complex at 'Ibqaiq southwest
of Dhahran, the Saudi port of Jubail on the Gulf, King Khalid Military
City, a large Saudi military base and military airport adjacent to the town
of Hafr al-Batin in northeastern Saudi Arabia near the Kuwait border,
and 'Isa military airport in Bahrain. The Iraqi communiques also noted

---

[36] In contrast to the language of the military communiques announcing
missile attacks on Israel, military targets in Saudi Arabia often were specifically
noted. For example, Communique No. 57 stated in part: "To take revenge on
the treasonous Saudi family and to deal with the military effort of the enemy
alliance, our heroic missile force directed two destructive strikes with Iraqi
missiles on the Saudi Khalid town [King Khalid Military City] and Khalid military
airport last night." (Armed Forces General Command, Baghdad Domestic Service,
February 22, 1991, as reported in FBIS, February 22, 1991 at 38.)

that missiles were fired at the "men, weapons and equipment" in various locations in Saudi Arabia, including Hafr al-Batin.[37]

Despite this, the communiques often used highly general language to describe some of the missiles launched at Saudi Arabia. For example, on January 20 "Iraqi missiles pounded...the city of Riyadh, the capital of the agent Sa'udi clan, and in the town of al-Dammam, where the corrupt and ignorant Sa'udi clan has gathered".[38] The Iraqi Armed Forces General Command described Riyadh as the target of an attack on January 25: "Before midnight last night, with God's help, a violent missile strike was directed at the city of Riyadh, capital of the corrupt Saudi rulers."[39]

THEMES: PUNISHMENT AND RETALIATION

As with statements about the attacks on Israel, themes of punishment and revenge appeared in Iraqi military communiques describing missiles fired at Saudi Arabia. For example, the aim of an attack on Riyadh on January 21 was to teach "the agents of Al Sa'ud...a lesson in good conduct."[40] The missiles fired at the city on February 11 were "to punish the agent traitors, infidel apostates, the rulers of Saudi Arabia...and to harass the traitors."[41] The Iraqi Armed Forces General Command stated that missiles launched at Riyadh on February 8 were

---

[37] Middle East Watch understands that the nonessential civilian population of Hafr al-Batin was evacuated prior to the start of the war by Saudi authorities.

[38] Communique No. 13, Baghdad INA in Arabic, January 21, 1991, as reported in FBIS, January 22, 1991 at 50.

[39] Communique No. 23, Baghdad Domestic Service, January 26, 1991, as reported in FBIS, January 28, 1991 at 30.

[40] Communique No. 16, Baghdad Domestic Service, January 23, 1991, as reported in FBIS, January 23, 1991 at 20.

[41] Communique No. 45, Baghdad Domestic Service, February 12, 1991, as reported in FBIS, February 13, 1991 at 19.

intended "to punish the traitor Al Sa'ud family" and "to disturb the sleep of the tyrants."[42] Such language suggests that at least some of the time Saudi cities and their civilian population were targets of attack, in violation of the customary-law principle codified in Article 51(2) of Protocol I. Moreover, because the language was also apparently intended to spread terror among Saudi civilians, it also violated the principle set forth in Article 51(2).

Iraqi statements also said that missiles were fired at Riyadh to avenge allied attacks on Iraq. An Iraqi military spokesman stated that missiles were launched at Riyadh on February 8 "[s]o that the rulers of the Sa'ud family may know that their masters' attacks on our civilian targets will not pass unpunished, a destructive missile strike with al-Husayn missiles was directed after midnight last night at the capital of the agents and traitors, the city of Riyadh."[43]

Iraq's claim that *some* of its missile attacks against Israel and Saudi Arabia were in reprisal for the allied bombing of Iraq is a tacit admission that it had in fact deliberately targeted civilians and civilian objects in those countries.

Conventional and customary international law prohibit direct attacks against the civilian population and civilian objects, and Article 51 (6) of Protocol I prohibits even "[a]ttacks against the civilian population or civilians by way of reprisals." However, this ban on reprisals is new law and not recognized by the United States and many other nations as binding customary law.[44]

---

[42] Communique No. 41, Baghdad Domestic Service, February 8, 1991, as reported in FBIS, February 11, 1991 at 34.

[43] Statement made by military spokesman, Baghdad Domestic Service, February 8, 1991, as reported in FBIS, February 8, 1991 at 19.

[44] Matheson at 426; *also see* Judge Abraham D. Sofaer, Legal Adviser at the U.S. Department of State, "The Position of the United States on Current Law of War Agreements," 2 *The American University Journal of International Law and Policy*, Fall 1987 at 469.

Reprisals during armed conflicts are "acts of retaliation in the form of conduct which would otherwise be unlawful, taken as a last resort, by one Party to the conflict against enemy personnel and property in response to grave and manifest violations of the law of armed conflict committed by the other Party, for the sole purpose of enforcing future compliance with" the laws of war.[45]

The *New Rules* notes that for reprisals to be legally justifiable they must satisfy, among other things, the following customary-law requirements:

> (a) other reasonable means to secure compliance must have been undertaken and have failed,
> (b) reprisals are acts of State and must be undertaken only at the direction of the appropriate political authority of the Party to the conflict,
> (c) there must be reasonable warning that reprisals will be taken unless the illegal acts are halted,
> (d) reprisals must be proportionate to the illegal act complained of and not excessive to the goal of ensuring enemy compliance with the law, and
> (e) reprisals must be terminated when the adverse Party abandons its unlawful policy.[46]

It is utterly implausible, when judged against these criteria, that Iraq's attacks against civilians and civilian objects in Israel could qualify as lawful reprisals. Israeli armed forces at no time during the Gulf conflict participated in the hostilities, much less committed any grave and manifestly illegal violation of the laws of war against Iraq -- the key requirement for valid reprisals. In fact, the initial missile attacks against Tel Aviv occured at 2 am on January 18, approximately 24 hours after the beginning of the allied air assault against Iraq. Instead, the purpose of Iraq's attacks was unquestionably to goad Israeli forces into actively

---

[45] *New Rules* at 311. *See* US v. Ohlendorf, 4 *Trials of War Criminals Before the Nuremburg Tribunals* at 493 (1950); Trials of Richard Bruns, 3 *UN Law Reports of Trials of War Criminals* at 21 (1948).

[46] *New Rules* at 312.

joining the conflict and, thereby, split the Arab members of the coalition. The inflammatory and punitive tenor of Iraq's rhetoric attending these attacks similarly belies the credibility of any claim of legitimate reprisals.

Iraqi military and civilian authorities bitterly complained throughout the air war that coalition forces were attacking the civilian population and civilian objects in Iraq.[47] Even if the Iraqis, in attacking Israel or Saudi Arabia, believed in good faith that the coalition was illegally targeting protected persons and objects, Iraq was nevertheless required to give reasonable warning to the coalition that it would undertake reprisals unless the allies halted their allegedly illegal acts against Iraq. However, no such warning was in fact ever given.

As in the case of Israel, the Iraqi government's own words with respect to its attacks on Saudi Arabia are the best evidence of its true intentions. These statements demonstrate that the attacks directed toward civilian areas were not undertaken to compel coalition observance of the laws of war, but rather for the impermissible purpose of punishing and terrorizing Saudi Arabia's civilian population.

---

[47] *See*, for example, Letter dated January 24, 1991 from Tariq Aziz, Deputy Prime Minister and Minister for Foreign Affairs of Iraq, addressed to the United Nations Secretary-General, included as an annex to Note Verbale dated January 25, 1991 from the Permanent Mission of Iraq to the United Nations addressed to the Secretary-General, U.N. Security Council S/22154, January 28, 1991. The letter stated in part: "The States that endorsed those [United Nations] resolutions for the motives indicated and you, personally, bear responsibility to history and to mankind for the heinous crimes being committed against the noble people of Iraq who are fighting for their freedom. Examples are given hereunder of the savage and premediated acts of aggression committed by the aggressor forces between 17 and 21 January 1991." (at 3.) The letter then lists incidents of bombing in residential areas and of bombing of other civilian objects, in some cases indicating deaths and injuries.

7
MEANS AND METHODS OF ATTACK AND DEFENSE

During the Gulf war Iraq launched its own modified version of a Soviet intermediate-range surface-to-surface ballistic missile widely known as the "Scud" -- the NATO code name for the Soviet SS-1c "Scud B" missile.[1] Iraqi military communiques stated that the missile attacks on Israel and the Gulf States used the "al-Husayn" surface-to-surface ballistic missile, an Iraqi modification of the Soviet Scud B (see below).

Saddam Hussein, in an interview with CNN on January 28, objected to Peter Arnett's use of the term *Scud* to describe the Iraqi missiles: "Why do you avoid calling things by their proper names?" he admonished. "Scud is your own system, which has a range of 270 km. As for this, it is an Iraqi missile called al-Husayn. Its twin brother, al-'Abbas, has a range of approximately 1,000 km and we are developing it to be ready for use in the numbers we might need." It appeared a sore point with Iraq that its modified missile was not recognized; on January 29 a statement was released that echoed Saddam's comments the day before:

> The enemies insist on calling the al-Husayn missile a Scud. By now they should be well aware that the missile they are trying to intercept is not a Scud missile and does not function in the same way as a Scud. Ours is the al-Husayn missile, a missile born in the steadfast land of Iraq.[2]

---

[1] Pyle at 131. The Scud B was "the most widely used and exported" of the four versions of the Soviet Scud, known as A, B, C and D. *See* Duncan Lennox, "Iraq--Ballistic Missiles," *Jane's Soviet Intelligence Review*, October 1990 at 438 [hereinafter Lennox].

[2] Baghdad Domestic Service, January 29, 1991, as reported in FBIS, January 30, 1991 at 22.

IRAQ'S MODIFICATION OF THE SOVIET "SCUD"

The only surface-to-surface ballistic missiles confirmed as having been exported to Iraq are the short-range Soviet FROG-7[3] and the intermediate-range Scud SS-1, "both of 1960s vintage."[4] Egypt and North Korea are believed to have acquired the capacity to manufacture Scud missile assemblies and, according to *Jane's Soviet Intelligence Review*, "it is most likely that Iraq developed a similar capability from about 1985/86."[5] *Jane's* states that "[t]he principal Iraqi effort in ballistic missile development appears to have centred around improvements to the Soviet designed SS-1 'Scud.'"[6]

Iraq is believe to have developed at least two modified versions of the Soviet Scud-B surface-to-surface ballistic missile, which has a range of about 175 miles and a 2,200-pound warhead.[7] The "al-Husayn" was first tested in August 1987; 150 of the missiles were later launched at Iran.[8] The chief improvement of the al-Husayn was its longer range -- 372 miles, compared to 186 miles for the Soviet Scud B; but the consequence of the longer range was a halving of the missile's warhead,

---

[3] Iraq also used Soviet-made FROG missiles during the Gulf war. The FROG -- an acronym for Free Rocket Over Ground -- is a short-range tactical missile with a solid fuel rocket. The FROG-7, which is not a true guided missile, has a maximum range of only 60 or 70 kilometers (Cordesman at 496-7). Middle East Watch is not aware of FROG missiles fired by Iraq at civilian targets during the war; Iraqi military communiques often noted when these missiles were used against military targets. On February 21, the Saudi Press Agency announced that Iraq fired two FROGs, one of which landed near a formation of Senegalese soldiers, injuring eight, two seriously.

[4] Lennox at 438.

[5] *Id.*

[6] *Id.*

[7] "Scuds: The Iraqi Missile Threat," *The Washington Post*, January 18, 1991.

[8] Lennox at 440.

from 455 pounds to 227 pounds, lessening its destructive power.[9] A second Iraqi modified Scud, the "al-Abbas," has a warhead of only 650 pounds, and is believed to have a range of about 500 miles.[10]

But both missiles are less accurate than the original Soviet version. In modifying the missiles Iraq traded greater range for less than half the accuracy of the original Soviet Scud B:

> Whilst the accuracy of the Soviet SS-1c 'Scud B' version is believed to be no better than 450 m CEP [circular error probable], the accuracy of the Al Hussein missile at 650 km is unlikely to be any better than 1000 m.[11]

Even with the smaller warheads, Iraq's missiles were capable of causing damage on the ground. Theodore A. Postol, professor of science, technology and national security policy at the Massachusetts Institute of Technology, said in testimony before the U.S. House Armed Services Committee that Iraq's Scud derivatives, traveling at high speeds, were capable of causing heavy damage on the ground from the warhead itself or from pieces of the body of the missile:

> An extended range SCUD that has burned all of its fuel during boost weighs between 5,000 and 6,000 pounds. Since the SCUD is moving at very high speed, at impact it has roughly half the destructive energy of its equivalent weight in TNT. Hence, although the approximately 500 pound SCUD warhead could be expected to do heavy local ground damage, similar to greater levels of ground damage could also be expected from high speed impacts of large pieces of SCUDs. However, heavy damage, serious injuries, or deaths from

---

[9] *Id.*

[10] *Id.*

[11] Lennox at 440.

such impacts will only occur within perhaps several tens
of meters from an impact.[12]

WHAT CAUSED THE DAMAGE ON THE GROUND?

The allies used 29 Patriot defensive missile batteries during the
war: 21 in Saudi Arabia; two in Turkey, and six in Israel; of the batteries
in Israel, four were U.S. batteries and two were Israel Defense Force
batteries, according to the Pentagon.[13] The Patriot system was used
to destroy incoming Iraqi missiles by exploding in extremely close
proximity of the missile and releasing over 300 small metal fragments;
but even in the case of a successful explosion, pieces of falling missiles
could send a rain of debris to the ground.[14]

The Pentagon has publicly noted that there was major political
significance in employing the Patriot system to shoot down Iraqi missiles:

> The political significance of the Patriot in assisting with
> the defense of Israel, Saudi Arabia, and other civil targets
> and in frustrating Saddam's most politically visible
> weapon was enormous.[15]

The Pentagon observed that the use of the Patriots had a positive effect
on the morale of the civilian population:

> [T]he Patriot system proved to be an effective counter to
> Iraqi Scud attacks on innocent civilians, boosting civilian

---

[12] Theodore A. Postol, "Lessons for SDI from the Gulf War PATRIOT
Experience: A Technical Perspective," Testimony before the House Armed
Services Committee, April 16, 1991 at 5 [hereinafter Postol].

[13] Pentagon Interim Report at 6-6.

[14] See, for example, James Schwartz, "How Patriots Destroy Scuds," The
Washington Post, January 26, 1991.

[15] Pentagon Interim Report at 6-6.

morale and enhancing Coalition cohesion. Patriots countered a sense of helplessness that civilian populations would otherwise have encountered. Without them, and without close communications established between the US and Israel during the war, Israel might have retaliated against Iraq, stressing the Coalition's political unity.[16]

But damage on the ground from the use of the Patriots, particularly in Israel,[17] was a sensitive issue during the war, and numerous questions about the Patriots' use and performance, particularly in relation to civilian casualties and damage on the ground, remain to be answered. In particular, the extraordinary amount of physical damage reported on the ground in and around the Tel Aviv metropolitan area is yet to be fully explained. The Pentagon's July 1991 preliminary report to Congress fails to provide detailed information about casualties or damage caused by Patriots:

> Many of the Scuds that were successfully launched went astray or were engaged by US missile defenses. Sensors detected Scud launches and sent attack warning and assessment information to Patriot batteries. The Patriot air defense missile system intercepted a high percentage of the engageable Scud missiles, although the warheads were sometimes not destroyed and debris fell on civilians.[18]

Elsewhere in the report, the Pentagon again provides information that lacks detail, claiming "[p]reliminary indications are that Patriot successfully intercepted the majority of Scud missiles that were within its

---

[16] Pentagon Interim Report at 4-4.

[17] Six Patriot batteries reportedly were in used in various locations in Israel, operated by U.S. and Israeli crews. (*See* William Claiborne and Jackson Diehl, "Patriots Launched to Meet New Scud Attack Over Israel," *The Washington Post*, January 27, 1991.)

[18] Pentagon Interim Report at 4-4.

engagement envelope."[19] But the report defines success in a manner that leaves obscured the important issue of civilian casualties and damage on the ground: "Intercept success is defined as preventing damage to the asset/protected area by killing the warhead and/or diverting the warhead off its intended trajectory."[20] No additional information is provided.

It should be noted at the outset that the Patriot system was never designed for area-wide defense of a large city but to protect surface-to-air missile sites in isolated areas.[21] Gen. Schwarzkopf, in testimony before the Senate Armed Services Committee on June 12, acknowledged that the Patriot system "is designed for purely military means for a point defense or to defend a very small area like an airfield or something like that. The Patriot was never a missile system that was designed to defend an entire city or an entire area or something of this sort."

Subsequent modifications of the Patriot system "were not radical enough to enable the Patriot to pulverize a tactical ballistic missile, an Army official said."[22] Patriot missiles, 17 feet long with a weight of one ton, have a range of less than 50 miles; in comparison, the Scud weighs eight tons and is 41 feet long.[23] One U.S. Army officer told *The Washington Post* that the eight-ton Iraqi missile was difficult to totally destroy with the smaller Patriot: "We're very accurate with our shots, but you just can't destroy the entire Scud because there's too much of it."[24] The *Post* reported that the Patriot system has "just seconds to compute a

---

[19] Pentagon Interim Report at 6-6.

[20] Pentagon Interim Report at 6-6.

[21] John Kifner, "Deadly Debris Shows Limits Of Patriot Missile Defenses," *The New York Times*, January 27, 1991.

[22] *Id.*

[23] Evelyn Richards and Barton Gellman, "Patriot Not Being Used As Designed," *The Washington Post*, January 26, 1991.

[24] *Id.*

trajectory and launch," and as a result, "sometimes is able only to knock an incoming missile off course."[25]

During the war, Brig. Gen. Uri Ram, who commands Israel's anti-aircraft artillery, acknowledged that in some cases Patriots had detonated "in a range that knocks the Scud around a bit but doesn't destroy it or doesn't destroy it completely."[26] Israeli officials told *The New York Times* that this may have occurred on January 22, when an Iraqi missile crashed into a three-story apartment block in Ramat Gan in Greater Tel Aviv, killing three people and injuring almost 100: "Israeli military officials speculated...that the Patriot fired [on January 22] exploded at the tail of the Scud missile, sending it off the intended trajectory but leaving the warhead intact."[27]

The Patriots were designed to be fired upward at a missile that is bearing down on a target at high speed:

> Defender missiles stationed at the target area are shot upward so they can meet an incoming missile head-on as it makes its final approach to the target. The Patriot carries a warhead weighing about 200 pounds that is designed to explode in proximity to the incoming missile, throwing off a spray of shrapnel that slices into the enemy missile and destroys it.[28]

A *New York Times* correspondent based in Tel Aviv during the war noted that interceptions often took place right over the target: "An incoming Scud usually follows a trajectory that causes it to fall almost straight down

---

[25] *Id.*

[26] Sabra Chartrand, "'Just Bad Luck' in Tel Aviv: Patriot Bumped Scud Off Path," *The New York Times*, January 24, 1991.

[27] *Id.*

[28] John Kifner, "Deadly Debris Shows Limits of Patriot Missile Defenses," *The New York Times*, January 27, 1991.

at the end of its path. And so the Patriots usually intercept them almost directly over the intended target, spewing debris below...."[29]

As indicated in Chapter Eight, some of these interceptions reportedly caused greater damage on the ground as missiles fell down in pieces over a wide area, rather than landing intact:

> A debate over the residual effects of Patriot missiles exploding against Scud missiles directly over Tel Aviv -- sometimes at an altitude as low as 140 feet -- has been fueled by witnesses to the missile clashes over the city and the pattern of damage on the ground that appeared to be spread out over an area larger than it would have been if the Scuds had not been intercepted.[30]

It has not been publicly disclosed how much damage was caused on the ground by the use of Patriot missiles to intercept incoming Iraqi missiles. Israeli Army spokesman Gen. Nachman Shai did acknowledge that in Tel Aviv "at least two Patriot missiles had been fired at every incoming Scud."[31] At a news conference on January 25, President Bush was asked to comment about reports from Israel of civilian injuries, and perhaps deaths, caused by Patriot missiles. He declined to supply information: "I will again express enormous confidence in the Patriots. They're doing very, very well. But whether this was debris falling down from an intercept or not, I simply don't want to comment because we don't yet know it for sure."[32]

---

[29] Joel Brinkley, "Patriots Stop Scud But Israeli Man Is Killed by Debris," *The New York Times*, January 26, 1991.

[30] William Claiborne and Jackson Diehl, "Patriots Launched to Meet New Scud Attack Over Israel," *The Washington Post*, January 27, 1991.

[31] Jackson Diehl and William Claiborne, "Scud Missile Attack on Israel Kills 1, Injures Dozens," *The Washington Post*, January 26, 1991.

[32] "Excerpts From Bush's Remarks on Moves in Gulf," *The New York Times*, January 26, 1991.

MIT's Professor Postol also noted that each time a Patriot surface-to-air missile was launched to intercept an incoming Iraqi missile during the Gulf war "there were at least 3 types of events that caused some level of damage on the ground."[33] First, in cases where Iraqi missiles were completely destroyed during an intercept, "they nevertheless resulted in some ground damage from numerous pieces of falling debris." This was acknowledged during the war by an Israeli missile expert:

> "It is a shortcoming, because the debris does what debris does and it causes damage," said Brig. Gen. Aharon Levran, a missile expert in the reserves....
>
> He said the Patriot's "deficiency seems to be that it intercepts a little bit too near. This is an inherent shortcoming, once they impact in densely populated areas."[34]

In a second group of cases, damage on the ground could be increased when an incoming missile was intercepted and broken apart in large pieces, which would then fall to the ground in multiple impact sites:

> The second type of event were intercepts that cut SCUDs into relatively large pieces that then fell in multiple locations. It appears that in some cases the SCUD warheads also fell intact and detonated, but the impact of large pieces could also do damage equal to or greater than that from the warhead. As a result, the pattern of damage was altered by these intercepts, but it is not clear that the total amount of ground damage was decreased. In fact, it is possible that in these cases the total amount of ground damage was increased.[35]

---

[33] Postol at 6.

[34] John Kifner, "Deadly Debris Shows Limits of Patriot Missile Defenses," *The New York Times*, January 27, 1991.

[35] Postol at 6.

In a third group of cases, falling Patriots caused damage on the ground, particularly from the warhead, which "contains metal fragments that are designed to inflict heavy damage at maximal range." Professor Postol described these cases this way:

> The third type of event was intercepts that resulted in either PATRIOTS falling to the ground or PATRIOTS chasing SCUD missiles or pieces of debris to the ground. The PATRIOT warhead probably weighs about half of that of the SCUD's, but it is almost certainly made from a more highly energetic explosive. In addition, the PATRIOT warhead contains metal fragments that are designed to inflict heavy damage at maximal range. When a PATRIOT hits the ground on a diving trajectory it could well be travelling at a higher speed than a SCUD, and although its mass is smaller than that of an expended SCUD, it is still about a thousand pounds of mass hitting the ground at quite high speeds. One would therefore guess that such events would almost surely result in ground damage per PATRIOT impact comparable to that from an unintercepted SCUD.[36]

More damage reportedly was sustained on the ground in Israel *after* the Patriot system began to be used. *The Washington Post* reported that the number of Patriot intercepts during the Gulf war is classified, but "U.S. officials acknowledged that fewer than half of the Patriots evidently struck Scud warheads over Israel."[37] On April 25, the Raytheon Company -- the manufacturer of the Patriot system -- said that about half of the warheads on Iraqi missiles fired at Israel were destroyed by Patriots.[38] A Raytheon official said that the information disclosed was prepared by the Israel Defense Forces. Raytheon also reported, in

---

[36] *Id.*

[37] R. Jeffrey Smith, "Effectiveness of Patriot Missile Questioned," *The Washington Post*, April 17, 1991.

[38] R. Jeffrey Smith, "Patriot Hit Half Of Scuds in Israel on Nose," *The Washington Post*, April 26, 1991.

contrast, that 90 percent of the warheads of the missiles launched at Saudi Arabia were destroyed.

8
CIVILIAN CASUALTIES AND DAMAGE: ISRAEL

According to the Israeli government, there were 18 separate Iraqi missile attacks[1] over a 39-day period during Operation Desert Storm, resulting in ground strikes in Israel and the occupied West Bank by 39 missiles.[2] In addition, "one or two" missiles reportedly landed in the sea. A spokesman for the Israel Defense Forces (IDF) told Middle East Watch that "many" of the Iraqi-modified Scud missiles were so poorly constructed that they broke up on re-entry into the atmosphere, resulting in several different "hits."[3] This multiplicity of impacts on the ground from a single missile complicates the problem of identifying the causes of damage.

The official Israeli statistics should be treated with caution. Israel-based journalists told MEW that the numbers provided by the authorities changed during the course of the war for no discernible reason. Running totals issued by different bodies -- the IDF, the Government Press Office (GPO) and the government-run Press Communications Center (PCC) set up during the war -- were often at variance with one another, and still cannot be fully reconciled.

---

[1] The figure is arbitrary, as Israel chose to classify attacks separated by a period of under an hour as one, but those of the night of February 2 to 3 and February 25 as two each. For classification purposes, as the last two attacks were only two hours apart, and may have landed in the same vicinity, MEW has chosen to treat them as one; 17 attacks are thus analyzed in this report.

[2] What remains unclear is whether these 39 were all separate missiles, some of which broke up into several parts, spontaneously or after collision with Patriots. A missile that landed between Yona and HaRoen streets in Ramat Gan on February 9, for instance, is also blamed for the complete destruction of the Burmese Embassy 400 meters away. Debris was scattered over a wide section of neighboring Bnei Brak. But only one hit was recorded that night by an Israeli TV crew on the spot.

[3] MEW interview with Col. Raanan Gissin, Tel Aviv, June 4, 1991.

This chapter presents a partial view -- not a comprehensive accounting -- of civilian casualties and damage in Israel from Iraq's missile attacks. The information was compiled from various official and unofficial sources, and from eyewitness accounts obtained by Middle East Watch during a fact-finding mission to Israel in June. Middle East Watch's reconstruction and analysis of the Iraqi attacks is based in part on a log kept during the war by a television crew in Israel.

* * *

According to the final official account, 13 Israelis were killed by the Iraqi attacks: one directly by a missile and another 12 from indirect causes, including heart attacks. However, these figures are also contradicted. On February 3, at the height of the conflict, Maj. Gen. Ehud Barak, then IDF Deputy Chief of Staff, spoke of two deaths directly attributable to missiles and 12 indirect deaths, making a total of 14. Other official sources spoke, at different times, of three or even four direct fatalities. Of the 18 attacks listed by official Israeli sources, 12 caused no casualties.

Estimates of injuries varied widely, even among official sources. Three attacks were said to have caused a substantial number of injuries: up to 96 were injured in the attack at 8:37 pm on January 22; up to 67 were injured in an attack at 6:02 pm on January 25; and another 27 or so were injured in an early morning attack on February 9. By MEW's calculation, the total number of injured civilians ranged from a minimum of 165 to a maximum of 334.

Of the 18 Iraqi attacks, official Israeli sources reported that nine caused no property damage. The other nine attacks, however, were reported to have caused substantial destruction. In Tel Aviv alone, according to the Hebrew daily newspaper *Maariv*, over 3,805 apartments were damaged, including 793 that were badly damaged.[4] *Maariv* also reported that in the city worst hit in the Dan region -- thought to be Ramat Gan -- 1,162 buildings were damaged, including over 3,700 apartments. Some 28 buildings were totally destroyed, including 118

---

[4] "The Missiles That Hit Israel: A Sum-Up of Damages," March 29, 1991. MEW translation from Hebrew.

apartments, and some 701 apartments in 129 buildings were in need of extensive renovation due to damage.

PATRIOT DEFENSIVE MISSILES: ADDITIONAL COLLATERAL DAMAGE?

Col. Raanan Gissin, an IDF spokesman, told MEW that the figure of 39 ground strikes did not include damage caused by Patriots which either misfired or broke up and exploded on the ground after striking incoming missiles.[5] He acknowledged that Patriots had been responsible for some damage in the Tel Aviv area, but would not go into details, other than to point out that the weight of the Patriots was only a fraction of that of the Iraqi missiles[6] and therefore bore less responsibility for the damage on the ground.

However, not all the damage caused by the Patriots followed mid-air collisions with the Iraqi missiles. On January 25, an ABC television reporter in Tel Aviv witnessed through video playback at least one Patriot rise into the sky from a battery located on open ground by the Yarkon River, between Tel Aviv proper and the northern suburb of Ramat Aviv, fly horizontally, below the level of taller office buildings, and then hit the ground again, exploding on impact.[7]

The Patriots have a built-in, self-destruct device. But the device apparently failed on at least this one occasion on January 25, raising the issue of the advisability of locating the air defense system so close to a major population center. The direction, and angle, of attack, together

---

[5] MEW interview, Tel Aviv, June 4, 1991.

[6] The 17.5-foot-long Patriot surface-to-air missile has a launch weight of 2,200 pounds. (Edward Luttwak and Stuart L. Koehl, *The Dictionary of Modern War*, Harper Collins:1991 at 451.) The Soviet Scud B, which Iraq modified, has a launch weight of 14,050 pounds. (*Id.* at 513.)

[7] MEW telephone interview with Leslie Cockburn, June 15, 1991. These details were also confirmed by the videotape of the incident.

with the Patriot's short range,[8] meant that interceptions were inevitably often going to take place over heavily built-up Ramat Gan, Bnei Brak and Givatayim -- due east of Tel Aviv -- with likely consequences in terms of civilian damage and casualties. Ironically, one possible conclusion of the evidence gathered is that there would have been less damage on the ground if the Patriots had not been deployed (see Chapter Seven for additional information on this subject).

It can also be argued that, by engaging incoming missiles suspected of carrying chemical warheads over densely populated areas, at an altitude that would generate the maximum dispersal of any chemical or biological agent, the U.S. and Israeli forces used the Patriots at great potential risk to the civilian population. On the other hand, there was no relaxation during the war of government warnings to Israeli citizens to act as if every attack involved a chemical weapon.

A NOTE ABOUT METHODOLOGY

The purpose of MEW's fact-finding in Israel was to document the damage caused by the Iraqi missile attacks and determine the extent to which this damage was the product of Iraqi violations of the rules of war.

Official sources of information used by Middle East Watch included releases from the Government of Israel Press Office; *Ricochet*, a published compilation of statements issued during the war by the Israel Defense Forces spokesman; data from the Press Communications Center set up temporarily during the war; and news broadcasts on the government-controlled Israel Radio and Television networks. *Maariv*, a mass circulation daily newspaper, published a useful, detailed chart of those missile attacks about which official information was disclosed. But, one week after the attacks began, the government began to restrict sharply what it permitted to be publicly disseminated, reducing the value of this and other journalistic accounts.

---

[8] Patriots have a maximum range of 37.3 miles and a height envelope of 500-78,750 feet. (Edward Luttwak and Stuart L. Koehl, *The Dictionary of Modern War*, Harper Collins: 1991 at 451.)

Private sources included dozens of Israeli citizens -- residents of affected areas and others, such as journalists, who gathered information about the missile attacks as they occurred but have not been at liberty to speak publicly. For obvious reasons, Middle East Watch has chosen to respect their confidentiality.

During MEW's visit to Israel, four months after the end of the war, the disclosure of any information about the missile attacks -- the precise location of impacts, whether military targets were in the vicinity, the amount of damage caused, and whether the Iraqi missiles were intercepted by the Patriot anti-missile system -- remained subject to Israeli military censorship. This constraint inevitably curbed the scope for independent on-the-ground research and complicated the task of reaching firm, reliable conclusions. It made Israeli citizens reluctant to speak in detail to a foreigner about damage in their neighborhoods, and it made the hunt for those missile impact sites about which least was disclosed during the war near impossible.

In the Tel Aviv area, a map of known impact sites was compiled from various sources. Some of these were evidently where entire missiles had landed. Others were caused by falling debris, including warheads, from missiles which had been partially destroyed. Complicating still further the task of assessing Iraq's responsibility was the fact that in some cases Patriot defensive missiles also fell to the ground. These often caused considerable damage, and casualties, but no Israeli official has been willing to admit as much, either at the time or subsequently. With the lapse of time, it was thus very difficult for Middle East Watch to make a precise distinction in each case between damage directly caused by Iraq's missiles and that caused by the Patriots. All the sites examined had been largely cleared up at the time of MEW's visit in June.

Five impact sites in various parts of Tel Aviv, Ramat Gan and the northern suburban districts of Ramat HaSharon and Tel Hashomer were selected to be visited. Bystanders, local residents and, where appropriate, shopkeepers and other workers were interviewed. It was explained to them why Middle East Watch was conducting this research. Most interviewees were cooperative, volunteering information about such matters as the extent of warning they had received from air raid sirens, how much damage had been caused and whether there had been any casualties. However, it should be emphasized that the sampling was not scientific and the picture obtained from these eyewitnesses was not necessarily complete. Some respondents were suspicious about the inquiries, preferring not to talk to a foreign human rights worker without official permission.

Interviewees were usually asked whether there were any military installations in the vicinity that could have been a possible target for the missile. Most said they did not know of any. Further information was obtained by driving around the area and by talking to foreign and Israeli journalists. Several interviewees pointed to the Kirya, the sprawling Defense Ministry complex which covers more than a square kilometer in the heart of Tel Aviv, as a likely target, but few doubted that the attacks were anything other than indiscriminate, intended to instill panic into civilians.

A CHRONOLOGY OF THE ATTACKS

The First Attack: Early Morning Hours of January 18
The first Iraqi missile attack occurred on Friday, January 18, at 2:20 am, Israeli time. A total of eight missiles were launched and all eight were recorded as striking ground. Since the U.S. Patriot batteries had not yet been installed, none of the missiles was intercepted.[9] Information collected by MEW indicates that six of the missiles landed in the Tel Aviv metropolitan area and two struck lower Haifa, not far from the port and its surrounding heavy industry. There were reports of moderate to heavy damage to civilian objects. *Maariv* reported that 668 buildings were damaged in Tel Aviv, 31 of which were scheduled for demolition, and 1,000 apartments damaged, 45 of which were totally destroyed.[10] In Haifa, 100 apartments were damaged as well as 100 shops and a large shopping center under construction.[11]

---

[9] U.S. Patriot batteries were installed after the first two attacks by Iraq. They were first fired against the incoming missiles on January 22 from positions on the northern and southern outskirts of Tel Aviv, near the coast.

[10] "The Missiles That Hit Israel: A Sum-Up of Damages," March 29, 1991.

[11] Id.

Reports of injured civilians varied, with 12 reported by the GPO, 20 reported by the IDF, 22 by the PCC, and 68 by *Maariv*.[12] The Government Press Office and other sources said no one died, presumably of direct causes. However, three elderly women and a three-year old Arab child were reported in the Israeli press to have suffocated to death while wearing their gas masks improperly, and a fifth indirect death may have occurred.

• TEL AVIV ATTACKS: CIVILIAN DAMAGE AND POSSIBLE MILITARY TARGETS: According to information collected by MEW, at least four of the six missiles launched at Tel Aviv and its vicinity struck relatively densely populated districts: Ezra, in southeast Tel Aviv; Givatayim, a municipality east of Tel Aviv; Tel Baruch, in north Tel Aviv; and Azor/Shikun Hadash, an industrial municipality south of Tel Aviv.

The fifth missile landed in a small suburban shopping mall, near both the Country Club and a major intelligence headquarters, under a kilometer away, within the Iraqi missile's estimated "circular error probable" of 1,000 meters. The explosion caused moderate damage, but no casualties. Enclosed within a large area of open ground covering several square kilometers, this secret and highly sensitive facility is located between the affluent municipalities of Herzliya-Pituach on the coast, and Ramat HaSharon, further inland.

Middle East Watch visited Ezra, a district in southeast Tel Aviv where one of the missiles landed. Bordered on two sides by the Ayalon Highway, an urban section of the Tel Aviv - Jerusalem highway, and the old main road to Lod, Ezra is located in the southern fringe of Tel Aviv. It is one of the poorest districts in the city, with much illegal, unregistered construction. A district of cheaply built, one and two-story houses with a few small groceries and a bakery, the poor quality of workmanship undoubtedly contributed to the scale of the destruction. Ethnically, the district is made up of Iraqi, Yemeni and Iranian immigrants.

---

[12] Many injuries in this attack resulted from panic and near absence of warning. A number of people are known, for instance, to have suffered from an anti-nerve gas agent with which they injected themselves.

According to Zahava, the 28-year-old headmistress of a local elementary school, the Amiel Rambam School, about 150 meters from the impact site, the missile made a direct hit on the house of an old lady. She was standing at the door of her house to see what was going on, a few seconds after the alarm was sounded. The blast pushed her outside and saved her life, while destroying her house entirely. The exact location has now been cleared of the worst damaged buildings, leaving an open space of about 1000 square meters.

Zahava herself lived two narrow streets away -- she estimates that she was less than 100 meters from the impact site -- and her house was severely damaged. She, and over a hundred others from the district, were temporarily relocated to 12 small hotels. While those whose damage was limited to broken windows and shutters have returned, at the time of MEW's visit in early June many remained in hotels, awaiting the completion of new government-built housing already going up nearby. In the midst of the rubble, reconstruction and new one-story row houses stand scores of freight containers. Each holds the personal contents of one destroyed house.

Considering that "over 100 houses were completely or partially destroyed," according to Zahava, the small number of casualties was remarkable. Both she and another older lady in her fifties, who would not give her name, said most injuries were cuts and bruises caused by the blast, particularly from flying glass. Only eight people were taken to the hospital. The older lady's house was about 300 meters from the impact site. Her windows were blown in.

Asked whether there were any conceivable military targets in the area, Zahava laughed and shook her head. "He made a mistake," she said, referring to Saddam Hussein. On being pressed, she noted that the Defense Ministry complex known as the Kirya was not far away in a straight line (about 1.6 km), but she could not come up with any possible target in the immediate vicinity. The south Tel Aviv railway station is barely 700 meters away on the outskirts of the city, but it is little used and there are no indications that this was the intended target of the missile.

A bakery stands on the edge of the empty lot created by the demolished and destroyed houses. Israel Wenger, an employee in his late

60's, was working in the building at the time of the explosion at 2 am. "There was just a second's warning," he said, "then the blast." The flimsy, corrugated iron roof of the bakery flew off, but there was no permanent damage to the equipment or building. He told MEW he was knocked to the ground, but unhurt.

An Iraqi military communique issued by the Armed Forces General Command about the attack used rhetoric that was to characterize Iraq's descriptions of subsequent attacks:

> After relying on the all-powerful and almighty God, our struggling missile forces pounded political, economic, and scientific targets in Tel Aviv, Haifa, and elsewhere in Israel. Let the United States hear the wailing of its daughter implanted in the heart of the Arab Homeland.[13]

The Second Attack: January 19

The second volley of missiles from Iraq hit Israel on January 19 at 7:15 am, with perhaps as many as five missiles fired.[14] None were intercepted, but only four were recorded as striking ground, and there was a maximum of three explosions on the ground.[15] The number of injured civilians was variously reported as 10 (IDF), 16 (GPO), 30 (PCC), and 47 (*Maariv*). Both the IDF and the GPO reported no fatalities, but MEW believes two people died of indirect causes.

Civilian property damage was extensive, with a total of approximately 1,400 buildings listed as damaged. A community cultural

---

[13] Communique No. 4, Baghdad Domestic Service in Arabic, January 18, 1991, as reported in FBIS, January 18, 1991 at 26.

[14] *Maariv*'s chart, published on March 29, 1991, stated that *five* missiles were involved, although it is not clear whether this represents missiles launched, or landed.

[15] From MEW's own observation, at least one missile -- the one which struck Allenby Street, in downtown Tel Aviv -- did not explode.

and sports center was also damaged in the poor Tikva district of south Tel Aviv.

Brig. Gen. Nachman Shai, the IDF spokesman, said on January 19 that "a number of surface-to-surface missiles fell in the Greater Tel Aviv area (Dan Region) and other parts of central Israel." These terms are quite general, in contrast to later descriptions by the Government Press Office, which are much more specific.

MEW collected information about three missile strikes within Tel Aviv proper at this date and time: in Yarkon Park, opposite the Exhibition Grounds in north Tel Aviv; in Hatikva, in south Tel Aviv; and on Allenby Street, in central Tel Aviv. However, *Maariv* spoke of a total of five missiles. It is therefore reasonable to infer that there were at least two other strikes outside the city itself, as implied by Gen. Shai, although there is a possibility that one or more missiles may have broken up in the final approach, with the parts landing in widely different locations.

One of the locations outside Tel Aviv hit at this time may have been a restaurant by a gas station in Rishon Le Zion, an upper-middle-class town southwest of Tel Aviv. Col. Gissin, an IDF spokesman, told MEW that a missile had struck this particular site, owned by someone he knew. He noted that Rishon Le Zion marked the southern edge of what he described as the "killing box" created by the Iraqi attacks. How much damage was caused and whether there were any casualties is not known, as MEW did not visit the site.

• THE ATTACK IN DOWNTOWN TEL AVIV: CIVILIAN DAMAGE AND POSSIBLE MILITARY TARGETS: Middle East Watch collected information about the missile that landed on Allenby Street in the heart of Tel Aviv's business district, an area of three-story older buildings dating from the 1930s, with shops below and apartments above, as well as purpose-built office blocks. The headquarters of some of Israel's leading banks are within a few hundred meters of the impact site. The Great Synagogue of Tel Aviv is 100 meters away, on the same side of the road. The Carmel market -- a crowded district of small stallholders during the week -- is less than 800 meters away. The city's main post office, which contains telecommunications equipment, is barely 50 meters away.

The impact site also was 1.3 km in a straight line from the Kirya. One of the previous day's missiles, which landed on the borders of Givatayim and Tel Aviv proper, was likewise 1.3 km away from the Defense Ministry buildings. These two missiles are the two that came closest to landing near the large complex. Two other missiles -- on January 19 in the Hatikva district, and January 26 on the beachfront in central Tel Aviv -- landed 1.6 km and 1.9 km away, respectively.

The January 19 missile landed on a three-story building, the upper-floor apartments of which were empty at the time. It went through two floors and came to rest in the middle level, above a jeweller's and a clothing boutique. In a humorous reference to an attack which did little damage, the jewelry store has erected a model Scud missile outside its window, showing it hitting the bullseye of a giant dartboard.

A salesgirl of Moroccan origin in the boutique told MEW that there had been no casualties when the missile struck, as the apartments were empty at the time. More important, the missile did not explode. Passers-by the day after the attack said the missile could be seen lodged in the upper floors of the building. Damage to the two apartments was extensive, but neither of the adjoining buildings on either side appears uninhabitable. The two shops on the ground floor were functioning normally, having suffered only minor damage.

An Iraqi military communique confirmed the January 19 attacks with the following words:

> These missiles poured out of the sky, making Tel Aviv and other targets a crematorium last night, the night of 18 January. The missile attack on Tel Aviv was repeated at 0800 and 0815 (0500 and 0515 GMT) this morning.[16]

---

[16] Communique No. 7, Baghdad Domestic Service, January 19, 1991, as reported in FBIS, January 22, 1991 at 45.

The Third and Most Damaging Attack: January 22

At 8:37 pm on January 22, Tel Aviv was hit by one Iraqi missile, which was not intercepted by the two Patriots fired at it.[17] It was reported that three civilians were killed in this attack, two of them from indirect causes.[18] The number of civilians injured was variously reported as 73 by the IDF, 85 by the PCC, and 96 by the GPO.

This was the most damaging single Iraqi missile attack on Israel, both in terms of the amount of destruction caused and civilian deaths. *Maariv* recorded damage to 357 buildings and 1,726 apartments, of which seven buildings and 61 apartments were completely destroyed. Significantly, it was also the first time the newly installed Patriot defensive missiles were fired at an incoming missile.

A detailed statement on civilian casualties was aired on IDF Radio: "A total of 98 wounded people were taken to five hospitals in the central district, of whom 48 have already been released.... 74 are slightly wounded; three sustained medium injuries; two are critically wounded.... Three women have died. One of them was taken to Ichilov Hospital in Tel Aviv, the second to Tel HaShomer Hospital, and the third to Beilinson Hospital. The dead woman who was taken to Ichilov Hospital died of crushing wounds as a result of the explosion. The two other dead women suffered heart attacks as a result of the missile impact."[19]

---

[17] At a press conference on January 23, the IDF spokesman said, *inter alia*, "An Iraqi Scud missile was launched on Tuesday evening, January 22, 1991, at 8.30 pm. The missile hit a densely populated residential area in the heart of the greater Tel Aviv area.... Two Patriot missiles were launched towards the Scud missile but did not succeed in downing it." *Ricochet*, publication of the IDF Spokesman's office, Tel Aviv.

[18] The IDF initially said that three deaths resulted from heart attacks suffered by elderly people. However, it later transpired that the woman taken to Ichilov Hospital in Tel Aviv died of being crushed by debris. This was a direct cause of death, meaning that the total number of direct fatalities from the attack should be increased from one to two.

[19] Jerusalem Voice of Israel & IDF Radio, January 23, 1991, as reported in FBIS, January 23, 1991 at 28.

The missile landed on the corner of Abba Hillel Silver Road and Bialik Street on the northern limit of Ramat Gan, within greater Tel Aviv. It struck a middle-class housing development of three-story apartment blocks. Some 600 meters from the impact site is the Diamond Exchange, two tall, twin towers which are among the most prominent landmarks in Tel Aviv and the nerve center of the country's most important export earner. Tel Aviv's northern railway station, the terminus of the main coastal line to Haifa, is about 1,150 meters away. In addition, the impact site was only about 1.5 km from the position where the northernmost set of Patriot batteries was located (another set was located south of the city).

Confusing any speculation about a possible military target of the missile is conflicting reports about whether the missile was intercepted or deflected by a Patriot. IDF spokesman Brig. Gen. Shai, in a live studio interview, said, "(t)he missile hit hard, very hard. It was a direct hit on a residential home and its immediate vicinity. All in all, approximately 20 buildings were hit." Asked whether Patriot missiles had been able to intercept the missile(s), Shai responded that two Patriots were launched from one of the batteries in the Tel Aviv area. As the incoming missile achieved a direct hit, he assumed that it had not been successfully intercepted; he therefore speculated that more than one missile was launched, one of which had been hit, while the other had continued unimpeded.[20]

Brig. Gen. Uri Ram, commander of the Antiaircraft Forces, later claimed that the Patriot had changed the trajectory of the Iraqi missile, and that it did not fall where it had been aimed. "After the collision, it was reported that the Scud was destroyed, but later it became apparent that its rear was hit, while the warhead continued on its trajectory and exploded in Ramat Gan."[21] The Israeli army stated later that the

---

[20] Jerusalem Israel Television Network, January 22, 1991, as reported in FBIS, January 23, 1991 at 27.

[21] Jerusalem Voice of Israel & IDF Radio, January 23, 1991, as reported in FBIS, January 24, 1991 at 30.

engine had been destroyed by a Patriot missile but that it had failed to destroy the warhead.[22]

The extent of the devastation caused by the impact and explosion of the missile was difficult to reconstruct with accuracy, as much of the rubble had been cleared away at the time of MEW's visit to the site in early June and reconstruction was well advanced. A large area of open ground, perhaps 150 by 150 meters, marks the impact site. Any crater had been filled in already. The missile hit a three-story apartment block on the edge of a small street, and four surrounding blocks -- each about 70 meters long by 25 meters deep -- were badly damaged, requiring extensive reconstruction.

An old woman who lives about 150 meters from the impact site described how the blast had brought a chandelier down on her head. She suffered only minor injuries, and there was superficial damage to her apartment. An Israeli of American origin, Irma Dothan, who works nearby, said the blast was felt for several hundred meters. Windows were blown out in a radius of at least 150 meters, she said.

An Iraqi military communique described the attack with the following words:

> For the sake of Palestine, and in implementation of the will of the heroes of the children of the stones, its strugglers, and its (word indistinct) and struggling women; for the sake of holy Jerusalem, and in revenge for the crimes of Zionism, our missiles slammed against the city of Tel Aviv, the city of vice and usurpation, to disturb the sleep of the Zionists and blacken their night, after they distorted the days of the Arabs and filled them with blood and peril, at 2115 last night. Our missile launchers then withdrew safely.[23]

---

[22] Joel Brinkley, "No Immediate Retaliation, Israelis Say," *The New York Times*, January 24, 1991.

[23] Communique No. 16, Baghdad Domestic Service, January 23, 1991, as reported in FBIS, January 23, 1991 at 20.

No Casualties in the Fourth Attack: January 23

This attack occurred at 9:50 pm on January 23. One missile was fired at the Haifa area[24] and was successfully intercepted; there were no civilian casualties. The IDF said on January 24 that "many pieces of debris were scattered throughout the area over which the Scud was destroyed, causing a certain degree of property damage."

According to Israel Radio, an Iraqi missile was launched at the Haifa area and intercepted by two Patriot missiles. There were no injuries, but, in many apartments, windows were shattered.[25] An Army spokesman claimed that the missile was successfully intercepted by Patriot missiles and that there were no casualties. There was some damage, however, "because the blast of the explosion and the shards of the missile were dispersed in all directions."

Although the IDF did not specify where over northern Israel the incoming missile had been intercepted, it is believed to have been on the prominent Carmel headland overlooking Haifa. The Carmel is an area of mixed Arab (primarily Druze) and Jewish settlement in small, widely scattered villages and other communities such as kibbutzim. Israel's main oil refinery, petrochemical plants, a shipyard and several other key industries are located around a bay below the headland, close to the city. High-tech defense industries are also nearby.

This was the first successful use of the Patriot during the Gulf war. According to a British businessman who visited the city regularly during the conflict, the Patriot batteries were placed in a location on the top of the hill over which Haifa spreads, commanding an excellent angle of fire at missiles coming in from the east. This defensive location, together with the difficult angle of access to key targets in and around Haifa and the thinly populated Carmel hinterland in front of the Patriot defensive batteries, account for the negligible success encountered by the Iraqis in attacking these targets in northern Israel as well as the ensuing small amount of collateral damage.

---

[24] IDF spokesman, January 24, 1991.

[25] The Government of Israel Press Office News Release, February 28, 1991, Information Department, Consulate General of Israel in New York.

Iraq did not name the targets in Haifa that were the object of this attack. A military communique issued by the Armed Forces General Command described the attack in the following terms:

> If they insist on denying the rights of our people in Iraq and Palestine...then we have no choice but to repel evil in kind and drive it back to those who have started in defense of our territories and dignity. Thus we struck yesterday and we will continue to strike until they stop their aggression....

> Our heroic missile force dealt a number of blows against selected targets in occupied Palestine as follows: a blow to selected targets in Haifa port inside the occupied Palestinian territories. Our missiles hit their targets and destroyed them at 2300 yesterday. [26]

Wide Collateral Damage in the Fifth Attack: January 25

The attack at 6:02 pm on January 25 was the first massive missile attack on Israel since the Patriot batteries were installed. Iraq may have fired as many as seven missiles,[27] of which an uncertain number -- estimates range from four to seven -- were intercepted by Patriots.[28]

---

[26] Communique No. 18, Baghdad Domestic Service, January 24, 1991, as reported in FBIS, January 24, 1991 at 25.

[27] Accounts vary, possibly due to at least one Patriot having misfired and landed in a built-up area of Tel Aviv without either striking the enemy missile or self-destructing. On January 26, the IDF referred explicitly to seven Iraqi missiles as having been fired. A log kept by an Israeli TV crew records eight possible missiles, the same number as that given by the Government Press Office.

On the other hand, MEW found concrete evidence for no more than five missiles as either having been intercepted in the air or exploded on the ground -- and there may have been fewer. Baghdad Radio refers only to four missiles, specifying that three were fired at Tel Aviv and one at Haifa.

[28] IDF spokesman Brig. Gen. Shai reported on January 26 that all of the Iraqi missiles "were hit in one way or another" by the Patriots. Other reliable press sources, however, insist that no more than four were intercepted. The discrepancies may indicate Israel's reluctance to admit to the likelihood that much

IDF Chief of Staff Lt. Gen. Dan Shomron, in a live interview, estimated that altogether seven missiles were fired,[29] but footnote 27 in this chapter lays out the doubts on this score. One missile was launched at Haifa[30] and the others at Tel Aviv. Middle East Watch was able to identify the locations where four of these missiles landed: Ramat Chen, a southern district of Ramat Gan; Shechunat Hillel, in central Ramat Gan; the central Tel Aviv beachfront; and the Geha junction near Tel Hashomer, a suburb north of Tel Aviv. All Israeli sources reported one fatality, but the number of injured was variously reported as 44 by *Maariv*, 66 by the IDF and 67 by PCC.[31]

Eyewitnesses -- both Tel Aviv residents and foreign journalists -- told MEW that "two or three" Patriots appeared to have been fired at each incoming missile. There could therefore have been anywhere from 15 to 20 missiles in combat over the heart of the city at the same time. Heavy collateral damage was inevitable. Eyewitnesses told MEW that debris and unexploded warheads from damaged missiles rained over a wide area that night.

Discussing the attack, Gen. Shai, the IDF spokesman, said it had been similar in scope to the first one: "The attack on our civilian population in the northern and central part of the country caused injuries to approximately 40 people -- most of whom suffered light wounds -- and

---

of the heavy damage caused by this attack was due to the use of an anti-missile defensive system over a major metropolitan area.

[29] Jerusalem Israel Television network, January 25, 1991, as reported in FBIS, January 28, 1991 at 49.

[30] Little information is available about the one missile believed to have been fired in the direction of Haifa. It is thought to have been intercepted by a Patriot, exploding either in the air or on the ground. *Maariv* reported that 700 apartments and 200 shops were damaged.

[31] All the casualties were in Tel Aviv, none in Haifa.

killed one man."[32] He added that a certain amount of damage was also
caused to property on the ground where missile debris fell and was
scattered over a wide radius.[33]

Analysis of the possible military targets that were the objects of
this attack is difficult, due to the discrepancy in the estimated number of
missiles involved and evidence that Patriot missiles were responsible for
a significant amount of damage and casualties. At least one Patriot
launched from the battery by the Yarkon river misfired, landing in a
built-up area of greater Tel Aviv.

The incoming missiles are likely to have been deflected off course
to varying degrees after collision with Patriots. Certain observations can,
nonetheless, be made: two of the four known hits -- those in Ramat Gan -
- were in densely populated residential neighborhoods, far from any
possible military target. A third missile landed on the beachfront within
a two-kilometer range of several important government buildings,
including the Defense Ministry complex. The fourth missile landed to the
north of the city in Tel HaShomer and could have been aimed at either
a major military industry complex or the intelligence headquarters
nearby, where several highly sensitive installations are located.

A major highway from Ashkelon to Haifa -- the principal artery
linking northern and southern Israel -- was 1.7 km away from the Ramat
Chen site. The Shechunat Hillel attack was even further from any
conceivable legitimate military target -- innocent civilians were the only
victims.

Middle East Watch obtained information about the missile that
landed in Tel Hashomer. Local residents and a driver who passed by the
scene of the explosion, none of whom wanted to be identified, told MEW
that the missile landed just east of the main Tel Aviv-Haifa highway, near

---

[32] It is unclear whether this person died as a direct result of the missile blast
or as an indirect result through, for instance, a heart attack. If the former, he
would be the third direct fatality.

[33] Jerusalem Voice of Israel & IDF Radio, January 25, 1991 as reported in
FBIS, January 28, 1991 at 48.

the important Geha junction, in the Tel Hashomer district. It apparently landed in an open area, alarming the few remaining drivers heading out of Tel Aviv at the end of the day for what was regarded as the relative safety of the northern suburban towns. The Jewish Sabbath had already begun, and most people would have already been home. The missile did not explode.

These partial accounts do not make clear, however, whether it was only a section of the missile which landed or the entire missile -- its warhead failing to explode. It also is not clear whether the missile was an Iraqi missile or a Patriot. While Patriots are known to have been fired from the Yarkon river batteries at incoming missiles, it was not possible for MEW to determine whether this particular missile had been intercepted and, if so, with what consequences.

Several potential military targets in the vicinity are worth noting. Less than a kilometer away to the west are the factories of Israel Military Industries (IMI) in Ramat HaSharon, an upper-middle-class town. IMI is responsible, among many other weapons systems, for the production of missiles and ordnance. A successful attack on this facility would almost certainly have resulted in heavy civilian casualties from secondary explosions. Another plausible target could have been the nearby army recruiting center in Tel Hashomer, the largest in the country. Equally possible, though, is that the missile could have landed on or near the large Tel Hashomer general hospital which is also in the immediate vicinity.

Iraq's military communique issued by the Armed Forces General Command provided no information about the military targets of these missiles launched on January 25:

> This is in reply to those who stand behind the aggression and encourage it and who directly participate in it with military, political and media efforts. With a spirit of determination and sacrifice, our mighty missile force carried out the following blows . . .

>> 1. A powerful missile blow dealt to the Zionists in their capital, Tel Aviv.
>> 2. A second missile blow also dealt to Tel Aviv.

3. A missile blow dealt to the occupied Haifa port.
4. A third missile blow also dealt to Tel Aviv.[34]

The Sixth Attack on January 26: Varying Figures, Unknown Targets
In the sixth attack, at 10:03 pm on January 26, Iraq reportedly launched some four to eight missiles;[35] of these, four reportedly were intercepted and possibly another four struck ground.[36] No civilian deaths were reported;[37] the IDF and the GPO said there were no injuries, and the PCC said two were injured. *Maariv* reported no damage from these attacks, while the GPO said damage was "minimal."

---

[34] Communique No. 22, Baghdad Domestic Service, January 25, 1991, as reported in FBIS, January 28, 1991 at 30.

[35] An Iraqi communique referred to five missiles, while Israeli estimates range from four to eight. A film crew's log refers to six, four of which were intercepted. The Government Press Office spoke of four missiles as having been launched, while Defense Minister Moshe Arens said in a live television interview that "seven, perhaps eight, Scuds had been fired". He added that Patriots had intercepted "some of them."
On February 3, Maj. Gen. Ehud Barak, then Deputy Chief of Staff, said that in the first nine days of the war (covering the attacks from January 18-26) "approximately 25 missiles were fired towards Israel." Retrospectively this gives a good fix on the actual numbers and suggests that the total on January 26 was no more than five, more likely four. By the same calculation, the previous day's attack can not have registered more than six enemy missiles, rather than the eight stated by the government.

[36] *Maariv* says three hits were recorded in "central Israel" and one in the vicinity of Haifa.

[37] The IDF said on January 26 that, to date, the Iraqi missile attacks had resulted in four deaths and 192 injuries. No further explanations were given as to how these figures were reached. Assuming that the criteria for evaluating deaths directly attributable to the enemy attacks had not changed, this infers that two of those injured in previous attacks subsequently died of their wounds. However, on February 3, Maj. Gen. Barak spoke of only two deaths resulting directly from missile hits, adding that there had been 12 deaths from indirect causes.

Least is known about this attack's targets, other than that they appear to have been widely scattered. The Press Communications Center referred to Tel Aviv and Haifa as the general target areas, while the IDF limited itself to saying, "a number of missiles were fired at Israel from western Iraq. The missiles were launched towards northern and central Israel...in two separate salvos marked by a short interval of time."

Gen. Shai said that a number of Patriots were fired at the incoming Iraqi missiles. There were no reports of casualties.[38] Even though all the missiles were said to have been intercepted, there was still, however, some slight damage. An IDF Radio report stated that pieces from an intercepted missile "fell in various areas, including Arab villages. There have been reports of shattered windows in the north."[39]

Possible targets in central Israel may have been Ben Gurion International Airport and its surrounding military installations, some 15 kilometers due east of Tel Aviv. These include an air base, the testing ground of Israel Aircraft Industries and several other defense factories. These are large, and obvious, military targets well away from civilian residential districts. But, in the absence of information as to the impact sites, no conclusions can be drawn.

An Iraqi military statement issued by the Armed Forces General Command used characteristic rhetoric to describe the attacks:

> [T]wo missile strikes were directed at Tel Aviv, which poured fire on the heads of the arrogant Zionists to avenge what their hands have committed. At the same time, and with God's help, a missile was directed at the occupied port of Haifa. After a short time, two missile

---

[38] Jerusalem Voice of Israel & IDF Radio, January 26, 1991, as reported in FBIS, January 28, 1991 at 50.

[39] *Id.*

strikes were directed at Tel Aviv to pound the positions of the filthy Zionists.[40]

Two Missiles Land in Occupied West Bank: January 28 and January 31
The next two attacks, involving one missile each, took place at 9:15 pm on January 28 and 6:05 pm on January 31. These attacks are grouped together here as they display similar characteristics. Each consisted of the firing of one missile, which landed in the occupied West Bank, not far from the 1967 "Green Line" border. One possible explanation for the fact that the missiles fell short of Israeli territory is the range from which they were launched. It may be that coalition bombing raids on suspected missile-launching sites in western Iraq from where the initial attacks were launched -- known as H-2 and H-3 -- forced Iraq to fire from further away, at the extreme end of the missile's range. Civilian damage is believed to have been minimal.

On January 28, a missile struck near the village of Deir Ballout, 22 kilometers due east of Tel Aviv and nine kilometers from the nearest major Israeli city, Petah Tikva, in the central Dan region of the country. An Israeli military spokesman said Iraq had fired a missile at "Israel's central sector and that its shrapnel had dispersed over Arab locations on both sides of the Green Line." He stated that no damage or injuries were reported and that no Patriot missiles had been fired.[41] The IDF was said to be investigating why Patriots were not fired during this missile attack.

Of all the attacks described in a chronology published by the Government Press Office, as distributed by the Israeli Consulate-General in New York, only the description of this attack specifically names the place hit. It was also the only attack for which the government-controlled radio announced the exact site of impact. An explanation for this may be the fact that it fell in the West Bank, Palestinians having given vocal support to Saddam Hussein.

---

[40] Communique No. 25, Baghdad Domestic Service, January 27, 1991, as reported in FBIS, January 28, 1991 at 31.

[41] Jerusalem Voice of Israel & IDF Radio Network, January 28, 1991, as reported in FBIS, January 29, 1991 at 28.

An Iraqi military communique said the missile was fired at Tel Aviv:

> With God's help, our heroic missile forces launched a missile strike against the dens of the enemy and the desecrators of the dear land of Palestine in the city of Tel Aviv before midnight yesterday.[42]

In the January 31 attack, a missile landed in, or near, the village of Harbata, five kilometers east of the Green Line. The nearest Israeli town is Lod, 12 kilometers away. Some reports the following day suggested that the missile had deviated from its course because of strong winds. Although there were no reports of casualties or serious damage, "a few window panes were shattered by the blast."[43] An Israeli Army spokesman said that the missile landed east of the Green Line, in the occupied West Bank, but he would not specify the exact location.[44] An Israeli television correspondent reported from the site of impact that the missile had fallen "near one of the Arab villages in Samaria [the official Israeli designation for the northern West Bank]," and that it struck "an open field."[45]

With this attack, the army said it would no longer announce whether Patriot missiles had been fired at incoming missiles, on the grounds that launches could tell the Iraqis where Patriot batteries were positioned and, by deduction, where missiles had landed.[46] As with the

---

[42] Communique No. 28, Baghdad Domestic Service, January 29, 1991, as reported by FBIS, January 29, 1991 at 14.

[43] *Mideast Mirror*, February 1, 1991 at 4.

[44] Voice of Israel & Army Radio, January 31, 1991, as reported in FBIS, February 1, 1991 at 29.

[45] Voice of Israel & Army Radio, January 31, 1991, as reported in FBIS, February 1, 1991 at 29.

[46] "Missile Fired at Israel," *The New York Times*, February 1, 1991.

attack of three days earlier, it is believed that Patriots were again not fired on January 31.

An Iraqi military communique said that the attack "pounded Tel Aviv with the giant al-Husayn rockets so that the Islamic, Arab, and Iraqi anger will fall on the heads of the Zionists."[47]

No Casualties or Damage Reported: Attacks on Night of February 2-3

Little information was released about these two consecutive attacks. According to the Israeli authorities, Iraq fired a missile at Israel on February 2 at 8:20 p.m. and hit an unsettled part of area *Hey*, the code word indicating the Negev desert.[48] IDF Spokesman Gen. Shai confirmed that one missile had been fired and that it had not caused any deaths or damage.[49] The report that the missile landed somewhere in the southern Negev desert was in sharp contrast to Iraq's claim that Tel Aviv was the target:

> In response to the enemy attacks and to avenge the Arab blood in Iraq and Palestine, your heroic missile force last night used al-Husayn missiles to deal a devastating blow to Tel Aviv, the capital of the usurper and occupying Zionist entity.[50]

---

[47] Communique No. 33, Baghdad Domestic Service, January 31, 1991, as reported in FBIS, February 1, 1991 at 19-20.

[48] *Hey* is the fifth letter of the Hebrew alphabet. In order to expedite civil defense orders while maintaining curbs on the disclosure of potentially valuable information, the country was divided into six regions. In this way, the army could designate generally which area had been hit without revealing where the missile had landed. The alphabetic designations were: *Aleph*/Tel Aviv; *Beth*/Jerusalem; *Gimmel*/Haifa; *Dalet*/nonurban areas in northern Israel; and *Hey*/Negev.

[49] Jerusalem Voice of Israel & IDF Radio, February 2, 1991, as reported in FBIS, February 4, 1991 at 52.

[50] Statement read by announcer, Baghdad Domestic Service, February 3, 1991, as reported by FBIS, February 4, 1991 at 33.

Later that night, at 1:37 am on the early morning of February 3, another missile was launched from western Iraq towards Israel. An IDF spokesman said that to the best of his knowledge, "there were no casualties and only minor damage, if at all."[51] An Iraqi military spokesmen said, again, that Tel Aviv was the target: "Further to the statement issued this morning, 3 February, our heroic missile force dealt another blow to the city of Tel Aviv with al-Husayn missiles at dawn today."[52]

Iraq Claims Another Attack: February 6

At least three Iraqi military communiques claimed that a missile strike was launched against the port of Haifa on the night of February 6. The Israeli Army, however, denied that any Iraqi missiles had struck Haifa or anywhere else inside Israeli territory:

> An alleged fresh Iraqi missile attack on the northern Israeli port of Haifa has apparently turned out to be an act of political propaganda by Baghdad this evening. 'Nothing is known of a missile attack here,' a spokesman for the Israeli Army told DPA in response to an inquiry. The sirens did not not sound in the Haifa area or anywhere else in the country.[53]

MEW has no independent evidence that this attack took place.

Iraq made repeated claims that the port of Haifa was hit in this attack. For example, an Iraqi military spokesman said that night:

> In response to the call of duty to our Palestinian Arab people and in triumph for the Iraqi martyrs who have

---

[51] Jerusalem Voice of Israel & IDF Radio, February 3, 1991, as reported in FBIS, February 4, 1991 at 52.

[52] Statement read by announcer, Baghdad Domestic Service, February 3, 1991, as reported in FBIS, February 4, 1991 at 33.

[53] Hamburg DPA, February 6, 1991, as reported in FBIS, February 7, 1991 at 20.

fallen victim to the bestial American-Zionist aggression, our heroic missile force dealt a destructive blow with al-Husayn missiles this evening on the heads of the wretched Zionists in the city of Haifa in occupied Palestine.[54]

Extensive Civilian Damage in the Eleventh Attack: February 9

One missile reportedly was fired at 2:40 am on February 9. It was reported as having been intercepted but also as having struck ground. Two explosions on the ground, in close proximity to one another, were recorded, suggesting that one might have been a Patriot warhead.

Civilians injured during this attack were variously reported as 20 (Israeli media), 25 (GPO), 26 (PCC), and 27 (*Maariv*). There were no fatalities. Civilian damage was extensive, given that only one enemy missile was involved. *Maariv* said that 287 buildings (with a total of 1,111 apartments) were damaged, and seven buildings were completely destroyed.

The location of the missile strike was the borders of Ramat Gan and Bnei Brak municipalities, east of Tel Aviv city. The impact site is recorded as having been off HaRoen, a major road in central Ramat Gan, but much of the destruction spilled over into Bnei Brak, with which this district merges imperceptibly. Bnei Brak is dominated by ultra-Orthodox Jewish seminaries and religious-student homes. The Burmese Embassy in Ramat Gan, 400 meters from the missile's point of impact, was virtually destroyed, according to Israeli eyewitnesses who drove along the main road a few days later.

As MEW was unable to inspect the embassy site, it is unclear whether a separate warhead was responsible for the embassy's destruction or simply a large piece of debris from a mid-air explosion. Breaking a

---

[54] Statement by military spokesman, Baghdad Domestic Service, February 6, 1991, as reported in FBIS, February 7, 1991 at 11. Also *see* statement by a military spokesman, Baghdad Domestic Service, February 7, 1991, as reported in FBIS, February 7, 1991 at 12; Communique No. 40, Baghdad Domestic Service, February 7, 1991, as reported in FBIS, February 8, 1991 at 19.

policy decision announced on January 31, an IDF spokesman said that several Patriot missiles were fired at the incoming Iraqi missile, and the government-controlled media acknowledged that large amounts of debris fell across a wide area of Bnei Brak and Ramat Gan.

No obvious military targets are in the vicinity of the impact sites. If the intended target was further west, in Tel Aviv proper, the only possible target of a military nature would have been the Defense Ministry complex. However, on the evidence of previous attacks, the chances of hitting even this large area with a missile fired from western Iraq were slim.

An Iraqi military spokesman said of the attack:

[O]ur heroic missile force at dawn today launched a destructive strike with al-Husayn missiles at Tel Aviv, the capital of the Zionist entity, to avenge the intifadah and Iraqi martyrs.[55]

To this, a military communique added:

[O]ur valiant missile force directed a destructive strike at the city of Tel Aviv, the capital of fornication, in implementation of the will of the children of the intifadah and the will of their brothers in Iraq....[56]

Two Attacks in Rapid Succession: February 11 and February 12
Two missiles were fired, at 6:52 pm on February 11 and at 1:27 am on February 12. One of the missiles was intercepted,[57] two were

---

[55] Statement by military spokesman, Baghdad Domestic Service, February 9, 1991, as reported in FBIS, February 11, 1991 at 34.

[56] Communique No. 42, Baghdad Domestic Service, February 9, 1991, as reported in FBIS, February 11, 1991 at 35.

[57] The missile fired on the early evening of February 11 was intercepted, but may have landed in the sea. The second missile, a few hours later, apparently aimed at the same vicinity, was not intercepted.

recorded as having struck ground,[58] and there was one explosion on the ground. No deaths were reported; injuries were put at six by the GPO and seven by the PCC. Damage to private housing around the area of impact of the second missile was extensive. According to *Maariv*, 375 houses were damaged in one form or another, 35 of them suffered moderate to severe damage. In addition, 436 apartments were slightly damaged from the effects of the blast.

The IDF Spokesman's office said the missile struck "a non-settled area in the center of the country," as a result of which windows in several buildings were smashed. A statement issued that day did not disclose whether an intercept had been attempted.

Local residents interviewed by MEW saw a missile flying overhead in the general area of Herzliya, but were unable to locate its impact site. They thought that it either ended up offshore -- some believed they saw a missile going into the sea -- or succeeded in striking a sensitive military target which the IDF did not want to reveal. The most important such target in the vicinity, as described in the attacks of January 18 and 25, would have been the intelligence headquarters a few kilometers away.

Gen. Shomron, IDF Chief of Staff, stated only that there were no casualties and no damage in this attack. When asked about the firing of Patriots, he replied, "We do not report on the firing of Patriots...."[59]

More details were publicly released about the second attack, six and a half hours later, after an inadvertent disclosure by the U.S. State Department in Washington that the missile had landed near the Savyon home of Defense Minister Moshe Arens, then visiting Washington.[60]

---

[58] The GPO chronology notes that the first missile landed, and the PCC speaks vaguely of "central Israel."

[59] Israel Television Network, February 11, 1991, as reported in FBIS, February 12, 1991 at 45.

[60] The Government of Israel Press Office News Release, February 28, 1991, Information Department, Consulate General of Israel in New York.

Such was the importance of the neighborhood that top officers rushed to the scene.

IDF Spokesman Gen. Shai reported, "I am now at the site of the attack. The chief of staff and other senior officers are also here. The situation at this moment is that a missile hit a residential area. There are several casualties who sustained light injuries, and one or two who might have medium wounds." Gen. Shomron, who was also at the scene, pointed out that there had been two attacks during a single night, "which is quite unique....There was a hit very close to a house."[61] The Army Radio said later that one man who had been completely buried under the rubble of his house was rescued unharmed -- a picture transmitted around the world.[62]

A wealthy residential suburb due east of Tel Aviv, Savyon is about nine kilometers northeast of Ben Gurion international airport and its surrounding complex of military facilities and factories. If these facilities had been the intended target (and there is no way of gauging the Iraqi intent from the evidence available) the attack was highly inaccurate.

An Iraqi military spokesman said of the two attacks:

So that the Zionists -- the instigators of all evil -- receive their share of just punishment, your heroic missile force used al-Husayn missiles to deal a destructive strike to Tel Aviv last night to sow death and alarm in the hearts of those who have isolated our women and children in the occupied land and who are today trying to commit aggression against Iraq's free women and its children....[63] After midnight last night, our heroic

---

[61] Jerusalem Voice of Israel & IDF Radio, February 12, 1991, as reported in FBIS, February 12, 1991 at 46.

[62] Id.

[63] Statement read by announcer, Baghdad Domestic Service, February 12, 1991, as reported in FBIS, February 12, 1991 at 26.

missile force directed a second blow at Tel Aviv, the capital of the Zionist villains.[64]

A military communique issued by the Armed Forces General Command added:

> [O]ur heroic missile force yesterday evening pounded the city of Tel Aviv, the capital of the Zionist entity, with al-Husayn missiles to spread death and terror among those who terrorized our nation, defied its will, and desecrated its holy shrines....[A]fter midnight last night, our heroic missile forces once again pounded the city of Tel Aviv with al-Husayn missiles.[65]

An Apparently Harmless Attack: February 16

Reportedly as many as four missiles were fired in this nighttime attack at 8:16 pm.[66] One of the missiles was intercepted,[67] and two were recorded as having struck ground, but the number of explosions on the ground is unknown. There were no reports of civilian casualties or civilian damage. According to the Government Press Office, the two missiles were launched in a coordinated attack. One was said to have landed in the south of the country in an open area. Parts of the other one

---

[64] Id.

[65] Communique No. 45, Baghdad Domestic Service, February 12, 1991, as reported in FBIS, February 13, 1991 at 18.

[66] Iraq claimed to have launched four: three in the Negev, towards Dimona, and the fourth towards Haifa. Gen. Shai, the IDF spokesman, confused the issue, however, by saying that while Iraq claimed to have fired *three*, Israel could confirm that only two had landed.

[67] One interception was recorded by a foreign television network as having taken place. This may have been the missile aimed at Haifa.

were officially said to have fallen into the sea in the north of the country. No injuries or damage were reportedly caused by either missile.[68]

Asked about Iraq's claim that one of the missiles was fired at the Dimona nuclear research and weapons plant, IDF Spokesman Gen. Shai replied, "I cannot go beyond that point, which is that one of the missiles landed in the southern part of the country." According to an Israeli journalist who asked not to be identified, one missile in fact struck the ground near the central Negev town of Arad, a small town of about 10,000 people 18 km southwest of the Dead Sea. Arad is the location of a major airbase. The Dimona nuclear plant is more than 30 km away, to the southwest. The IDF confirmed Iraq's claim that a modified Soviet Scud, dubbed by Iraq the *hijarah al-sijjil,* had been responsible for the attack in the south.

Another missile was fired towards Haifa. But, as with previous attacks, it failed to reach its destination. An IDF account spoke of a missile as having "fragmented," suggesting that this one broke up of its own accord prior to hitting the ground.

Baghdad Radio said the following day that Iraq had used a new missile to attack Israel on February 16: "It named the missile as the *Hijarah al-Sijjil* (shale stone), a reference to a story in the Koran in which God sent giant birds to drop shale stones on invaders who attacked the Kaaba, Islam's holiest shrine."[69] A military communique issued by the Armed Forces General Command stated:

> Since the Zionists are behind every crime that is committed against the sons of Iraq and the nation and they stand behind this aggression...our heroic missile force directed the following strikes missiles [sic] at the Zionist entity:

---

[68] The Government of Israel Press Office News Release, February 28, 1991, Information Department, Consulate General of Israel in New York.

[69] *Mideast Mirror,* February 18, 1991 at 2.

Three destructive strikes on Dimona, in the south of occupied Palestine, where the Israeli reactor dedicated to war purposes is located, yesterday evening with Hijarat al-Sijjil ... missiles. One strike on the port of Haifa, on the Mediterranean, in occupied Palestine, yesterday evening, with al-Husayn missiles.[70]

The Fifteenth Attack: February 19
This attack was recorded at 7:55 pm, with one missile fired. According to Israeli data, there were no civilian casualties or damage. Little is known about this attack, except that Patriots apparently successfully intercepted the Iraqi missile somewhere over "central Israel." An Iraqi military statement said:

> [S]ince it is Zionism which stands in the way of the peace opportunities provided by Iraq, in expression of our country's capability, in embodiment of its invincible power by the will of God, and in implementation of our people and nation's determination to take revenge from all criminal tyrants, our heroic missile force has dealt a destructive blow to the city of Tel Aviv, the capital of the Zionists. Our missiles destroyed their targets.[71]

Sixteenth Attack: February 23
One missile came in at 6:50 pm on February 23; it was not intercepted and was recorded as striking ground and exploding. There were no civilian casualties and only "minimal" damage, according to the GPO.

Information gathered by MEW from reliable Israeli sources is that the missile landed, apparently unimpeded, near the moshav (rural cooperative) of Bareket, in central Israel, four kilometers east of the perimeter of Ben Gurion international airport. This attack marked the

---

[70] Communique No. 52, Baghdad Domestic Service, February 17, 1991, as reported in FBIS, February 19, 1991 at 46.

[71] Baghdad Domestic Service, February 20, 1991, as reported in FBIS, February 20, 1991 at 24.

closest known hit to the airport and its surrounding military facilities. (Apart from the Savyon attack on February 12, Israeli censorship of the precise locations hit by the three other missiles said to have landed in "central Israel" makes difficult the task of determining whether there was a pattern of attacks near the airport.)

The official Israeli word was that this missile landed in an unpopulated area in the center of the country, where it caused a fire to break out.[72] An Iraqi military spokesman described the attack with the following words:

> With the aim of punishing the Zionist scoundrels, who are behind every crime, plot, and aggression committed against this nation and the great people of Iraq, and because the Zionists have conspired through their intrigues and puppets against the chances for peace Iraq called for, our heroic missile force this evening dealt a destructive strike to Tel Aviv, the capital of the Zionist entity, with al-Husayn missiles.[73]

The Last Missiles: Early Morning Hours of February 25
The last missiles launched at Israel by Iraq were fired in the early morning of February 25. It was reported that one missile was fired at Israel at 3:37 am and caused no damage or injuries as it fell in an unpopulated area in the south.[74] A second missile was fired about two hours later, at 5:36 am, and also hit a region in the south. Like the

---

[72] The Government of Israel Press Office News Release, February 28, 1991, Information Department, Consulate General of Israel in New York.

[73] Statement by military spokesman, Baghdad Domestic Service, February 23, 1991, as reported in FBIS, February 25, 1991 at 36.

[74] The Government of Israel Press Office News Release, February 28, 1991, Information Department, Consulate General of Israel in New York.

first, it was reported by Israel to have fallen in an open field. There were said to be no casualties, and no damage was reported.[75]

Later, however, the IDF claimed that only one missile had fallen in southern Israel and that it had caused no damage or casualties.[76] MEW has no independent evidence as to the exact location of these strikes, or explanation as to why the initial reference to a second missile was dropped.

An Iraqi military spokesman said that the intended target was, once again, the Dimona nuclear facility:

> [O]ur heroic missile force directed a destructive blow with the al-Husayn, al-Hijarah missiles at the Zionist entity, specifically at the Dimona area, the site of the Zionist nuclear reactor used for military purposes.

LEGAL STANDARDS AND CONCLUSIONS

Middle East Watch believes that we are aware of the precise or general location of impact of two thirds (26) of the missiles that Iraq fired at Israel during the war. Fourteen, or nearly half, of these 26 were not intercepted by defensive missiles, according to eyewitnesses, Israeli journalists or the government's published account. Assessments of accuracy, or the extent to which the Iraqi military planners may have taken into account the possibility of civilian casualties when aiming missiles at targets in Israel, are therefore drawn from this base of unintercepted attacks.

A further seven of the 26 missiles are known to have been knocked off course to varying degrees by Patriots after mid-air collisions or explosions, negating their significance for interpretative purposes.

---

[75] Army Radio, February 25, 1991, as reported in FBIS, February 25, 1991 at 70.

[76] The Government of Israel Press Office News Release, February 28, 1991, Information Department, Consulate General of Israel in New York.

Confusion exists over whether the remaining five Iraqi missiles were intercepted, and they are thus also excluded from this analysis.

In assessing the intent of Iraq's missile strikes, the quality of information at Saddam Hussein's disposal as to the location of military targets in Israel needs to be taken into account. In this context, the following statement by the Iraqi leader -- made in the spring of 1990 to the visiting PLO chief Yasser Arafat -- is of significance:

> Iraq is familiar with every inch of Palestine, every [Israeli] airfield, base, factory and research facility. We have been able to photograph all the targets we need, deep inside Israel. We started to do this when the war with Iran ended. Israel knows, and we know she knows.[77]

Despite this confident comment, the estimated 39 Iraqi missiles failed, to the best of MEW's knowledge, to strike a single military target.

Attacks on Civilian Targets

Many of the Iraqi missiles appear to have been directed at civilian targets. The marked preference for targets in the heavily populated region around Tel Aviv, when numerous military targets were available outside these urban centers, suggests a deliberate decision to harm civilians. This conclusion is only reinforced by the rhetoric accompanying the missile attacks, which suggested that the Iraqi military had at best an indifference to the plight of the civilian population of Israel, if not a deliberate desire to cause as much civilian damage and suffering as possible. Firing missiles with the purpose of harming civilians flatly violates the customary-law rule that "[t]he civilian population as such, as well as individual civilians, shall not be the object of attack" (Article 51(2) of Protocol I).

Given the apparent targeting of residential areas, Iraq also appeared to select times to launch attacks when most Israelis would be at home, and thus the likelihood that civilian casualties would result from attacks on civilian residences would be greatest. All attacks against Israel

---

[77] *Al-Muharrir* (a pro-Iraqi newspaper published in Beirut), May 10, 1990.

took place during the hours of darkness, between 6:00 pm and 5:30 am, with one exception: the second attack, on January 19, which occurred at 7:15 am. While an obvious reason for these nighttime attacks was the Iraqi desire to avoid allied aerial surveillance in western Iraq, an intention to maximize harm to civilians may also have played a role. A similar rationale may have played a role in the bunching of Iraqi missile attacks (eight of the 17 separate attacks registered by MEW) during the Jewish Sabbath, either Friday evening or Saturday morning. These actions are in violation of the duty to take all feasible precautions to avoid civilian casualties (Article 57, Protocol I).

There is also evidence to suggest that Iraq was targeting Jewish civilians in particular. Apart from the obvious effort to avoid sending missiles toward Jerusalem -- which apart from its large Palestinian population also has some of the holiest sites in Islam which the Iraqis would have been loath to hit -- care appears to have been taken not to direct missiles toward exclusively Arab population centers in Israel. While 22 of the 39 missiles struck different parts of Tel Aviv, none came within a kilometer of Yafo (Jaffa), the largely Arab-populated municipality in the southwest of the metropolis. Two Iraqi missiles fell short of Israel and landed in the occupied West Bank on January 28 and 31, while at least one other caused indirect damage to Arab villages in eastern Israel, not far from the Green Line, on January 26. However, technical difficulties or problems of range may have accounted for these deviations from the usual pattern.

The Use of Indiscriminate Missiles

Even many of the missiles that might have been directed toward military targets were indiscriminate, in violation of the laws of armed conflict, in that they could not reasonably have been directed away from civilians and civilian objects. For example, the four missiles fired during the first two rounds of attack, on January 18 and 19, before the arrival of the U.S. Patriots, landed within 1.5 kilometers of the Defense Ministry complex, the Kirya, suggesting that some effort may have been made to hit this facility. Similarly, three missiles landed between one and two kilometers from Israel's intelligence center, north of Tel Aviv, near Ramat HaSharon -- if one missile believed to have gone into the sea near Herzliya-Pittuach and another intercepted missile are included.

However, as noted, the customary-law principle codified in Article 51(4)(b) of Protocol I prohibits attacks as "indiscriminate" which use "method[s] or means of combat which cannot be directed at a specific military objective" and thus "are of a nature to strike military objectives and civilians or civilian objects without distinction." The Iraqi-modified Scud missiles used against Israel and Saudi Arabia had a circular error probable (CEP) of 1000 meters, meaning that 50 percent of the missiles launched could be expected to fall within a 1000 meter radius of the point targeted. While a CEP of this magnitude may be adequate if the military object targeted is either very large or is located in a desolate area without a surrounding civilian population -- such as the possible attacks on the Dimona nuclear facility -- it is wholly inadequate if used against a relatively small target in a populated urban area such as Tel Aviv and its environs, since 50 percent of the missiles would not come within even one kilometer of the target.

In fact, when missiles exploded on the ground without interference from any defensive system, they rarely succeeded, to MEW's knowledge, in getting even within one kilometer of any possible legitimate military target, despite the fact that central Israel is densely packed with military bases and defense factories. None of the attacks investigated by MEW, or studied on the basis of reliable information provided by Israelis, resulted in damage to a military facility.

The condemnation of these attacks as, at best, indiscriminate -- and quite possibly direct attacks on civilians -- does not depend on an assessment of Iraq's goals in attacking Israel or Saudi Arabia. Although Iraq might claim in the case of Israel that it sought a military advantage from its missile attacks -- to split the military coalition against it by prompting Israel to attack Iraq -- those objectives do not justify indiscriminate attacks on civilians. Just as it would be illegal for allied forces to harm Iraqi civilians with the aim of encouraging them to overthrow Saddam, as explained in Part Two of this report, so it is improper for Iraq to target civilians in Israel or Saudi Arabia with the aim of furthering Iraq's military or political objectives.

Terrorizing the Civilian Population

The rhetoric accompanying the Iraqi missile attacks on Israel suggest an effort to terrorize the civilian population. For example, an official Iraqi military communique of January 19 described the previous night's attack on Tel Aviv as "missiles pour[ing] out of the sky, making Tel Aviv and other targets a crematorium." A similar image was conjured up by Saddam Hussein in his April 1, 1990, speech, when he threatened to "make fire eat up half of Israel" if it attacked Iraq. An Iraqi military communique issued on January 23 stated that a purpose of an attack the previous night was "to disturb the sleep of the Zionists and blacken their night." Following a missile launching on February 11, Radio Baghdad said that the strike was intended "to sow death and alarm in the hearts of those who have isolated our women and children in the occupied land," a reference to the round-the-clock curfew in force in the West Bank and Gaza Strip at the time. The Iraqi Armed Forces General Command stated that the missiles launched against Israel on February 12 were intended "to spread death and terror among those who terrorized our nation."

These comments, when coupled with ongoing missile attacks and the ever-present possibility that these missiles might be armed with chemical weapons, appear to have been made deliberately to spread terror among the civilian populations, in violation of the customary-law principle codified in Article 51(2) of Protocol I. This would be a violation regardless of whether any particular attack was aimed at a military or civilian target.

The Role of the Patriots
While the Patriots provided an obvious psychological boost to Israelis who felt helpless in the face of the Iraqi missile barrages, their use may have contributed to greater harm to civilian life and property than would have been the case had no attempt been made to defend against the incoming missiles. In at least one case, on January 25, a Patriot misfired, failed to connect with an enemy missile, and landed in a built-up area; neither the Israeli nor the U.S. government has acknowledged this malfunction. Moreover, in the case of Tel Aviv, the Patriots, even when they functioned properly, intercepted Iraqi missiles over densely populated areas, with the result that debris, at times explosive, fell on civilians. The practice of launching several Patriots to meet an incoming Iraqi missile compounded this effect. However, this was not a problem in the case of Haifa, because the configuration of the city and the placement of the Patriots allowed them to intercept the incoming Iraqi missiles over territory that was lightly populated.

9
CIVILIAN CASUALTIES AND DAMAGE:
SAUDI ARABIA

Based on information released by official Saudi sources, Iraq launched 37 missiles[1] at Saudi Arabia during the war. In addition, one missile was fired toward Bahrain[2] on February 22 and one toward Qatar on February 26. All told, the missile attacks took a mercifully low toll on Saudi Arabia's civilian residents: only one civilian was reported killed, on January 25 in Riyadh, and another 77 were reported injured, most of them lightly. There were no reports of civilian casualties or damage after an attack on February 14 that slightly injured four people in Hafr al-Batin. On the other hand, the missile attack on the U.S. Army barracks in Dhahran on February 25 killed 28 U.S. soldiers and injured 97.

The Iraqi missile strikes began at dawn on January 18 and continued throughout the war until 1:00 am on February 26. It appears that most of the Iraqi missiles were aimed at military targets in Saudi Arabia. First, U.S. military officials have admitted that in some cases military targets were the objects of Iraq's attacks (see Overview to Part III). Second, one Iraqi missile, not challenged by a Patriot, precisely hit a legitimate military target: the U.S. military barracks in Dhahran on February 25. A month earlier, a six-story Interior Ministry building in Riyadh was totally destroyed on the night of January 25 by what the U.S. command said was the warhead of an Iraqi missile that "careened into the building" after the missile itself was hit by a Patriot. The number of reported successful Patriot intercepts of other incoming Iraqi missiles

---

[1] In the second Iraqi attack on January 20, official Saudi sources issued conflicting statements about the number of missiles launched in the direction of the Eastern Province. MEW has used the lower figure, two missiles, in our tabulations.

[2] British Tornado aircraft that bombed targets in Iraq operated from Bahrain. *See* David Fairhall and Martin Walker, "Scuds fired at allied air base," *The Guardian*, January 21, 1991.

over Saudi Arabia makes it impossible to definitively ascertain the objects of the other attacks.

However, based on official Saudi accounts, there were at least ten separate attacks -- involving a reported 15 or 16 Iraqi missiles -- "towards the Eastern Province," perhaps a reference to the air base at Dhahran. Another six missiles were fired, in three separate attacks, at Hafr al-Batin, where the military base and airport at the adjacent King Khalid Military City served the allied forces. If Iraq in fact was aiming at these military targets, the use of its surface-to-surface ballistic missiles cannot be condemned under the laws of war as an inappropriate means of attack. With a reported "circular error probable" of 1,000 meters, the Iraqi missiles could be expected to land within the boundaries of a legitimate military target such as a large air base. But the same missiles -- with the same wide "circular error probable" -- must be viewed quite differently when fired at substantially smaller targets in populated sections of Riyadh.

A missile that is expected only 50 percent of the time to fall within a radius of 1000 meters from an intended target lacks sufficient accuracy to be used to attack individual military targets in an urban environment, in violation of the customary-law requirement to discriminate between military targets and civilian objects. Moroever, in some cases, Iraqi military communiques indicated that the purpose of the attacks on the Saudi capital was to "pound" the city, to "punish" and "harass" the population, and "to disturb the sleep of the tyrants," language clearly suggestive of an intent to target and terrorize the civilian population. This is only reinforced by the substantial proportion of missiles sent toward Riyadh.

The information in this chapter is based on statements issued by the official Saudi Press Agency (SPA) daily English Service in Riyadh. Press accounts are cited when they provide information supplemental to the official Saudi news statements and military communiques. Middle East Watch did not conduct its own field research in Saudi Arabia on this subject.

A CHRONOLOGY OF THE ATTACKS

The First Attacks: Dhahran Air Base

The first Iraqi missile fired at Saudi Arabia was aimed at the sprawling Dhahran air base in the Eastern Province, the major allied air base in the country.[3] Philip Shenon of *The New York Times*, reporting with a dateline "in Saudi Arabia" on January 18, wrote that a Patriot "blew an Iraqi Scud missile out of the sky over one of Saudi Arabia's largest air bases," clearly referring to Dhahran.[4] Shenon interviewed the crew that fired the Patriot. Again, not mentioning Dhahran by name, he wrote that the crew "had been working this morning at their launch site on the deserted stretch on the outskirts of the base now being used by American forces." *The Times* also reported that Saudi officials "had no immediate reaction to the attack."[5] *The Times* subsequently reported that the Pentagon acknowledged the Dhahran airfield was the target:

> The Pentagon said a Patriot shot down an Iraqi missile in flight as it headed for an airfield in Dhahran, Saudi Arabia, on [January 18], the same morning that eight Iraqi missiles hit in the Tel Aviv-Haifa area.[6]

According to Shenon's report, the U.S. Army crew manning a Patriot surface-to-air missile battery on the outskirts of the facility saw the missile on their computer screens just after 4 am on January 18; a Patriot was

---

[3] David Fairhall and Martin Walker, "Scuds fired at allied base," *The Guardian*, January 21, 1991.

[4] Philip Shenon, "Incoming Iraqi Missile Destroyed Over Saudi Base," *The New York Times*, January 19, 1991.

[5] Judith Miller, "Riyadh Prepares for New Dangers After Iraqi Attack on Israel," January 18, 1991.

[6] Joel Brinkley, "Israel Says It Must Strike at Iraqis But Indicates Willingness to Wait," *The New York Times*, January 20, 1991.

fired at 4:28 am and it destroyed the Iraqi missile.[7] A Saudi military spokesman said that the missile was launched from Basra and that there were no casualties or damage.[8] The spokesman did not identify the target, saying simply that the missile was fired "toward the Saudi eastern region."[9]

In the second attack, at 10 pm on January 20, two Iraqi missiles were reportedly fired "at the direction of the Eastern Province," presumably again at the Dhahran base.[10] The official Saudi statement provided no other details, except to note that the missiles were destroyed in the air by Patriots and there were no casualties. Neither Saudi nor other allied military spokesmen claimed that these first missiles were indiscriminately fired at civilian areas.

There was conflicting information about whether Iraq had launched two or three missiles in the January 20 attack. A spokesman for the Saudi joint command reported that on January 20, at around 10:00 pm, *three* missiles were fired at the eastern region of the country and were intercepted and destroyed in the air before hitting their targets.[11] The following day the Saudi Press Agency issued two conflicting reports, one in which a spokesman for the joint command stated that *two* missiles had been launched at the Eastern Province, and another in which Col.

---

[7] Philip Shenon, "Incoming Iraqi Missile Destroyed Over Saudi Base," *The New York Times*, January 19, 1991.

[8] Joint Forces Communique No. 2, Riyadh Saudi Arabia Television Network, January 18, 1991, as reported in FBIS, January 22, 1991 at 30. Also *see* Riyadh Domestic Service, January 18 1991, as reported in FBIS, January 18, 1991 at 20.

[9] Saudi Press Agency, January 18, 1991.

[10] Saudi Press Agency, January 21, 1991.

[11] Joint Forces and Field of Operations Command Communique No. 4, Riyadh Domestic Service, 21 January 1991, as reported in FBIS, January 22, 1991 at 30-31.

Ahmed Mohammed Al-Rubayan, chief spokesman for the Joint Forces, said that *three* missiles were launched toward the Eastern Province.[12]

First Missiles Fired at Riyadh on January 21, Twelve Injured
The Saudi capital of Riyadh was the headquarters of the allied military command, and the old Riyadh airport serves as a military airbase, although the airport is surrounded to the south and west by residential areas.[13] During the war Riyadh was attacked at least ten times by Iraqi missiles, most of which were intercepted and destroyed by Patriots with little reported civilian damage on the ground.

In the first Iraqi missile attack on Riyadh, U.S. military briefers said that of seven missiles launched at 12:45 am on January 21, four were fired at Riyadh; two others were fired at Dhahran and one fell into the Gulf waters off the coast of Dhahran.[14]

• CONFLICTING INFORMATION ABOUT THE CAUSE OF DAMAGE ON THE GROUND: The Saudi military spokesman said that the missiles fired toward Dhahran on January 21 were intercepted and destroyed by Patriots before reaching their targets; similarly, he stated that all of the four missiles launched toward Riyadh that night "were intercepted and destroyed by Patriot missiles."[15] He also noted that a crater in one of Riyadh's suburbs, caused by an explosion, was being investigated.[16] At a U.S. military briefing in Riyadh, journalists asked about the crater in Riyadh and were told that "right now U.S. [Central Command] has not

---

[12] Saudi Press Agency, January 21, 1991.

[13] David Fairhall, "The Scud may have a feeble payload but it packs a heavy political punch," *The Guardian*, January 22, 1991.

[14] "Excerpts From Sessions On Missiles and Goals," *The New York Times*, January 21, 1991.

[15] Saudi Press Agency, January 21, 1991.

[16] *Id.*

received any such information." The briefer stated categorically that "the ones in the Riyadh area -- all four were engaged and destroyed."[17]

What may well have been responsible was a Patriot missile that misfired. (During a fact-finding mission to Israel, Middle East Watch obtained a similar account to the one that follows; *see* Chapter Eight). Jeffrey Lenorovitz, the European editor of *Aviation Week & Space Technology*, who had witnessed test firings of Patriots in the United States, reported that he saw one Patriot misfire. "I'm not 100 percent sure, but just watching the Patriots, it did not launch properly," he said. He then visited the impact site and saw a 15-foot-wide crater, five feet deep, where he believed the Patriot had landed:

> [H]e witnessed the launching of a Patriot anti-missile missile and saw the missile crash after traveling horizontally less than two miles....[he] said the missile landed in a vacant lot next to an apartment building in central Riyadh, near the old airport in the capital. The windows of the apartment bulding were shattered, he said, and some residents appeared to be slightly injured. No ambulances were present, he said, adding that he had arrived at the site soon after the missile had hit.[18]

Other reporters also saw the crater, which they described as 10 feet deep and 15 feet wide, near the military base at the old Riyadh airport. An office building in front of the crater and a smaller building next to it were damaged, apparently by an explosion.[19] But *The New York Times* reported that "a Pentagon official said he had no reports of any missiles

---

[17] "Excerpts From Sessions On Missiles and Goals," *The New York Times*, January 21, 1991.

[18] R.W. Apple, Jr., "U.S. Foils Missile Attacks on 2 Saudi Cities," *The New York Times*, January 21, 1991.

[19] Molly Moore and Edward Cody, "Scuds Shot From Saudi Sky; Iraqi Targets Still Elusive, *The Washington Post*, January 21, 1991.

landing in Riyadh, and added that the military was investigating."[20]
The findings of this investigation was never publicly released, to Middle
East Watch's knowledge.

The Saudi Press Agency reported the following day that the
Interior Ministry said twelve people had been slightly injured in the
attack on Riyadh, as a result of "some shrapnel" which "fell on a building
in one of the districts of Riyadh." The injured were brought to hospitals
and ten were released immediately, while two others required
treatment.[21] No information was released, however, about whether the
damage was caused directly by the impact of the Iraqi missile or by debris
from a Patriot interception, or whether this was the same site where the
crater was seen. The Pentagon refused to provide data about the number
of Patriots used to intercept the Iraqi missile barrage on January 21, but
one U.S. government official told *The New York Times* that 35 Patriots
were launched, at a total cost of $35 million.[22]

Iraq used a flourish of characteristic rhetoric to acknowledge the missile
attacks:

> [O]n the night of 20 January, the roaring sound of Iraq's
> missiles pierced the ears and blinded their eyes with the
> light of truth. Iraqi missiles pounded the dens of sin in
> the Dhahran base, symbol of Jewish domination, in the
> city of Riyadh, the capital of the agent Sa'udi clan, and in
> the town of al-Dammam, where the corrupt and ignorant
> Sa'udi clan has gathered....[23]

---

[20]R.W. Apple, Jr. "U.S. Foils Missile Attacks on 2 Saudi Cities," *The New York
Times*, January 21, 1991.

[21] Saudi Press Agency, January 22, 1991, as reported in FBIS, January 22,
1991 at 33.

[22] Michael R. Gordon, "Iraq's Military Report Hurt But Not Halted in 5
Days' Raids," *The New York Times*, January 22, 1991.

[23] Communique No. 13, Baghdad INA in Arabic, January 21, 1991, as
reported in FBIS, January 22, 1991 at 50.

An Iraqi military communique issued two days after the attack did not identify the targets in Riyadh but stated: "At 0045 on the day before yesterday, our missiles rained on the city of Riyadh, the capital of the agents of Al Sa'ud, to teach them a lesson in good conduct."[24]

The Second Attack on Riyadh, No Civilian Casualties
In the early morning hours of January 22, three missiles were fired "towards the Eastern Province," and two "towards" Riyadh, according to the Saudi Press Agency.[25] There were no injuries from these attacks, although debris from one missile fell in Riyadh.

The two missiles fired toward Riyadh were launched at 3:45 am. Two Patriot missiles were launched and one was seen meeting an incoming target.[26] According to the Saudi Press Agency, "one of the missiles was intercepted and destroyed before reaching its target," although the target was not identified.[27] Regarding the second missile, the Saudi Press Agency stated that it "was also intercepted and destroyed," but "searching is continuing for obtaining more information on the second missile."[28] A Saudi Press Agency report the next day said that one of the missiles "was intercepted and destroyed in the air of Riyadh City. The debris of the second missile, which crashed in the city, is being analyzed as part of the investigations."[29] Asked on January 23 about the remains of the missile lying on a street in Riyadh, a Saudi military

---

[24] Communique No. 16, Baghdad Domestic Service, January 23, 1991, as reported in FBIS, January 23, 1991 at 20.

[25] Saudi Press Agency, January 22, 1991.

[26] Martin Walker and David Fairhall, "Army chief claims air superiority achieved," *The Guardian*, January 24, 1991 at 1.

[27] Saudi Press Agency, January 22, 1991.

[28] *Id.*

[29] Saudi Press Agency, January 23, 1991.

spokesman said it might be part of the Iraqi missile or its fuel reservoir.[30]

Of the three missiles launched at the Eastern Province, one was intercepted and destroyed, while the two others "were allowed to land harmlessly in non-populated areas."[31] At 10:00 p.m. that night, another missile was fired at the Eastern Province and "crashed into the waters of the Arab Gulf."[32]

Five Missiles Fired on January 23, No Civilian Casualties Reported

An hour before midnight on January 23, Iraq launched five missiles at Saudi Arabia: two at Riyadh, two at the Eastern Province and one at Hafr al-Batin, the site of a military base near the Iraqi border southwest of Kuwait.[33] All the missiles were reportedly intercepted and destroyed by Patriots, with no casualties reported.

One missile was reportedly destroyed in the air "over the military base of Hafr al-Batin."[34] Eyewitnesses in Dhahran saw Patriots "knock out one incoming missile low over an airport runway and another at higher altitude over the nearby town of al-Khobar."[35]

An Iraqi military communique stated that the air base at Dhahran was one of the targets, but did not identify the possible targets in Riyadh: "Iraqi missiles were raining on the heads of the Al Sa'ud traitors in Riyadh, their capital. At the same time our missiles pounded the

---

[30] Id.

[31] Saudi Press Agency, January 22, 1991.

[32] Saudi Press Agency, January 23, 1991.

[33] Saudi Press Agency, January 24, 1991.

[34] Mideast Mirror, January 24, 1991 at 25-26.

[35] Id.

imperialist base at Dhahran, one of the staging posts for the aggression on our country."[36]

First Civilian Killed as Missile Levels Wing of Interior Ministry Building in Riyadh on January 25, 30 Injured

In a nighttime attack at 10:28 pm on January 25, Iraq launched two missiles at Riyadh. While one missile was successfully intercepted by Patriots, the other was not. Middle East Watch obtained information about the damage caused by the second missile from a resident of Riyadh. He stated that the missile totally destroyed one wing -- about 10 meters by 10 meters -- of the six-story Civil Records building of the Ministry of Interior on al-Washem Street.[37] The remainder of the building was damaged but not leveled. The building is located in the densely populated al-Murabba' residential neighborhood of Riyadh, about 5 km southwest of the old airport and located off the old airport road, a major north-south thoroughfare. The area surrounding the building is totally residential and the windows of many houses were shattered from the attack. The Saudi Defense Ministry complex is located some two and a half km away from the Civil Records building and the Ministry of Commerce is about one and a half km distant.[38] The U.S. command said a Patriot hit the Iraqi missile but did not destroy the warhead, which "careened into the building."[39]

Saudi public statements did not identify the target that was destroyed. A military communique stated that there had been two missiles launched at Riyadh, that they were detected, and that Patriots were fired in response. Part of one of the missiles fragmented and "landed on a populated district of Riyadh. As a result, one Saudi citizen was killed and

---

[36] Communique No. 18, Baghdad Domestic Service, January 24, 1991, as reported in FBIS, January 24, 1991 at 25.

[37] MEW interview, July 29, 1991.

[38] Also *see* Malcolm Browne, "2 Office Buildings Leveled In Riyadh; Body Recovered," *The New York Times*, January 26, 1991.

[39] *Mideast Mirror*, January 29, 1991 at 13.

30 persons of different nationalities were injured."[40]   The injured
included 19 Saudis with broken bones and other slight wounds, and 11
lightly injured foreigners: five Egyptians; two Jordanians; one Sudanese
woman, and three Bangladeshis.[41]   Official Saudi reports did not say
that the Interior Ministry building was destroyed.

The New York Times reported that apparently there were no
casualties inside the Interior Ministry buildings. In addition to the fact
that the attack took place at 10:30 pm, many Government buildings were
closed, including the two buildings that had been destroyed or damaged,
because it was the Muslim Sabbath.[42]

Iraqi military communiques issued after this attack did not
identify the target:

> Before midnight last night, with God's help, a violent
> missile strike was directed at the city of Riyadh, capital of
> the corrupt Saudi rulers.[43]...With God's help, before
> midnight last night, a missile strike was directed at the
> city of Riyadh, the capital of the agents and slaves from
> the Saudi clan.[44]

Whether the missile that hit the Interior Ministry buildings in Riyadh had
been deflected by a Patriot or precisely targeted by Iraqi forces, the direct

---

[40] Communique No. 9, Riyadh Domestic Service, January 26, 1991, as
reported in FBIS, January 28, 1991 at 23.

[41] Riyadh Domestic Service, January 25, 1991, as reported in FBIS, January
28, 1991 at 24.

[42] Malcolm W. Browne, "7 Iraqi Missiles Are Fired at Cities in Israel and 2
at Saudi Arabia's Capital," *The New York Times*, January 26, 1991 at 6.

[43] Communique No. 23, Baghdad Domestic Service, January 26, 1991, as
reported in FBIS, January 28, 1991 at 30.

[44] Communique No. 25, Baghdad Domestic Service, January 27, 1991, as
reported in FBIS, January 28, 1991 at 31.

hit does not alter the indiscriminate nature of the weapon used. As noted, the best available information suggests that only half of of the modified al-Husayn missiles launched by Iraq could be expected to fall within a 1000-meter radius of the targets at which the missiles were aimed.[45] While the laws of probability will nonetheless allow an occasional direct hit, such inaccuracy is incompatible with the customary-law duty to discriminate between civilian and military targets if Iraq aimed its missiles at relatively small targets -- individual buildings, for example, compared to large military airbases -- in urban areas.

The Next Two Attacks: No Reported Casualties or Damage

According to the Saudi authorities, one missile was intercepted on the morning of January 26, aimed at the Eastern Province.[46] An Iraqi military communique said that the attack "was directed at the city of Dhahran and its air base."[47] Two days later, at 9 pm on January 28, one missile was fired at Riyadh; it was reportedly intercepted and destroyed, causing no injuries.[48] A joint forces communique the following day stated that although the missile was destroyed in the air, debris fell on a farm in the suburbs of Riyadh.[49] (Middle East Watch learned that the farm was located in al-Hayer, south of Riyadh.) Reporters who went to the scene said the debris "appeared to include a spent Patriot warhead."[50]

---

[45] Duncan Lennox, *Jane's Soviet Intelligence Review*, October 1990 at 440.

[46] Communique No. 9, Riyadh Domestic Service, January 26, 1991, as reported in FBIS, January 28, 1991 at 23.

[47] Communique No. 23, Baghdad Domestic Service, January 26, 1991, as reported by FBIS, January 28, 1991 at 30.

[48] Saudi Press Agency, January 29, 1991.

[49] Communique No. 12 issued by the command of the Joint Forces, Riyadh Domestic Service, January 29, 1991, as reported in FBIS, January 30, 1991 at 17.

[50] *Mideast Mirror*, January 29, 1991 at 5.

29 Injured in Riyadh: February 3
     Iraq launched one missile toward Riyadh at 1:00 a.m. on February 3. The Saudi Press Agency issued the following report:

> As a result of an explosion of a missile, which was launched by the Iraqi aggressor at 0100 am (local time), Sunday, toward Riyadh City, a bulk of the missile fell down after its explosion on a residential area in Riyadh City, causing slight injuries to 29 persons, most of it due to splinters of glass-windows, disclosed a responsible source of the Interior Ministry here last night to the Saudi Press Agency. The source said all injured persons were given medical treatment, adding that all of them were discharged from the hospitals in good health.[51]

The statement added that the injured were 14 Saudis, six Jordanians, four Syrians, three Yemenis, one Kuwaiti and one Pakistani.

No Casualties in February 8 Attack
     One missile was fired in the direction of Riyadh at 1:48 on February 8 and was intercepted and destroyed in the air by Patriots.[52] The Iraqi statement about the attack indicated that the missile was fired at the Saudi capital to avenge allied attacks on Iraq:

> So that the rulers of the Sa'ud family may know that their masters' attacks on our civilian targets will not pass unpunished, a destructive missile strike with al-Husayn missiles was directed after midnight last night at the capital of the agents and traitors, the city of Riyadh.[53]

The Iraqi statements about the Riyadh attack clearly were designed to terrorize the civilian population. The Iraqi military communique did not

---

[51] February 3, 1991 statement.

[52] Saudi Press Agency, February 8, 1991.

[53] Statement made by military spokesman, Baghdad Domestic Service, February 8, 1991, as reported in FBIS, February 8, 1991 at 19.

identify the object of the attack in Riyadh but stated that its aim was "to disturb the sleep of the tyrants":

> To punish the traitor Al Sa'ud family, who have allowed the sanctities of the Arabs and Muslims to be violated by the atheists and polytheists, and who have relinquished their land and wasted their funds on vides, debauchery, and on aiding the nation's enemy against the nation, our heroic missile strike at the city of Riyadh, the capital of the atheist Al Sa'ud family, to disturb the sleep of the tyrants.[54]

Two Foreign Workers Injured in Riyadh: February 11

A single missile was fired at Riyadh on the night of February 11, according to the Saudi authorities. Although it was intercepted by a Patriot missile, shrapnel fell in a suburb of Riyadh and "broken glass slightly injured two guest workers in the Kingdom, an Egyptian and an Indian."[55] According to the Interior Ministry, the debris fell near a "populated quarter in Riyadh suburb" and two people were slightly injured.[56] Another report identified the injured as two guards on a university campus, and said the falling debris destroyed a building housing a swimming pool.[57] Middle East Watch learned that the debris fell on the campus of Muhammed Ibn Saud University, located in a suburb near the new international airport.

An Iraqi military spokesman said the attack was designed to punish Saudi Arabia's ruling family:

---

[54] Communique No. 41, Baghdad Domestic Service, February 8, 1991, as reported in FBIS, February 11, 1991 at 34.

[55] Saudi Press Agency, February 12, 1991.

[56] Riyadh Saudi Arabian Television Network, February 11, 1991, as reported in FBIS, February 12, 1991 at 20.

[57] *MidEast Mirror*, February 12, 1991 at 19.

> So that we can inflict the punishment of the nation and
> the people on the Al-Sa'ud family--the atheists, traitors,
> and corrupt--our missile force used al-Husayn missiles to
> strike at Riyadh before midnight last night.[58]

Saudi Col. Ahmed al-Rubayan, the spokesman for the Joint Forces and
Theater of Operations, said on February 13 that Iraq's missile attacks
were aimed "at terrorizing the citizens...and added that these missiles have
no military signficance."[59]

Four Slightly Injured in Daytime Attack on Hafr al-Batin: February 14

In a rare daytime missile attack, Iraq launched two missiles at
Hafr al-Batin on February 14 at 11:45 am. Hafr al-Batin, a remote
desert town of about 30,000 residents in northeastern Saudi Arabia less
than 100 kilometers from the Iraqi border, is also the location of King
Khalid Military City, which served as a major base for Arab military
forces during the war. As noted above, Hafr al-Batin's nonessential
civilian population was evacuated prior to the start of the air war.

The Saudi Press Agency reported that "the missiles divided into
pieces while at midair without [being] intercepted and five pieces of them
fell down on a residential area at Hafr al-Batin region."[60] The
statement also reported that four people suffered minor injuries, three
cars caught on fire and one house and a workshop were destroyed.

An Iraqi military communique said that six -- not two -- missiles
were launched in an attack on military targets in Hafr al-Batin:

> The Iraqi missile force has directed six destructive strikes
> at the Hafr al-Batin area, where the atheist aggressors
> are massed....to take revenge on those who applauded the
> aggression -- the despicable, shameless, and godless

---

[58] Statement read by announcer, Baghdad Domestic Service, February 12,
1991, as reported in FBIS, February 12, 1991 at 26.

[59] Saudi Press Agency, February 13, 1991.

[60] Saudi Press Agency, February 14, 1991.

rulers of Saudi Arabia -- our missile force directed six fierce and destructive missile strikes today at the enemy's sectors and concentrations of its men, weapons and equipment in the Saudi area of Hafar al-Batin, on the other side of our international borders in Kuwait Governorate. The al-Husayn missiles pounded their targets violently, inflicting heavy human and material losses on the savage criminals who have assassinated the children.[61]

THE REMAINING IRAQI MISSILE STRIKES: NO CIVILIAN CASUALTIES OR DAMAGE REPORTED

The Hafr al-Batin attack on February 14 was the last reported firing of Iraqi missiles that caused civilian casualties or damage in Saudi Arabia or elsewhere in the Gulf. Following the February 14 attack, Iraq reportedly launched an additional nine missiles, from February 16 through the early morning hours of February 26. None of these attacks caused civilian casualties or damage.

Based on reports from the Saudi Press Agency, the chronology of these attacks is as follows: February 16, 2 am: one missile fell into the Persian Gulf off Jubail, with no casualties or damage; February 21: three missiles fired at Hafr al-Batin with one intercepted, one exploding spontaneously prior to interception and one crashing harmlessly without interception -- no casualties or damage reported from any of the missiles; February 22, 2:30 am: one missile launched in the direction of the island nation of Bahrain intercepted and destroyed, with debris falling into the Gulf; February 23, 5:05 am: one missile fired toward the Eastern Province exploded in midair without interception and debris fell harmless in the desert; February 24, 9:30 pm: one missile fired toward Riyadh intercepted and destroyed -- debris falls on empty street and no casualties or damage sustained; this report was contradicted by a subsequent Interior Ministry statement which said debris fell on a school and caused

---

[61] Baghdad INA, 14 February 1991, as reported in FBIS, February 15, 1991 at 20.

some damage[62]; February 25, 8:32 pm: one unintercepted missile directly hits a warehouse at the Dhahran air base that had been converted to a military barracks, killing 28 U.S. servicemen; and -- the last attack -- February 26, 1:26 am: one missile, fired toward Qatar, crashed in the Persian Gulf.

LEGAL STANDARDS AND CONCLUSIONS

With regard to Iraq's missile attacks against Saudi Arabia, it appears that in the majority[63] of cases Iraq was aiming at military targets, particularly the allies' air base at Dhahran. The use of a missile with a 1,000-meter circular error probable against large and isolated military targets such as air bases or similar military installations, where the possibility of civilian casualties or damage would be remote, is not a violation of the laws of war.

At the same time, insofar as Iraq launched the same missiles at smaller military targets -- known as "point targets" -- located in or near civilian population centers, that presents different legal issues entirely. The use of such an inaccurate weapon in these situations must be condemned because these weapons do not have the technological capability to distinguish between civilian objects and military targets in populated civilian areas, as required by the laws of war.

Moreover, the language used in official Iraqi statements about some of the attacks suggested indicated that the civilian population in

---

[62] Saudi Press Agency, February 24, 1991, as reported in FBIS, February 25, 1991 at 25.

[63] Based on the accounts in this chapter from Saudi Press Agency statements, the majority of missiles were not fired at Riyadh but, presumptively, at military targets in Dhahran and Hafr al-Batin. Here are the numbers of missiles fired:

Toward Dhahran/Eastern Province:	15-16
Toward Hafr al-Batin:	6
Riyadh:	15
Into Gulf waters:	1
Toward Bahrain:	1
Toward Qatar:	1

Saudi Arabia itself was the object of attack. Again, this would be a violation of the customary law duty not to target civilians codified in Article 51(2) of Protocol I. Iraqi rhetoric accompanying the missile launches also appears to have been designed to terrorize the Saudi population -- an independent violation of the principle set forth in Article 51(2).